The New York Times

GUIDE TO
WHERE TO LIVE
IN AND AROUND
NEW YORK

The New York Times

GUIDE TO WHERE TO LIVE IN AND AROUND NEW YORK

Edited and with an Introduction by

MICHAEL STERNE

Times
BOOKS

Designed by Linda Kosarin
Manufactured in the United States of America
9 8 7 6 5 4 3 2
First Edition

ACKNOWLEDGMENTS

The true genesis of this book was the decision of the publisher and senior editors of *The New York Times* to redesign and expand the paper's Sunday Real Estate section. The new section was to be in no sense a trade journal for investors, developers, and operators of real estate. Rather, it was unequivocally to serve the needs of the consumers of real estate, among them individuals and families seeking homes.

The decision to proceed with the new section was made late in 1981, and early in 1982, A. M. Rosenthal, executive editor of the *Times,* appointed me the section's editor. My first task was to create features in the new consumerist mode of the section, and the first one I proposed was a weekly article that would introduce readers to the infinitely varied communities that make up the New York area. Such articles would tell readers what they would have to know if they were to make an informed decision on whether or not to live in a community. The articles would provide an inventory of the housing stock, taxes, local government, population, public transportation, schools, libraries, shopping resources, recreational amenities, problems, and pleasures. They also would say something about each community's history and style, the more elusive qualities that nevertheless are important in deciding where to put down roots.

Mr. Rosenthal accepted this proposal and then gave these pieces their name, "If You're Thinking of Living in . . ." The first appeared in the inaugural issue of the new section on March 28, 1982, and another has been published every Sunday since then. From the first, these "Living in" articles, as my colleagues and I have come to call them, have been the most popular feature of the new section. Soon after they appeared, I began getting requests for extra copies of the articles from readers, residents, company relocation officers, and real-estate professionals. I also got many calls and letters from mayors, city managers, development officers, heads of chambers of commerce, and presidents of real-estate boards proposing their communities as subjects for future articles. Others suggested that I collect the articles in a book that could serve as a permanent guide to the communities of the New York area. That thought also had occurred to me, but I realized that such a book would have to wait until enough articles had been produced to make such an undertaking useful. That moment came last year, and this book is the result.

All the "Living in" articles have been written by members of the *Times* staff or by regular *Times* contributors, and the reporting and writing have been what readers expect of the paper. Inevitably, mistakes creep into every piece of writing, but judging by the post-publication comments of residents and officials of the communities we profiled, there have been few. Those few have been corrected in the course of reediting the articles for this book.

I am grateful to all the colleagues who accepted assignments to write these articles for the Real Estate section, did them so well, and then allowed me to republish them here. This is much more their book than mine. I also am grateful to Gordon T. Thompson, the copy chief of the section, and Wilbur A. Hollander, the copy editor, who, with intelligence and sensitivity, helped to shape the articles for publication in the *Times*. And I am especially grateful to Gene Rondinaro of the Real Estate news staff, who not only wrote two of the articles but also helped me to update prices, rents, taxes, travel times, and other essential data and checked hundreds of niggling details as I prepared these articles for republication. I owe many thanks, too, to John Forbes, the section's picture editor, who ordered the maps illustrating the articles and then collected them for inclusion here, and to Andrew Sabbatini, manager of the *Times* map department, and his skillful staff, who designed and made most of the maps. Additional maps were drawn by Stephen Hadermayer.

Readers who compare what follows with what first appeared in the *Times* will find that the articles are basically the same but somewhat different. Events and controversies in the news at the time of publication but of only transitory interest have been eliminated. Basic data on prices, rents, and taxes have been updated, but all are volatile and may change again by the time a reader consults this book and then goes into a community to seek a home. Nevertheless, such data should prove useful for a long time because this guide is being published in a period when inflation, the main generator of change, has slowed to a modest pace. The introductory sections are all fresh material that has not been published before. For whatever errors of fact or emphasis are found in those sections, or in the articles as I have reedited them, I am fully responsible.

Michael Sterne
New York
1985

CONTENTS

(Commuting times given are to midtown Manhattan during rush hours as shown on carriers' schedules. For communities not located along rail, bus, or subway lines, additional time to get to such transportation by car, bus, or foot has been added.)

MODES

B—Bus
F—Ferry
S—Subway
T—Train
W—Walk

The New York Times
GUIDE TO
WHERE TO LIVE
IN AND AROUND
NEW YORK

INTRODUCTION
I.

The title of this book means just what it says: it is a guide for individuals and families who are seeking a place to live "in and around New York." "In New York" means the five boroughs of New York City; "around New York" means what often is called the metropolitan area, that is, all those communities—cities, suburbs, and exurbs—that lie within commuting range of midtown Manhattan.

These outer communities are in northern New Jersey; in Orange, Rockland, and Westchester counties at the southeastern end of New York State; in southern and western Connecticut; and in Nassau and Suffolk counties on Long Island. There are, literally, hundreds of them, but not all are profiled in this book. Many are too small to warrant a separate article. Others are so troubled or unattractive that most people of middle-class income and tastes would not want to live in them. But the one hundred and one communities discussed in the following pages are among the most popular and desirable in the area, and in one or another of them almost everybody should be able to find a satisfactory home. Those who wish to explore others will, by reading this guide, acquire realistic criteria against which to measure them.

A widely shared misconception is that there is a shortage of good housing in and around New York. On the contrary, there is a plenitude of good housing in the area, and it is affordable by all except poor people. (The poor, whether dependent or working, are badly housed everywhere except where government reallocates the resources of society to provide decent living accommodations for them; such people must hunt for housing in a separate, subsidized market that is not covered in this book.) But for the great middle of society and for the upper-middle and rich segments, the metropolitan area offers housing aplenty, and in many forms. Moreover, much new housing is being developed throughout the area, adding to the choices open to those who already live here and those who are planning to relocate.

Why, then, is it widely believed that a housing shortage exists? Because there is a true shortage of apartments in the most sought-after neighborhoods of Manhattan. In this narrow segment of the huge metropolitan area housing market, even people who have large incomes and substantial resources find it difficult to buy or rent an apartment. It is not folklore but fact that seekers of Manhattan cooperatives with more than a million dollars to spend often find, when they get to a broker's office, that there are few listings from which to choose. And companies that bring executives to New York and are ready to pay thousands of dollars a month to house them in mid-Manhattan apartments often find that few are available. Apartment seekers with less to spend find even fewer choices. (For the borough as a whole, the apartment vacancy rate was only 2.12 percent in 1984.)

The Manhattan shortage is the product of a strong demand that seems to be limitless—that is, there apparently is no end to the number of people wishing to live in the borough, for reasons given below—and extraordinary inhibitions on the ability of developers to create more housing. Sites are few and expensive, building costs are high, zoning regulations are restrictive, and tenants in small, older buildings that could be replaced by new, larger ones have uninvadable rights to remain that are protected by rent regulations going back to World War II.

In part, the strong demand for living space in the heart of the city is the result of a local form of madness called the Manhattan Obsession. It is the passionately held conviction of many New Yorkers and would-be New Yorkers that the only acceptable places to live are the Upper East Side or Upper West Side, Murray Hill or Greenwich Village, East End Avenue or Sutton Place. To such people, anywhere else is as remote as Sandusky, Siberia, or the Sahara.

Those afflicted with this obsession go to extraordinary lengths to find Manhattan apartments. They bribe superintendents and building managers; they put signs on lampposts offering rewards for information leading to a rental; they sublet on tenuous terms that clearly are illegal in the hope that a landlord will let them stay if they already are in place; they endure affronts to their dignity from agents and brokers and then pay dearly for the privilege in excessive commissions; they spend 40 and even 50 percent of their incomes on rent or mortgage payments; and they seize with whoops of joy small, pokey, dark, noisy, ill-maintained living quarters that would be rejected as uninhabitable anywhere else in the country. Some even give up the hope of raising families because there is no room for children in the tiny apartments they can afford. Manhattan is the only place in the United States where couples routinely pay more than $1,000 a month for a one-room studio with bathing and cooking facilities attached.

A great deal of this madness is attributable to sheer snobbery, but there also are real reasons to crowd into Manhattan's prime residential districts, if one can afford them. One is the not ignoble desire to be at the heart of the city's life and to be touched by its glamour. Most of the best of New York really is at the center, and to live in propinquity to it is to own a perch on the thin edge of excitement and to fare daily on truffles and champagne. It is what New York success is all about, and those who want to experience it to the full consider the pleasures well worth the cost.

A more practical reason is the desire to be able to walk to work. Most of the best jobs are in Manhattan's central business district, which runs from 59th Street to the Battery, and more good jobs are being created there than anywhere else in the metropolis. To many who hold those jobs or hope to hold them, the prospect of a long journey each morning and evening on a commuter bus or train is daunting. They know they can find attractive homes at costs they can more easily afford outside the city, but they also know all the horror stories of maddeningly erratic schedules, of railway cars that roast commuters in summer and freeze them in winter, of buses that get stuck for hours in the choking air of the tunnel crossings, of days being made or unmade on the basis of finding or not finding a seat. Commuting by car into Manhattan's over-trafficked streets is a possibility, but it has its own little agonies, and it usually takes only a few trips to convince those who try it that driving is not the way they will want to commute for the rest of their working lives.

Upper Manhattan and the outer boroughs also are alternatives, but the state of public transportation in the city ranges from barely acceptable to shameful. Many New Yorkers who might find remote neighborhoods attractive refuse to consider them if they have to commute to them on the subways. They perceive the system to be dirty, unreliable, and sometimes dangerous. In fact, the system is dirty, unreliable, and sometimes dangerous, and the outlook for improvement is not good. Though the financing is in place for modernization and large capital expenditures are being made, the Transit Authority, which runs the system, still is snarled in antiquated union rules, unproductive work practices, and its own sluggish administrative practices, all of which make better service difficult to achieve. And though the system still succeeds on most working days in moving millions of people to and from their jobs without mishaps, the on-time and safety records are worsening, and the utter ugliness of it all turns away thousands of potential riders.

So there are both psychic and practical reasons for the Manhattan Obsession, but there also is a cure. It is an exploration of the outer borough and suburban alternatives to Manhattan. They are so vast and so varied that when people consider them seriously they come to realize that there is, indeed, no housing shortage in and around New York, and that the trade-offs may not be as bad as they seem.

This is not idle or Pollyannaish advice. Thousands of families and individuals now are living in outlying communities and finding that the better housing they enjoy and the money they save are worth the agonies of commuting. And though they do not have the convenience and pleasure of living next door to the Metropolitan Museum of Art or the theater district or *haute cuisine* restaurants, they find that they still can enjoy the amenities of Manhattan in the evenings, at the end of their working days, before boarding subways, buses, or trains to go home.

Moreover, many also are learning that the alternatives to Manhattan are not just the traditional, vanilla-flavored suburbs of single-family houses on neat plots of mown grass. They are moving to old and, until recently, decaying neighborhoods in New York City and to older, small cities throughout the area. The investment of their housing dollars in these communities is revitalizing them. And by their presence, they are creating a demand for Manhattan-like amenities that is bringing them into being outside Manhattan. Beaujolais nouveau, goat cheese, fresh pasta, grainy breads, kiwi fruit, and mange-tout are available just about everywhere, as are stylish clothes, art films, and picture galleries. Park Slope and Fort Greene in Brooklyn, Stapleton on Staten Island, Astoria in Queens, Jersey City, Paterson, and Hoboken in New Jersey, and Norwalk in Connecticut are examples of older urban areas that are being made over into vibrant and attractive living places by new middle-class and upper-middle-class residents.

And the traditional suburbs are themselves not as traditional as they used to be. Many are homes now to swinging singles, young professionals, and empty-nesters who are building new life-styles around fitness, athletics, clubs, amateur theaters, gardening, crafts, and ambitious cookery. Moreover, the shape of suburban housing is changing, too, from the freestanding single-family houses that need the intensive labors of husbands and wives. New developments feature clustered condominium town houses that require no lawn mowing or do-it-yourself maintenance.

But traditional or new style, the suburbs that are easiest to commute from also are the most expensive. In a rough way, then, home seekers can calculate that in and around New York they will be trading travel time for either dollars or space. That is not always true—some distant communities have a special cachet that makes them more expensive than closer-in communities—but it is almost always true. And the corollary also is almost always true: people with lower incomes can get more house for their limited dollars the farther out they settle.

Bergen County, New Jersey, for example, which is just across the Hudson River from New York, has few new houses that sell for less than $125,000. But in Morris and Somerset counties, which are much farther from the city, developers are creating tracts of clustered town houses selling for as little as $60,000. Similarly, brownstone town houses that sell for $1 million or more in Manhattan may be bought for $500,000 in Brooklyn Heights, the closest-to-Manhattan Brooklyn community, and for $250,000 in Park Slope, which is fifteen minutes or so farther into Brooklyn by subway. The houses are roughly the same; it is the geography that changes.

Indeed, one of the most heartening developments in the metropolitan area in recent years has been the growing acceptability of older neighborhoods that were hit by turbulent social and demographic change in the 1960's and abandoned by middle-class families. The first reaction to those wrenching events was an attempt to squeeze into Manhattan, which began the dramatic rise in housing costs there, or into the nearby suburbs, which also saw sharp price increases for housing. The second reaction, as thousands of families and individuals found themselves unable to afford either Manhattan or a nearby suburb, was the resettlement of old urban neighborhoods. That process continues today, with gentrification spreading outward from central Manhattan in concentric rings. Already, the closest neighborhoods have become too expensive for many families. The solution for them is to go farther. In Brooklyn, for example, Flatbush and Fort Greene are considered the new frontiers for those who cannot afford the Heights. In New Jersey, those who are priced out of Hoboken are moving into Jersey City and Paterson.

It also must be said that no matter how much they may spend for their housing, the people who live in and around New York get less for their money than those who live in most other parts of the country. The tiny studio renting for a thousand dollars a month in Manhattan is kin to the cramped, 1,500-square-foot new houses selling for $100,000 in the suburbs, just as the million-dollar co-op on Central Park West is related to the million-dollar center-hall colonial in Greenwich. All are the product of economic and population pressures that have pushed housing costs in this part of the country to extraordinarily high levels.

A survey of the thirty-seven major metropolitan areas done late in

INTRODUCTION

1984 by the National Association of Realtors showed that New York ranked just below San Francisco and Los Angeles as the areas with the highest prices for resale houses. The same study also showed that prices had advanced 14.9 percent in the New York area since the previous year, a rate topped only by Boston, where house prices had advanced 19.4 percent.

New houses, too, are more expensive in the New York area. A 1984 survey done by the Meredith Corporation analyzed costs across the country for a new 1,600-square-foot house with three bedrooms and one and a half or two baths in a desirable neighborhood. It found the highest average price, $290,000, in a New York suburb, Darien, Connecticut, and the second highest price, $255,000, in another Connecticut community, Ridgefield.

Manhattan apartment costs by now are legendary and are comparable to nothing else in the country. In the 220 mostly older cooperative buildings managed by Douglas Elliman-Gibbons & Ives, one of the city's leading brokers and managing agents, the average cost per room in 1984 was $107,000. At that level, a two-bedroom apartment (counted as five rooms) would cost $535,000. Most new Manhattan apartments are created as condominiums, and the prices range upward from $300 a square foot. In such buildings, a small one-bedroom apartment of only 600 square feet—and many are built that small—would cost a minimum of $180,000.

With costs so high for families of all income levels, it becomes harder year by year to weigh alternatives and to find the best places to live. That is the principal reason this book has been written. It offers sound advice by *New York Times* reporters and contributors on what can be found where. But before readers turn to the community profiles, they might find it profitable to read further into this introduction for brief analyses of some of the considerations they should weigh before beginning their searches for a home.

RENTING

In the suburbs that surround New York City and in urban and suburban areas across the country, most people own the homes they live in. In New York City most of the residents are renters. And though in recent years thousands of New Yorkers have been buying apartments, owners still are a minority of the population. Only 30 percent of the housing units in the city are owner-occupied.

History and geography explain this phenomenon. The agglomeration of people that makes New York what it is has been created only by crowding the population onto a limited amount of available land at high densities. The dimensions of a standard block in Manhattan

INTRODUCTION

are 200 by 600 feet (120,000 square feet), or 2.75 acres. Even in the 1880's, before the development of steel-framed high-rise buildings, as many as 3,500 people were living in low-rise tenements on single blocks of Manhattan, a density of more than 1,270 people to an acre.

Multifamily buildings were the only way to organize living space in so dense a city, and such buildings were too expensive for most people to own. Rather, most of the housing units in the city were owned by developers and investors who ran them as businesses. True, the cooperative form of apartment living got its start in New York more than a century ago, but until recently it was available only to the rich or the upper middle class. The condominium form, which originated in Europe, was not introduced until 1964.

As a result, most New Yorkers became renters, and the persistence of rent regulations for more than four decades has kept them renters, even when many apartments became available for ownership. The reason is not hard to find. Rent control, which began during World War II, and rent stabilization, which began in 1969, have kept the cost of housing to tenants far below its true market cost. In fact, low rents and the nickel subway ride were for many years the only real bargains in a city of high living costs. Now, with the subway fare up to 90 cents, only regulated rents are a bargain, and mostly for people who have lived in their apartments for many years. But the system of regulation, while it is amended and tinkered with by the Legislature almost every year, is considered unrepealable by most politicians. Too many voters have a stake in keeping things as they are.

But just as there is no free lunch, there also are no benefits without costs. Landlords who were getting a return that they considered inadequate stopped investing new capital in their buildings, with the result that the buildings deteriorated. Development of new rental buildings slowed to a pace far below the demand. And when buildings slipped into the red, as some began to do when energy and financing costs rose sharply, landlords began converting them into cooperatives and condominiums. That was their way of withdrawing their own capital from an unprofitable situation and forcing the tenants to invest their own.

There are legal limits on converting rentals into co-ops or condominiums, as will be seen in the next section, but conversions are nevertheless proceeding at a rapid pace. They began with the best buildings in the best neighborhoods, and then spread to more modest apartment houses in other neighborhoods. In the first three quarters of 1984, plans were filed for converting more than 15,000 apartments. This followed filings for 33,000 apartments in 1983. As a result, the rental stock of the city is shrinking, making it even harder to find an apartment.

For more than two decades, the differences between regulated

9

rents and market rents have been so wide that tenants who are lucky enough to live in rent-regulated apartments just do not move. Almost every New Yorker knows a family of empty-nesters who are remaining in an apartment too large for their needs because it is cheaper than the smaller apartment they want but cannot afford. Likewise, almost every New Yorker also knows a couple with young children who are crowded into a small apartment because they cannot find a larger one they can afford. And in every rent-regulated building, tenants are paying vastly different rents for equivalent apartments because the apartments have different histories of occupancy. Those that have been held by a single tenant for many years have low rents; those that have had several tenants have high rents because the landlord was legally entitled to raise the rent with each change in tenancy.

In short, the benefits of the system are distributed unequally, creating a mismatch between needs and availabilities. The system provides artificially low rents for tenants in place and forces everyone else to seek housing in the free market, where strong demand and keen competition for living space keep rents at high levels, especially in Manhattan.

By 1983 the system had developed so many anomalies that it had become an administrative nightmare. There were two parallel systems, one for rent-controlled apartments and the other for rent-stabilized apartments, with separate administrations and procedures. Tens of thousands of complaints of overcharges had been filed by tenants and thousands of requests for hardship increases had been filed by landlords. The Omnibus Housing Act of 1983 sought to correct the worst of these problems, and the new system came fully into effect in 1984, with one major exception. The act provided for the writing of a new administrative code of rules and procedures to give effect to the new law. But the code as drafted by landlord representatives was rejected by Mayor Edward Koch, and an amendment to the act giving the city veto power over another draft to be written by the state was rejected by Governor Mario Cuomo. This left the code in limbo, and the system has been limping along without one while a compromise is sought in the State Legislature.

Nevertheless, a single agency, the State Division of Housing and Community Renewal, now administers the 218,000 rent-controlled apartments and the 943,000 rent-stabilized apartments in the city. Together, they constitute 61 percent of the occupied housing units. And when the computerized registration program being set up by the division is operating fully, it should be possible to determine instantly the legal rent and range of services mandated by law for every one of these apartments. This should eliminate a lot of the acrimony and suspicion between landlords and tenants, and it will give confidence to new tenants that the rent they are being asked for is correct.

When rent-controlled apartments are vacated, they pass out of rent control and the rents may be raised to market levels. As the law is written, that means the new rent should be comparable to what a similar apartment would bring in the same neighborhood. Thereafter, the apartment is subject to rent-stabilization rules, which means that as leases expire rents may be raised only as much as allowed by the city's Rent Guidelines Board. The board, which has both landlord and tenant representatives, sets new guidelines effective in October of each year, with different increases allowed for one- or two-year leases. In the year ending September 30, 1985, for example, rents may be raised 6 percent on one-year leases and 9 percent on two-year leases. An additional increase may be allowed if there is a change of tenancy and a new lease is written. Similar rules apply to rent-stabilized apartments elsewhere in New York State, but the local rent guidelines boards set their own increases and they vary considerably from place to place. In Westchester, for example, the board granted no increases in 1984, an act that outraged landlords in the county.

Subletting of rent-stabilized apartments is permissible under law, but the new housing act limits its use for people who are seeking a permanent home. A sublet may last no more than two years, which means that it is most useful for people who want a temporary home. And though many take sublets with the hope that the prime tenant will not return, the landlord is not obliged to give a subtenant a permanent lease. The law also sets limits on the rent a subtenant may be charged. It is the rent paid by the prime tenant, plus no more than a 10 percent surcharge for furnishings.

For most newcomers to New York, rent-stabilized apartments are a tantalizing but elusive goal. Because they are so desirable, they are hard to find. Friend tells friend when there is to be a vacancy, and landlords often have their own lists of friends and relatives to whom they let vacant apartments. Or the landlords list the apartments with brokers and agents who charge them nothing, do all the work of screening, and load the charges onto the incoming tenant. Some agents demand commissions as high as 20 percent of the first year's rent and seek an additional commission if the lease is renewed. Persistence, watching the newspaper ads religiously, word of mouth, and a lot of luck may help a few to hit the jackpot.

For the rest, the alternative is free-market apartments or houses. In these, rents and the other terms of tenancy are set in direct negotiations between landlord and tenant. Such apartments are found in small buildings with five or fewer units that are not covered by rent stabilization. Or in two- or three-family houses that also are unregulated. Or in single-family houses, in the city or in the suburbs, which are let, usually on short leases, while their owners take a temporary job assignment out of town or overseas. Or, increasingly, rental apartments are found in new condominiums that have been bought by investors. Apartments for let in cooperatives are rare because the house rules of most co-op buildings limit sublets to maintain the active interest of owner-occupants.

But free-market or rent-regulated rental apartments are in short supply in the city. The vacancy rate in 1984 stood at only 2.04 percent, according to a study done for the city's Department of Housing Preservation and Development. Vacancy rates are not much higher in other New York State communities where rent-stabilization rules apply. More rental apartments are available in New Jersey, where some communities have a limited form of rent control, and in Connecticut, where there are no controls.

What all this means is that home seekers in and around New York will find more to choose from if they consider buying rather than renting.

OWNING

Owning a home in and around New York is no different from owning a home anywhere else in the country, except that it is likely to be smaller. Not smaller in the absolute sense—there are lots of large houses and apartments to be had—but in the relative sense that people of the same income levels, spending more or less equivalent amounts on their housing, generally get less living space for their money in this area than they do elsewhere. New York and its environs are crowded, making land costs high. Building costs also are high. And though incomes are high as well, so, too, is the cost of living.

All of this means that newcomers to the area would be wise to approach what they are offered here with the expectation that a $100,000 house or a $200,000 apartment is not going to be the last word in spaciousness and luxury, or even the next to the last word. In fact, what they will be offered at those prices is likely to seem small and disappointing when they compare it with what all those dollars would buy for them back home. Corporate relocation officers who bring middle and upper managers to New York to work in company headquarters here know this phenomenon well. All have had their desks used as wailing walls by relocatees who complain that even with the generous raises they have received to compensate for New York's higher living costs, their standards of housing have to fall.

INTRODUCTION

For New Yorkers, this is an old story, but even they, if they have not looked with attention at housing costs for a while, may be surprised by how little big sums buy. For them, the shock usually comes when they shop for the new housing being developed here. Quite costly condominium apartments in the city, for example, often have their kitchens in little crooks or corners off living rooms, with one wall open to the living rooms because there are no windows in the kitchens. Often the open wall is called a pass-through and is presented as a convenience because the area on the other side will have to serve as the dining room. Or the open wall is explained as "the loft esthetic," a reference to the large open-plan living spaces that artists have created in commercial lofts in old Lower Manhattan factory buildings. Loft living in SoHo has a cachet in New York, and developers are not averse to a SoHo loft association that helps to sell uptown apartments.

And it is not just the kitchens that are small. Bedrooms, too, are built on a Lilliputian scale, say, 10 by 11, while the hyperbole used to describe them, "spacious" and "sweeping," is Brobdingnagian. Closets that are called walk-in often are not, and ceilings usually are low, no more than eight feet high.

On the other hand, bathrooms are Sybaritic, with marble replacing tile on walls and floors, sinks set in vanity tables and tubs that are talented, ready to caress tired bodies with swirls of water. In fact, some bathrooms are so lavish they actually exceed in size the bedrooms they adjoin. And the kitchens, though small and short of counter work space, are jammed with such equipment as microwave ovens and dishwashers. Many new apartments also have little wall-mounted television monitors connected to the lobby that allow tenants to see callers before admitting them to the building by buzzer.

Detached, single-family houses exist in great numbers and still are being produced in the metropolitan area, and those who prefer that kind of living space will find it in all the boroughs of the city except Manhattan, as well as in outlying communities. Among the in-city neighborhoods that offer attractive one-family houses are Forest Hills and Bayside in Queens, Riverdale and Pelham Parkway in the Bronx, Todt Hill and Tottenville in Staten Island, and Midwood and Flatlands in Brooklyn. Indeed, some of these sections of the city are true suburbs, in the sense that they were developed when there was open space between them and Manhattan, and they still retain the open feeling and grassed-over look that most people associate with suburban communities. In most such sections, two-family houses also are available, offering an opportunity to live in a suburban setting while sharing the costs with a tenant.

Increasingly, however, the new housing that is being developed in the outer boroughs and in the rest of the area is in the form of the clustered condominium town house. There are advantages for both builder and buyer in this form. It is cheaper to develop and maintain, and it preserves open land. Moreover, it also suits households in which there are two working spouses or older couples because all the exterior work associated with a house—painting the shutters, mowing the lawn, sweeping the walks, clearing the gutters and downspouts—is done by the condominium management. The disadvantage is that there is less privacy.

Newer houses often are smaller than older ones, with the average size shrinking from about 1,750 square feet to about 1,600 square feet. Many are being designed with open plans to disguise this fact or make it more acceptable. The suburban analogue to the urban loft is the "great room," a large space that incorporates living room, dining room, and kitchen. Such a room affords a sense of spaciousness that would not be possible in a small house if the space were cut up by walls. And so popular have these multipurpose "great rooms" become that in some developments they are being built into quite large and expensive houses that could easily accommodate more separate rooms. Privacy, again, is lost in such an arrangement, but many home buyers apparently do not miss it.

Some home seekers who are prepared to accept the physical shape of condominiums are confused by their legal status. What, they wonder, will they own if they do not own the land under their units? And how can they own the space within their walls but not the walls themselves? Such questions arise frequently because the condominium form of ownership in the United States is only two decades old, and it really has been only a few years since condominiums have been developed in large enough numbers to make an impression on the American psyche.

Actually, a condominium unit is as much a piece of real estate as a freestanding, single-family house, and it may be financed with a mortgage in exactly the same way. In most condominiums, however, all the owners share a common interest in the land, and they also share the costs of maintaining the property through monthly dues payable to the condominium association. The common interest in the land and its appurtenances, like swimming pools, lawns, tennis courts, and walks, is indivisible, and the monthly common charges paid by the owners include a share of whatever taxes are payable on that property. But the owners of the units are assessed separately on their living spaces, and they are free to sell them whenever they wish. To retain some control over who moves into a development, however, many condominium associations write into their rules the right of first refusal on a sale. This means that if an owner agrees to accept, say, $125,000 for his unit from a buyer, the association may buy it instead so long as it pays the same price.

Some home buyers are uncomfortable with the usual condominium arrangements and dislike not owning their own piece of land. To accommodate them, condominiums also are being developed in the "fee simple" form. In this form, the land directly under the unit, and perhaps a narrow strip in front or in back, is sold along with the unit, and only the lawns, walks, and other shared property are held as an undivided interest of the condominium association. Such developments often are called homeowner associations.

In the city and in some suburban areas, condominiums also are developed as high-rise apartment houses, and the legal principles governing them are the same as those governing clustered townhouse condominiums. In apartment condominiums, the common interest includes not only the land under the building but also the mechanical systems, the lobby and public areas, and the corridors and elevators. The cost of maintaining them is shared by the unit owners.

Cooperative apartments, however, are a quite different form of ownership. Strictly speaking, a cooperative apartment is not real estate at all. Rather, what the buyer gets for his purchase price are shares in the corporation that owns the building and a proprietary lease on his apartment. The costs of heating and operating the building, the taxes on the property, and the payments on the building's mortgage all are paid by the corporation and then apportioned as maintenance charges among the tenant owners. However, the shareholders are permitted under federal law to deduct from their taxable income whatever they pay to the corporation toward its real-estate taxes and mortgage interest. Thus they get the full tax benefits of home ownership.

Financing is not as easy for co-op buyers as it is for condominium buyers. Lenders now are willing to write long-term mortgages on co-op units and accept the pledge of the owner's share as security. But because there may be difficulty in selling the shares in the event of a foreclosure, such mortgages are not fully salable in secondary mortgage markets, and for that reason, lenders often charge slightly more for a co-op loan than a loan on a condominium. Another difficulty is that the bylaws of some co-ops forbid financing and insist that a buyer pay the full price of an apartment before taking over the proprietary lease. Other buildings will allow only a third or a half of the purchase price to be financed. Few allow more than three quarters of the price to be financed.

Co-op owners also may have more trouble selling their apartments because the law and their own bylaws give the boards of cooperatives full power to screen potential buyers. At a time like the present, when the demand for cooperatives exceeds the supply, boards sometimes act capriciously and reject would-be buyers on quite flimsy grounds. Some have run their buildings as if they were private clubs, refusing to admit applicants whose life-styles did not match their own. And rejections on racial and religious grounds are not unknown, even though discrimination of that kind is illegal. But most boards look for only two qualities in buyers—financial resources to assure their ability to pay their maintenance charges and the promise of a quiet tenancy.

Cooperative and condominium living are waxing in the city, and tenancy is on the wane. As explained earlier, many rental buildings are being converted by their owners as a way of withdrawing capital from an enterprise that may be losing money or earning less than can be earned in other forms of investment. And almost all new housing is being developed for sale rather than for rent.

For home seekers trying to determine whether renting or owning is the better course, there are a few simple criteria. If they can find a rent-stabilized apartment with a below-market rent, then renting is worth considering. But if the only rental apartment they can find has a market-level rent, then owning probably is more advantageous. People with middle-class incomes derive tax benefits from home ownership that lessen the cost of their housing dramatically. In addition, ownership gives them the opportunity of profiting on the long-term appreciation of whatever property they buy, of sheltering some of that gain, and of paying the lesser capital-gains rate on the gain that is not sheltered. Moreover, owners may remodel their living spaces and adapt them to suit their needs in ways that renters may not.

One common way renters become owners is by purchasing the apartment they are renting when a building is converted. Conversion plans are examined and monitored by the state Attorney General's Office, and while the attorney general's permission to proceed with a plan does not necessarily mean it makes sense economically, it does mean that the sponsor of the plan has fully disclosed what tenants have to know to make an intelligent decision. Often that decision will depend on how much deferred maintenance is needed to make the building sound and how large a fund the sponsor will provide to do the work.

Conversions go forward as either eviction or noneviction plans. Under an eviction plan, if 51 percent of the tenants agree to buy their apartments, the plan becomes effective and tenants who do not want to buy must leave within three years. The exceptions are handicapped people and people sixty-two years old or older, who may remain as tenants as long as they like. Under a noneviction plan, only 15 percent of the apartments must be sold for the plan to become effective, but tenants in the other apartments may remain as renters.

Because it often is difficult to get tenants to buy their apartments, sponsors usually offer them at a discount or insider's price. Sometimes these prices are pegged as much as 50 percent below market value. At that level or anything close to it, buying at an insider price is a real opportunity, although not all tenants are in a position to seize it.

CHOOSING A PLACE TO LIVE

Making the right decision about where to live in and around New York is difficult. It takes thought, research, and a lot of looking. But those who invest the time and effort to do it right will make the right choice.

People who already live in the metropolitan area will have an easier time because they have a home that can serve as a base while they make a leisurely survey of the neighborhoods and communities that interest them. Those who are coming to the area for the first time, or who have made only brief visits, often must conduct their search under the impetus of time constraints. They may be living temporarily in an expensive hotel or staying with friends or relatives who will not welcome a long visit. Or they may have young children who have to be enrolled in a school as soon as possible.

But no matter what the home seekers' situation, they should keep in mind the most important bit of commonsense advice offered in this book: they should look beyond the four walls of any home they are considering to the setting in which it stands. People live not only in a house or an apartment; they also live in a community, and that community becomes their home as much as the living spaces they choose. That, indeed, is the major point of all the articles that follow.

To make an intelligent choice, home seekers also should consider carefully their life-style and their needs and interests. If, for example, there are children in the family, the availability of good schools becomes of paramount importance. Indeed, even people who do not have school-age children should look into the quality of the schools in any community they are considering because good schools add value to a home and bad ones take away value. Though the buyer may not be using the schools and may even look on the taxes he will be paying to support them as a burden, he will welcome them as a selling point if he ever puts his home on the market.

The criteria for assessing a good school system are themselves confusing. It is interesting to note, for example, how often the school officials who were consulted by the writers of these articles cited how well their high-school graduates do on the Scholastic Aptitude Test or how many get into prestigious colleges. An emphasis on that kind of achievement may be just what some families want. But top achievers always are a minority, and a system that puts its best efforts into helping them achieve even more may not be doing enough for the great middle group or for those who have special learning problems. On the other hand, if the pride of a school system is its marching band and its basketball team, will there be enough emphasis on academic achievement? These are difficult questions, and they can be answered only by home seekers who take the time to visit schools, talk with alumni and other parents, and carefully assess the needs of their own children.

Commuting is another issue that should be addressed with care. Certainly it is worth every home seeker's time, before committing himself to a new home, to try out the bus line, subway, or suburban train that he will be depending on to get him to and from work each day. It was meant as a joke, but the final laugh in the film *Mr. Blandings Builds His Dream House* was a situation that has been replicated all too often in real life. The hero discovers, after building a house in Connecticut, that he will have to get up long before dawn each day to catch the only commuter train that can get him to his Madison Avenue advertising agency on time. Others have found that the paperwork or reading they hoped to accomplish during the ride to work is impossible because they almost never get a seat. Or that the bus service from their new home puts them down in the Port Authority terminal on the West Side when their office is another bus ride away on the East Side.

Home seekers also should consider how they will get to whatever is important to them outside working hours. If, for example, music is what gives them most pleasure, it would be foolish to settle in a place from which a trip to Lincoln Center or Carnegie Hall would require a bus, a train, a taxi, and two hours of travel time. If live theater is the passion of their lives, they should think of how to get to not only the theater district in the West 40's but also the Off-Broadway and Off-Off-Broadway theater centers in other parts of town.

In these times of rampant secularism, many families do not consider church or synagogue affiliations important, but those who do find them of primary concern. Or affiliation may become important to them in a few years when a child has to be prepared for confirmation. Surely, such a family will want to settle close to where there is a church or synagogue that fits its sense of what is right and appropriate.

There is no better way to try out a community than to spend a weekend actually living in it. Almost every place has a hotel or motel that can be used as a temporary base from which to explore shops, restaurants, the library, and the hospital. The exploration should be done, at least in part, on foot. A through-the-windshield tour may save time, but nothing gives the feel of a place more accurately than a stroll down its main street. And a careful perusal of the local newspaper is also useful.

INTRODUCTION

A list of what to look for in a community could be expanded to great length, but readers who have read this far will already have seen the point. They should make their own inventories of what is important to them and then look at what is accessible in or near or within relatively easy commuting of the place they are considering. Those choices are personal and must be made to each home seeker's tastes and needs.

One final point that may not be obvious is taxes. All the articles that follow give either the tax rate in a community or an example of the average tax bill on a house in the median price range for that area. This is useful information, but it is not the full picture. As readers go through this book they will be struck by the fact that property taxes in New York City are quite low. They are, indeed. One-, two-, and three-family houses are assessed at 17.35 percent of market value and the rate is $9.10 for each hundred dollars of asset valuation. That means a house with a market value of $100,000 will be assessed at, say, $17,000, and taxes will be about $1,540 a year. In many cases, taxes will be even lower because reassessments often lag far behind advancing market values. Taxes also are low on cooperative and condominium apartments.

If, however, a home buyer weighs his tax burden only by considering the taxes he might pay on his home, he would be making a serious miscalculation. What must be weighed is the totality of the tax burden attendant on living in a community. Yes, New York City residents generally pay low property taxes, but the city is the only jurisdiction in the area that has its own income tax, and New York State also has an income tax. Moreover, the city and the state have sales taxes that for city residents come to 8.25 cents on the dollar on almost everything that is bought except food.

By contrast, Connecticut has no tax on earned income, although it does tax interest and other forms of unearned income. It also has a tax on automobiles, boats, and other forms of personal property, and it has a 7.5 percent sales tax. New Jersey has a tax on earned and unearned income, but it is lower than New York's. New Jersey also has a sales tax, but at 6 percent it is lower than New York's and Connecticut's, and it is not levied on such important purchases as clothing. In both New Jersey and Connecticut, however, and generally throughout the New York suburbs, property taxes are higher than in New York City.

In making choices, then, what home seekers must do is inquire diligently into what taxes they would be exposed to if they moved into a community. A good source of advice is a local broker, banker, or accountant. Comparisons cannot be generalized, and each community is a tax world unto itself.

MANHATTAN
II.

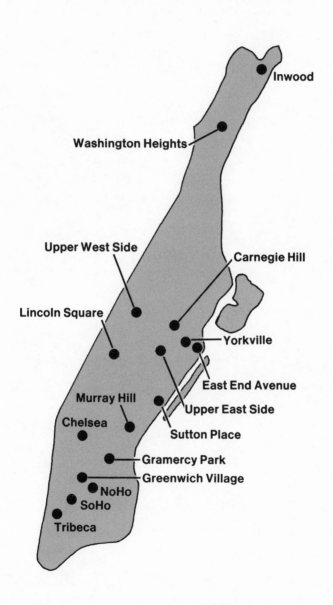

Inwood

Washington Heights

Upper West Side

Carnegie Hill

Lincoln Square

Yorkville

East End Avenue

Murray Hill

Upper East Side

Chelsea

Sutton Place

Gramercy Park

Greenwich Village

NoHo

SoHo

Tribeca

CARNEGIE HILL

To midtown Manhattan: Bus or subway 30 minutes

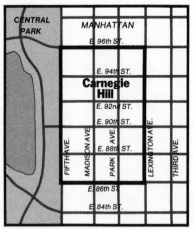

In 1901, Andrew Carnegie, the industrialist and philanthropist, built a palatial mansion on a rise at Fifth Avenue and 90th Street, an area then occupied by shanties and generally considered beyond the pale. Today Carnegie Hill, encompassing roughly the area from 86th to 96th Street between Central Park and Lexington Avenue, is a comfortable, family-oriented neighborhood. It retains many of the mansions and town houses built by millionaires and social figures who followed in Mr. Carnegie's wake, and it has a preponderance of the city's exclusive private schools. Many of the apartment houses are spacious prewar buildings well suited to family living.

"It's a part of town surprisingly few New Yorkers appreciate, a little neighborhood all on its own," said Brewster Ives, of Douglas Elliman-Gibbons & Ives, which manages some of the cooperatives in the neighborhood as well as its first condominium, Carnegie Hill Tower at 94th Street and Madison Avenue.

Recent years have seen a revitalization, particularly on Madison Avenue, where chic boutiques and fancy restaurants have proliferated. "I love what has happened to Upper Madison," stated Liz Bader, a Carnegie Hill resident for almost thirty years. She recalled a time when "you could barely buy a pair of socks in the neighborhood."

But recent construction—in particular a forty-story apartment

23

building at Madison and 89th and a thirty-two-story building at 50 East 89th that supplanted brownstones and modest apartment houses—has not been welcomed by residents, who jealously guard the character of their elite enclave. "My fear is that the character of the neighborhood will be spoiled—I'm concerned about the fragile balance," said Herbert P. Rickman, a special assistant to Mayor Koch and a Carnegie Hill resident.

The sliver building was seen as the particular threat of the 1980's until its development was sharply limited by amended zoning rules. One, however, at 14 East 96th Street, former site of the Stanley Isaacs town house, got in under the zoning wire and is a continuing source of regret to neighborhood activists who fought it.

Carnegie Hill is an active place, with children at play in the tree-lined side streets, cyclists on their way to and from Central Park, and everywhere joggers, whose headquarters is the New York Road Runners Club at 9 East 89th Street.

Groups taking Sunday walking tours can be seen gawking at such sights as the Soviet Mission to the United Nations, at 9 East 91st Street, the former John Henry Hammond residence; at 72 East 91st Street, where Secretary of State John Foster Dulles lived; at the gray frame houses at 120 and 122 East 92nd Street, dating to 1871 and 1859, that are reminders of more rural times; and at 75 East 93rd Street, the headquarters of the Russian Orthodox Church Outside of Russia and the Cathedral of Our Lady of the Sign. The church office and cathedral occupy the former residence of George F. Baker, Jr., whose private railroad car could be shunted to a siding under his house from the tracks passing under Park Avenue.

Many of the Madison Avenue shops cater specifically to the children attending such schools as Spence, Dalton, St. David's, the Lycée Français, Nightingale-Bamford, and the Convent of the Sacred Heart. For suitably preppy clothing, there are J. McLaughlin and Park Bench I; for toys, the Penny Whistle and Dollhouse Antics. Among the holdover shops from earlier times is the eight-decades-old family-oriented Bristol Market at 1110 Park Avenue, which still closes at 1:30 P.M. on Thursdays, traditional maid's afternoon off.

The hub of the neighborhood's cultural activity is the 92nd Street Y on Lexington Avenue, with concerts, dance programs, and poetry readings. And Carnegie Hill is smack in the middle of Fifth Avenue's Museum Mile, with the Yivo Institute for Jewish Research at 86th, the Guggenheim at 88th, the National Academy of Design at 89th, Cooper-Hewitt in the Carnegie mansion at 90th, the Jewish Museum in the Warburg mansion at 92nd, and the International Center of Photography at 94th.

There is a Public Library branch on 96th and the American Alpine Club library at 113 East 90th Street, with its collection of 8,000 mountaineering books and periodicals.

Restaurants are particularly plentiful on Madison Avenue. Among them are Summerhouse, Bailiwick, Devon House, Nodeldini's Park East, Adam's Son, Jackson Hole (for hamburgers), and Piro's. The tiny Table d'Hôte at 44 East 92nd Street and the Hsing Hua Chinese Restaurant at 1108 Park Avenue also have their adherents, as does the Rose Bud, a restaurant with a French menu and fresh flowers on every table, that formerly was the coffee shop in the Wales Hotel.

The hotel itself, on Madison at 92nd Street, attracts a predominantly European and South American clientele, but many neighborhood residents value it as a convenient place for their out-of-town guests to stay.

Public transportation is adequate, with crosstown buses on 86th and 96th, downtown buses on Fifth and Lexington, and uptown buses on Madison and Third. There are IRT subway stops on Lexington at 86th and 96th. Midtown is less than a half hour away.

Since most apartment buildings are cooperatives or in the process of being converted, rentals are at a premium, and prospective tenants are often put on waiting lists for up to a year. Nancy Packe, president of the Feathered Nest rental agency, said that brownstone apartments run from $900 to $1,000 a month for studios, $1,400 to $1,800 for one-bedrooms, and $2,400 to $3,000 for two-bedrooms.

Town houses, according to Frances Hedin of Albert B. Ashforth, range from $950,000 to around $4 million.

Roger W. Tuckerman, executive vice president of Douglas Elliman, said prices of cooperatives have gone up faster than in surrounding areas on the East Side. Apartments on Fifth Avenue in the 90's cost an average of $100,000 a room, with maintenance charges of around $2,100 a year. Resale apartments in the 220-unit condominium at Madison and 94th, he said, have been listed at about $360 a square foot. Even on Lexington Avenue, a location once considered less desirable, as much as $650,000 is being asked for a seven-room co-op.

Real-estate agents often tell their clients that children moving into the area can attend Public School 6, where some pupils are dropped off by limousines and others are bused in from poorer neighborhoods in East Harlem. But Charles Wilson, superintendent of District 2, said only children in the southern portion of the neighborhood may attend this well-known school. Others would attend P. S. 198, where about half the students read at or above grade level, as opposed to well over 80 percent at P. S. 6. The appropriate junior high school is J.H.S. 167, where reading scores are one to two years above grade level. For gifted children there are the Hunter College Campus Schools at Park Avenue and 94th Street.

Within the confines of Carnegie Hill lie two irregular sections designated as the Carnegie Hill Historic District. They include midblock areas between Fifth and Madison from the north side of 92nd

Street to the north side of 94th Street and between Madison and Park avenues from the north side of 90th Street. Community Board 8 has approved and recommended to the city's Landmarks Preservation Commission that the district be extended to include the area between Fifth and Madison avenues from the north side of 94th Street to the north side of 96th Street.

"The architecture you walk past every day," said Ronald Spencer, former president of Carnegie Hill Neighbors, "has a profound effect on how you feel about where you live."

—RUTH ROBINSON

C H E L S E A

*To midtown Manhattan: Subway
10 minutes or walking 20 minutes*

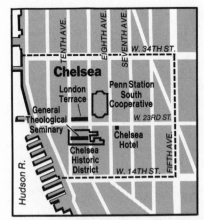

For Chelsea, the 1970's
and early 1980's were something of a second childhood, a frenetic
period of growth in which many of the area's brownstones were
converted, rehabilitated, or restored. New residents, many of them
young professionals priced out of more costly areas of the city,
poured into this West Side neighborhood, changing its character.

But local officials say that most of the brownstones in Chelsea
now have been restored and that the creation of new housing units—
mostly through the conversion of larger apartment buildings and
lofts on the fringe areas of the neighborhood—has leveled off. The
result has been steady price and rent escalations, as current and
would-be residents compete for a limited housing stock.

"It's slowing down only because there practically isn't anything
left to upgrade," said Sidney Rubell, a real-estate broker who has
been doing business in Chelsea for forty years. "The market is still
very hot. Prices are very high. There seems to be no limit to what
renters are willing to pay."

Although prices in Chelsea are still not as high as on the Upper
West Side, to which the neighborhood is often compared, they have
climbed rapidly in the last few years. For a studio, $900 a month rent
is common on the more desirable blocks. In one of the few newly
constructed buildings, a forty-four-unit condominium completed in

1983 on 23rd Street between Eighth and Ninth avenues, studios started at $125,000. Duplexes sold for up to $350,000.

Compounding the apartment shortage are the many older, long-term Chelsea residents who occupy rent-controlled or rent-stabilized apartments. Two huge apartment complexes in Chelsea—London Terrace and Penn Station South—have long waiting lists for apartments. At Penn Station, a co-op between Eighth and Ninth avenues and 23rd and 28th streets, one resident said she waited twelve years.

"If the landlord hears you're moving out, he'll have somebody all ready to move in the day you're gone," said Irene Williamson, who has lived in Chelsea with her husband, Raymond, for the last thirty years. "A lot of people are stuck in their apartments. They can't afford to move."

Not that the Williamsons would move if they could. Like many other residents, they are sentimental about their neighborhood—and about the fact that it is still largely a neighborhood, despite the influx of so many new faces.

"We haven't lost our neighborliness," stated Mary Swartz, who moved to Chelsea from Greenwich Village in 1976. "There are block parties, and people come out to help. There was a lost cat on my block the other day. Lots of people got involved in that, trying to find it."

Generally, the boundaries of Chelsea are considered to be 14th Street on the south, 34th Street on the north, Fifth Avenue on the east, and the Hudson River on the west. That location puts it within a twenty-minute walk or a ten-minute subway ride of the midtown office district. There are bus lines on the avenues and main cross-town streets and subway lines on Sixth, Seventh, and Eighth avenues.

Chelsea is an old and historic swath of the city that strongly resists classification. It has blocks of gracious brownstones that seem snipped from an 1830's real-estate circular, and blocks of dingy former factories moldering on its western fringes. It is primarily residential, but it still has more than 12,000 manufacturing jobs in a special industrially zoned area west of Tenth Avenue, according to an unpublished study by the Department of City Planning, and the area north of 24th Street is more industrial than residential.

"There's an interesting economic mix in Chelsea, and it seems to be holding up," said City Councilwoman Carol Greitzer, who represents Chelsea. "Some people are alarmed at the commercial gentrification, which has been very rapid, but I think the community has been very careful to preserve its stock of modest-income housing. There's a very strong pro-tenant movement."

Although there was a brief wave of construction in Chelsea in the 1920's and 1930's, most of the housing stock in the central areas south of the intersection of 23rd Street and Eighth Avenue was built between 1830 and 1880. The Chelsea Hotel, home for a time to a long procession of writers, including Mark Twain, was built in 1884.

The area was named by Captain Thomas Clarke in honor of the Royal Chelsea Hospital in London, a home for retired soldiers founded in the seventeenth century. In 1750, Captain Clarke, himself a retired British soldier, bought his beloved Chelsea estate, which at its greatest extent covered the area between 19th and 24th streets and from about Eighth Avenue to the Hudson. In the 1830's, Captain Clarke's grandson, Clement Clarke Moore, a theologian most often remembered for the humorous poem he wrote for his children, "A Visit from St. Nicholas," began subdividing the estate into private housing.

Mr. Moore, who donated the land for both St. Peter's Church and the General Theological Seminary, both on 20th Street within the Chelsea Historic District, sought to maintain strict control over the type of development in Chelsea. Under his supervision, most of the brownstones were built in the Anglo or Anglo-Italianate style. The historic district is bounded by Ninth and Tenth avenues and by 20th and 23rd streets, though some sections east of Ninth Avenue also are protected.

In the late 1920's and early 1930's, Henry Mandel, the builder of the London Terrace complex, dreamed of building an apartment building on every corner of Seventh Avenue between 14th and 23rd streets, and for a while, it almost seemed possible. At one point, Mr. Mandel was reputed to own 45 percent of the land fronting Seventh Avenue along the nine-block stretch.

But in 1932, after only four buildings in the series had been constructed (one at 15th Street and three at 16th), Mr. Mandel's empire collapsed. He filed for bankruptcy, claiming liabilities of more than $14 million against assets of only $380,602.

Now a new owner of one of the so-called Chelsea Corners buildings has filed a plan for noneviction conversion to cooperative ownership. It is the first of the Mandel buildings to be converted, but it surely will not be the last Chelsea apartment house to be switched from rental to co-op status.

Today, much of the pressure once brought to bear in Chelsea by patrons like Mr. Moore is wielded by local community groups, historical societies, architectural preservation leagues, and tenant-protection groups, some of which are quite well organized. Late in 1984, for example, a proposal for an eleven-story building was withdrawn after groups led by the Chelsea Coalition on Housing, a tenant group, protested that the project, which included a 180-car parking garage, would cut the amount of light to the street and increase traffic.

Despite such concerns, most residents seem to agree that the changes in Chelsea have been for the best. For instance, the Police Department's Crime Analysis Unit says the crime rate in the 10th Precinct, which includes Chelsea, has declined sharply in the last few years in most categories.

Education has also improved with the reopening last year of the former Charles Evans Hughes School as the High School for the Humanities. The old school, on 18th Street west of Eighth Avenue, was phased out beginning in 1981 and restructured with a stiffer curriculum. There are also two elementary schools and Intermediate School 70. Enrollment has leveled off for the last five years, with the number of Hispanic children decreasing, and the numbers of black and white children increasing.

Local residents have a wide variety of restaurants from which to choose, including the Art Deco Empire Diner and several others beginning to sprout near the industrial areas on Tenth Avenue. There are many Japanese restaurants, including That's It, which opened while still under construction, on 23rd Street and Tenth Avenue. Health food also seems popular, with restaurants like Healthy Chelsea, farther east on 23rd.

Several city officials have voiced concern that more restaurants may be opening than can be supported by the local population. Some are expected to fail unless more outsiders can be attracted to Eighth Avenue boutiques. Many have opened in the last few years along 23rd Street as well, and brokers say their expansion is continuing.

Along with clothing stores like Camouflage at 17th Street and Eighth Avenue, there are movie-rental shops like La Boom Video on 23rd Street and specialty stores like the purveyor of athletic shoes that opened recently on Eighth just south of 23rd.

—KIRK JOHNSON

EAST END AVENUE

To midtown Manhattan: Walking and subway 25 minutes

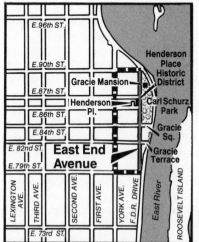

ast End Avenue is the spine of a small, almost private residential enclave that is so far off the beaten tourist path that few visitors to Manhattan ever stumble upon it and even many New Yorkers never set foot in it. The avenue that gives the neighborhood its name and cachet parallels the East River along 79th and 90th streets and has no bakery, no bus line, no post office, and only one bank, one restaurant, one supermarket, and one dry cleaner.

What it does have is an abundance of luxurious living spaces, many with unobstructed river views, in some of the city's most selective buildings, including the most selective of all, Gracie Mansion, where a would-be tenant must be elected mayor of New York to move in. Gloria Vanderbilt lives in the neighborhood, as do Constantine Sidamon-Eristoff, Benno Schmidt, Osborn Elliott, and a host of well-connected New Yorkers whose names are known only to other well-connected New Yorkers.

Though the East End name applies properly only to the eleven blocks of the avenue, the neighborhood also includes Gracie Square and Gracie Terrace (the easternmost blocks of 84th and 82nd streets) and the crosstown blocks running west to York Avenue.

In all, the enclave encompasses only two dozen square blocks, with most of the local shopping and services on York Avenue and tall apartment houses lining East End Avenue and 79th and 86th streets.

31

Crosstown buses on those two streets provide the main public transportation access to the neighborhood. Cruising cabs are hard to find at any hour and the nearest subway, the Lexington Avenue IRT, stops a good half mile away at 77th and 86th streets.

For residents, the remoteness is a trade-off for privacy and quiet. Traffic noises from the Franklin D. Roosevelt Drive are muffled, since its route through the area is mostly underground along the river. Boat whistles are heard more often than police sirens. "It's almost as if you are living on a dead-end street," said Elizabeth Hagen, who has lived on East End Avenue for twenty years.

Some residents, among them Brewster Ives, the octogenarian real-estate broker, can remember when residents could walk down to the river. Now they view it from a walkway built over the drive, which was completed in 1942.

"Renovating Gracie Mansion was the first real improvement to the area," Mr. Ives recalled. "There was a residential colony called Henderson Place where the town houses are now. There was a hospital. The Good Shepherd Home for the Aging was there at 89th Street. Robert Moses, the commissioner of parks who designed the F.D.R. Drive, lived at 7 Gracie Square. It became a fashionable avenue when the apartments were built."

According to Christopher Gray, the architectural historian, that transition began in the 1920's, when "Park Avenue–type buildings with elevators and doormen" began going up. The first, he said, were 520 and 530 East 86th Street, erected by Vincent Astor, who later built several others nearby. The new character of the area was confirmed by a rezoning in 1928 that limited development of East End Avenue below 84th Street to residential uses.

Among the early believers in the future of the avenue was Maria Bowen Chapin, founder of the Chapin School, who moved her growing academy for girls to a Georgian-style building she erected at the 84th Street corner in 1928. Brearley, another independent girls' school, followed a year later to a riverfront site on 83rd Street. Both remain neighborhood anchors.

A longtime resident who recalls that era is Louis Jones, proprietor of the Park View Market grocery at 83rd Street, opened by his father in 1889. He remembers when many of the Irish, English, and German working-class families who had lived in the neighborhood since the 1890's began moving out to Queens in the 1920's. For a while, he said, the neighborhood died. "Then the building started—1 East End, 25 East End, 1 Gracie Square, 10 Gracie Square, 520 East 86th Street, 120 and 130 East End—until 1929 and the stock-market crash."

Residential construction resumed after World War II, and the demolition of the Third Avenue el in 1954 brought a wave of redevelopment throughout the Upper East Side. Hundreds of tenements were demolished and new high-rise apartment houses went up. East End Avenue got many tall new buildings at that time, and only a shortage of clear building sites has prevented further redevelopment.

The newest apartments are in Asten House, a cooperative completed in 1983 at 515 East 79th Street, and 2 East End Avenue, a co-op created out of a former warehouse in 1979.

There are thirty-three cooperative buildings in the area and all are expensive. One-bedroom apartments begin at about $130,000, according to Edith Sachs, vice president and director of sales for J. I. Sopher & Company, and prices in excess of $1 million are not unusual for three-bedroom units. The owner of one co-op with a grand library overlooking the river recently listed the apartment for $7 million.

Rentals also are expensive, ranging upward from $1,000 for a studio, according to J. I. Sopher, but there also are some hard-to-get rent-regulated apartments, a few on the avenue but most on the side streets, with more moderate rents. Town houses range upward from $750,000.

Many residents send their children to Chapin, Brearley, and other private schools scattered throughout the Upper East Side. Others choose among well-thought-of public schools nearby—P.S. 158 at 78th and York; P.S. 190 on 82nd between First and Second avenues; Wagner Junior High School between Second and Third on 76th; and the Hunter College Campus Schools at 94th and Park Avenue, to which students are admitted by competitive examination.

The neighborhood's major recreational resource is Carl Schurz Park, a 14.9-acre tract of greenery and paved playground that runs along the river between 84th and 90th streets. Within it, behind a fence to ensure the mayor's privacy, is Gracie Mansion, built as a country seat by Archibald Gracie in 1799, enlarged by him in 1811, and enlarged again by the city in 1966.

On fine spring and summer weekends, hundreds of sun-seekers pour into the park and take perches along its riverfront promenade to watch the passing parade of tugboats, tankers, yachts, and cabin cruisers. Despite crowds of strollers and sitters who often fill every bench, a day in the park is for many as refreshing as a day in the country. The promenade extends to the Queensboro Bridge and is a jogger's haven.

Opposite the park, on the 86th to 87th Street blockfront, are twenty-four small Queen Anne–style houses, the remnant of an enclave of thirty-two built in 1881, that now constitute the Henderson Place Historic District.

When residents want to dine out near home, they walk to York Avenue (where some of the restaurants have sidewalk tables in the summer) and choose among Francesco's, Arturo's, Gold Medal 83, Wilkinson's Seafood Cafe, and other dining places or walk farther west along 86th Street to the bustling heart of Yorkville near Third Avenue, where there are traditional German restaurants such as the Ideal, specializing in potato pancakes, and the Cafe Geiger.

There is a bus line on York that runs as far south as 59th Street and links the neighborhood to the shopping hub around Bloomingdale's. And there is express bus service to Wall Street from 79th and York. For those who work in the midtown area, there is either a brisk ten-minute walk or a crosstown bus ride of equal length to Lexington Avenue and then a fifteen-minute subway ride downtown on the IRT.

Among the entertainments in the neighborhood are mayor-watching and its concomitant, watching the celebrities who visit the mayor.

Beatrice Morse, who lives on 85th Street, often walks her dog past Gracie Mansion to see who may be calling and not long ago saw Zhao Ziyang, the prime minister of China. "It's comforting to know Gracie Mansion is here," she said. "I walk the dog from one to two in the morning and feel safe."

—MAX KLEIMAN

GRAMERCY PARK

To midtown Manhattan: Subway 10 minutes or walking 20 minutes

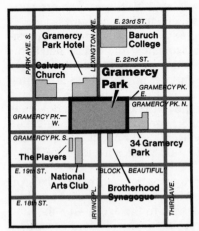

To the Reverend Stephen Garmey, sorting out the lore of Gramercy Park is like keeping a family album. From the archives of Calvary Church to what he hears on the streets, he collects stories about the park, tidbits of information—even fables—and recounts them with affection.

He tells of being caught in a neighborhood traffic jam and spotting a brass plaque on the side of a building on East 20th Street. "On this site in the year 1897," it was inscribed, "Sir Arthur Sullivan wrote 'The Pirates of Penzance.'"

"Amazing, isn't it, what surrounds us in this neighborhood," said Mr. Garmey, who is associate rector of Calvary, the Episcopal church at the corner of 21st Street and Park, which was built in 1846. "And all the stories are bits and pieces that fit into a mosaic of life that is changing and exciting."

The land that Samuel B. Ruggles deeded to New York City in 1831 as a private park remains under lock and key, accessible only to those who live in buildings on the perimeter. Inside the wrought-iron gates of the park elderly people sit on the benches chatting and mothers play with children as they might have a hundred years ago.

"The inside of the park hasn't changed at all," said Mr. Garmey, "but Gramercy Park has not been static. It has a fascinating history, and history is nothing if not strange."

Technically, the Gramercy Park neighborhood comprises only the blocks directly facing on the park, that is, 21st and 20th streets (called Gramercy Park North and South, respectively), and Gramercy Park West and Gramercy Park East. Leading out of the north side is the start of Lexington Avenue, which Mr. Ruggles named for the Revolutionary War battle site, and out of the south side runs Irving Place, which he named for Washington Irving.

Practically, however, the neighborhood embraces a larger area running between 23rd and 17th streets and from Park Avenue South to Third Avenue. In fact, as far away as 14th Street, owners have used the name Gramercy to lend panache to their buildings.

"The name is borrowed very liberally," stated Peter Ryan, president of Gramercy Neighborhood Associates, the oldest neighborhood association in the city. "Real-estate agents realize that people like the idea of living in Gramercy Park, even if it means stretching the term."

Although it is limited, housing in the larger Gramercy Park area is available, according to Hank Sopher, president of the real-estate concern of J. I. Sopher & Company. Rentals for one-bedroom apartments start at $1,000 a month and co-op resales average $50,000 a room.

Apartments in Gramercy Park proper command prices that, on the average, run 25 percent higher, Mr. Sopher said, but, he added, "most of those apartments never make it to the agent—it's the kind of thing you have to hear about from the inside." More accessible are newer apartments in loft buildings along and adjacent to Park Avenue South and in the high-rises that dot Third Avenue. Although the appeal of the park lures many new residents, they often are not aware of its rules.

"The number-one question I get asked is whether they can get a key to the park," remarked Mr. Ryan. "Once I explain that the only people allowed to have keys are those who live on the fringe of the park, there is disappointment, but most people understand."

The residents entitled to keys are responsible for paying the annual $39,600 in maintenance fees and $1,000 in taxes on the property. It is a park unadorned by recreation facilities, but even though the rules forbid ball playing, the paid supervisor has been known to ignore unidentified flying objects. "The park is the most essential feature to the cohesiveness of this neighborhood," said Fay Moore Donoghue, an artist known for her paintings of thoroughbred racehorses, who lives in the National Arts Club at 15 Gramercy Park South.

Founded in 1898, the club moved into its current residence, the mansion of Governor Samuel J. Tilden, in 1906. Mr. Tilden was the only presidential candidate to win the popular vote but lose the election in the electoral college, where Rutherford B. Hayes edged him out by one vote in 1876. The club is home to about fifty tenants, most of them writers and artists. It is also host to cultural events, including the Gramercy Park Flower Show, which has been held annually since World War II.

Next door, at 16 Gramercy Park South, is The Players. The actor Edwin Booth bought the building in 1888 and had it redesigned by Stanford White as a club for fellow thespians. Mr. Booth died in his room in the club on June 7, 1893, and the room remains as it was on that date. "The legend has it that there was a clap of thunder at 1:35 A.M.," Mr. Garmey said, "and he went with it."

At 28 Gramercy Park South is the Brotherhood Synagogue, an austere building that was erected for Quakers in 1859 as the Friends Meeting House. Across the street is 34 Gramercy Park, which in 1983 celebrated its centennial. It is the oldest co-op apartment house in the city, and a gloved operator still pulls on a cable to activate the original hydraulic elevator.

On the west side of the park, Nos. 3 and 4 are marked by lacy iron porticoes and ornamental gas lamps. On 20th Street is the birthplace of Theodore Roosevelt.

History is a benign presence in many buildings, but it was not too long ago that relics like the Third Avenue el were a blighting influence on the neighborhood. Since the el was torn down in 1954, however, much of Third Avenue has been redeveloped with tall apartment houses, and it now is lined with boutiques and service stores that make it an attractive shopping thoroughfare.

Outrageous attire is featured at the Wild Game boutique, and gift items for the home can be bought at Wilburt's. There are sources to satisfy virtually any gastronomical whim, from baked goods at the Gramercy Pastry Shop to cheeses, breads, and assorted delicacies at the LaMarca Cheese Shop.

Residents laud the opening of newer restaurants like 65 Irving Place and Cafe Society, but they still frequent established neighborhood eateries like Pete's Tavern and Sal Anthony's. Both of these restaurants on Irving Place lay claim to being the spot where O. Henry wrote "The Gift of the Magi."

The area also is home to Baruch College, the City University business school, and the Police Academy is on 20th Street just to the east of the neighborhood. The presence of these two institutions aggravates the already tight parking situation.

But the neighborhood is accessible by public transportation. The IRT Lexington Avenue subway stops at 23rd Street and 14th Street, and there are buses that run along Second and Third avenues and 14th and 23rd streets. Midtown offices and shopping are only a twenty-minute walk or a ten-minute subway ride away.

The area even has its own hostelry, the Gramercy Park Hotel, which borders the park on its Lexington Avenue corner and has a residential annex as well. Rates average $85 a night for a single and $90 for a double.

Public School 40, at Second Avenue and 20th Street, is the local grade school, although many children in this predominantly upper-middle-class neighborhood attend private schools.

One of the most notable neighborhood features is the stretch of 19th Street between Irving Place and Third Avenue. It has been dubbed "Block Beautiful" by the American Institute of Architects, and the varied styles of its houses give it a special charm.

"Gramercy Park is very much like a small town," Mr. Garmey said. "Because there are no skyscrapers, people are close to the streets. There is a feeling of community that is somehow connected to the park itself that makes this a fascinating neighborhood."

—ESTHER B. FEIN

GREENWICH VILLAGE

*To midtown Manhattan: Subway
15 minutes or walking 30 minutes*

In 1948 a young woman from Spokane, Washington, arrived in Manhattan, got into a taxicab, and told the driver, "Take me to the Village." She roamed the streets near where he set her down and saw a "For Rent" sign on a quaint, red-brick Federal house in Grove Court. She went in, rented an apartment from the mistress of an actor, and lived happily in the Village for several years.

Like many Villagers, she has since departed for married life in the suburbs and would have a fit if her own daughter came to Greenwich Village under the same circumstances today. But although life in New York has changed a great deal since then, the Village remains a symbol of a kind of spontaneous, unconventional life-style that came to be known as Bohemian.

The Village is a maze of crisscrossing streets, narrow byways, winding lanes, and tree-shaded, cobblestoned cul-de-sacs below 14th Street, above Houston Street, and between the Hudson River and Fourth Avenue, although some Villagers now call the area west of Hudson Street "The Far West Village" and think of it as a separate neighborhood. The exact boundaries of the Village often provoke arguments, during which someone is bound to declare that the geography does not matter—that the Village is a state of mind.

"State-of-minders" vaunt the fact that the Village has been the home and workplace of generations of writers, painters, sculptors,

39

playwrights, theater producers, and other creative and rebellious individualists whose influence has spread nationwide.

It is still a mecca for the adventurous. On dozens of stages in small theaters, church basements, lofts, cellars, and vacated stores, Off-Broadway productions carry on in the spirit of Eugene O'Neill, Edna St. Vincent Millay, Susan Glaspell, George Cram Cook, and Robert Edmond Jones. And like Helen Westley and her Washington Square Players, and Eva Le Gallienne and her Civic Repertory, they, too, sometimes move uptown and win Pulitzer prizes.

But the Village is also a cohesive community of handsome homes in turn-of-the-century apartment buildings, modern high-rises, stately post–Civil War mansions, and Federal town houses. Many of the mansions and town houses have been remodeled into apartments, as have lofts and factories, a former church, a former firehouse, a former power station, a former library, and a lot of former stables. Backyard gardens, tree-lined streets, window boxes, and public land lovingly tended by volunteer gardeners abound.

Like the eclectic mix of housing, restaurants with food from all nations flourish, die, and reappear under new management, while old neighborhood bars and taverns serve the descendants of the original patrons.

Chumley's, a speakeasy during Prohibition, is still serving food and drink on Bedford Street. So, too, are the century-old White Horse Tavern on Hudson Street, where Dylan Thomas, the poet, caroused and emoted with Welsh vigor, and the Cedar Tavern on University Place, where Mark Rothko and other painters discussed Abstract Expressionism.

Operatic arias still enliven Asti's, on East 12th Street, when a waiter or a customer suddenly becomes inspired and cash-register bells ring out the accompaniment. For gourmet dining, there is nothing finer south of midtown than the Coach House, on Waverly Place, according to restaurant critics, who also give high ratings to La Tulipe on West 13th Street.

The Village traces its origin to the era after the Revolutionary War, when merchants and bankers who lived and worked at the tip of Manhattan built country places farther up the island. Later, in the nineteenth century, Manhattanites fled to the Village to escape smallpox, yellow fever, cholera, and other plagues. The wealthy built handsome town houses, while craftsmen erected more modest two-story homes.

In 1969 the city designated a major part of the Village a historic district. In its report on the designation, the Landmarks Preservation Commission said there were more than 1,000 buildings built before the Civil War in the Village, including "one of the greatest concentrations of early New York residential architecture to be found anywhere within the five boroughs."

GREENWICH VILLAGE

Some of the houses built for the wealthy remain on the northern border of Washington Square Park, which was once a burial ground for the poor. Henry James, author of *Washington Square,* was born on the park in 1843. His friend Edith Wharton, who wrote of old New York society, lived on Washington Square.

Because of the landmark designation, developers are deterred from replacing row houses and low-rise apartment buildings of historic interest with new buildings. But on the edges of the Village, where the designation does not apply, there is a booming transformation of commercial buildings into residences, with an accompanying burst of shops and restaurants.

The Village is, in the words of Marc Cassuto of Sulzberger-Rolfe, "an area of strong demand" for those seeking to turn residential buildings into cooperatives. "The present level of prices for town houses and cooperative apartments is the highest in the twenty-eight years I have been specializing in the sale of Greenwich Village property," said Eduard A. Griggs, who lives and has an office in the Village. "The same applies to apartment rentals. However, the quality of life in the Village has also reached its highest level."

"Rentals are scarce and expensive," he stated, "generally starting at $750 for studios, $900 for one-bedroom apartments, and $1,500 for two-bedroom apartments. Town houses in the Fifth Avenue area between University Place and Avenue of the Americas cost an average of $900,000. Those between Avenue of the Americas and Hudson Street average $750,000 and those west of Hudson Street somewhat less."

According to Mr. Griggs, "the prices of cooperatives range from $40,000 to $125,000 a room, depending on their condition and location, with condominiums somewhat more expensive."

Young people and Bohemians, who have traditionally given the Village its flavor, often have a hard time paying such prices. But they still manage to live there by doubling up and sharing rents, house sitting, or living in dormitories.

The Village has a large population of homosexuals, who set some of its tone, but it also is a neighborhood of families and children. It has superior public schools and a variety of parochial and private schools from preschool through postgraduate, including the Little Red School House, St. Luke's, Friends, and Grace Church schools, New York University, and the New School for Social Research.

Among the well-regarded public schools are Intermediate School 70, which has been sending more than 40 percent of its students on to the city's special high schools for the talented, and Public School 41, where more than 70 percent of the students read at or above grade level.

The Village, however, does not have much open play space for children. There are plots of greenery and paved-over school yards here and there, but the only large open space is Washington Square Park, and it is so heavily used and cut up into seating areas that it is more suited to casual Frisbee tossing than an organized game of baseball or field hockey. Nevertheless, the park is the Piazza San Marco of the Village, and despite its occasionally threatening alcoholics and drug traders, it continues to draw great throngs of residents and visitors.

Few blocks in the Village are exclusively residential, and most have at least a few small shops. But the neighborhood also has clusters of specialty stores. One is on Sixth Avenue north of 8th Street, where Balducci's, the Jefferson Market, and the Jon Vie Pastry Shop offer delights for gourmets and gourmands; another is on Bleecker Street, where small, family-run enterprises offer Italian breads, pastries, cheeses, sausages, and pastas. Bookshops and clothing boutiques are almost everywhere.

Another attraction of the Village is its relative safety. Villagers walk to and fro without fear after dark because most of the streets are brightly lit and filled with people. From their bit of Bohemia, Villagers also may walk downtown to jobs in the financial district or uptown to offices in the midtown area. Either way, the walk takes about a half hour, or, if they prefer, they can get to work in those areas in about fifteen minutes on the IND, IRT, or BMT subway lines that run through the neighborhood.

But one of the Village's greatest attractions remains its mix of creative residents. Among them are Leontyne Price, Agnes De-Mille, Joseph Papp, Mikhail Baryshnikov, James Coco, Elliott Gould, James Beard, and Charles Kuralt.

One of the most dyed-in-the-wool Villagers is Mayor Edward Koch. The city provides him with a handsome residence uptown— Gracie Mansion—where he lives most of the time. However, he has kept his cozy one-bedroom penthouse apartment in the Village, returning to it often enough to keep the plants watered.

—EDITH EVANS ASBURY

INWOOD

To midtown Manhattan: Subway 45 minutes

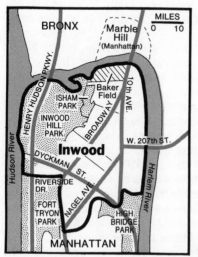

Depending upon the sort of New Yorker one is talking to, Inwood is either where Columbia University plays its football games or it is the area that lies below the south anchor of the Henry Hudson Bridge, or it is ultima Thule on the A train. In all cases, it is the narrow northern tip of Manhattan, and it is emblematic of change that today midtown cab drivers know where it is and do not stubbornly insist that Payson Avenue or Cummings Street or Indian Road is across the Spuyten Duyvil Creek in Riverdale. The traditional rejection of the reality that Inwood is part of Manhattan probably stems from the state of mind depicted in the W.P.A. *Guide to New York City,* published in the 1930's. It said that Inwood's "rivers and hills insulate a suburban community that is as separate an entity as any in Manhattan."

A minor symbol of Inwood's wider window to the south is the recent opening of a carrot-cake bakery with a tiny sidewalk cafe on Broadway at 214th Street not far from the Gallo Auto Body Shop. The arrival of trendy carrot cake among the rugelach, black-and-whites, and jelly doughnuts favored in old Inwood supports the belief that new people are filtering in, looking for reasonably priced pleasant places to live, where commutation is not a day's work.

Inwood fits its name: it lies north of Washington Heights and Fort Washington, claiming a short strip in the Broadway valley between;

it is two fifths greenbelt, with park filling its northern and western borders along the Harlem and Hudson rivers.

The grounds, trees, and gardens of Columbia's Baker Field on the north flow into Manhattan's only primeval park, Inwood Hill, at the Harlem-Hudson confluence. This seamlessly joins Isham Park, once the Isham Estate, whose gatehouse below on Broadway, in a typical piece of Inwood adaptation, now shelters the Gallo shop. The southern end of Inwood Hill Park meets Fort Tryon Park at Dyckman Street.

Inwood's spine is Broadway, and the elevated line of the No. 1 local of the Broadway–Seventh Avenue IRT joins it at 218th Street. The A train of the Independent line ends underground at 207th Street, which, like Dyckman Street, is a main cross street for the area. By either line, the trip to midtown Manhattan takes about forty-five minutes. Inwood now also has a stop at 207th Street for the $3 East Side express bus run by Liberty Lines.

Just north of the 218th Street intersection is the area where the Presbyterian Hospital plans to put its new $106 million community hospital, with 300 beds. This will take 4.3 acres of Baker Field's 26 acres, under present plans. Presbyterian Hospital, which now shares a medical center with Columbia at 168th Street, is also collecting land in a commercial strip along the Harlem River, on the east side of Broadway. John Brian Murtaugh, the assemblyman who represents the neighborhood, believes that the hospital will help Inwood, by stimulating investment in the area, by upgrading the Harlem River waterfront, and by providing sorely needed off-street parking for the community at night.

Another major project in the neighborhood is the upgrading of Baker Field. With the gift of $3 million from Lawrence A. Wien, an alumnus, the university already has replaced the larger grandstand on the east side of the field. Another stand will be erected on the west side, and an eight-lane, 400-meter track with a synthetic surface will be created. When completed, the facility will be opened to track and field teams from other institutions.

Although change is clearly afoot, Inwood retains many of the characteristics it had when it was intensively developed in the 1930's. Before that, it had been unfolding much as expected by Frederick Law Olmsted and his partner, J. James R. Croes, who in a plan submitted in 1876 envisioned it as a residential neighborhood for "fairly comfortable people."

A few of the comfortable buildings of earlier times have recently fallen to the wrecker's ball, but others are being bought up and privately renovated, with the apartments offered for sale as co-ops. But the low-rise and light density character persists. Tucked among the low-rises are one- and two-family houses with trees and tiny yards.

INWOOD

The neighborhood bubbles with children and schools: Good Shepherd and St. Jude's Roman Catholic elementary schools, the Northeastern Academy of the Seventh-Day Adventists, St. Matthew Lutheran School, and a public elementary school and junior high school keep the buses full and the pizzerias busy.

For all its suburban quality, Inwood is not homogeneous. On the east side of Tenth Avenue, it is a transport hub and provides some necessary and gritty services for the greater city. Auto wreckers and repair shops adjoin bars. Gas stations abound, although some have folded. An ancient brick barn for city buses sprawls on Broadway. Much of the Harlem River shoreline on the east is filled with a Con Edison generating station and subway yards. A kennel and a pet crematory sit next to an auto laundry.

One result is that the area is more active around the clock than a suburb. After shifts, workers emerge from the end of the IND line and from the bus barn, and this means coffee shops keep late hours. Bars that are drowsing at 10 P.M. sometimes are swinging by midnight. And the supermarket that replaced the Miramar swimming pool on 207th Street operates twenty-four hours a day.

It may be this mechanical heart that has held gentrification at bay. Residential Inwood has classically been a rental area, save for its private houses, a cluster of Mitchell-Lama limited-profit co-ops at the southern end, and Park Terrace Gardens near Isham Park. But, according to Joseph H. Green, a broker active in upper Manhattan, the pressure for affordable housing in all of Manhattan and the prospect of housing needs for the new hospital have led the owners or new purchasers of a dozen or so older buildings west of Broadway to offer the apartments as co-ops. The prices begin at about $7,500 a room. "Investors who formerly worked only downtown are coming into the area," Mr. Green said. "They are putting a lot of money into the buildings. There is even a shortage of commercial space now."

Buildings that are still rental properties tend to have rents in the area of $170 and $300, which sounds more like the 1960's than the 1980's. Indeed, the area has few vacancies and many residents represent the third generation of their families to live on the same street, and even in the same building. Under rent ordinances, this stability has kept the rents from rising out of sight.

Inwood's private houses turn over seldom, and then usually quickly. Two recent sales were at prices that are typical for the neighborhood: one was a two-family house for $160,000; the other a small one-family brick house for $130,000.

The neighborhood has some architectural treasures. Dyckman House, Manhattan's surviving eighteenth-century farmhouse, is a city museum set upon a rise over Broadway. Some of its old family objects were lost in a trade with Boscobel, another Dyckman home up the Hudson, but children never fail to be amazed on finding that the setting is part of the house: the wall along the interior stair is one of Inwood's many bare granite outcroppings.

West of the farmhouse, the apartment houses of Seaman Avenue, Beak Street, and Payson Avenue are sprinkled with gems of Art Deco doorways, modernistic fire escapes, and courtyards with fountains.

Inwood has one grave lack besides the paucity of parking space in an auto-owning neighborhood: although it has a Chinese restaurant and Formica-tabled eating places, it has no midtown-class restaurant. Assemblyman Murtaugh worries about this a lot. "If I could just get the O'Neals interested," he said. "Otherwise, we really have everything."

—BETSY WADE

LINCOLN SQUARE

To midtown Manhattan: Walking, subway, or bus 15 minutes

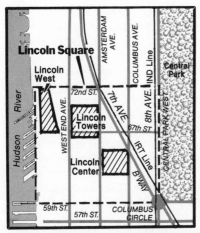

Dancers step gracefully along the walks, their slippered toes pointed outward, their hair tightly pulled into chignons and pinned into place. The sounds of street music complement their movements. The Chagall murals of the Metropolitan Opera House loom and the crowds lean forward with anticipation. This, after all, is Lincoln Center, and this is all happening outdoors, a sort of street-show appetizer to the real shows going on inside the center's many theaters.

"Living in this area is like living on a stage all the time," said Tamara Roberts, a computer programmer who lives on West 69th Street. "You see performers on their way to work, or dancers and musicians on their way to Juilliard for classes, or people all glitzed up to go watch a show. It's an electric neighborhood."

It is difficult to imagine the Lincoln Square neighborhood without Lincoln Center, without the plaza fountain spewing, without banners flapping in the wind advertising the current programs, without ticket holders rushing to make an 8:00 P.M. curtain. But before Leonard Bernstein conducted Beethoven and Mahler in the first performance at Philharmonic Hall (now Avery Fisher Hall) on September 23, 1962, Lincoln Square was a wasteland, cultural and otherwise.

Run-down buildings and neglected tenements covered the blocks from 62nd to 66th Street between Amsterdam and Columbus ave-

47

nues. The music the area knew then was mothers lulling babies to sleep or radios blaring from stoops in hot weather.

But what was once an example of urban decay now is a monument to urban growth and development. Lincoln Center, with its twelve concert halls, museum, public library, bandshell, and park, has inspired the rejuvenation of the entire Lincoln Square neighborhood, which spreads from Columbus Circle to 72nd Street between Central Park West and the Hudson River.

With specialty food shops like Pasta and Cheese and cafes like Fiorello's and Opera Espresso catering to affluent residents and visitors, it is easy to forget that behind the Lincoln Center complex there are still low-income housing projects. Amsterdam Houses are directly behind the center on Amsterdam Avenue, and the eight buildings known as Phipps Houses, built in 1904, are on 63rd and 64th streets between Amsterdam and West End avenues.

There is also a large middle-income complex, Lincoln Towers, a 3,900-unit rental apartment development on West End Avenue between 66th and 70th streets. It takes years to get to the top of the waiting list for these well-designed rent-stabilized apartments, and all attempts so far to convert the buildings into cooperatives have been unsuccessful. But that may change now that the owner of the complex, the MacArthur Foundation of Chicago, has put it up for sale; the most likely buyers are converters.

The predominant form of housing in the Lincoln Square area, however, is luxury. "If you're thinking of living in the Lincoln Square area," said Ethel Sheffer, the chairman of the local Community Board 7, "you'd better have a lot of money."

The Lincoln Square Special District, established by the City Planning Commission early in the 1970's to encourage the development of the neighborhood around Lincoln Center, comprises six blocks in the area from 62nd to 67th Street between Broadway and Columbus avenues.

Developers were granted additional floor space in buildings on these blocks in return for providing pedestrian bonuses, such as arcades and plazas. But the spirit of Lincoln Square—and the prices—extend to the entire Lincoln Square neighborhood.

Rents start at $1,000 for a one-bedroom apartment, and co-op prices at $60,000 a room. Among the newest buildings in the area are a twenty-six-story condominium on 66th Street between Broadway and Central Park West, a thirty-one-story condominium at the corner of Columbus Avenue and 67th Street, and a high-rise apartment building at 67th and Amsterdam.

"It's a good address," said Rose Seda, a manager at Rodman & Associates, a real-estate agency. "It's a neighborhood that's up there already. There are good restaurants and shops and, of course, there's the center itself."

LINCOLN SQUARE

The biggest proposed construction in the area is Lincoln West, a 4,300-unit, seventy-six-acre complex between 59th and 72nd streets on the old Penn Central rail yards hugging the Hudson River. Although Community Board 7 voted against the huge project, the Board of Estimate approved it in 1983.

The Argentine developer of the project, however, ran into financial difficulties and late in 1984 agreed to sell out his interest to Donald Trump. Mr. Trump wants to change the scope and size of the project and is drafting new plans, which will have to be submitted to the Community Board and city officials.

The earlier plan called for contributions to neighborhood amenities by the developer, among them renovation of the 72nd Street and 66th Street stations of the IRT. Though the stations are shabby, the trains provide an efficient link to midtown Manhattan, just to the south of the neighborhood. The area also is served by the IND subway line, running along Central Park West, and several bus lines. By foot, subway, or bus, midtown is less than fifteen minutes away.

Residents of the Lincoln Square area can buy trendy clothes at Charivari and classic haberdashery at Banbury Cross, gourmet cheese and breads while browsing through antiques at Maya Schaper, and exotic flowers at the Southflower Market. And they can swoon over Gable and Garbo at the Regency movie theater, which runs festivals of old films, or philosophize over first-run foreign films at the Lincoln Plaza Cinema. All this is the blessing.

What dilutes that blessing is that lots of other people in the city want to eat in the chic new restaurants, shop in the elegant new stores, and be the first to catch the new Italian movie. Still, the crowds that come to experience Lincoln Square and Columbus Avenue (locals sometimes call it "an East Side avenue misplaced on the West Side") keep the area lively and dynamic.

Central and Riverside parks, which buttress the Lincoln Square area to the east and west, are frequented by walkers, bikers, and runners. The 63rd Street Y.M.C.A. serves as a cultural and artistic center. Squash and racquetball courts at the Manhattan Squash & Racquetball Club at the corner of 66th Street and Columbus Avenue supplement the athletic facilities at the Y.

Crime in the area, which is covered by the 20th Precinct, has been declining, according to Henry Martin, a crime analyst for the Police Department. He attributed the decline in part to the hiring of private security guards by some block associations and to the proliferation of attended buildings. He also pointed to the stabilizing influence of Lincoln Center, the ABC-TV complex, and other nearby institutions, such as Fordham University's West Side campus and Roosevelt Hospital.

Children can attend Public Schools 191 or 199, where about 60 percent of the students score at or above grade level on city reading tests. The nearest high schools are Martin Luther King, Jr., where about 70 percent of the graduates last June were accepted at institutions of higher education, and Louis D. Brandeis, where the figure was 76 percent.

There are also several private schools, among them the Ethical Culture School and the Professional Children's School. The Fiorello H. La Guardia High School of Music and the Arts, which encompasses the High Schools of Music and Art and Performing Arts, opened on Amsterdam Avenue, behind Avery Fisher Hall, in September 1984.

But despite the revolving-door traffic, there is a community of Lincoln Square. "When the weather is nice, I see the same elderly people sitting under the trees in Damrosch Park, eating their lunch," said Doreen Lown, who works at Lincoln Center. "You see mothers strolling their kids around the complex and couples sitting on the edge of the fountain and you realize that Lincoln Center is very much a part of this community."

—ESTHER B. FEIN

MURRAY HILL

*To midtown Manhattan: Walking
10 minutes*

You can eat a fish-and-raw-egg Japanese breakfast in Murray Hill, read a Gutenberg Bible, buy a pornographic birthday card, or swim on a rooftop. You can protest political repression outside the Polish consulate or pump iron in a basement health club.

You can get home delivery of a pastrami on rye and a kasha knish at 4 A.M. You can buy flowers on your way into the Queens-Midtown Tunnel and, coming out, you can get your windshield washed—like it or not—by a persistent street urchin.

What you can't easily get is a really great loaf of freshly baked bread.

As New York neighborhoods go, Murray Hill—loosely defined as the area of about 20,000 residents between 34th and 42nd streets and Madison Avenue and the East River—has pretty much everything, including a Japanese hotel, the Kitano, and a profusion of foreign consulates. But a special dimension, Murray Hill's pervasive nineteenth-century flavor, sets it apart from neighboring communities on Manhattan's trendy East Side. Behind the boutiques and traffic-choked streets, the Gilded Age is still to be experienced in the rows of million-dollar brownstone mansions, wide-doored carriage houses, gas lamps, and leafy backyards.

"It's full of little jewels," said Louis Harris, the pollster, who lives in one—a brick Federal town house built by a cousin of President Martin Van Buren in 1858 and set behind its own ivied courtyard at 152 East 38th Street. Murray Hill, he stated, is a kind of small town:

"It's the embodiment of the city as a series of neighborhoods. It's the opposite of Los Angeles and T. S. Eliot's *Waste Land.*"

Stephen A. Weingrad enthusiastically agrees. Breakfasting on a small terrace at the rear of his town house at 233 East 35th Street, the lawyer and president of the Murray Hill Committee instructed a visitor: "Listen to the pulse of the city."

For a moment there was no sound. Then the silence was broken by the burbling of a fountain in the flower garden below, the peal of a church bell, the flutter of wings under a weeping willow.

Murray Hill takes its name from Robert Murray, a Quaker merchant who moved from Pennsylvania to New York in 1753 and built a farmhouse on what the Dutch called Beacon Hill, near what is now the corner of 37th Street and Park Avenue. When the British attacked the city in 1776, Mrs. Murray and her beautiful daughters— or so the story goes—persuaded General Howe to dally long enough to cover the escape of Washington's trapped troops.

Seeking to preserve the residential nature of the community, Murray's descendants drew up a pioneering zoning covenant in 1847 that barred slaughterhouses, museums, theaters, or circuses. The standards were still being enforced more than half a century later by the financier J. P. Morgan, who had put up a brooding chocolate-colored mansion on Madison Avenue at 37th Street and who founded the Murray Hill Association in 1914 to police his vision of an ever-sheltered Murray Hill.

The Morgan mansion still stands, now housing the offices of the Lutheran Church in America, which shares a grassy plot with the neo-Renaissance Morgan Library, erected in 1906. Open to the public, the library exhibits such eclectic treasures as della Robbia terra-cottas, period rooms, and one of the world's forty-eight remaining Gutenberg Bibles (another one and part of a third also are part of the library's collection).

Less ostentatious, but every bit as distinctive, is the toylike Sniffen Court, a flagstone mews of Civil War–era remodeled carriage houses and town houses on 36th Street just west of Third Avenue. A plaque outside the court, whose two- and three-story residences are valued by real-estate brokers at around $2 million each, marks its designation in the National Register of Historic Places. "When I moved in twenty-five years ago, there was still a horse stabled across the way," recalled Isabelle Bacon, another owner.

Sniffen Court is also home to one of the city's better-kept secrets, the Amateur Comedy Club, founded in 1884. Quartered in two former stables, the club mounts six productions a year for members and invited guests in a miniature, 115-seat theater in the clubhouse at 150 East 36th Street. There are no female members, although women do take stage roles; Julie Harris, then an amateur, appeared in a club production of *The Devil's Disciple* in 1946. The rolls are limited to a hundred active members—players—and 250 supporting associates. Would-be joiners "just have to wait for someone to die," said John Steinway, the piano maker and club archivist who lives in nearby Gramercy Park.

But Murray Hill is not just for the patrician, although newcomers seeking to move in these days might wonder. Conventional four-story brownstones on the side streets, when available, tend to go for $825,000 and up, and newly erected apartment buildings are asking phenomenal rents. The Feathered Nest, a rental agency, lists studios and one- and two-bedroom apartments in town houses for $1,200 to $2,800 a month.

Apartments at lower rentals sometimes are available in high-rise rent-stabilized buildings. The area has been the focus of a great deal of condominium development in recent years, and owners often let those apartments at rentals comparable to those for town-house apartments. Three-bedroom and larger units are scarce; when they are available, the rents start at $4,000 a month.

There are also a number of ancient tenements. The 1980 census, for example, turned up 442 apartments renting for $50 to $100 a month and 661 for $100 to $150.

According to a recent survey by the Corcoran Group, a real-estate brokerage, of the 333 residential buildings in Murray Hill, 227 containing 8,649 apartment units are rental buildings; 19, with 988 apartments, are co-ops; and 15, with 2,248 apartments, are undergoing co-op conversion. The remaining 72 buildings are single-family town houses. Reflecting the low-rise character of the neighborhood, more than a third of the buildings have ten or fewer apartments and 25 percent have between eleven and fifty apartments, the survey showed.

The Corcoran survey found that Murray Hill co-ops have been selling at an average price of $46,000 a room, lower than prices elsewhere on the East Side and a reflection, according to Barbara Corcoran, head of the agency, of Murray Hill's "sleeper" status.

Murray Hill has a single public elementary school, P.S. 116 at 220 East 33rd Street. The original building dates from 1927, but there is a more modern addition built in 1951. About half of the 432 pupils read at or above grade level. There are also a dozen or more well-regarded private schools in or around the immediate neighborhood.

As elsewhere in the city, crime is an issue in Murray Hill, although the police and many residents feel the busily trafficked neighborhood has fared well by contemporary New York standards. Of particular concern have been the bands of youths who cluster at corners of streets leading to and from the Midtown Tunnel and dart out to insistently wipe motorists' windshields for tips.

—RALPH BLUMENTHAL

N O H O

*To midtown Manhattan: Subway
15 minutes*

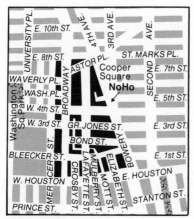

The area north of Houston Street known as NoHo is a mixture of graceful turn-of-the-century buildings, some dilapidated and others beautifully restored, and spacious factories and warehouses that have attracted many artists, filmmakers, and people from other walks of life looking for affordable loft living space in Manhattan. Once strictly reserved for light manufacturing and industry, and occupied by a goodly number of hat factories, hardware shops, and textile concerns, this sliver of a neighborhood has in the past decade undergone many changes.

These days it is not unusual to see big black cubes of sculpture being carted down the street or dancers in leg warmers bounding into a cafe or filmmakers shooting a brief scene. It is also the sort of place where theater companies and trendy restaurants proliferate, where fashionable clothing shops and late-night cafes draw huge weekend crowds, and where the full-time residents have learned to live with the sheet-metal shops, plumbing concerns, gas stations, and truck-rental companies that remain.

"Many people in NoHo have alternate life-styles—they are filmmakers, actors, dancers, and creative professionals," said Star Sandow, a writer and president of the NoHo Neighborhood Association. "But we now have many families with children, professionals, singles, and people sharing lofts moving in."

N O H O

NoHo, which stands for North of Houston Street, is northeast of SoHo (for South of Houston Street), with Little Italy to the south and Greenwich Village to the north and west. Community Board 2 in Manhattan defines its boundaries as Houston Street on the south, 8th Street and Astor Place on the north, the Bowery on the east, and Broadway on the west, though many residents consider Mercer Street the western border.

NoHo's name is said to have been invented by some of the early refugees from SoHo who arrived in the 1970's in search of large loft spaces and cheaper rents. Like SoHo ten to fifteen years ago, NoHo is an area that is swiftly being gentrified.

"The place is going crazy," stated Debra Sillaro, director of sales at Herbert H. Kliegerman, a real-estate broker in NoHo. "The change is bordering on the unbelievable. Prices have gone up substantially. Four years ago the price of a loft that was 2,000 square feet was anywhere from $60,000 to $80,000, but we are now selling such lofts for as high as $300,000 to $500,000."

"I bought a 1,500-square foot loft twelve years ago for $3,500," said Selma Anderson, a local real-estate agent. "Today that loft would go for $150,000 to $175,000." Renting a similar loft could cost more than $2,000 a month, she added.

Much of NoHo is zoned for mixed use, with artists-only residences. Newcomers can legally move into lofts only if a household member has been certified as a working artist by the city's Department of Cultural Affairs. But real-estate brokers say those not connected with the arts have found ways around the rule, and one said housing demand is so strong that even doctors and lawyers are finding ways of gaining certificates and moving in.

Between 1970 and 1980 the residential population increased by 185 percent, according to census data supplied by Community Board 2.

"It's like night and day," said Barbara Contardi, director of The First Amendment Comedy and Improvisational Theatre Company on Bond Street, just off Broadway. "Four years ago we were so isolated, people didn't know that anyone lived here." Then came Tower Records, she noted, and all that changed.

Tower Records—a four-floor repository of jazz, rock-and-roll, video, and classical music recordings at Broadway and East 4th Street—is open until midnight seven nights a week. It has brought lively activity—and strong lighting—to Broadway below 8th Street. The shop is in a mixed-use building that houses condominiums and commercial offices.

Other signs of expansion have been a dormitory for New York University Law School students at the site of the former Broadway Central Hotel, at 240 Mercer Street; and the construction of the Mercer Square Apartments, 270 units in nine loft buildings on Mercer Street and Broadway between 3rd and 4th streets, notable for the Richard Haas trompe l'oeil mural in its courtyard.

Although NoHo once was an urban frontier, the sort of place where one had to walk fifteen to twenty blocks to find a pharmacy or buy a quart of milk, there now are a fair number of service shops in the area. On Mercer, there is a large Sloan's supermarket, and on Broadway and nearby, there are gourmet delis, a discount drugstore, a flower shop, an international newspaper and magazine kiosk, a Chinese-food take-out, a Blimpie sandwich shop, a bicycle shop, a locksmith, and a personal computer store. In the last few years or so late-night restaurants such as Caramba!, the Blue Willow, and the twenty-four-hour Astor Place Riviera Cafe have also opened.

Despite the changes, residents say that NoHo will never become another trendy, high-priced area like SoHo or Tribeca (for Triangle Below Canal Street). "What distinguishes NoHo from SoHo and Tribeca is the presence of the men's and women's shelters," said Keith Crandell, a NoHo resident and a member of the Community Board.

According to the NoHo Neighborhood Association, social-service agencies in the area include the Women's Shelter at 350 Lafayette Street and the Men's Shelter at 8 East 3rd Street. On a recent night, the Men's Shelter provided lodging to 832 homeless men in nearby hotels, and on that same evening, the nearby Women's Shelter housed forty-five women.

Among privately operated shelters are the Volunteers of America, the Bowery Mission, the Lower Manhattan Sobering-Up Station, the Alcoholism Center, and the Salvation Army. There also are several soup kitchens and single-room-occupany hotels along the Bowery. One of the latter, the Kenton, was recently taken over by the city and is now used to lodge homeless men, despite strong community opposition.

For these reasons, Ms. Sandow, the neighborhood association president, said, those who move to NoHo must be willing to live with neighbors who are vagrants and panhandlers, though residents say that crime is no worse than in other sections of Manhattan. The twenty-four-hour nature of the neighborhood, the presence of theaters and many late-night cafes, helps deter crime, they note.

Some NoHo residents accept the presence of homeless people and vagrants. "The concentration of homeless people has held down rents and allowed a lot of people to stay in the neighborhood who might otherwise have had to move," Mr. Crandell said.

Despite the transient population, new residents keep settling in and the neighborhood does get more trendy. Newcomers find many attractions, not the least of them plentiful public transportation. The Lexington Avenue IRT gets them to midtown in fifteen minutes, and there are also northbound, southbound, and crosstown buses. They get a little more space and elbow room for their money than in more congested neighborhoods to the north and south. And they live as neighbors with such important cultural institutions as the Public Theater, New York University, and Cooper Union.

There are no schools in NoHo, but many parents send their children to P.S. 41, at 116 West 11th Street, in Greenwich Village, where more than 70 percent of the students read at or above grade level; and P. S. 3, at 490 Hudson Street, where more than 65 percent read at or above grade level. At Intermediate School 70, at 333 West 17th Street, it is about 70 percent. Also accessible are the Grace Church School at 86 Fourth Avenue and other private schools in Greenwich Village.

"This is an area where the space is still considerably cheaper than uptown," said Ms. Anderson, the real-estate agent. "NoHo has become a respectable neighborhood with shoe stores and record shops, and you no longer have to walk miles for a pack of cigarettes. Now, it's just like a little suburb."

—KATYA GONCHAROFF

S O H O

To midtown Manhattan: Subway 15 minutes

Perhaps there is no better measure of the protean nature of New York City than SoHo. In less than fifteen years, a squalid, industrial area known for noisy factories and choked streets has become a central symbol of the city's avant-garde culture. Just as the phrase "made in Japan" has changed from an indicator of shoddy labor and cheap goods into a certificate of excellence, the name SoHo—once synonymous with grime—has come to signify artsy sophistication and glamour.

"I don't think anyone could have dreamed that SoHo would come this far so fast," said William Robertson, who follows the SoHo housing market for the realty firm, J. I. Sopher & Company. "It's become New York's Montmartre—people from around the world come in here every day looking to move in."

But if today's SoHo—crammed with fashionable boutiques, art galleries, and a growing number of renowned restaurants—has attracted a new group of wealthy young professionals, the neighborhood's success has also made things difficult for the same community of artists who first moved there late in the 1960's. These artists, most of whom came to SoHo for its exceptionally large, cheap living and work spaces, have seen rents soar far beyond their reach.

"The SoHo pioneers resent many of the changes that have occurred here," said Charles Leslie, who has long been active in the

S O H O

SoHo Artists Association and has lived in the neighborhood since 1968. "I prefer the dynamism of change—it's inevitable. But parts of the city have a way of self-destructing, and we don't want to see that happen here."

The area was first settled during the colonial period, when it was farmland. Early in the nineteenth century, it became a residential neighborhood as the city expanded northward. But by the end of the century, the area had become predominantly light industrial, ushering in a period of slow decay that finally stopped in the 1960's.

Since 1971, when the city adopted a zoning resolution allowing joint living-working quarters for artists certified by the Department of Cultural Affairs, it has been legal to live in SoHo only if at least one member of a household is certified. By 1976, another amendment increased the number of buildings that could be converted to residential use; about that time, chic began to blossom in SoHo.

While it is still illegal to move without certification into most of the thirty-three-block area south of Houston Street—hence the area's name—the law is often sidestepped. (The other boundaries are Canal Street on the south, West Broadway on the west, and Lafayette Street on the east.) Suzanne O'Keefe, executive director of the Loft Board, which was established late in 1982, stated that in 1978, the last time the city produced comprehensive figures, 92 percent of New York's loft residents were illegal tenants.

In 1982 the legislature effectively legalized most residential loft tenants and set guidelines for converting lofts into legal residences. But the law does not provide for residents without artist's certification, and some residents are angered by the changes in the neighborhood.

"The very nature of art has changed," said Gerhardt Liebmann, a painter drawn to SoHo fourteen years ago by abundant space at minimal rent. "I can't work on an easel in a small room. When I do a piece that's twenty feet long I must have space and light. We all found that in SoHo."

But rising real-estate values have lured a new constituency to the neighborhood in the last few years—those often more at home in the world of high fashion and *haute cuisine* than with the trucks that still clog the narrow streets. Population doubled in twenty years to 8,400 in 1980, and the price of real estate has grown almost as fast as the population. According to local brokers, residential space now costs $190 to $235 a square foot to purchase, while the monthly rent for a 1,500-square-foot loft can range from $1,700 to $2,500.

One recently converted condominium at Prince Street and West Broadway has apartments both for rent and for sale. The apartments that will rent for $1,200 a month are priced to sell at $260,000, and there are triplex apartments with twenty-two foot ceilings that will rent for $4,000 a month and sell for up to $400,000.

SOHO

Anyone planning to move into SoHo with children should note that neighborhood amenities have not always kept pace with development. There are only three public grade schools, and Chelsea Vocational High School, the public high school that serves the community, also accepts students from throughout the city. There are fifteen private and parochial schools in the neighborhood, and most residents send their children to one of them, according to Herbert Sacher, deputy superintendent of Community School Board 2.

And, of course, there are the restaurants, galleries, and shops that help to define the neighborhood. From the famous (the SoHo Charcuterie, O. K. Harris Gallery) to the less well known (Rangoon Burmese Kitchen) to that which is unique to SoHo (Parachute, the massive high-tech clothing warehouse on Wooster Street), to walk in SoHo is to be assaulted by variety.

SoHo is still zoned for a mix of residential and commercial purposes, and a considerable amount of light manufacturing industry remains. Some residents cherish the physical contrasts this creates, but increasingly people who have invested large sums of money in their lofts and apartments have complained about the noise and dirt that is an inescapable part of a manufacturing community.

"This is not Park Avenue, and there are no white picket fences here either," said Rita Lee, district manager for Community Board 2, who has noted a steady increase in noise complaints as SoHo has become more residential. "SoHo is not a sleepy residential community, and people who are attracted to it should know there are drawbacks as well."

One irony that SoHo residents must face is that while it has never been easier to find a good brioche or an arrangement of cut flowers in the neighborhood, there is only one dry cleaner, and the nearest grocery store for such mundane daily needs as a quart of milk and a bar of soap can be many blocks away. Pharmacies and coin laundries also are few compared to many other Manhattan communities.

Although the streets of SoHo are often deserted at night, crime is not a major problem, other than an increase in thefts that officers of the First Precinct attribute to the growing number of expensive stores. Public transportation is fairly good, since both the IRT and the BMT subway lines run nearby. The ride to midtown takes about fifteen minutes.

Lack of new housing space is acute because the entire area, with its distinctive cast-iron facades, gained landmark status in 1973.

Nestled between Greenwich Village to the north and Chinatown and Little Italy to the south and east, SoHo would appear to have something for everyone: easy access to several ethnically diverse neighborhoods, exposure to the excitement of the city's art world, a quiet remove from—but within easy distance of—the speeding tempo of the financial district.

S O H O

Like so many other neighborhoods these days, finding affordable space can be the biggest barrier to living in SoHo. To live there requires plenty of money or an energetic devotion to that urban folk art, apartment hunting. Often, both are necessary. But to live happily in SoHo also calls for a certain sense of abandon and a willingness to experiment. In the words of David Johansen, the New York rock star, somehow SoHo manages to remain "funky but chic."

—MICHAEL SPECTER

S U T T O N   P L A C E

*To midtown Manhattan: Walking
10 to 15 minutes*

Above the buzz of the Franklin D. Roosevelt Drive, landscaped lawns and gardens slope down from the expensive, deceptively small private houses and the big apartment buildings of Sutton Place, Sutton Square, Riverview Terrace, and Sutton Place South. Between these elegant blocks, which form an enclave running from 53rd to 59th Street, nearly every crosstown street ends in a tiny public park or terrace overlooking the East River. To share in the scenery as well as the ambience, knowledgeable outsiders head eastward with books, toddlers, snacks, or someone to hold hands with. The views include the Queensboro Bridge, the gentle traffic of riverboats, the reach-out-and-touch-it activity on Roosevelt Island and its tramway.

"It's mid-Manhattan convenience here but off the beaten path—there's no hurly-burly this side of First Avenue," said Lois Levine, formerly of Manhasset, Long Island, and now of Sutton Place. Like many residents, she and her husband moved to the area when their children were grown.

Sutton Place proper is only two blocks long, between 57th and 59th streets one block east of First Avenue. But as a synonym for costliness and class, the name reflects its glow south to 53rd Street, west to Second Avenue, and even a bit farther west on 57th Street.

It is a neighborhood where the evening parade of limousines begins just as housekeepers and nursemaids—those who don't live

62

in—depart, where twenty-four-hour doormen announce visitors in fountain-splashed lobbies, and where fashion photographers and movie makers come for the cachet of its backdrops.

Its residents, present or recently past, include former Senator James L. Buckley, Pat Kennedy Lawford, J. Peter Grace, Clint Murchison, and Charlotte Ford. Marilyn Monroe was married to Arthur Miller in her apartment at No. 2 Sutton Place South, which extends south of 57th Street to 53rd Street. Some say the neighborhood includes the easternmost block of 52nd Street, where Greta Garbo lives and where River House, the elegant twenty-six-story-plus-penthouse cooperative built in 1930, is home to the Henry Kissingers, the Joshua Logans, and the Angier Biddle Dukes. Others say River House is a neighborhood to itself.

It was Sutton Place pride—and clout—that got city planners to save the cliffside gardens and create parks when the East River Drive was built in 1940, according to Carole Rifkind of Sutton Area Community, the major neighborhood association. "To this day, the alternation of private and public gardens remains an example to the city of how to plan a waterfront," said Ms. Rifkind, who is chairman of the committee seeking the designation of Sutton Place as a historic district.

For more than fifty years, town houses and other low-rise residential buildings have been replaced with increasingly tall and bulky apartment towers. Recent construction includes a thirty-two-story condominium, St. James's Tower at 450 East 53rd Street; and two rentals—the nineteen-story Branford at 333 East 56th and the thirty-eight-story River Tower, a dogleg angling between 53rd and 54th streets midblock between Sutton Place South and First Avenue. Such buildings are likely to feature marble bathrooms, saunas, wine cellars, and heavy security systems.

St. James's Tower has sold all of its 106 units except the two penthouses. The smaller, on the north, is priced at $3.5 million. The south one, with 6,000 square feet, costs $7.5 million.

Rents for River Tower apartments range from $1,400 for a one-bedroom on a low floor to $8,000 for a high-floor five-bedroom. Few of the 317 units are vacant.

In its farther reaches, the area has such co-ops as the forty-seven-story Excelsior at 300 East 57th and the forty-story Plaza 400 at 400 East 56th, both built in the late 1960's, and the forty-eight-story Sovereign at 425 East 58th, opened in 1974.

Among the smaller side-street buildings, two newly converted six-story cooperatives on 58th between Sutton Place and First Avenue offer studios or one-bedrooms from $91,000 to $130,000, with maintenace ranging to $500 monthly. On the same block, Myron A. Minskoff is developing a twenty-seven-story condominium with seventy-five units.

SUTTON PLACE

Barbara DiMona, chairman of Sutton Area Community's zoning and development committee, said one reason the neighborhood was "a prime target" for new apartment towers was its zoning. The area from 49th to 59th Street between First Avenue and the river is zoned for the highest residential density the city allows.

For all its present prestige, Sutton Place got its slow start as a chic address only in the 1920's. Once simply called Avenue A, it took its now-famous name from Effingham Sutton, who tried in the mid-1870's to upgrade the area from factories, meat-packing plants, and workers' tenements.

Artists brought the first sort of gentrification, and, in the New York pattern, people with money followed. In the early 1920's, Mrs. William K. Vanderbilt (Anne Harriman) and Anne Morgan, sister of J. P. Morgan, deserted Fifth Avenue to buy and rebuild, respectively, No. 1 Sutton Place—Sutton's original home—and the double house at No. 3–5.

The latter is now the official residence of the secretary-general of the United Nations. No. 7 is the home of Robert Goelet, president of the American Museum of Natural History, and No. 11, of I. M. Pei, the architect. In that block-long row of nineteenth-century houses, between 57th and 58th streets, one recently sold for $3 million. Town houses on side streets are valued at $1 million to $2 million.

In 1925, Henry Phipps built No. 1 Sutton Place South, which covers the entire block between 56th and 57th. Any unit in the co-op now "commands in the millions," according to Diana Ponzini, a broker who specializes in the area. She estimated the same for 25 Sutton Place, at the corner of Sutton Square (at 58th Street), which is the only other apartment house on the river side of the street built before World War II.

Longtime residents talk about buying in the area "before the prices went crazy" and say new buildings are making side streets into "concrete canyons." They distinguish carefully between "prewar" and "postwar" buildings, regarding the former as more luxurious and prestigious. So do real-estate brokers.

"One-bedroom apartments in good postwar buildings sell for an average of $325,000," said Aimee Eden of Sulzberger-Rolfe. "Two-bedrooms go for $500,000–$550,000 and three-bedrooms up to $850,000."

First Avenue is where many residents shop for daily necessities at D'Agostino's and a Food Emporium with a "Butcher Shoppe" and deli. On a recent day the deli offered such specialties as cognac liver pâté, vegetable pâté, and duck liver mousse.

The Police Department regards the Sutton Place area as "fortified," with twenty-four-hour doormen and security systems. "Security is on their minds here," said Officer Richard Hauser of the 17th Precinct. "Burglaries," he said, "most often coincide with occupants' absences"—often long and frequent. He called First and Second avenues "a supermarket for car thieves" looking for luxury cars and accessories.

Many parents send their children to private schools outside the neighborhood, although there are public schools nearby—P.S. 59 at 228 East 57th Street and the High School of Art and Design at 1075 Second Avenue. The Cathedral High School for Girls, a parochial school, is at 350 East 56th Street.

Among the favorite neighborhood restaurants are Le Perigord, on 52nd Street in the vast Sutton House, and several on First Avenue and on 57th, among them Billy's, the Mayfair, and the new Metropolitan Cafe.

"People do go to Second Avenue to eat," said Ms. Levine, the former suburbanite, "but somehow it's not really one's neighborhood."

—LAURIE JOHNSTON

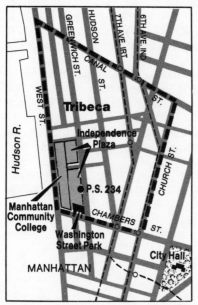

*To midtown Manhattan: Subway
20 minutes*

There is something desolate in the streets of Tribeca. They flow like gray rivers of cobblestone, their banks lined by warehouses.

Five years ago, cars were so rare that seabirds wheeled inland from the river, unafraid. Now, the automobiles have come and the birds have gone, but a stroller can still pause on a fine spring Sunday and find himself utterly alone.

Tribecans like it this way. "People come down and look at the warehouses and go 'yuck,'" said Carole De Saram, a decade-long resident and former chairman of Community Board 1. "But if you live down here, it's like having a little part of Manhattan all to yourself."

Tribecans like the neighborhood not only for the solitude but for the vibrancy it belies. They mobilize ferociously—hundreds of residents, thousands of dollars—in defense of their turf. They have waged successful battles against a move by the State Parole Board to Hudson Street, the building of a jail in neighboring Chinatown, and the construction of an access ramp by Manhattan Community College through the middle of Washington Market Park. But they lost the battle against the fumigation of the Port Warehouses on Vestry Street with lethal methyl bromide gas.

They shop in gourmet food stores, brunch in restaurants with names like The Acute Cafe and Laughing Mountain, do their laundry at The Laundry Loft on Leonard Street, and refer to anything north of Canal Street as "uptown."

"There is everything in the world down here," said John Perella, president of the South of Canal Association, a community group, "and it never sleeps."

Tribeca is an acronym for the Triangle Below Canal, about forty square blocks bounded on the north by Canal Street, on the south by Chambers Street, on the west by the Hudson River, and on the east by Church Street. (The city officially puts the southern border at Park Place, but residents insist on Chambers.)

Most Tribecans also scorn their appellation, although it sticks. "The people who live here want to recall the historical nature of the area and refer to it as Washington Market," said Lois Mazzitelli, an urban designer with the City Planning Commission.

The Washington Market merchants, who began selling produce in 1880, have long since moved on to Hunts Point, but Tribeca remains the city's major butter, egg, and cheese depot. On weekdays the streets belong to the trucks and the air belongs to the Martinson's factory on Franklin Street, which sends passersby into ecstasy with its daily roasting of coffee beans. On weekends the trucks vanish and the air smells faintly of river.

Harmony is achieved by mixed-use zoning, which has legitimized most of the early, illegal loft-dwellers, protected existing businesses, and preserved the industrial aura. And thus it is that instead of the proverbial front stoop, Tribecans have the loading dock.

Tribeca is co-op country, with the single, looming exception of Independence Plaza. The three 40-story apartment towers, which abut Manhattan Community College, cover three blocks from North Moore to Duane Street and between West and Greenwich streets. They opened in November 1974 and languished, unrented, until October 1975, when federal housing subsidies took effect for all but eighty-eight of the 1,332 apartments.

"We were incapable of marketing the apartments at that time on an open-market rental," said Jerome Belson, president of Jerome Belson Associates, which manages the complex. "Today we could. The area has dramatically improved." Rents are low—the nonsubsidized pay a maximum of $937 for three bedrooms—but the waiting list for apartments is almost three years' long.

The complex has swallowed what once was Washington Street, where there was a row of elegant little Federal houses built from 1804 to 1828. In 1975 the houses, now privately owned, were trucked around the corner to Harrison Street and renovated, creating a courtly area amid the towers.

But it was not zoning or Independence Plaza or even the advent of thrice-weekly sanitation pickups three years or so ago that made Tribeca a legitimate neighborhood. It was a supermarket—the Food

Emporium, to be precise, which opened in Independence Plaza in 1982. Before that, Ms. De Saram said, "I got used to drinking my coffee black because there were no stores around here."

There was, of course, Earl Morgan's deli, on Hudson Street at Reade Street, which grew from take-out to small grocery as the middle class came to roost, and a few gourmet stores. But serious shopping demanded a weekly trek outside the neighborhood.

The rest of Tribeca is a grid of warehouses and factory buildings, low and solid and old. The main floors are usually businesses, with lofts above—many renovated by early, illegal pioneers, whose clandestine lives included lugging bags of garbage to distant corners by moonlight. These residences took root in the early 1970's as artists spilled over from the saturated SoHo area, northeast of Tribeca; soaring real-estate values have limited Tribeca to higher-income tenants.

Most lofts are now sold prerenovated. They tend to cost less than SoHo lofts, according to Creative Leasing Concepts, a Tribeca realty concern, but prices depend on both the luxury of the loft and of the building. Loft prices range from $150 to $200 a square foot, and hard-to-find rentals run about $1 a square foot per month.

There are lofts for sale on Duane Street, and conversion is under way at 67 Hudson Street, at Jay Street, a small white building that got its start as New York Hospital. Sprouting out of the back of 67 Hudson is an overhead bridge spanning a tiny two-block-long alley called Staple Street and ending at what was once a two-story stable; patients were brought to the stable by carriage and trundled over the bridge into the hospital.

Tribeca has two schools: the private Washington Market preschool in Independence Plaza and P.S. 234, at 334 Greenwich Street. A public high school is planned on an empty lot between Hubert and Beach streets, near the river. Eleven houses of worship serve the area, although many lie outside the Tribeca boundaries, and there are, more than anything else, restaurants and galleries.

Cafes like Capsouto Frères and the Washington Street Cafe crowd their loading docks with tables in good weather, and the Odeon draws a lunchtime clientele from midtown Manhattan. Galleries and artists have taken over several historic buildings, including the former Mercantile Exchange on Harrison Street, now owned by the nonprofit Dia Art Foundation.

Another sign of the growth of ordinary amenities in this rather extraordinary neighborhood was the opening of a park, Tribeca's first, on a rainy Sunday in 1983. This corner plot, called Washington Market Park, is at Chambers and Greenwich streets, and it has courts for tennis, volleyball, and basketball, as well as a gazebo, gardens, and grassy areas.

Tribeca, being north of Wall Street, had subway service long before it had a live-in population to use it. The IRT Seventh Avenue and IND Sixth and Eighth Avenue lines both traverse the neighborhood. Residents who work in the financial district can walk to their offices; for those who work in midtown, the subway trip takes about twenty minutes.

The influx of artists and middle-class people seeking large living spaces into an area that only ten years ago shut down at 5 P.M. also has drawn its share of the criminal element. The population in Community District 1 more than doubled between 1970 and 1980, rising to 16,322. Some residents blame crime on the discotheques that draw hundreds of drinkers and dancers to Tribeca on weekends; one, The Gotham, closed after a murder occurred on its premises. But for the most part, said Phil Nuzzo, district manager of Community Board 1, "this is a quiet area—you can walk down the street in the middle of the day and see no one there."

—DYLAN LANDIS

UPPER EAST SIDE

To midtown Manhattan: Walking 20 minutes

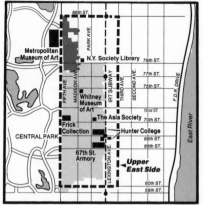

The Upper East Side is New York City's prime residential neighborhood. No other section has its glitter and glamour, its cachet and chic. To be at home in this enclave of a hundred square blocks bounded by 60th and 86th streets, and Fifth and Third avenues, is to have at your door some of the best New York has to offer.

There are affluent and successful New Yorkers who choose to live in other neighborhoods, and their reasons say something about what the Upper East Side is and is not. Some prefer the less buttoned-up atmosphere of Greenwich Village. Others like the mélange of ethnicities to be found on the West Side, or the opportunity to live an alternate life-style afforded by SoHo, or the sense of the city's ongoing history to be had in such older parts of town as Murray Hill and Brooklyn Heights.

The primary advantage of the Upper East Side is superior housing. Along Park and Fifth avenues and on the cross streets is clustered the city's largest stock of luxury-class prewar apartment houses. Prewar is the essential characteristic: almost nothing built since the 1930's affords the same amenities—large rooms, high ceilings, windowed kitchens and baths, redundant closets, working fireplaces.

The standard three-bedroom apartment in such a building contains, besides the bedrooms and their adjoining baths, a drawing room, a dining room, an entrance gallery, a big kitchen, a pantry,

70

two small maids' rooms, and a maids' bath. Some also have a library and a servants' hall. In fact, they are the equivalents of spacious houses, stacked one on another in twelve- to fifteen-story buildings.

In today's overheated co-op market, most such apartments sell for $1 million or more, and it would be hard to find one for less than $850,000. The maintenance charges range upward from $18,000 a year. Almost all were either built as co-ops or have been converted. The few rentals that remain are hard to find and cost a minimum of $3,500 a month. Much larger and more expensive apartments also are available, but two-bedroom units, priced at $500,000 and more, are about as small as they get in prewar buildings.

The neighborhood also has a large stock of town houses. Most were built of limestone or Georgian red brick and are wider and grander than the narrow, high-stooped brownstones so characteristic of the West Side. Many have been divided into apartments, with rents for studios beginning at $1,200 and floor-throughs at $2,500. Some of these, too, have become co-ops, with prices roughly equivalent to those in high-rise buildings.

Single-family town houses still exist, with prices in excess of $1 million, but they have a major drawback. They cannot be left alone for a weekend without risking a burglary. The Upper East Side is a prime target for the city's accomplished burglars, and for that reason, many families prefer to live behind the well-guarded portals of an apartment house with round-the-clock doormen.

Because so much of the area was developed with tall apartment houses before World War II, it has not seen the waves of new construction that have swept over other parts of the city. Further inhibiting new building was the creation of the Metropolitan Museum and the Upper East Side historic districts, which conferred landmark status on most of the neighborhood and ensured that its architectural riches would not be ravaged.

Nevertheless, some new buildings were erected, and it is in them that smaller apartments may be found. Many of these buildings, too, are being converted into co-ops, with $250,000 about the minimal price for a one-bedroom unit. When they are available as rentals, one-bedrooms cost $2,000 a month or more.

Judging by what is available to newcomers, it would seem that the Upper East Side is home only to the rich. This is not true, but it is becoming more true year by year. Yet there are many families of more modest means living in the neighborhood who bought their apartments before the run-up in co-op prices began a decade ago, or who were able to buy at low insider prices when rental buildings were converted into co-ops. Others are tenants in rent-stabilized buildings who enjoy apartments at rents far below market levels. But because such apartments are bargains, they do not often change tenancies and are available to new families only rarely.

Those who are able to move in find themselves part of an expensive way of life. There are good public and parochial schools in the neighborhood, notably P.S. 6 at Madison Avenue and 83rd Street, which is rated among the city's best, but many Upper East Side families send their children to private schools, where the tuition is $7,000 a year, or to boarding schools, where the annual cost is $10,000.

Dining out close to home is expensive, too. The restaurants that have opened in recent years, among them La Petite Ferme, Jack's, and Mortimers, post prices that make dinner for two, with wine and tips, cost well over $100. Rising rents have closed many of the cheaper restaurants, and more are disappearing year by year.

And the level of consumption among many Upper East Siders is so high that it can be intimidating and even distasteful. Nevertheless, living next door to the rich has its advantages, not the least of them the general level of cleanliness of the neighborhood. The streets get no more attention from the Sanitation Department than those of other sections, but sidewalks and gutters on many blocks are swept twice daily by the doormen and porters of well-maintained buildings.

Two great feats of nineteenth-century engineering laid the basis for the development of the Upper East Side. One was the creation of Central Park, which drew fashionable New Yorkers up Fifth Avenue, first to baronial town houses and then to the grand apartment houses that replaced them. The park remains the preeminent amenity of the neighborhood—indeed, of the whole city—and East Siders are in the forefront of efforts to preserve it. The other was the submerging of the New York Central's railroad tracks below Park Avenue—once called Fourth Avenue—which created a broad boulevard along which more apartment houses could be erected. Except for a scattering of institutions, hotels, and town houses, the whole of both avenues from 60th Street northward is developed with high-rise apartment buildings.

A generation ago, Madison Avenue was the service street for Park and Fifth. It was then lined with butchers, grocers, hand launderers, dressmakers, domestic help agencies, and the like. Many closed for the summer while their customers were away. Today, almost all those uses have been pushed off Madison by high rents and the avenue has become the city's best retail address, outshining even Fifth Avenue.

Now a stroll on Madison is a window shopper's delight, affording tantalizing glimpses of art, jewels, fashions, and antiques. There is a cost in convenience in all this, however. Except for the three Gristede's markets left on Madison and a few others, residents have no place left to get a quart of milk short of a hike to Lexington Avenue or Third.

By contrast, nothing could be handier than the neighborhood's collection of cultural institutions. One of the delights of being an Upper East Sider is the opportunity to drop in at the Whitney, the Metropolitan, the Asia Society, the Frick Collection, and the New York Society Library. (The library, which sets its family dues at $60 a year, has a collection of 200,000 volumes in its 79th Street town house.) And just north of the neighborhood are the Guggenheim and the Cooper-Hewitt.

The northern boundary at 86th Street is less firm than it used to be. Social geographers once ranked East Side families by how far uptown they lived, with 86th the very edge of respectability. Now such distinctions are derided, but the area above 86th retains a separate identity and is called Carnegie Hill.

The eastern boundary also has shifted. It now parallels Third Avenue, which was blighted by the el until it was demolished in 1954. The clatter of trains stopped development of first-class buildings on most streets at Lexington Avenue, and for many years it was the neighborhood's eastern limit. Once the el was razed, however, redevelopment followed quickly, and now Third is lined with expensive high-rises. It is there that many younger people live, close to the boutiques, take-out food stores, and trendy restaurants that line the avenue.

The midtown office district begins just below 60th Street, and for many Upper East Siders, being able to walk to work is worth every penny of the high cost of their housing. They flow down Park Avenue in a tide every morning at 8:30. Nevertheless, the area is well served by public transportation. There are bus lines on all the avenues except Park and all the major cross streets. And there also is the Lexington Avenue IRT, essential for Wall Streeters, but grotesquely overcrowded at rush hours.

Curbside parking is restricted by meters or alternate-side rules, forcing residents who keep cars into garages. Spaces are as hard to find as apartments, and the rates are $200 a month and up.

It is not apparent to outsiders, but the Upper East Side is a church- and synagogue-going community. It supports such handsome and well-attended places of worship as St. James' Episcopal, Madison Avenue Presbyterian, All Souls Unitarian, Temple Emanu-El, and St. Vincent Ferrer.

These institutions are woven into the life of the neighborhood, and, surprisingly, they find themselves increasingly dealing with the problems of the poor. They and others recently established the Neighborhood Coalition for Shelter to succor homeless women who have drifted into the Upper East Side. These women have been drawn to the neighborhood by its relatively safer streets, which is one of the reasons rich people live there.

—MICHAEL STERNE

UPPER WEST SIDE

*To midtown Manhattan: Subway
20 minutes*

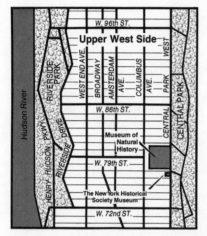

When urban renewal began on Manhattan's Upper West Side, recalled Austin Haldenstein, a real-estate broker, eleven brownstone houses were put up for sale. "We couldn't move them for $25,000 or $35,000."

But that was twenty years or so ago. When he speaks of current brownstone prices in the neighborhood he says the "middle range" goes from $500,000 to $600,000.

To its surprise—and not much to its liking—the Upper West Side has become, as they say, an "in" place. It has always been an individualistic place, but today, in a world replete with stories of communities that try to keep out racial minorities or the poor, its residents are girding to resist the rich.

Some might say that since the poor have pretty well moved out, the people who are there have a good thing going and don't want to share it. Some might say that the West Side is middle-class in attitude and fears dilution. In any case, the point is that residents are wary.

"Another population is rolling its way northward," Ethel Sheffer, chairman of Community Board 7, warned at a neighborhood planning session one recent evening. "It is an affluent, luxury population, nonfamily."

Many of the people now living in the neighborhood are hanging on tenaciously to some of the city's best housing bargains—controlled and stabilized apartments in fine old buildings with rents far below market levels. They almost never surrender their apartments. They either die in place or try to sneak in friends, relatives, or strangers willing to part with lots of cash. As a result, there is almost no standard rental market in the heartland of the West Side, but the picture is beginning to improve because of new construction.

"The market is shifting from regular rentals to condominiums," said William Robertson, general manager of J. I. Sopher & Company, which opened a new office in 1983 at 230 West 74th Street. According to Mr. Robertson, many people are buying condominiums for investment, then renting them out at whatever prices the market will bear. "A studio will go for $800 or so," he said, "a one-bedroom apartment for $1,000 to $1,200, and two-bedrooms start at $1,600."

Even at those prices, the market is tight. A recent renter said that besides a one-month finder's fee, she was asked by an agent for $4,500 "key money" and by another for sexual favors. "I found another agent," she stated.

Co-ops do become available, but they, too, are costly. Elliot D. Sclar of Columbia University's Division of Urban Planning, coauthor of a historical study of the neighborhood, says prices rose about 6 percent a month from 1979 to the end of 1982. Since then, prices have continued to rise, but less sharply, he said. In the best buildings along Central Park West, prices in excess of $1 million are being achieved for three-bedroom apartments with park views.

More modest apartments are available, too. According to Mr. Haldenstein, a floor-through co-op in a brownstone on a good block would cost $225,000 to $275,000. His average purchaser is a young professional couple with two incomes.

The West Side is defined variously, and strictly speaking it includes everything west of Central Park. But the heart of the neighborhood in all its undiluted west-sidedness is between 72nd and 96th streets. The blocks to the south are now thought of as a separate Lincoln Center neighborhood, and the area immediately to the north is linked to Morningside Heights.

Within the West Side proper are rows of side-street brownstones, their homey facades fronting in many cases for warrens of tiny studio and one-bedroom apartments. Developers already eye hungrily the few remaining dilapidated blocks, mostly side streets just west of Broadway. And the forerunners of gentrification—antique stores and chic take-out food shops—are supplanting bodegas along Amsterdam Avenue. Columbus Avenue already has been gentrified as far north as the 80's, and it has become the place to be seen for younger, trendy West Siders.

On Riverside Drive, West End Avenue, and Broadway are comfortable 1920's-era apartment houses with sunken living rooms, Art

Deco lobbies, and sprawling layouts that could not be duplicated today. Many are agitated by rumors of plans to go co-op. Co-oping is expected to double to 20 percent of the area's housing stock in the next few years, according to Dr. Sclar's study.

Central Park West has some of New York's best-known apartment buildings, with prices that more than amply reflect their chic. Among them are the Majestic at 72nd, the San Remo at 74th, the Beresford at 81st, and the Eldorado at 90th. Best known of all is the Dakota at 72nd Street, built in 1884. It is forbiddingly gloomy outside, but opulently comfortable inside, and it still is attracting such celebrities as Leonard Bernstein.

The notable public buildings in the neighborhood are the turreted Museum of Natural History on Central Park West at 77th Street and its neighbor, the New York Historical Society. They, along with Central and Riverside parks, are the West Side's great resources, and most residents make use of them often.

Two precincts cover the area—the 20th and the 24th—with 86th Street the line dividing them. Both have high rates for burglaries.

Jack Berberian, Jr., superintendent of School District 3, covering the area west of Central Park between 59th and 122nd streets, said his district's all-day kindergarten program had been so successful that "we were the model for the other thirty-one districts—we made the training film."

While student performance in both mathematics and reading is slightly below grade level in the district overall, 90 percent of the students at P.S. 87, on West 78th Street, are above grade level in math and 75 percent are better than average in reading.

There also are several private schools in the neighborhood, among them Trinity on 91st Street and Collegiate on 77th.

"The West Side is a neighborhood that always seems to embarrass the fashionable," said Richard Shafer, cocurator of the Columbia study with Dr. Sclar. Much of it was a shantytown until the Ninth Avenue elevated line moved north in 1878 and brought the first wave of development. The IRT moved north under Broadway, the Independent line under Central Park West, and by the 1930's the neighborhood looked very much as it did until glitz began to grip Columbus Avenue. One big exception is the urban-renewal area in which high-rises replaced houses on twenty blocks between 87th and 97th streets and Amsterdam Avenue and Central Park West.

To the uncommitted, the West Side's avocation of advocacy— from opposition to the Vietnam War to boycotting nonunion grapes—could be pretentious and pesky. But the corollary of the relentless activism is that the West Side is organized to defend its turf.

"This is a neighborhood," Kent Barwick, president of the Municipal Art Society, said admiringly, "that can take a significant—if not a dominant—role in determining its own future."

The determination to do so was clear at the community forum that Ms. Sheffer addressed, sponsored by the Municipal Art Society in the auditorium of Congregation Rodeph Sholom, 7 West 83rd Street, as the participants deplored the cuteness that is afflicting Columbus Avenue.

A walk north along the avenue is like drowning in whipped cream until, at 86th Street, a lunchroom and a check-cashing office side by side bring a sudden sobering reminder of what it was like in ancient times, less than a decade ago.

Participants at the forum also seemed determined to rewrite the zoning regulations so that, in effect, the only sort of new buildings permitted in the neighborhood would be essentially identical to the buildings already there.

"I can tell you, whatever is built will have to be built on top of something else," said Doris Rosenbloom, district manager for Community Board 7. "There isn't a single inch left. Now we're a fashionable place to live."

—MAURICE CARROLL

WASHINGTON HEIGHTS

To midtown Manhattan: Subway 20 to 35 minutes

From the gray of the George Washington Bridge to the green of Fort Tryon Park, Washington Heights is a collection of contrasts—young and old, recent immigrants and third-generation residents—and its steep hills and wide vistas make it the part of Manhattan that feels least like New York. Along 181st Street, the main commercial strip, the accents are German, Greek, Russian, and Spanish, with a smattering of Irish brogues. The avenues are filled with commerce—hardware stores, vacuum-cleaner repair shops, discount-clothing outlets—while the quiet, winding side streets hide carefully tended gardens.

To many New Yorkers, the Heights remains little known, and the rent for a two-bedroom apartment in a prewar elevator building can be as low as $250 a month. "It's an open secret," said Margaret Martin Maggs, director of community relations for Community School Board 6 and a twenty-year Heights resident. "The only problem is the rents are going up."

The rising rents are a sign of renewed confidence in the area, which fills most of the northern sliver of Manhattan, from 155th to Dyckman Street and the Hudson to the Harlem River. A combination of public and private redevelopment in the last five years seems to have stemmed the decline of the 1960's and 1970's, and real-estate agents and residents say the neighborhood is fairly stable, although some areas remain run-down.

For years a stronghold of working- and middle-class families of German-Jewish and Irish descent, Washington Heights still is a family place, although its ethnic composition has changed. Blacks moved north from Harlem in the 1930's and 1940's, replacing families who left for the suburbs. In the 1950's, Cubans and Puerto Ricans began migrating to the neighborhood. Now more than 50 percent of its residents are Hispanic, said Anne S. Loftus, district manager of Community Board 12. The most recent arrivals are Dominicans and Soviet Jews.

Many of the older residents have remained, however, and 17 percent of the population is more than sixty-two years old, according to 1980 census figures. But the area is also one of the few in the city with a growing school-age population, with 24 percent of its residents under seventeen. The mix of ages and cultures has caused conflicts. Parts of the Heights have been plagued by crime, mostly burglaries and robberies, but the police say the rates have been stable during the last few years.

"We do have our problems like any mix of people learning to live together with a diversity of languages and cultures," Ms. Loftus said. "But one of the outstanding things about Washington Heights as a community is that people do try to work together, live together, and sometimes play together with a certain amount of respect for each other in the midst of a very urban environment."

Living together may be made easier by the almost 600 acres of parklands that Washington Heights shares with Inwood, the neighborhood to the north. There are also outstanding museums, from the historic Morris-Jumel Mansion, which was used as headquarters by George Washington during the Revolution, to the Cloisters, a branch of the Metropolitan Museum of Art set on a hill at the northern end of Fort Tryon Park.

The Washington Heights Museum Group, at Broadway and 155th Street, includes the Museum of the American Indian, the Hispanic Society of America, the American Numismatic Society, and the American Academy of Arts and Letters, the nation's honorary society for artists and writers. The neighborhood is also home to Columbia-Presbyterian Medical Center and Yeshiva University.

Columbia, already a major presence in the neighborhood, is planning a $120 million research and commercial complex adjacent to its medical center. The five-building complex, to be called Audubon Research Park, will stretch from 165th to 168th Street between Broadway and Aubudon Avenue. The heart of the complex will be the former Audubon Ballroom on 165th Street, where the black activist Malcolm X was assassinated in 1965. The first floor of the ballroom will be converted to retail space and the second to laboratory space.

Mostly because of the low rents, new arrivals come to the Heights and longtime residents remain. Paul Maslin, a retired real-estate broker and owner who has specialized in upper Manhattan properties for twenty years, said the housing market, still largely rental, is tight. "If you're looking for a place to live in Washington Heights, you really have to look." He quoted prices ranging from $544 a month for a six-room apartment near Columbia-Presbyterian to $105 for a two-room apartment in a 1930's elevator building on Thayer Street.

Because the rental market is so tight, there is also a growing demand for cooperative apartments, and several buildings have recently been converted. "A year ago I used to get one call a week for co-ops, and now I get ten to twenty calls a day," stated Joseph H. Green, a broker in the area for fifty years. He said a two-bedroom co-op in one of the better sections costs from $50,000 to $75,000, with a monthly maintenance charge of $450 to $500. One of the older cooperative developments is Hudson View Gardens, a Tudor complex on Pinehurst Avenue at 183rd Street built in the 1920's. Its stone walls, wrought-iron fixtures, and terraced flower gardens look more like Stratford-on-Avon than Manhattan-on-Hudson.

Commercial rents in the area have increased dramatically in the last ten years. Mr. Green said a 750-square-foot store on 181st Street that rented for $500 a month in 1974 can now bring in $5,000 or more a month. Ms. Maggs said one of the community's greatest concerns is that the higher rents will drive out longtime merchants who have given the neighborhood its family atmosphere.

In 1978 the city designated Washington Heights and Inwood a "neighborhood strategy area." Since then the city has helped pay for a refurbishment of 181st Street and other projects. In 1979 forty local businesses and institutions formed the Washington Heights–Inwood consortium to provide private support for development and employment.

Community groups sponsor a variety of events, from an annual medieval festival at the Cloisters to a mediation program that settles tenant disputes. "It's a neighborhood that can rally together," Ms. Loftus said.

The neighborhood is linked to midtown Manhattan by a twenty-minute ride on the IND A train or a thirty-five minute ride on the IRT No. 2 train.

The public schools serve an enrollment that is 80 percent Hispanic and includes the greatest number of students in English-as-a-second-language classes of any New York City district, according to Ms. Maggs. Reading scores for elementary and intermediate school pupils are among the lowest in the city, but this does not mean most are poor students, she said, only that many still have limited proficiency in English.

George Washington High School, whose alumni include Henry A.

Kissinger and Jacob K. Javits, is the local secondary school. About 65 percent of its graduates go on to some form of higher education. There are also about twenty private schools serving 6,000 children from elementary through high school. One of them is Mother Cabrini High School, named after Saint Frances Xavier Cabrini, the first American saint and the founder of the Missionary Sisters of the Sacred Heart. Her remains are buried there.

Washington Heights is actually two ridges of bedrock—Fort Washington on the west and Fort George on the east—and the valley between them. The natural path through the valley between was originally an Indian trail and was later known as the Boulevard. In 1899 it was renamed Broadway.

The high ground was the scene of struggles during the Revolution. On November 16, 1776, the British captured more than 2,000 of Washington's best troops, who were left behind when the general retreated from New York. The remains of the fort are discernible in Bennett Park at Fort Washington Avenue and 183rd Street, and a plaque marks the site. At 267 feet above sea level, it is the highest natural elevation in Manhattan.

In the nineteenth century, prominent New Yorkers, including John James Audubon, the naturalist, and James Gordon Bennett, the publisher of *The New York Herald,* built country estates in the Heights. Many of these estates disappeared when the anchorage for the George Washington Bridge and its approaches were built more than half a century ago.

—TODD S. PURDUM

YORKVILLE

*To midtown Manhattan: Subway
15 minutes or bus 20 minutes*

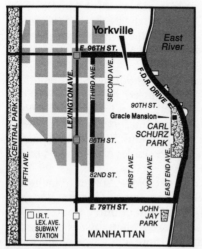

From a neighborhood that in 1900 was second in the world only to Berlin in the number of German residents, the area on the east side of Manhattan known as Yorkville has been transformed into a mostly upscale community that is more silk stocking that *lederhosen.* The dispersion of the Germans—and the Hungarians, Irish, and Slavs who also once lived in the neighborhood—resulted from the demolition of the Third Avenue el in 1954 and the ensuing boom in high-rise apartment construction. Rising housing costs altered the neighborhood's character, bringing more of a cross section of people to live in an area that now includes million-dollar cooperatives and elegant rental apartment houses side by side with smaller rent-stabilized apartment houses and shabby tenements.

Today's Yorkville is a bustling area, with streets that provide the diversions that a moneyed, heterogeneous community desires. Gimbel's Department Store rises eleven stories at 86th Street and Lexington Avenue. There are squash clubs, first-run movie houses, and restaurants that offer all varieties of cuisine.

But Yorkville is more than its "action" for those who settle there. The area possesses a certain cachet. It is not yet the Upper East Side, which adjoins it, but year by year it is taking on more of that neighborhood's character.

Assemblyman Alexander B. Grannis, a Democrat who represents

the area, describes Yorkville as "a very solid community. It's perceived as safe. It's got good transportation. It's been a traditionally strong neighborhood, with more of a sense of community and stability—even with the real-estate boom. A solid community made up of people with a degree of social conscience. These are the kind of people that elected Lindsay and Koch."

Yorkville's boundaries are shifting, but they generally are thought of as 79th and 96th streets, Third Avenue and the East River. The area has long been associated with the German community that lived and worked there and gave its streets (particularly those around 86th Street and Third Avenue) their ethnic character.

The German influence was well established by the mid-1800's by prosperous families like the Rupperts, Ringlings, and Ehrets, who had their homes in Yorkville. Brownstones and tenements began to go up as early as 1835 following the opening of the New York and Harlem Railroad and a stagecoach line. The new housing attracted both prosperous and working-class Germans, and many laborers found employment in Yorkville's factories and breweries.

The ethnic legacy of Germans, Hungarians, and others can be seen amid the high-rise developments, the smart shops, and antique stores. Notices posted outside churches advise that services are offered in German and Hungarian. In a few stores, Yorkville old-timers still buy delicacies that were once common staples.

Schaller & Weber, on Second Avenue between 85th and 86th streets since 1937, sells wieners, knackwurst, bockwurst, bauernwurst, and varieties of kielbasa and hams, as myriad "pork stores" in the neighborhood once did. From the front door of Lekvar-by-the-Barrel, at First Avenue and 82nd Street since 1926, drift the scents of spices and herbs—including the Hungarian paprika that the store's catalogue boasts is "perfect for soups, salads—and, of course, the most popular Hungarian dish of all—goulash!"

Bremen House, at 220 East 86th Street, does a brisk business not only in gourmet fare, but also in German-language magazines and records. And for those whose palates are enticed by Wiener schnitzel and sauerbraten, there are German restaurants like Cafe Geiger at 206 East 86th Street and, for a less formal atmosphere, the Ideal Cafe at 238 East 86th Street.

"Yorkville back when the Third Avenue el was up was delightful," recalled Helen Banyai, who grew up in the neighborhood and still attends services with her husband at the Hungarian Baptist Church. "There were different ethnic groups and wonderful odors from the restaurants and bakeries, and you could stroll past doorways where continental music could be heard—performed by violinists and gypsy musicians."

The economic pressures on the community's housing stock brought on by a growing population is one of Yorkville's biggest concerns. Sprinkled among the middle- and upper-middle-class buildings are many old rent-controlled tenement buildings and walk-ups occupied by poor and elderly tenants, many of whom are being bought out or harassed into moving to make way for new high-rise buildings.

When walk-ups and railroad flats are vacated, they rent for $700 to $900 a month, according to local real-estate brokers. Dennis Ryan, director of rentals at J. I. Sopher, said rents on one- to three-bedroom apartments in elevator buildings with doormen range from $1,200 to more than $3,200. Even one-room studios rent for as much as $800 a month.

Edith Sachs, vice president and director of co-op sales for Sopher, said it was still possible to find a "miracle" one-bedroom apartment in a recent conversion in a midblock location for $135,000 and two-bedrooms for $200,000, but for the most part, one-bedrooms sell for a minimum of $175,000 and two-bedrooms for a minimum of $250,000.

By comparison with other parts of the city, Yorkville is not particularly afflicted by violent street crime; its most conspicuous problems—prostitution and drug sales—are visible on East 86th Street. Burglaries are numerous, particularly in old tenement and walk-up buildings, which offer an intruder easy access. But overall, said Detective Jack McGuire of the 19th Precinct, "it is a neighborhood that is safe to go out and walk in."

It also has good public transportation. Buses run on Lexington, Third, Second, and First avenues and on 79th, 86th, and 96th streets, and the IRT Lexington Avenue line has stops at 96th, 86th, and 77th streets. The midtown office district is fifteen minutes away by subway, twenty minutes by bus.

Yorkville still has the conveniences and comforts that attracted hordes of young people late in the 1960's before the rental market stiffened. Many of those residents say they intended to move to larger apartments elsewhere but found themselves with Yorkville as their permanent address.

"That's when people realized they had to take charge of their lives and not depend on government," said Paulette Geanacopoulos, director of community services at the Lenox Hill Neighborhood Association. "The feeling was, 'Hey, we're here now, and we're going to be here in five years because we can't afford to be anywhere else. In five years, the problems are going to be worse, so let's start working on them now.'"

That meant working with the neighborhood's block associations, which, by establishing programs to beautify streets, aid the elderly, and curb crime, have at least partially restored the community feeling for which Yorkville was once famous. "One way we fight crime is to put stickers on store windows," said Dawn Sullivan, president of

YORKVILLE

the 400 East 80th Street Block Association. "These stickers let people know this is a place they can go to if they are being followed, a place where they can use the telephone or just wait until the danger passes."

Yorkville has more than two dozen public, parochial, and private schools, including P.S. 158, which ranks among Manhattan's best schools in reading scores. Many parents tend to send their children to private schools after the sixth grade. But Wagner Junior High School gets high praise from Charles N. Wilson, superintendent of Community School District 2, who said the majority of its graduates go on to such specialized high schools as Stuyvesant, Bronx Science, Brooklyn Tech, and Music and Art.

Yorkville has recently responded to the growing problem of the homeless, with organizations like the Neighborhood Coalition for Shelter, Lenox Hill Neighborhood Association, Jan Hus House, The Common Pantry, and the Stanley Isaacs Neighborhood Center working to give street people places to stay. In Assemblyman Grannis's words, "Yorkville is socially compassionate."

In that neighborly spirit, Manhattan Savings Bank, on Third Avenue and 86th Street, offers daily music for a mostly elderly audience that gathers midday to hear a pianist play on bank premises.

And for those who love the outdoors, there are other amenities. At Carl Schurz Park, a walkway overlooking the East River is trafficked by joggers, strollers, and bench jockeys who watch the gulls and barges go by. In 1984, Yorkville got a new recreational amenity, the Asphalt Green, at Franklin D. Roosevelt Drive and East 90th Street. It has a gymnasium and indoor track in a former municipal asphalt plant and five and a half acres of playing fields.

—LESLIE BROOKS BERGER

BROOKLYN
III.

Greenpoint

Cobble Hill

Brooklyn Heights

Fort Greene

Boerum Hill

Park Slope

Carroll Gardens

Flatbush

Bay Ridge

Flatlands

Midwood

Sheepshead Bay

BAY RIDGE

*To midtown Manhattan: Subway
60 minutes*

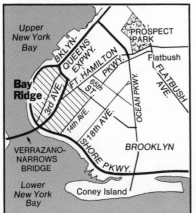

Bay Ridge is an enclave of churches, children, and quiet streets on the western edge of Brooklyn, where the view of New York Bay is almost as spectacular as the pale blue Verrazano-Narrows Bridge that looms above it. Residents of this tightly woven community of 116,000 think of it as a small town. Many of them can walk down their streets and know just about everyone they see. And that, they say, makes Bay Ridge special.

From a tiny settlement planted by the Dutch in 1636, Bay Ridge has grown to cover a broad area. It is bounded by 65th Street on the north, Fourteenth Avenue on the east, and the Brooklyn shore on the west and south. In 1898, Norwegians seeking religious freedom gave the neighborhood a lasting Scandinavian flavor, but it has become home to many other peoples as well, among them Italians and Irish and, more recently, Lebanese, Greeks, Asians, and Hispanics.

There is hardly a religious denomination not represented among the community's thirty-two churches and one synagogue. But for all its ethnic and religious diversity, it has remained an almost totally white enclave. According to the 1980 census, 95 percent of the population is white, and only 0.6 percent is black. The remainder is Asian, American Indian, and others.

Bay Ridge is politically conservative and is one of the few areas in New York City that traditionally votes Republican.

BAY RIDGE

"There are many generations of families that live here," said Kathy Wylde, a community leader who is assistant to the president of Anchor Savings Bank. "That contributes to stability."

Such stability extends to Bay Ridge's housing market, which has been virtually unchanged for decades. Two recent residential projects met stiff opposition from the community. Two 14-story towers for the elderly called Shore Hill were sponsored by the Lutheran Medical Center and dedicated in 1977. The other project, a 210-unit cooperative called Watersview, at the foot of the Verrazano-Narrows Bridge, is the only new nongovernment-assisted residential construction in at least twenty years.

A previous attempt to erect high-rise apartments on the site, which adjoins John Paul Jones and Leif Ericsson parks, was defeated and led to a zoning rule limiting the height of new buildings to three stories on side streets and six stories on main streets.

The bridge, which opened in 1964, was also vigorously opposed by residents who feared that the extra traffic—as well as the demolition of 800 houses for approach roads—would ruin the neighborhood. The bridge displaced some 7,000 residents. Today, however, the bridge has become a community icon, its image emblazoned on store signs and even on ashtrays and coffee cups in diners.

Views of the bridge and the Narrows are a selling point for apartments and houses, especially along Shore Road, which is known as the Gold Coast of Brooklyn. There, many rental apartment buildings are being converted to cooperatives. Frances Gaudio of F. Gaudio Realty said listings for recently converted co-ops on Shore Road range from $60,000 to well over $100,000.

Single-family detached homes near the water sell from $200,000 to as much as $500,000. Typically, they have three or four bedrooms, a two-car garage, and a finished basement. Two- and three-family houses—semidetached dwellings of brick—sell for between $150,000 and $200,000, depending on location. As in the rest of the city, taxes are low. Owners of one- or two-family houses pay $1,000 to $2,000 a year.

From Shore Road, it is a short walk to Third Avenue, a busy shopping area that in the last few years has sprouted boutiques, bars, and restaurants. Al Nahas, a community leader and merchant, said the boom began about the same time the film *Saturday Night Fever* brought notoriety to disco dancing, another sort of Bay Ridge nightlife.

Though the disco craze has abated, 2001: Odyssey, the disco featured in the film, is still open and tourist traffic persists. Third Avenue is frequently clogged with cars on weekend nights. The neighborhood has other commercial strips on Fourth and Fifth avenues and 86th Street.

Cars are part of life in Bay Ridge, and many houses have garages.

BAY RIDGE

Though the area is served by the BMT subway line (the RR local runs along Fourth Avenue to its terminus at 95th Street–Fort Hamilton), many residents complain that the trip to Manhattan is slow and can take as long as an hour.

Crime is not much talked about, partly because it is not a major problem. Sergeant John Granite of the 68th Precinct said that burglaries and auto thefts were the area's most serious crimes, but that "from 65th Street to 101st Street is one of the safest areas in Brooklyn."

For most residents, crime is something that comes from elsewhere, which explains their determination to keep the neighborhood as it is. Many were born and grew up on the same street and stayed on to raise families of their own.

Longtime residents remain an active force in Bay Ridge, according to Ms. Wylde of the Anchor Bank, who said the annual Ragamuffin Parade, held in October, began as "an intergenerational effort by some of the older folk to acknowledge the importance of children." It has become a community event almost as important as the May 17 Norwegian Independence Day parade.

Most of the threads of neighborhood life come together in the Bay Ridge Community Council. More than a hundred civic, trade, and block associations are represented on the council.

Bay Ridge is part of School District 20, which includes Bensonhurst, Borough Park, and part of Sunset Park. According to Lucretia Marcigliano, whose three decades and more on the district's school board constitutes, by her own account, "the longest service in the history of the city school system," the area's public schools are cherished "like children."

She said a twenty-five-year dream to build a new elementary school to replace two obsolete buildings was fulfilled in 1982, when the Luis Muñoz Marín School at Third Avenue and 59th Street was dedicated. Though technically in the Sunset Park area, the school serves many Bay Ridge children. The school, complete with what Ms. Marcigliano calls "a gorgeous gym," accommodates 1,700 preschool to sixth-grade children. There are also many parochial and private schools in the area, among them Polytechnic Preparatory Country Day School and Adelphi Academy.

Violet Mamary, who was born in Bay Ridge, and with her husband, Edward, raised three children in her house here, is not at all tempted to leave. "When the kids grow up," she said, "we'll move to Shore Road and take an apartment with a balcony. Our roots are here."

—LAWRENCE JOSEPHS

91

BOERUM HILL

To midtown Manhattan: Subway 30 minutes

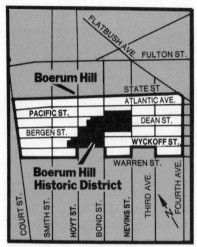

When Patricia Snyder and her husband moved to Boerum Hill twenty years ago, many of the deteriorating brownstones in the neighborhood just south of downtown Brooklyn were scheduled for demolition. The old families were either moving out or dying off and were replaced by absentee landlords or real-estate speculators. Banks were writing mortgages only reluctantly, if at all.

It was hardly the setting for an urban revival. But the prices of real estate today in Boerum Hill—named in the early 1960's by one of its earliest middle-class pioneers in an attempt to put it on the map with some respectability—reflect its survival as a residential neighborhood. Restored four-story brownstones are now fetching as much as $275,000, according to Nat Hendricks, a seventeen-year resident of the area and a real-estate broker whose agency bears his name. Ten years ago, he said, a comparable building would have cost $100,000.

Shells are now selling for between $65,000 and $90,000, up from $20,000 a decade ago, and one- and two-bedroom floor-through apartments are now renting for $450 to $960 a month, up from $150 ten years ago. One-bedroom floor-through co-op apartments—which became available in the neighborhood only about five years ago as the Brooklyn Heights co-op market spilled over—are fetching from $50,000 to $125,000, up from about $40,000 only two years ago, Mr. Hendricks said. "These prices say that Boerum Hill has been recognized as an attractive neighborhood," he added. "People like it for its ambience, its convenience to transportation. Shopping is getting better. The neighborhood is becoming a real community in its own right."

But while Boerum Hill is often spoken of in the same breath as its more prosperous neighbors, Brooklyn Heights and Cobble Hill, major differences exist. "I think we are going to see a strong middle-class and upper-middle-class enclave here," said William Harris, a broker with Renaissance Properties who has lived in the neighborhood since 1970. "But it is not here yet."

As defined by the Boerum Hill Association, the neighborhood is bordered by Court Street on the west, Fourth Avenue on the east, State Street on the north, and Wyckoff and Warren streets on the south. The thirty-block area includes a six-block historic district roughly bounded by Pacific, Nevins, Wyckoff, and Hoyt streets and encompassing a set of buildings on nearby State Street. The association would like to add to the district Wyckoff between Bond and Nevins, two blocks of Dean between Smith and Court, and two blocks of State between Bond and Third Avenue. The present district was designated by the Landmarks Preservation Commission in 1973, when the commission described Boerum Hill as a "pleasant residential neighborhood of low building heights, uniform roof lines and continuous iron railings at street level."

But while the neighborhood's roof lines may be uniform, its economic and social mix is not. There are historically protected brownstones but also two large subsidized housing projects and more than a dozen social-service facilities.

The neighborhood's proximity to downtown Brooklyn has also made it vulnerable to the economic and social forces affecting that area. Only recently has this become an advantage as the downtown neighborhood is experiencing its own economic revival, aided in part by the planned relocation of many state and city offices from the World Trade Center.

"This is never going to be like Brooklyn Heights," Ms. Snyder said. "It will never be sanitized. But most everyone who moves here expects that mixture. And it's a viable mixture."

For Bill Taylor, a social worker who runs a residential program for delinquent boys and young men in Bedford-Stuyvesant, "the racial and economic mix" of the neighborhood was among the factors that led him to buy an 1848 Greek Revival brownstone in Boerum Hill in 1977. "When I was thinking of moving here, I found a house that I loved, but I wasn't sure of the neighborhood," he said. "I walked by it maybe three hundred times, at three in the morning and nine at night, and sat on the stoops and talked to people. That sold me. I saw the same people. People recognized me. They offered to share a beer with me, and I liked that stoop culture. I'm from a rural area in

BOERUM HILL

Michigan, and it meant something to me to see this kind of mixed community working."

According to Brendan James, president of the Boerum Hill Association, the ethnic mix is the ultimate melting pot: white Anglo-Saxon Protestants, Puerto Ricans, Chinese, Arabs, and third-generation Irish and Italians. "And everyone gets along," he said.

The neighborhood has passed through many phases since its row houses started going up in the 1840's. According to the Long Island Historical Society, the neighborhood had its most rapid growth between the 1840's and the 1870's when middle-class tradesmen, small businessmen, and politicians began building three- and four-story row houses, mostly in the Greek Revival and Italianate styles. Before that, the neighborhood was farmland, settled first by the Dutch and later the British. It was named for the Boerum family, which owned a farm in the area during colonial days.

The deterioration of the neighborhood, according to the historical society, intensified between the Depression and the end of World War II. In the 1960's, however, middle-class artists and professionals, mainly from Manhattan, began to be drawn to the area by the still salvageable brownstones, low prices, and good subway links to Manhattan. In setting out to reclaim the area, they had to convince not only city demolition experts—by 1960 the city had targeted the neighborhood for demolition and high-rise urban-renewal projects—but also local bankers who saw little hope for the neighborhood and little reason to offer mortgages there. And they also had to contend with the ire of the neighborhood's poor residents, who argued that the new people were driving up rents and forcing them out.

Today, Boerum Hill is, as Mr. James of the Boerum Hill Association describes it, "slightly in transition, like Columbus Avenue" in Manhattan. The so-called antidisplacement battles with the area's poor have ebbed, bankers now readily lend mortgage money in the neighborhood, and the middle class has a firm hold. "The people coming in are now mainly Manhattan refugees looking for a better quality life that is less expensive," said Mr. James, who called the area "a fine mix of the West Village, SoHo, and Little Italy."

The neighborhood has two public elementary schools: P.S. 38, where about 45 percent of the students are reading at or above grade level; and P.S. 261, where about 50 percent read at or above grade level. Sarah J. Hale High School is also in the neighborhood. Many Boerum Hill parents send their children to private elementary and high schools in Brooklyn Heights—Packer Collegiate Institute, St. Ann's School, and the Friends School.

Boerum Hill does not lack for good places to eat, notably the Lisanne Restaurant on Atlantic Avenue and the Boerum Hill Cafe on Hoyt Street. And for an evening's cultural entertainment, the

B O E R U M   H I L L

Brooklyn Academy of Music is a short distance to the east in the nearby Fort Greene section.

The neighborhood's subway connections provide easy links to Manhattan. The IRT, BMT, and IND subways all have stations in the neighborhood. Wall Street is less than fifteen minutes away, midtown about thirty minutes.

There has been a decline in robberies, burglaries, and car theft in the last several years, according to Captain James Danaher of the 76th Precinct, which covered much of Boerum Hill until the beginning of 1984. (Now it is covered by the 84th.) "The people are very active and that enhances the community," Captain Danaher said. "The more people put into a neighborhood, the better it gets, and these people are putting in."

—JOAN MOTYKA

B R O O K L Y N   H E I G H T S

*To midtown Manhattan: Subway
30 minutes*

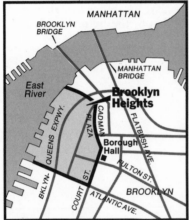

Longtime residents, and very often new ones, use words like stability and dignity to describe Brooklyn Heights. They also say it is convenient. The neighborhood is a fifty-square-block plateau studded with well-preserved and elegant brownstone houses just across the East River from Manhattan. From many of the brownstones there are spectacular views of New York Bay and of lower Manhattan's financial towers, where many Heights residents work.

But the Heights is more than bankers and brokers. Its pleasant brownstones have attracted a diverse population that includes such people as Norman Mailer, who lives and writes there, and Victor Gotbaum, the leader of the largest municipal union, District Council 37 of the American Federation of State, County, and Municipal Employees.

It is a five-minute subway ride from the Heights to Wall Street and about a half hour to midtown, but people who work in Manhattan had made the area New York's first suburb long before the commuting was that easy.

What is now Brooklyn Heights was the entire area of the town of Breukelen established by Dutch settlers in 1657. As early as 1659 a ferry was operating between Manhattan and the Heights. It was only a rowboat then, and passengers summoned it with a horn that hung from a tree. Commuting took a big jump early in the 1800's when

Robert Fulton set up a ferry service with his new steamboats. Developers began selling 25-by-100-foot lots and soon what had been a gathering of farmhouses began to look much like today's urban community of 21,500.

An example of the stability people talk about is the house built in 1820 that still stands at the corner of Willow and Middagh streets, its gray clapboard and wooden stoop pretty much the way they were originally.

The Heights extends from the Brooklyn Bridge south to Atlantic Avenue. On the east, its boundary is Cadman Plaza as far as Brooklyn's Borough Hall and then on Court Street to Atlantic. The East River, overlooked by the Esplanade, the broad and pleasant walkway facing Manhattan, marks the western boundary.

Not all of the Heights is brownstones. There are well-kept apartment buildings, such as the Breukelen at 57 Montague Street and 2 Montague Terrace, put up before the Heights became a historic district. On the eastern boundary there are the soaring towers of the city-financed Cadman Plaza cooperative apartments.

Preservation has long been practiced in Brooklyn Heights, where some 700 houses date from 1820 to the Civil War. In 1966 the Heights became the first neighborhood to be designated a historic district by the city's Landmarks Preservation Commission.

Kenneth Boss of Boss Realty Company, who has been in business for forty years in the Heights, said that housing costs continue to rise there. A two-bedroom apartment in a newly renovated building rents for $900 to $1,500 a month. Brownstones that have not yet been modernized sell for $400,000 to $500,000 and require an additional investment of $125,000 to $150,000 for renovations. For a brownstone in move-in condition, the prices often exceed $600,000.

The rising cost of living space in the Heights has stirred concern about its being a community for only the well-to-do. Several organizations, among them the Brooklyn Heights Association, have mounted efforts to keep lower-income people from being evicted from moderate-rental dwellings that landlords are eager to turn into co-ops for greater return.

Ted and Tina Ells, who grew up in suburban Connecticut, moved to the Heights in 1969, to a fourth-floor walk-up. By 1974 they owned a brownstone on Garden Place, one of the area's choicer streets. "Ted was working downtown and it was the shortest commute," Ms. Ells said. She said she and her husband, a corporate lawyer, also liked the idea that the Heights combined the best of the city and a country community. "One can be anonymous and still feel close to people."

The Ellses have become so attached to the Heights that they stayed when his company moved, first to midtown Manhattan and then to Stamford, Connecticut. Mr. Ells now commutes to Stamford.

BROOKLYN HEIGHTS

The Ellses have three children, all of whom have gone to St. Ann's Episcopal School at 129 Pierrepont Street, a private institution that draws children from many parts of the city and even the suburbs. The other major private school in the Heights is the Packer Collegiate Institute at 170 Joralemon Street.

The only public school in the Heights is P.S. 8, at Middagh and Hicks streets. Although housed in a seventy-five-year-old building, it is one of the city's better public schools. In the reading tests, about 80 percent of its students read at or above grade level, compared with 50.8 percent citywide.

The main Heights shopping thoroughfare is Montague Street, which has everything from boutiques and bookstores to major supermarkets and restaurants of every kind. In a one-block stretch, between Henry and Clinton streets, there are more than a dozen eating places, including Armando's, which specializes in Italian food, at 143; Chuan Yuan, a Sichuan place at 128; Hebrew National at 139; Old Hungary at 142; Foffe, which specializes in wild game, at 155; and even a Burger King, with a tastefully restrained front to comply with landmark regulations, at 135.

Along Atlantic Avenue, on the Heights' southern boundary, there is a string of Far Eastern and Near Eastern restaurants, such as the Moroccan Star at 205, Son of the Sheik at 165, Dar-Lebnan at 151, and the Bali Rice Shop at 145.

Heights residents can stroll a few blocks into downtown Brooklyn to shop at a section of Fulton Street that has been turned into a mall. Variety specialty shops there sell everything from stereos to blue jeans. The mall also has one of the city's major department stores, Abraham & Straus.

Gage & Tollner's, the landmark restaurant, stands nearby at 374 Fulton Street where it was established in 1879. It still uses gas lamps.

In the other direction, a short walk to the river from the Heights brings one to the relatively new River Cafe, riding on a barge moored at the river's edge and offering sparkling views of Manhattan.

Another panoramic view is from the Esplanade, the 1,825-foot-long walkway high above the river. The Esplanade was a fringe benefit for Brooklyn Heights when Robert Moses built the Brooklyn-Queens Expressway after World War II. The expressway slashed mercilessly through many communities. But, at much extra cost, it was made to curve gently around the edge of the Heights and decked over to provide the Esplanade.

—DAVID BIRD

CARROLL GARDENS

To midtown Manhattan: Subway 30 minutes

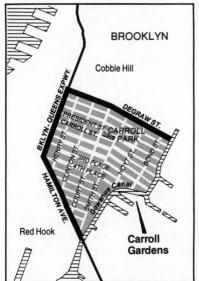

BROOKLYN

Cobble Hill

BKLYN-QUEENS EXPWY.

DEGRAW ST.

PRESIDENT ST.
CARROLL ST.
CARROLL PARK

HENRY ST.
CLINTON ST.
3RD PLACE
4TH PLACE
COURT ST.
SMITH ST.
Governur Canal
HOYT ST.
BOND ST.

HAMILTON AVE.

Red Hook

Carroll Gardens

It was, said Salvatore
Scotto, a surprise. Early in the 1960's, brownstoners began to
trickle in, first into Cobble Hill, across Atlantic Avenue from Brooklyn Heights, and then farther south into his neighborhood, an Italian
enclave that had its own identity but not a name, a place that some
called South Brooklyn and others simply "the neighborhood."

"All of a sudden doctors were moving in," stated Mr. Scotto,
founder and president of the Carroll Gardens Association, a group
that gave its name to the community in the mid-1960's. "We were
used to poor Italian immigrants and these brownstoners were something different. They came from Ohio, Wisconsin, God knows
where. They didn't have families or church ties here." More than
that, he added, they were considered oddities by old-timers in the
neighborhood, who believed "that if you were a professional, you
didn't move in, you moved out."

Now in Carroll Gardens, brownstoners and professionals are no
longer considered unusual and the old-timers no longer move out for
social advancement. Italian-Americans continue to predominate, as
they have since late in the last century, but within the last decade
there has been an influx of young, middle-class and upper-middle-
class professional couples, drawn by the same forces that keep local
residents from moving out.

Crime is low, houses with the deep front gardens that distinguish the area are well maintained on streets that are clean, people know their neighbors, and shopkeepers call their customers by their first names.

There are two public elementary schools, where more than 40 percent of the pupils read at or above grade level, and a junior high school in the neighborhood. There are also three parochial grammar schools. Local children also attend P.S. 29 in nearby Cobble Hill, where more than 60 percent of the pupils read at or above grade level, as well as private institutions in Brooklyn Heights such as St. Ann's and Packer Collegiate Institute, both of which have elementary and high schools.

For many newcomers, transportation into Manhattan also is a major attraction. Using the IND F train, via the Carroll Street station, the trip to midtown takes about a half hour.

"When we first came here we thought: This is what we can afford and we can move somewhere else when our salaries increase," said Tom Swain, an investment banker who in 1979 moved into a four-story Federal house on Sackett Street with his wife, Ann, a commercial banker. "Now we wouldn't move."

The neighborhood, which adjoins Cobble Hill, is bounded by De-Graw Street, Hamilton Avenue, the Brooklyn-Queens Expressway, and the Gowanus Canal. On the other side of Hamilton Avenue and considered a separate neighborhood is the waterfront area of Red Hook, the setting for Arthur Miller's *A View from the Bridge*.

Carroll Gardens is named for Charles Carroll, a signer of the Declaration of Independence. His connection to the neighborhood, says the Long Island Historical Society, is tenuous: both he and a regiment that during the Revolutionary War defended the Old Stone House at Gowanus, a local landmark, were from Maryland. That was enough to warrant the naming of a local street, a park, and later the neighborhood for Carroll. But he never owned property in the area.

Like much of Brooklyn, the neighborhood was originally settled in the 1600's by the Dutch. By 1846, according to the historical society, its residents were prosperous burghers who resided in large, comfortable houses. The row houses were built after the Civil War and their first owners were of many nationalities. But by 1901, according to the historical society, Carroll Gardens had become a mostly Italian neighborhood and was one of eight major Italian settlements in Brooklyn.

Today, the commercial heart of the neighborhood is Court Street, a busy stretch of small shops—pork stores, greengrocers, funeral homes, bakeries, and florists. Its food stores draw much local admiration.

"There are fabulous things to eat here," said Anne Trigg, who moved to the neighborhood from Manhattan with her husband in 1981. There are homemade pastas, cheeses, and sausages, as well as such Italian specialties as ricotta and rice balls spiced with prosciutto sold in the delicatessens. The greengrocers are not Korean, as they are in many other neighborhoods, but Italian-American.

Most of the residential blocks contain long, well-kept rows of three- and four-story brick and brownstone buildings. Two streets—Carroll and President, bounded by Smith and Hoyt—have been designated historic districts by the city's Landmarks Preservation Commission.

According to Penelope Karagias, who lives in the neighborhood and owns the real-estate agency bearing her name, 95 percent of the buildings in Carroll Gardens are owner-occupied. On some streets, such as Third Place between Court and Clinton, they are 100 percent owner-occupied.

House prices have been rising, Ms. Karagias said, and one—four stories on a 20-foot lot and mechanically perfect—sold recently for $350,000, perhaps a record for the neighborhood. But most houses are not in such good shape and sell for considerably less, $175,000 to $225,000. Such houses, she said, might need total rewiring but the plumbing usually is sound.

The neighborhood pattern is for owners to take the bottom two floors or the top three floors for themselves and rent out the rest. A duplex apartment on the top two floors of a row house, with four bedrooms, would rent for $1,000 to $1,400 a month, she said. A one-bedroom, floor-through apartment, with a second, smaller hall bedroom, would range from $550 to $850 a month.

The increase in home prices in the last decade, primarily in the last several years, has been a mixed blessing for longtime residents. "The cost of brownstones escalated to the point that many people are unable to afford to stay," Mr. Scotto stated. "Because of rent control, this is still an Italian neighborhood, but for second-generation kids who wanted to stay, prices were just too high. Neighborhood kids who got married had to move."

To address that problem, the Carroll Gardens Association is encouraging the development of co-ops, but they are still a rarity in the neighborhood. The best known, the nine-story former Doehler Die factory on Court Street, went on the market in 1981. Unable to sell the required number of apartments, the building has been converted into 123 rental units. The rents range from $645 for a studio to $1,300 for three-bedrooms.

"It's either too high-priced or it's deteriorating," said Mr. Scotto of his neighborhood. The part of Carroll Gardens that extends from Fourth Place to Cobble Hill is considered the "luxury" section. But south of Fourth Place, bordering the Gowanus Canal, there are dilapidated buildings, empty lots, houses from which "the Italian poor moved out, replaced by the black and Hispanic poor," according to Mr. Scotto.

In an effort to stem deterioration, the association and other groups have become involved in development. Construction is expected to begin soon on a hundred units of housing for the elderly on Carroll Street between Hoyt and Bond.

Despite deterioration and change, crime is not considered a problem. According to the Police Department, the 76th Precinct, which covers Carroll Gardens and Cobble Hill, has been experiencing fewer felonies than other Brooklyn precincts. "People watch out for one another here," said Detective Timothy Cole.

—JOAN MOTYKA

COBBLE HILL

*To midtown Manhattan: Subway
30 to 40 minutes*

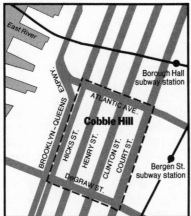

For years Cobble Hill was
called a poor man's Brooklyn Heights, but no longer. "Not when
you've got houses selling for $425,000," said Penelope Karagias, a
local real-estate broker. "That's not remotely the case anymore."

Cobble Hill, a twenty-two-block area south of Brooklyn Heights
bordered by Atlantic Avenue and Hicks, DeGraw, and Court streets,
has long drawn people priced out of the Heights. Its blocks of tidy
three- and four-story row houses, its brownstone ambience, and its
proximity to Manhattan extend the lures of Brooklyn Heights past
Atlantic Avenue.

Cobble Hill's new identity evolved from the brownstoning revival
that began in the 1960's. Now, brownstoners coexist with the Arab
and Italian immigrants who came before them, and stockbrokers,
bankers, and advertising executives live side by side with butchers,
small merchants, and Italian grandmothers who spend hours surveying the streets from upper-floor windows.

The neighborhood's commercial center is Court Street, which is
lined with small shops. But its culinary heart is Atlantic Avenue,
where Arab restaurants and shops redolent of exotic spices and
coffees long have been dominant.

"There's a big difference between Brooklyn Heights and Cobble
Hill and it's one of the reasons people like Cobble Hill so much,"
said Frank Farella, a local developer. "Brooklyn Heights is not a

community; it's very transient. But in Cobble Hill, people know their neighbors and help each other out. They shop locally. They stay and set down roots."

That "hometown" atmosphere is undergoing some dilution, however, as real-estate prices keep rising and more buildings become cooperatives. According to Ms. Karagias, a renovated four-story brownstone with a triplex apartment for the owner and a one-bedroom garden floor-through rental sells for $425,000, with the rental bringing in $950 a month for the owner. Five years ago, she said, a comparable house would have sold for $150,000, with the garden rental fetching $450. Prices for a similar place would start at about $550,000 in the Heights.

Many buildings are now being turned into co-ops. "Anything developers can get their hands on is being co-oped," Ms. Karagias stated, including parochial schools, a yeshiva, a Jehovah's Witnesses meeting hall, and a factory.

One example is a recently converted building on Atlantic Avenue between Henry and Clinton streets where life preservers once were made. In a joint venture, Gris Associates and the Central Federal Savings and Loan Association of Long Beach, Long Island, have created sixty-five apartments and twelve commercial units, including nine doctors' offices at a cost of $6.5 million. The building now is known as Cobble Court. The co-ops range in price from $85,000 for a studio to $271,000 for two-bedroom simplexes or duplexes.

Elsewhere in the neighborhood, co-op prices start at about $115,000 for a two-bedroom apartment, with maintenance charges of about $420 a month. Generally, Ms. Karagias said, prices are a bit lower than in the Heights, where a similar apartment might begin at $125,000.

The co-op push has some longtime residents concerned. "With all these buildings becoming residential and high-density, people are worried about increased traffic and transients," observed Joanne Nicholas, a member of the executive board of the Cobble Hill Association, a neighborhood betterment group. "Not transients as in bag people, but transients who would move out in two or three years. This has been a community where people stay and raise families, and now the neighborhood is starting to move away from having that family quality."

Maria Favuzzi, who bought a house on Henry Street in 1976, also feels the high prices of co-ops and houses threaten Cobble Hill's identity. "As you begin to price out the people who made the neighborhood what it was—the Arabs who work in the restaurants on Atlantic Avenue, for example—you lose some of the character."

That character has long been in the making. The neighborhood traces its history to the early Dutch farmers who settled much of

COBBLE HILL

Brooklyn in the seventeenth century. Its name was derived from Cobleshill, a steep hill at what is now Atlantic Avenue and Court Street. The hill was turned into Cobble Hill Fort by American soldiers during the Revolutionary War. George Washington used it as an observation point and from it saw his troops defeated in the Battle of Long Island. British troops then captured the fort and lopped off the top of the hill to strip it of its value as a vantage point.

It was not until 1836, however, when ferry service began from the foot of Atlantic Avenue to Manhattan, that Cobble Hill's real development began. By that time the small estates and farms had already been divided into lots for row houses. In a few years, the row-house construction then in full flower in the Heights had moved past Atlantic Avenue.

Architecturally, the neighborhood flourished. Some of the finest remaining examples of Gothic Revival, Greek Revival, and Italianate structures in the city can be found in Cobble Hill. Large brownstones were built along Henry and Clinton streets, while more modest row houses were built along the side streets.

The neighborhood claims one of the earlier low-rent housing projects in the city, a sociological experiment that was urged by Walt Whitman and sponsored by Alfred Tredway White, a nineteenth-century Brooklyn merchant and philanthropist.

The red-brick Tower and Home buildings on Hicks Street, now overlooking the Brooklyn-Queens Expressway and lower Manhattan, were built in 1876 and 1877 as examples of early tenement-house reform. They were designed for working people of modest income, with central courtyards for recreation that let air and light into the apartments, a revolutionary idea for low-income housing.

After extensive renovation in the late 1970's and a name change to Cobble Hill Towers, the two six-story, walk-up buildings now have 188 apartments that rent for $300 to $600 a month. "We tried to restore this as housing for working people," said Mr. Farella, the project's developer. There is a one-year waiting list for an apartment.

Behind the Tower buildings is another project sponsored by White: a group of twenty-six two-story brick cottages on Warren Place built for workingmen. The cottages are now privately owned.

Cobble Hill once was home to Thomas Wolfe, the writer, who lived for a time on Verandah Place; and Jenny Jerome, the mother of Winston Churchill, who was born on Amity Street in 1854. The neighborhood continues to draw new people and its schools are one reason. At P.S. 29, more than 60 percent of the pupils read at or above grade level. The school has a strong Parent-Teacher Association.

Many parents, however, send their children to Packer Collegiate

C O B B L E   H I L L

Institute and St. Ann's School in Brooklyn Heights. Only one parochial school, Sacred Hearts of Jesus and Mary, remains in the neighborhood—as an elementary school.

There is an easy commute into Manhattan. Many residents catch subways in Brooklyn Heights, with an estimated travel time on the IRT Lexington or Seventh Avenue lines of about a half hour from Borough Hall to midtown and ten minutes to Wall Street. The F train from the Bergen Street station takes a little bit longer.

—JOAN MOTYKA

FLATBUSH

*To midtown Manhattan: Subway
45 minutes*

Flatbush, stretching through central Brooklyn, is, in its contrasts, a quintessential New York neighborhood: well-kept gabled houses with oak wainscoting, wide porch swings, and deep window seats stand just around corners from boarded up storefronts.

The community is many things to many people. The Flatbush Development Corporation defines it as an area of 2.5 square miles bounded by Prospect Park and Parkside Avenue on the north, Avenue H and the Long Island Railroad cut on the south, Bedford and Flatbush avenues on the east, and Coney Island Avenue on the west.

Traditionally, however, the neighborhood boundaries are considered to stretch even farther, from Ocean Parkway on the west to New York Avenue on the east. And it is a neighborhood with two distinct sides: 3,500 private one- and two-family homes and 700 apartment houses.

The heart of Flatbush, according to the development corporation, is the three landmark neighborhoods: the two-block Albemarle Terrace–Kenmore Terrace area; the Prospect Park South section, bounded by Church Avenue, Beverly Road, Buckingham Road, and Stratford Road; and Ditmas Park, whose boundaries are Ocean Avenue, East 16th Street, Dorchester Road, and Newkirk Avenue.

What distinguishes these areas are their houses. They are turreted

107

and columned, one resembling a Japanese temple, another a Southern plantation mansion, many as whimsical as daisies pushing through cracked pavement, all of them rambling—and none reincarnated as rooming houses. Some date from the turn of the century, when the Brooklyn, Flatbush, and Coney Island Railroad—now the BMT Brighton Beach line—spurred a real-estate boom that transformed farmland into subdivisions.

Before that development, Flatbush retained a rural character little changed from the sleepy settlement founded in 1634 by Dutch farmers who called it 't Vlacke Bos—wooded plain—and Midwout. Those names were later anglicized to Flatbush and Midwood. (Some residents consider Midwood part of Flatbush and others do not.)

Today, Flatbush is a neighborhood in transition. It has suffered wrenching changes that saw its demographics shift radically between the 1970 and 1980 census counts. From a population that was heavily Jewish and white in 1970—89 percent of the neighborhood was white and 11 percent nonwhite—Flatbush in 1980 was 30 percent white, 50 percent black, 7 percent Asian, and 13 percent Hispanic.

The migration of many old-time Flatbush residents led to an exodus of many of the merchants who supplied them. Now the 3,200-seat Loews Kings movie house, with its Art Deco chandeliers, is closed and Dubin's bakery, famous for its challah and Jewish rye, is gone. And some would say that the lovingly portrayed Flatbush of William Styron's *Sophie's Choice,* set in the late 1940's, is only a memory.

Civic leaders, however, say that the neighborhood is stabilizing, that new businesses are coming in, and that landlords are investing in their properties once again. The changes can be seen in the new stores, in the thriving Korean groceries and West Indian restaurants that replaced Jewish delicatessens. Among the commercial hubs of the area are Flatbush and Nostrand avenues, near Brooklyn College, and Flatbush and Church, near the eighteenth-century Dutch Reformed Church, one of the area's landmarks.

"When it starts going downhill, it's hard to stop," said Bob Blank, the development corporation's executive director, "and when it goes the other way, it's hard to stop, too. You just have to create the conditions. We've turned the corner, and the momentum is now moving in the positive direction." With the help of the corporation and city funds, many merchants have spruced up their shops.

Some of that momentum is reflected in the rise in house prices in the historic areas. According to Mary Kay Gallagher, a local real-estate broker who has lived on Marlborough Road for twenty-five years and raised six children there, houses that sold for about $75,000 in 1979 are now fetching $110,000 to $200,000. Those houses, with seven or eight bedrooms and three baths on three floors, typically stand on lots measuring 60 by 100 feet, and include a driveway and garage. Heating costs run about $2,000 a year on average. Houses can be bought for less than $110,000, Ms. Gallagher said, "if you're willing to do a lot of work," although not a total renovation.

Ilene Gross and her husband, Jay Touger, were renters in Park Slope for eight years before moving to the neighborhood. They had hoped to buy in Park Slope, but found prices too high, and turned to Flatbush, where they purchased a three-story, seven-bedroom Tudor house in 1981 for less than $40,000 at auction. But the house, at the corner of Buckingham Road and Church Avenue, had been abandoned and vandalized and needed a total renovation, most of which they did themselves.

Ms. Gross, an audiologist, and Mr. Touger, a high-school chemistry teacher, typify many of the young couples moving into the neighborhood. In recent years, Ms. Gallagher said, she has done a brisk business selling to couples tired of cramped apartments and to many people from the Middle West and around Boston, who say the houses and the neighborhood remind them of home. Another type of buyer who has turned up with increasing frequency in recent years is the loft-dweller. "They hate to give up the lofts," she noted, "but when they have children, they're finding that the loft areas simply don't have places where kids can play. They don't want to give up the space and they don't want to leave the city. So they come here."

Not all Flatbush residents own their own homes, however. There is a heavy preponderance of renters in the area, many of whom live in the prewar buildings that either border or are part of the historic districts. Rents, according to the Flatbush Development Corporation, range from $400 to $800 for a one-bedroom apartment. The corporation has found that many of the apartments are taken by couples whose children have grown and who no longer need large homes but want to stay in the neighborhood.

The schools are considered strong. Board of Education records show that District 22, which covers Flatbush, is one of the higher-ranking districts in the city's annual reading achievement tests. Among high schools in the area is Erasmus Hall, founded in 1787 by Alexander Hamilton, Aaron Burr, John Jay, and others, one of the oldest schools in the country. The school, which has been part of the city school system since 1896, still harbors a clapboard academy building in its courtyard, now being used by the school for administrative offices. Another school, Midwood High, has a highly regarded medical-science program.

Getting into Manhattan is relatively easy, since all three subway systems traverse Flatbush. The ride to midtown takes about forty-five minutes. Express buses to Manhattan also stop in the area.

Flatbush, with its twelve neighborhood associations and as many

F L A T B U S H

block associations, is one of the most community-active neighborhoods in the city. The seventy-five-year-old Prospect Park South
neighborhood association is said to be the oldest civic association in
the country.

Yet, Flatbush also reflects more current concerns, of which crime
is foremost. "Crime is the number-one problem," said Cathy Paull,
who lives in the Prospect Park South area. "What else is there to be
concerned about? Everything else is perfect."

Flatbush is covered by three precincts, the 63rd, 67th, and 70th.
Most of the neighborhood and block associations have organized
volunteer and paid patrols to maintain a "presence" on the streets.
"Those patrols can only be an asset in stabilizing crime in the area,"
said Police Officer Donald Asfar of the 70th Precinct.

—JOAN MOTYKA

FLATLANDS

To midtown Manhattan: Bus and subway 75 minutes

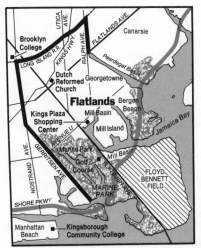

In the 1630's the Dutch farmers who settled in Brooklyn at what is now the corner of Flatbush and Flatlands avenues looked around them, saw marshes, a bay, and very little high ground and appropriately named the area Flatlands. Not until the building boom that followed World War II did Flatlands become a heavily populated residential area, but when it did, the builders who erected houses took a page from the book of the settlers. They built simply and efficiently, mainly one- and two-family, attached and semidetached homes. Block after quiet, tree-lined block, those homes now house almost 100,000 people in greater Flatlands.

The portion of Flatlands nearest the end of the IRT line at what residents call "the Junction," the intersection of Flatbush and Nostrand avenues, blossomed into a residential section in the 1920's. Many streets were developed with brick and shingled houses on small lots while four- and six-story apartment buildings were erected along Flatbush Avenue and side streets from the Junction south to Kings Highway.

Greater Flatlands encompasses not only what Brooklynites know as Flatlands itself but also five related communities along the area's southern fringe. The westernmost of these is Marine Park; to the east are Mill Basin, Mill Island, and, on the eastern edge of Flatlands, Georgetowne and Bergen Beach, both of which border on Paerdegat Basin.

111

FLATLANDS

In Mill Island, a peninsula south of Avenue U where waterfront properties sell for $450,000 to $600,000, many of the residents are able to keep boats tied up at their own docks. In Mill Basin, where houses are in the $175,000 to $300,000 range and apartments rent for about $140 a room, the attractions are several yacht clubs on Flatbush Avenue and the eighteen-hole Marine Park golf course.

The Marine Park section grew up around the land for which it is named, the largest city park in the neighborhood. The park has a two-mile oval for runners and cyclists, baseball diamonds that are home to the area's several Little Leagues, and handball and basketball courts.

The semidetached homes that predominate in Marine Park sell for between $95,000 and $120,000, according to Marie Keenan, manager of the Fillmore Realty Company office at 2280 Flatbush Avenue. "It seems everyone is asking for Marine Park these days," she said. "People say they find it affordable and still kind of unspoiled." Renters pay about $120 a room.

Georgetowne is one of the few areas in Brooklyn where new houses are to be found. The Kings Plaza Homes Corporation recently built twenty-four two-family houses in the area, priced at between $195,000 to $210,000.

Bergen Beach was a summer amusement area in the early twentieth century, and most of its houses were custom-built, according to Frank Seddio, district manager of Community Board 18. There houses are priced at between $175,000 and $350,000, Ms. Keenan said.

The boundaries of Flatlands, as defined by Community Board 18, are the Long Island Railroad on the north, Ralph Avenue and Paerdegat Basin on the east, Jamaica Bay on the south, and Nostrand and Gerritsen avenues on the west.

The northwest portion of the area is among the longest-settled land in New York, with land grants dating back to 1636. The Flatlands Dutch Reformed Church on Kings Highway just west of East 40th Street, the third oldest congregation in the country, was organized in 1654. It is said that Lord Cornwallis marched his troops past the church before the Battle of Long Island in August 1776.

This neighborhood and its mix of housing appeal to many residents. "It has the best aspects of urban and suburban life," said Representative Charles E. Schumer, who lives in the Phillip Howard Apartments on Flatbush Avenue. "We have many different kinds of people, you don't need a car to go places, and there's a true sense of neighborhood. And we also have greenery and space."

Homes in this section sell for between $75,000 and $110,000, according to Ms. Keenan, and a two-bedroom apartment rents for around $440.

As in the rest of New York City, the tax rate is $9.10 per $100 of assessed valuation, and houses are assessed at 17.35 percent of market value. Thus, the owner of a house with a market value of $80,000 would pay $1,263 a year in taxes.

Houses throughout Flatlands are close together, and while acreages are not great, interactions are. "It's a homey-type neighborhood," said Jerry Bisogno, a homeowner in Mill Basin for fourteen years and president of the Civic Association. "People really care about what goes on."

The public schools in the area are thought to be among the best in New York City. The district ranks high in standardized reading and mathematics examinations. Most of the schools participate in the Eagle program, an accelerated course for gifted children that runs from kindergarten through ninth grade, according to Ralph Brande, district superintendent.

The area's teenagers attend James Madison, Midwood, and South Shore high schools, all of which are just outside the neighborhood's borders. There also are independent, Catholic, Protestant, and Jewish schools in the area.

Flatlands falls within the boundaries of the 63rd Precinct. "We have our share of burglaries, but we also have a lot of homes in the precinct," said Louis Mangone, an administrative aide at the precinct. "Basically, we're running par for the course," he added, noting that the number of reported burglaries has been declining.

Several civic associations, concerned about car thefts and home burglaries, have hired private security guards to patrol the streets.

Shopping is relatively easy for Flatlands residents. The neighborhood's main streets—Flatlands, Flatbush, Nostrand, Utica, and Ralph avenues and Avenue U—are all major shopping arteries, and there are clusters of small stores on many other streets. The Kings Plaza Shopping Center, which includes Macy's and Alexander's, is at Flatbush Avenue and Avenue U.

A half-dozen city bus lines reach the mall and provide connections with the IRT lines at the Junction and on Eastern Parkway, and the Brighton Beach line all along East 16th Street. From the Junction, it takes about an hour and fifteen minutes to reach midtown Manhattan.

The private Command Bus Company provides express service to midtown. By car, Manhattan can be reached in thirty to forty minutes when traffic along the Belt Parkway is moderate.

There is not much nightlife in Flatlands, although there are several movie houses and a wide variety of bars, diners, delicatessens, and Chinese, Italian, and American restaurants.

The large number of school playgrounds—there are fifteen convenient to residents—and the city parks make the neighborhood a daytime delight for athletes and parents.

—MARK SHERMAN

FORT GREENE

To midtown Manhattan: Subway 35 minutes

T here is a Fort Greene in Brooklyn that brings to mind drab housing projects, crime, and poverty, There is another that is gracefully restored and preserved brownstones.

"There are two Fort Greenes," said Roberta Kyle, a writer who moved to the neighborhood in 1970. "Whenever there is a murder, the papers say it happened in Fort Greene, even if it happened someplace else, because it's a label for all of the bad stuff. But there is a lot of good stuff happening."

After a period during which crime was on the rise, Fort Greene now is considered a stable area, said Captain Anthony De Vito, the commander of the 88th Precinct. "It's an area that's being rebuilt, an area that shows great promise."

The brownstone section of Fort Greene, with a population of about 40,000, is on the edge of downtown Brooklyn, bounded on the south by Atlantic Avenue, the north by Myrtle Avenue, the east by Vanderbilt Avenue, and the west by Flatbush Avenue. The area radiates from Fort Greene Park, which, like Central Park in Manhattan and Prospect Park in Brooklyn, was designed by Frederick Law Olmsted and Calvert Vaux and is considered one of their masterpieces.

The neighborhood encompasses two adjacent historic districts—Fort Greene and the Brooklyn Academy of Music—that were designated in 1978 by the city's Landmarks Preservation Commission. At the time, James Marston Fitch, a professor at the Columbia University School of Architecture, described the area as an "encyclopedic collection of buildings 125 years old."

Although several other brownstone neighborhoods around downtown Brooklyn have taken on new names, such as Cobble Hill, Carroll Gardens, and Boerum Hill, in an effort to put them at arm's length from a decayed past, Fort Greene has remained Fort Greene. "No one moved to change the name," Ms. Kyle said, "because it would look like a gentrification kind of thing and could lead to chic and trendy boutiques and hanging plants. People who moved here didn't want to kick the indigenous population out. If black people and white people are ever to live in harmony, it will be in places like Fort Greene."

Another brownstoner, Alfred R. Muglio, believes the neighborhood shows how gentrification can work because it attracts the new black middle class as well as the white. "For every new white who moves into the neighborhood a black moves in," he said. "Fort Greene's strength is in its racial integration."

Many people have been part of Fort Greene's history. George Washington led his troops through it in retreat from the British. Walt Whitman lived there, and it was his editorials in *The Brooklyn Eagle* that are credited with bringing about the creation of Fort Greene Park.

Marianne Moore, the poet, moved into Fort Greene with her mother in 1929. In a 1961 essay she recalled that time: "An atmosphere of privacy with a touch of diffidence prevailed; as when a neighbor in a furred jacket, veil and gloves would emerge from a four-story house to shop at a grocery or meat market. Anonymity, without social or professional duties after a life of pressure in New York, we found congenial."

While Fort Greene grew rapidly in the last century as people sought to escape Manhattan, the decline came with the exodus to the suburbs. By the 1950's many of the graceful homes had been hacked into dank rooming houses. Ms. Moore moved back to Manhattan six years before her death in 1972.

In the late 1960's, the middle class began to return to Fort Greene, and real-estate prices have been driven up. But brokers say there are still bargains compared with other areas. "I get clients coming in every day from Manhattan and Brooklyn Heights who are looking for nicely renovated places at more affordable prices," said Anita Pins of Renaissance Realty in Fort Greene.

Prices of renovated two-family brownstones run from $150,000 to $250,000, according to Ms. Pins. Cooperative apartments, she added, are $30,000 to $50,000 for one bedroom and $50,000 to $80,000 for two bedrooms. Rentals, Ms. Pins said, range from $500 to $750 for one bedroom and $700 to $1,200 for two bedrooms.

Families have a choice of sending their children to public schools or to several private schools nearby—Packer Collegiate, St. Ann's, and Brooklyn Friends.

"We've probably made the greatest improvement of any district in the city in the past decade," said Dr. J. Jerome Harris, the superintendent of Community School District 13, which includes Fort Greene as well as Brooklyn Heights and part of Bedford-Stuyvesant.

As measured by standardized tests, about 55 percent of the pupils in the district's nineteen elementary schools are reading at or above grade level. That level is highest, about 80 percent, in P.S. 8 in Brooklyn Heights. Usually pupils from Fort Greene would not go to P.S. 8 but they may if they apply and there is room, Dr. Harris said.

Of downtown Brooklyn's brownstone areas, Fort Greene is perhaps the most convenient to public transportation, with major subway lines and the Long Island Railroad converging at the Atlantic Avenue and Pacific Street stations. By subway, midtown Manhattan is about thirty-five minutes away.

Martin Alter moved from Manhattan three years ago to a Fort Greene brownstone he had renovated for himself and his advertising and promotion firm. He is buying the house next door, an empty shell that he plans to remodel.

There is one thing he misses, he said: "I can't just walk down the street and fall into a great Italian restaurant like I used to. But that's a small price to pay for all the space and the living arrangement I have now."

Mr. Alter now has to walk a little farther than down the block, but there are good Italian restaurants not far away—Joe's Place on Waverly Avenue, for instance, where the owner prepares everything himself to a background of classical music in the kitchen.

There are many other restaurants within a dozen blocks or so. On Fifth Avenue, the Old Havana has authentic Cuban food. On Atlantic Avenue, Lisanne, with a French-inspired menu, has drawn good reviews. Farther down Atlantic Avenue is a clutch of good Middle Eastern places.

For entertainment there is the Brooklyn Academy of Music, on Lafayette Avenue between Ashland Place and St. Felix Street, featuring outstanding programs of dance, theater, and music.

The Brooklyn Academy Local Development Corporation, a private group financed primarily by foundation grants and donations, has raised funds for two projects. One is the conversion of the former Lafayette Hotel, across Lafayette Avenue from the academy, into apartments. The other is a park, diagonally opposite from the academy, that will have extensive plantings of flowering shrubs and trees and a gazebo.

Also in Fort Greene is the Williamsburgh Bank Building, the tallest in Brooklyn. An observation deck on the twenty-sixth floor offers a panoramic view of Brooklyn and Manhattan.

For food shopping, there are large supermarkets in nearby Park Slope. In Fort Greene there are neighborhood groceries and bodegas, as well as at least one gourmet shop, Fowler Square on Fulton Street. Fowler Square stocks imported cheeses, smoked fish, and Petrossian beluga caviar.

—DAVID BIRD

GREENPOINT

*To midtown Manhattan: Subway
20 minutes*

On a Sunday morning in Greenpoint, the streets are empty but the churches are full. The dozen or so local churches, which sponsor dances, bingo games, and annual Easter and Christmas parades, are an important element in the life of this quiet, predominantly working-class community of 67,000 on the northern end of Brooklyn.

Another is the Polish heritage shared by a large proportion of the residents. At St. Stanislaus Kostka Church on Humboldt Street, as in some of the other Roman Catholic churches in the area, the masses and hymns are in Polish.

Polish families maintain ties with relatives at home, and people fleeing repression in Poland still arrive in the area, where a network of Polish-American organizations and churches tends to their needs.

Another recent influx—though it is still small—has been of people attracted by Greenpoint's low housing prices, its safe streets and neighborhoods, and its accessibility to Manhattan.

"Greenpernt," as it is sometimes called (folk linguists credit it with being the area where "Brooklynese" originated), has changed very little since Polish, Italian, and Irish immigrants arrived in the nineteenth century to work in its factories. Many of their descendants now work in the warehouses, oil-storage facilities, and light manufacturing enterprises lining the East River waterfront.

Urban development came in the 1830's when Neziah Bliss, a ship-

118

builder, bought land and had it surveyed and mapped into streets. A turnpike connecting the area with Williamsburg and Astoria ended its bucolic isolation.

Later in the century, Greenpoint became a major shipbuilding center. Its yards turned out steamships for inland waterways and, during the Civil War, blockade vessels for the Navy. The ironclad *Monitor,* residents note with pride, was built in Greenpoint in 1862.

Shipbuilding declined after the war, but some of the street names, such as Java and India, recall the trade in coffee and spices. Other industries were established—among them porcelain, china, glass, pottery, machinery, and oil refining.

The area is bounded on the north by Newtown Creek, which separates Brooklyn and Queens; on the west by the East River; and on the south and east by Meeker Street, an extension of the Brooklyn-Queens Expressway.

Greenpoint is a neighborhood where children play in quiet, tree-lined streets. Mothers take toddlers in their strollers to Monsignor McGoldrick Park, a leafy enclave that recalls the words of Peter McGuiness, a local political leader who once called Greenpoint "the garden spot of America." Few buildings are taller than five stories.

Families live in the same houses for generations, and housing officials and real-estate dealers say the percentage of owner-occupied houses with rental units is unusually high. Pride in the neighborhood is reflected in neatly trimmed lawns and freshly painted doorways.

About a third of the houses are one- or two-family dwellings, a third have three or four units, and the rest have five units or more, according to the Department of City Planning. Two thirds are built of brick or a combination of brick and wood frame, and the rest are frame houses.

The Friends of Greenpoint recently succeeded in obtaining designation as a historic district for an area roughly bounded by Kent, Franklin, Calyer, and Leonard streets, which contains many of the homes put up by Greenpoint's wealthy shipyard owners. The group tries to attract new residents by sponsoring annual house tours, according to its president, Thomas Diffley. Although the facades of some frame houses may have lost their charm because of new siding, he said, the interiors are usually in their original condition, with fine plaster moldings, high ceilings, parquet floors, and marble fireplaces.

Turnover is low. "In order to get a house in Greenpoint on a particular block or a particular kind of house," Mr. Diffley said, "you almost have to wait until there is a death somewhere, and then it's word of mouth."

David Russell, a lawyer who works in Manhattan, bought a four-story brick house on Kent Street in the historic district in 1978 for $55,000. He and his family live in the top three floors and rent out the bottom floor.

Today, a house is likely to cost much more, brokers say, although prices are still relatively low. Two- and three-family frame houses cost from $90,000 to $150,000, and brownstones can cost as much as $200,000. There are bargains to be had to the north of the historic district, between India and Ash streets, where two- or three-family frame houses cost between $90,000 and $100,000.

Craig Stankus, a researcher on Wall Street, decided to move to Manhattan several years ago from Babylon, Long Island, but was discouraged by the rentals. He turned to Brooklyn but was unable to find anything he could afford until he looked in Greenpoint. In 1979 he and his wife rented a large three-room apartment in a two-family house on Milton Street for $260 a month. They occupy the ground floor and have use of the garden in the front.

Rents have advanced since then but still are moderate compared to better-known Brooklyn neighborhoods. Apartments, mostly of the railroad flat type, can also be found in four- or five-story walk-ups. Julian J. Borak of Greenpoint Realty pointed out such apartments still can be had for $500 a month or less.

Most residents think of Greenpoint as a small town. "It's not the kind of place you happen through," Mr. Stankus said. "You have to be heading for it." The most direct subway route to midtown Manhattan is the BMT LL line to one of three points on 14th Street, then changing to uptown trains. This takes about twenty minutes. The Williamsburg Bridge and Queens-Midtown Tunnel are within a few minutes' drive, as are the Brooklyn-Queens Expressway and the Long Island Expressway.

According to Ina Schulman, a crime analyst for the 94th Precinct, Greenpoint is one of the safest residential areas in the city. "It's something out of a storybook," she stated. "It's a very quiet neighborhood." Civilian patrols organized by the area's many block associations help insulate Greenpoint from the crime in adjoining areas of Bushwick and Williamsburg.

Most basic shopping needs can be met on Manhattan Avenue, a busy strip of small stores in the heart of the neighborhood. Shoppers can be heard speaking Polish in the Poznanski Bakery or the Nassau Meat Market, a source of kielbasa, or Polish sausage. The Zakopane Gift Shop sells painted wooden Easter eggs and other imported handcrafts.

One restaurant advertises "Polskie Obiady," or Polish meals, and signs saying "Polska Mowa," or Polish spoken here, are posted in many shop windows.

The section of Humboldt Street in front of St. Stanislaus Kostka Church has been renamed Pope John Paul II Square. The pope visited the church in 1969 when he was cardinal archbishop of Krakow, and the event was commemorated with a bronze plaque after he became pope.

The church runs one of the four parochial elementary schools to which many Roman Catholic families send their children. Tuition is about $400 a year. There are also three public elementary schools and a junior high school in Greenpoint. A majority of the children in these schools are at or above grade level in reading and math, according to Nicholas Stefanizzi, a member of the board of Community School District 14.

But parents "have a big decision to make" when it comes to sending their children to high school, Mr. Stefanizzi said. "They have no confidence in the schools around here." These include two vocational schools, Eli Whitney and Automotive, and the local high school, Eastern District. As a result many send their children to schools out of the neighborhood.

In a predominatly blue-collar area, there is little in the way of amenities of a more genteel kind. "There's no place for Sunday brunch," Mr. Russell stated. "There are no fancy restaurants or boutiques." But he added that because of the safety and accessibility of the area, and particularly because of the low real-estate prices, "I wouldn't consider living anywhere else."

—CHRISTOPHER WELLISZ

MIDWOOD

*To midtown Manhattan: Subway
60 minutes*

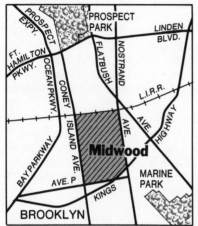

Once a wilderness of thickets in the southern part of Brooklyn, the Midwood section today is a community notable for its well-kept private homes, suburban appearance, and abundant towering trees. One resident, known as the "Tree Lady," has inventoried the more than 8,000 trees in Midwood, and neighbors often ask her advice on their care.

"One of the reasons we live here is because it's not far from the city and it's beautiful," said the "Tree Lady," Elaine McPartland. She lives in a red-brick house on the outskirts of Brooklyn College. There is a neatly groomed patch of lawn in front of her house and a vegetable garden in back. The block, like so many in this villagelike community, is shaded by Norway maples.

"Compared to Manhattan, Midwood is very suburban," said Mary Cosgrove, a neighborhood resident and director of urban services for Citibank. "It's really an urban forest."

Surrounded by the Flatbush, Borough Park, Bensonhurst, Sheepshead Bay, and Flatlands sections, Midwood is a middle- to upper-middle-class community that residents describe as a cultural hodgepodge. "On my block, East 9th Street, we have every ethnic group that you could possibly think of, and they all blend in very nicely," said Saul Klein, president of the Midwood Civic Action Council.

The Midwood Development Corporation, a community-service

group, defines the neighborhood's boundaries as Coney Island Avenue on the west, Nostrand Avenue on the east, the Long Island Railroad cut to the north, and Avenue P and Kings Highway on the south. Within those lines are many blocks with old and comfortable houses graced with inviting facades.

As "Midwout," a Dutch word for Middle Woods, the area was sufficiently populated by 1652 to gain a patent of township from Peter Stuyvesant, but the neighborhood did not develop rapidly until the 1920's. According to *The New York City Handbook,* by Gilbert Tauber and Samuel Kaplan, the area between Ocean and Nostrand avenues is the largest expanse of detached private houses in Brooklyn.

There is a great range of house prices in the community. Some detached and semidetached one- and two-family houses sell for as little as $110,000 to $115,000, but others are priced at more than $450,000. Many are on fairly large plots.

The neighborhood also has a stock of four-, five-, and six-story apartment buildings along Ocean Avenue. One-bedroom apartments rent for about $400 a month and two-bedroom apartments for $500 to $550, according to Bruce Dwork of Dwork & Korn Real Estate. Rents in luxury buildings like the Premiere House on Ocean Avenue range up to $700 for two-bedroom apartments.

Unlike other parts of the borough, where brownstone town houses abound, often in block-long rows, Midwood has none. Instead, there are many freestanding houses in a mixture of architectural styles, including Georgian, colonial, Tudor, and Spanish stucco.

The Midwood Development Corporation says that while Midwood is primarily a community of families, a large proportion of its population is elderly. Of Midwood's 50,000 residents, 25 percent are over the age of sixty-two.

"Our little pocket is a stable neighborhood that is changing," said Dorothy Rabinoff, a member of Midwood's Nottingham Civic Association. "A great many Syrian and Hasidic Jews are moving in from Borough Park, Crown Heights, and Williamsburg. Many of them do not affiliate with existing temples. Instead, they form their own."

City Councilman Noach Dear, whose district includes Midwood, said that at least fifty *shteibels,* or small synagogues, have been established in the neighborhood. Many are in private homes and have congregations of fewer than a hundred members.

"This is a new phenomenon," said Hyman Sardy, a Midwood resident who is professor of economics at Brooklyn College. "In Borough Park, *shteibels* exist in a massive way. In Midwood, this was unheard of five years ago."

Another resident, Alan Silverstein, agreed that the Jewish community is growing in Midwood, but, he added, "there is also a cultural mix." Explaining the attraction of the section for him, he said: "What I like is that I have a little slice of the suburbs but lower taxes and less commuting."

The property taxes on a house worth $120,000 would be about $1,300, according to Martin Meltzer of Best Realty in Midwood.

Residents can catch an M or D train at the elevated station at 15th Street and Avenue M for a trip of about an hour to midtown Manhattan. Downstairs, the twenty-four-hour newsstand carries more than fifty periodicals, everything from computer magazines to the local paper, *The Kings Courier.*

The IRT No. 3 or No. 4 trains can be boarded at "the Junction," the intersection of Flatbush and Nostrand avenues, and the F train stops on McDonald Avenue between Avenues M and J.

It takes thirty minutes to drive into Manhattan, but up to twice that long during rush hour. Also available are express bus runs to Manhattan offered by the Command Bus Service.

The main commercial strips are Avenue J and Avenue M, where there are many delicatessens, a twenty-four-hour bagel shop, fresh fish and fruit stores, a Shop-Rite, several Waldbaums, and a Jerusalem Pizzeria. Many residents also shop at the Kings Plaza mall south of Midwood in Mill Basin.

Among the popular local restaurants are Captain Gayle's, which has Dixieland music and New Orleans–style food; Szechuan Omei; the Genovese House; and Caravilles, a Greek establishment.

The local police precincts (Midwood is covered by three—the 61st, 63rd, and 70th) report that it is a low-crime area. One reason is the crime-prevention efforts of Midwood's six civic associations. Since the mid 1970's, they have sponsored four volunteer car patrols and two paid security patrols that cruise the neighborhood night and day.

There are several well-regarded public schools, among them 193, 197, and 199 and Hudde Junior High School. In all, about 70 percent of the pupils read at or above grade levels.

The two Roman Catholic churches in the neighborhood, Our Lady Help of Christians and St. Brendan's, both run schools, and there are, in addition, several yeshivas, including the Shulamith School of Girls at Avenue M and East 14th Street.

In the early 1900's, the Shulamith School was the home of Vitagraph Studios, where Rudolph Valentino, Norma Talmadge, and Erich von Stroheim once worked. Props for some of the silent films were borrowed from nearby householders, and local residents were occasionally called upon to work as Vitagraph extras. Today, part of what used to be Vitagraph property is owned by NBC and is used as a soundstage for the videotaping of *Another World,* the soap opera.

One of the two local secondary schools is Midwood High, where

MIDWOOD

Woody Allen was graduated in 1953 and where Rena Gordon, a first-prize winner of the Westinghouse Science Talent Search, was graduated in 1982. The other, Edward R. Murrow High School, is a communication arts school with its own TV studio.

Behind Murrow is General George Wingate Field, better known as Midwood Field, which offers free outdoor concerts on summer nights. In years past such notables as Rosemary Clooney and Eddie Fisher performed there. On other nights, teenagers in the area use the field to practice "popping" or break dancing.

While to many residents, Midwood is a cozy, undeniably Brooklyn neighborhood, it has a slightly different appeal to Peter Wehrwein, a fairly new resident of the neighborhood. "Kids playing out of doors, tricycles roaring up and down the streets," he said, "Midwood reminds me of where I grew up—Evanston, Illinois."

—KATYA GONCHAROFF

PARK SLOPE

To midtown Manhattan: Subway 40 minutes

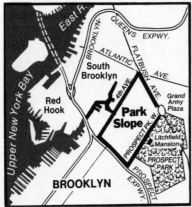

The talk in Brooklyn's Park Slope section these days is of change, of new people coming in and driving up the average price of brownstone houses well past the $250,000 mark. But at the same time, there is a realization that although some other parts of the city have been all but devastated by major upheavals, Park Slope has changed very little in recent years. Most residents seem to agree it is just that feeling of security in the midst of chaos, that lack of sharp change, that is drawing new people to Park Slope. Many newcomers come from Manhattan to escape rents that have soared beyond their means. Others come to find more space for their children and perhaps even a place to park their car.

Park Slope, a parallelogram roughly five blocks by thirty blocks, lies in the northwest section of Brooklyn. It is bounded by Flatbush Avenue, Fourth Avenue, the Prospect Expressway, and Prospect Park West. Its name is a perfect description of its geography: the land slopes gradually away to the west from Prospect Park's high ground.

According to the 1980 census, non-Hispanic whites numbered more than half the area's total population of 65,202, with 19,286 Hispanics and 7,757 blacks. By comparison, whites constitute slightly less than half the population of the entire borough.

In the middle of the last century, Park Slope was virtually vacant land when Edwin C. Litchfield bought up large tracts and started settling the area. He began developing industry along the Gowanus Canal, beyond the lower end of the gentle slope. At the top, where there was a commanding view of the whole of Brooklyn extending even into Manhattan, Litchfield built his mansion in 1857.

By 1871 he had joined with the city of Brooklyn to build Prospect Park, one of the bright creations of Frederick Law Olmsted and Calvert Vaux—a brighter gem, some say, even than their Central Park. The mansion remains as a borough headquarters for the Parks Department.

In 1892 the dramatic Grand Army Plaza with its Arc de Triomphe—like arch was added, and today visitors can climb up inside for a spectacular view of the park and the neighborhood.

By the turn of the century, Park Slope had become a social ladder for upwardly mobile groups: Italian immigrants were settled in houses at the bottom, earlier Irish immigrants had moved a rung up to the middle, and old Dutch and English families lived at the top of the ladder, the Gold Coast along the park. By the 1930's and 1940's, the Irish had moved up to the top and the Italians up to the middle slope, while blacks and Hispanics had moved into the houses vacated at the bottom.

Only the top Gold Coast area of the Slope has been designated by the city's Landmarks Preservation Commission for protection as a historic district. In its designation, the commission called it "one of the city's most beautiful residential areas," adding: "Finest in the city and among the most outstanding in the nation are the Romanesque revival row houses, town houses and mansions. The Venetian Gothic Montauk Club at Eighth Avenue and Lincoln Place is the architectural treasure of the Slope."

Today, newcomers are arriving at all levels of the Slope, while the area south of 9th Street, once considered a working-class neighborhood, is where people displaced by high Manhattan rents are settling.

Many came with dreams of graceful Victorian mansions and had to settle for a lot less. Increased prices have led to talk of gentrification, the process whereby affluent families take over homes once occupied by the poor. There also is concern that Park Slope is becoming a community for childless couples with two paychecks.

The cost of schooling in the Slope can also be an added burden, with many families preferring to send their children to private schools than to public ones. One private school, the Carroll Street School, was started fifteen years ago by then-new brownstoners. In 1982 it merged with the Berkeley Institute, a ninety-seven-year-old Park Slope institution.

Public schools present a mixed picture: at P.S. 321, a relatively new building in the middle of the Slope, more than 60 percent of the pupils read at or above grade levels, while at I.S. 83, only about 40 percent read that well. The Slope's public high school, John Jay, has acquired a reputation as a tough school, but the principal, Enzo Togneri, said he is cracking down on troublemakers. But he added that he did not expect the new middle-class residents of the Slope to make much difference at John Jay. "People who buy a $300,000 brownstone will probably not send their children to any public school no matter what it has to offer."

Rental apartments are especially hard to find now because demand is so high. And houses in prime areas of the Slope that sold for less than $100,000 in the mid-1970's now are going for more than $200,000, and in some cases for as much as $500,000.

Allan H. Bowie of Bowie & Keegan Real Estate, who has dealt in Slope real estate for many years, said rental apartments sometimes come on the market for as little as $550, but they are not in the better parts of the area and rent quickly. His listings go up to $1,300 a month for an attractive duplex.

Mr. Bowie also said he still had some houses for sale for less than $100,000, but they, too, were not in the best part of the neighborhood, and most would require extensive renovations.

Slope real-estate brokers often use the word *spillover* these days; it refers to the movement by professionals and managers into areas long occupied only by working people. Spillover is also being actively encouraged by developers who are turning older buildings— some of which never were residential—into cooperative apartments.

In 1982, for example, the massive Ansonia Clock Factory, long abandoned, was successfully remodeled into apartments. One of the developers was Kenneth Patton, who headed the city's Economic Development Administration under Mayor John V. Lindsay and now is senior vice president and director of operations for Helmsley-Spear, the big Manhattan real-estate company.

Mr. Patton, who rehabilitated a Park Slope brownstone and lived in it for fourteen years, now resides on Prospect Park West, in one of the luxury apartment houses on the edge of the park. Like most residents of the Slope, he commutes by subway—the IND and IRT lines serve the community—to his office in midtown Manhattan. When schedules are met, the trip takes forty minutes.

Some people have moved into Park Slope after a disappointing time in the suburbs. Susan Motley, a financial and economic planner for the City Planning Commission, returned from Princeton, New Jersey, with her husband and two children four years ago. "In Princeton we had a split-level house and we'd just landscaped our backyard. We were living like all bourgeois colored folks did, but it was boring. I walked in and I fell in love," she said of their Park Slope house. "It had everything I wanted—wonderful parquet floors, the original chandelier in the hall. It had a modern kitchen but it still had the nice old cabinets."

Sean Callery, a writer who was born in the Slope in 1925 and has lived there almost all of his life, remarks on how many of the old establishments have remained despite the influx of boutiques and fancy restaurants.

There is, for example, L'Espirit d'Homme, a haberdashery that formerly was simply Freddie's. There are also restaurants like Le Parc Gourmet where rack of lamb goes for $25. But there are also old Irish bars like Farrell's and Mooney's.

Surveying Seventh Avenue, the Slope's main commercial street, Mr. Callery picked out a corner establishment that he remembers as the old Blue Eagle saloon. "It's now called Minsky's," he said, "and I don't call that progress."

—DAVID BIRD

SHEEPSHEAD BAY

To midtown Manhattan: Subway 45 minutes

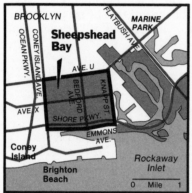

At the turn of the century, Sheepshead Bay was a favored resort of the rich. Most came for its racetrack, its fine seafood restaurants, and the salubrious sea breezes that blew in from the Atlantic. Lillian Russell, Diamond Jim Brady, and Lillie Langtry were among the famous folk who frequented Sheepshead Bay, and they were often seen strolling along the Emmons Avenue promenade overlooking the harbor.

The racetrack has long since been replaced by houses and apartment buildings. And today, the waterfront, with its restaurants and fishing boats, is more reminiscent of a Cape Cod village than the typical middle-class neighborhood Sheepshead Bay resembles farther inland. There, the predominant style of building is a two-story, two-family attached or semiattached brick house of a kind that is typical of the southern end of Brooklyn.

Harold Meckler, president of Exclusive Buys, a local real-estate brokerage, said the average cost for such dwellings ranges from $150,000 to $175,000. These houses are still available for those who want to buy, but rentals are scarce both in multifamily homes and the low-rise apartment houses in the neighborhood. "A two-bedroom apartment goes for an average of $550," Mr. Meckler stated. "Add an additional $100 a month for a third bedroom and consider yourself lucky if you can find either. It's rare for vacancies to go for as long as thirty days."

130

SHEEPSHEAD BAY

Few of Sheepshead Bay's buildings and land parcels are undeveloped or underutilized, according to Deborah Friedman, executive director of the Greater Sheepshead Bay Development Corporation, a state-assisted housing agency.

The community, roughly 2.5 square miles in size, is situated above a narrow inlet directly north of Manhattan Beach, a smaller, more affluent community on Brooklyn's southern shore. Many residents say its boundaries are Coney Island Avenue on the west, Emmons Avenue on the south, Avenue U on the north, and Knapp Street on the east, although Assemblyman Daniel Feldman, Democrat from Brooklyn's 45th District, said Kings Highway is the proper northern boundary.

From midtown Manhattan, the district is accessible by car via the Brooklyn-Battery Tunnel and the Belt Parkway, a drive of about thirty minutes; the time to midtown Manhattan by the D or QB subway trains on the Brighton line is about forty-five minutes.

According to the 1980 census, Sheepshead Bay's population is 130,482. Though minority-group residents constitute only 7 percent of the population, school officials say the community's elementary schools are well integrated because of busing. Minority students in the neighborhood's four elementary schools and the district's only junior high make up more than a quarter of the enrollment of about 3,500. At the highly regarded Sheepshead Bay High School, nearly a third of the 2,700 students are nonwhite.

"Our schools are among the best in the city," said Ralph Brande, school superintendent of District 22. "The facilities are safe and secure. Social conduct is good and our students are high achievers." In both reading and mathematics achievement tests, junior high and elementary school students score well above national averages.

Although its schools are an important attraction to parents, Sheepshead Bay's larger lures are sports fishing and waterfront seafood restaurants. Together, fishing and food draw about 100,000 visitors a year, according to John Hall, president of the Sheepshead Bay Boatowners Alliance. The organization's twenty-four members, he said, maintain the largest collection of party fishing vessels on the eastern seaboard.

Amateur anglers come during the warm seasons, stated Ethel Lentino, the proprietor of Jean's Clam Bar, at 2123 Emmons Avenue, a modest establishment, family-owned for nearly forty years, where lobster fra diablo is a specialty of the house. "But the true diehards come year-round, even in the sleet and snow, when it's so cold they have to chop ice to get the boats out of the harbor," she said. "I call those guys the purple people because of the way they look when they get off the boats—their hands are shaking and their teeth are chattering."

Most party boats are about seventy-five feet long and can carry as many as seventy-five passengers. The boatowners offer trips of eight or nine hours, day or night, and sometimes offer amenities to pacify fishermen when fish cannot be found. On the *Tampa VI*, a cabin cruiser, for example, the owner has advertised heated railings, color TV, and even a rock band after 7 P.M.

The waterfront has other nightlife offerings beyond the usual array of waterfront bars and seafood spots. Pips Comedy Club, at 2005 Emmons Avenue, a showplace for standup comics, includes Rodney Dangerfield, Robert Klein, and David Brenner among its alumni. Mr. Brenner returned in 1981 to help the owner, George Schultz, celebrate the club's twentieth anniversary.

For residents, there is convenient and varied shopping along Sheepshead Bay Road, with a cluster of boutiques on the block between East 13th Street and Voorhies Road.

Though such business from transients is important for the local economy, Maurice Kolodin, chairman of Community Board 15, said heavy traffic put a burden on public facilities, particularly on Emmons Avenue. "We don't want to cut down on this business," he stated, "just improve our facilities for attracting more."

In summer particularly, traffic jams tie up Emmons Avenue on weekends. With the help of Mr. Kolodin and the community board, the Departments of Ports and Terminals and Transportation are working to improve parking facilities and the traffic flow. "Eventually we hope to rehabilitate many of the piers and bulkheads, some of which have been deteriorating for forty years without repair," said Ray Gordon, project manager for Ports and Terminals. "We will also have to install new water and electrical lines."

Henry Sloan, assistant transportation commissioner, said his agency's improvements would include roughly a mile and a half of Emmons Avenue between Ocean and Shore avenues. "Our hope is to start reconstruction of the roadway and sidewalks by 1985." There also will be new sewers, water mains, and tree plantings.

The city has budgeted only about $20 million for the project, but officials said the total cost could run at least twice as much.

A key feature of private plans for the area is the renovation of Lundy's Restaurant, a neighborhood landmark and once one of Brooklyn's most popular eating establishments. The restaurant, whose massive Moorish-styled building can seat more than 2,000 patrons, has been vacant in recent years. It and about twenty-two acres of adjoining property were purchased by the Litas Investing Company for about $10.5 million in 1982, and the new owners said they planned to open two or more restaurants in the space. However, since then Litas has offered the property for sale, and new schemes for redevelopment are being proposed.

Some years ago, Mr. Kolodin stated, the community board successfully appealed to the city for a special zoning district that limits the height of both residential and commercial buildings. As a result, none of the forty apartment buildings arrayed along Ocean Avenue in the most densely populated section of the neighborhood is more than six stories tall.

"After all, what Sheepshead Bay needs most is to be left alone, at least sometimes," Mr. Kolodin reflected. "We're not unfriendly—on the contrary—but the people of Sheepshead Bay have always considered this to be the country, and we want to keep it that way."

—GEORGE W. GOODMAN

BRONX
IV.

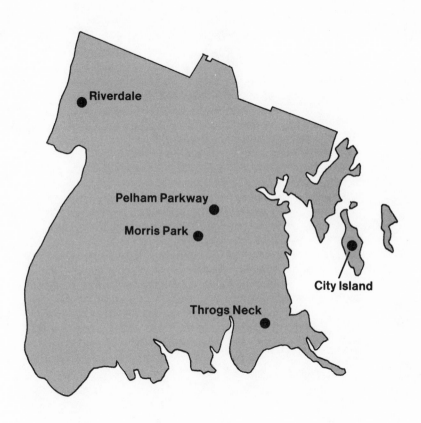

Riverdale

Pelham Parkway

Morris Park

City Island

Throgs Neck

CITY ISLAND

To midtown Manhattan: Bus and subway 50 minutes

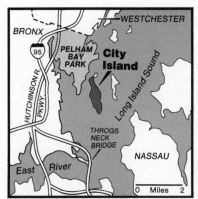

Cut off by Long Island Sound from the world—and, perhaps more important, from the rest of the Bronx and its woes—City Island is a yachting center with New England charm. Since World War II the island has been a haven not only for yachts and yachtsmen but also for middle-income families fleeing decaying and crime-ridden sections of the borough. But even today, it has more boats than people.

It is one of the few places in New York City where mansions and humble homes stand side by side, and there is a form of wealth that every islander shares—what residents call "the water." (Never "Eastchester Bay" or "Long Island Sound," it is always just "the water.")

City Island, a mile and a half long and a half mile wide, has only one through street, City Island Avenue. And City Island Bridge, at the north end, is the only way on and off the island. The cross streets start and end at the water, some at beaches where dinghies lie in the sand, ready to ferry an islander out to a boat bobbing at a mooring a few yards offshore.

Shipyards and marinas ring the island, and related businesses— sail lofts and ships' chandlers—line the avenue. These businesses, which lure mariners from the city's five boroughs and its suburbs as well, have long generated the island's coin and character.

Traditionally, the residents have owned their own homes. Few

137

rent, and the idea of a condominium has been alien. To some devout City Islanders, covetous of what they have and suspicious of any change, condo conjures up the idea of transient, a dirty word to the longtime islanders, who are known as clamdiggers.

But all that may be changing. A waterfront complex of seventy condominiums—ranging in price from $199,000 to $255,000 but averaging $227,000—is being built on the site of the once-bustling United Shipyard. Appropriately named The Boatyard, the complex has kept United's 500-foot pier and is giving each buyer a slip.

"Everyone is watching to see how the new condominiums do," said Isabelle Egdorf, former managing director of the City Island Chamber of Commerce and a member of Planning Board 10. "If the condos do well, then the boatyards and marinas are all going to go."

Jacqueline Kyle Kall, a City Island real-estate broker, said that the island already has changed and is ready for a new breed of islander, replacing "the fireman with five kids that my mother sold to." She stated that more than a hundred doctors and other health professionals affiliated with the Albert Einstein College of Medicine and the Montefiore Hospital and Medical Center have moved onto the island.

City Island was once a popular place for policemen, firemen, and other municipal employees, for although the island is in New York City, it is a universe away from the crime-infested, arson-razed neighborhoods where many policemen and fire fighters work. But, Ms. Kall said, "they can't afford to live here today." She noted that houses were selling for between $135,000 and $200,000, and some waterfront homes are going for as much as $560,000. When houses are let, she said, the rent tends to be about $1,500 a month.

Mary McDonnell, a lawyer and real-estate broker who has lived on City Island since 1928, stated that "homes under $110,000 are the exception." She said her listings of two- and three-bedroom houses range upward to $225,000.

City Island's houses are an eclectic mix, Ms. Egdorf noted, from "ultramoderns to shanties that have been renovated." There is only one apartment building, Pickwick Terrace, a seven-story structure erected before a 1976 zoning change banned anything over three stories.

City Islanders are quick to point out their community's flaws—no supermarket and no movie house, for instance—but they also take pride in its assets. Among these they cite P.S. 175, with about 300 pupils, and St. Mary Star of the Sea School, a Roman Catholic institution with about 200 pupils. Both take students through the eighth grade. The average reading scores of P.S. 175 pupils are among the highest in the public schools of the Bronx, and the school ranks among the leading public schools in New York City, according to Ena Ellwanger, the principal. Sister Margaret O'Sullivan, principal of St. Mary's, said that all her pupils tested on or above grade level. Tuition is $640 for one child and $700 for all the children in a family. Parishioners pay $100 less. There is no high school on the island.

City Island has three churches and a synagogue as well as a public library branch, an American Legion post, a fire station, a post office, and a monthly newspaper, *The Island Current.*

It is hard to imagine how isolated City Island can be and still be a part of New York City. When an islander crosses the bridge to the mainland, he doesn't find himself in another Bronx community, but in what has been called "the Everglades of the North," Pelham Bay Park, the biggest park in the city. (Central Park has 840 acres. Pelham Bay Park has 2,117 and dwarfs City Island, which covers only 230 acres.)

The No. 10 bus links the island to the mainland. The first stop the bus makes after leaving the park is the Pelham Bay IRT elevated station, normally a ten-minute ride. From there, the IRT's stop at Grand Central Terminal is twenty-five minutes away.

Islanders without cars shop in the Pelham Bay section or on Fordham Road, a much longer trip. Most with cars drive to Westchester and shop in New Rochelle, a twenty-minute drive. Midtown Manhattan is thirty-five minutes away by car.

Nobody stumbles across City Island. You have to be going there to get there, and each year 700,000 visitors do. On hot summer weekends, traffic frequently slows to a snail's pace as visitors pour onto the island to partake of its seascapes and seafood. Sixteen restaurants line City Island Avenue, with the biggest of them, Johnny's Reef, offering seating for hundreds at picnic tables right on the Sound.

Clashes between the visitors and young islanders have led to the assignment of police patrolmen to the island on warm summer weekends. The major crime problem is burglaries of both homes and businesses. But most City Islanders walk their streets without fear, and the crime New Yorkers dread the most, mugging, is all but unheard of.

Everyone seems to think the island is at a crossroads. Will it continue on its nautical course, marked by boatyards, marinas, sailmakers, diving and sailing schools, yacht brokers, and chandlers? Or will the island yield to more intensive residential development?

The Minneford Yacht Yard—which has built four defenders of the America's Cup—typifies what City Islanders are afraid of losing if developers buy up waterfront property.

When H. Schieffein Sayers founded the yard in 1926, yacht building was a matter of hard wood and hard cash. Today, the founder's son, Henry Sayers, presides over a shipyard at a time when factories mass-produce plastic boats and yachtsmen pay their bills with plastic cards. But despite the changes, Mr. Sayers said he is confident that Minneford will survive. "There will be smaller boats, but more of them. And somebody has to fix them."

—FRANK EMBLEN

MORRIS PARK

To midtown Manhattan: Subway 40 minutes

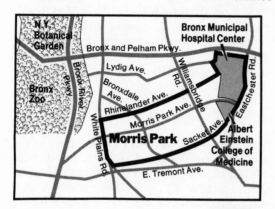

Something in the scene at Angelo & Sons Luncheonette captures the spirit of Morris Park. Joe Minotti, who was at the counter not long ago dealing with a sandwich and coffee, said cheerfully that Angelo's has "the worst coffee in the world." But Mr. Minotti has been drinking it since 1954, according to friends at the counter. That was the year Angelo converted his ice-cream parlor at Morris Park Avenue and Radcliff Avenue into a luncheonette.

Joe Minotti hasn't left Morris Park. Nor has Angelo. And apparently many others, their children, and their children's children haven't left, either. This is a cohesive, mostly Italian, middle-class community in the northeast Bronx that has remained virtually untouched by the urban decay that has blighted so much of the rest of the Bronx.

"It's probably the most stable neighborhood in the Bronx, a neighborhood to itself," said Ralph Iacontini, a real-estate dealer for the last fifteen years who moved in 1983 into a new office at 957 Morris Park Avenue. He attributed the low turnover rate in the neighborhood's housing to the fact that residents take pride in their homes and are reluctant to sell. When houses do change hands, the buyers often turn out to be the sons and daughters of Morris Park parents, who provide leads they pick up on the local grapevine. That makes it hard, but not impossible, for outsiders to acquire a home here. One-

141

family houses cost about $100,000, Mr. Iacontini said, and two-family houses about $140,000. The rent for a two-bedroom apartment averages $500 a month.

Shady lanes run past houses of brick and clapboard. Backyards are small. In the summer young people play stickball or wiffle ball on side streets, where traffic is light. In time-honored New York tradition, fenders of parked cars and manhole covers serve as bases. Parents, grandparents, aunts, and uncles watch from nearby porches, cool drinks in hand.

Small shops—many under the same ownership for decades—line Morris Park Avenue, which bisects the neighborhood east to west. Customers double-park in front of stores like Frank's Deli, Scotti & Sons Meat Market, Scaglione Brothers Bakery, and Tony's Pizza Shack.

The neighborhood's Italian specialties attract shoppers from as far away as New Jersey, according to Thomas J. Brown, the district manager of Community Board 11. Sal's A & S Pork Store and Deli at 1044 Morris Park Avenue, for example, sells homemade ricotta cheese, and Enrico's Pastry Shop across the street is known for its Italian cookies and pastries.

Morris Park is a lopsided rectangle just east of the New York Botanical Garden. The boundaries vary, depending on who describes them: The City Planning Department lists Rhinelander Avenue as the northern edge, but most residents say the neighborhood extends at least to Lydig Avenue. To the east is Eastchester Road; to the west, White Plains Road; and to the south, Sacket Avenue.

The shopping hub of Morris Park Avenue runs east to Williamsbridge Road, and that road, another major thoroughfare, runs north-south and angles through the eastern section. A lattice of narrow one- and two-lane streets completes the neighborhood.

The population of 21,000 is 97 percent white and is primarily Italian, Mr. Brown said. Only 15 percent is over sixty-five, making Morris Park one of the youngest neighborhoods in Community Board 11. Included in the housing stock are 1,500 one-family houses, 3,200 two-family houses, and 3,100 houses with more than two families.

Ted Weinstein, the director of the local neighborhood preservation office within the city's Department of Housing Preservation and Development, stated there were about 700 apartment buildings with more than seven apartments in Morris Park. Most have seven to twelve apartments.

Parents may send their children to any of three public and four parochial elementary schools, one public and one parochial junior high school. The local high school is Christopher Columbus.

The nearby Van Nest branch of the New York Public Library, at 2147 Barnes Avenue, houses more than 31,000 books and 1,100 recordings. There are two hospitals in the neighborhood—Bronx Municipal and one at the Albert Einstein College of Medicine.

Morris Park dates to 1889 when John Albert Morris, the wealthy thoroughbred racehorse hobbyist after whom the community was named, built a chic racetrack on 307 sparsely populated acres he had bought the year before. Hotels sprang up around the track after train and buggy service from Manhattan was initiated, and the city's social elite made frequent pilgrimages to the track. The old Laconia Hotel and Restaurant, circa 1890, is still standing and is now a home at 1571 Bronxdale Avenue, between Sacket and Pierce avenues.

After Mr. Morris died, his heirs sold the land to a real-estate syndicate that later went backrupt. The city took over Morris Park and by 1910 had built Morris Park Avenue and some adjacent streets. Trolleys ran to Bronxdale Avenue at the neighborhood's edge.

The Aeronautic Society of New York held air meets on the site of the old racetrack. Alexander Graham Bell was among the entrants whose plane never left the ground.

Morris Park turned residential in 1913 when the city auctioned plots of land to more than 1,500 people, including the Astors and other notable New York families. As late as the 1930's, the neighborhood was still a "wilderness," according to Frank La Lumia, a plumber who has lived in the area for seventy-two years, thirteen in his Hone Avenue house. "It was all my sister-in-law's farm." During the Depression, he recalled, the trolley line was extended across Morris Park to Williamsbridge Road. But passengers had to pay a second nickel to enter Morris Park. Few did. But when the economy picked up after World War II, he said, many families from Italian neighborhoods in lower Manhattan moved to Morris Park.

The trip to midtown Manhattan on the No. 5 Lexington Avenue IRT takes about forty minutes—the same as the trolley trips of old. There is also an express bus service to midtown, which takes about the same amount of time; it makes stops along Morris Park Avenue.

Crime is almost nonexistent in Morris Park, Mr. Brown said. "It's a fairly close community. There aren't a lot of strangers that walk through, and they are readily recognized."

"There's a tendency for neighbors to look out for each other," said Sergeant Edward Moran of the 43rd Precinct, who has worked in Morris Park for more than a decade. Auto theft was the only crime on the rise in the neighborhood, he noted. The major complaint in Morris Park during the summer, according to Sergeant Moran, is about teenagers hanging out on street corners. "I get hundreds of complaints about kids playing their radios."

The Morris Park Community Association acts in part as a surrogate parent watching over the neighborhood's youths. "Kids want to have things to do, but if you don't steer them, they just want to hang around," said the association's president, Pat Quaranta, who moved to Morris Park forty-four years ago. "If you give them something to do, they'll get involved."

The association runs organized softball, basketball, and touch football leagues for more than 500 children and teenagers, he stated. It also invites the elderly to the community center to play bingo and watch cable television. More than sixty parents and teenagers donate their time to the association, which also runs one of the Bronx's oldest community patrols to help keep crime at a minimum.

—MARK B. ROMAN

PELHAM PARKWAY

*To midtown Manhattan: Subway
45 minutes*

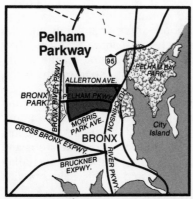

On Lydig Avenue in the Pelham Parkway section of the Bronx, huge trucks still deliver rattling cargoes of seltzer bottles to dairy restaurants and kosher delicatessens. On quiet afternoons, the gossip of the neighborhood can still be heard in Yiddish and Russian as the area's older residents sit on wooden crates at street corners to talk and pass a pleasant hour or two.

At a time when many other Bronx neighborhoods have disintegrated or are fighting to ward off the ravages of abandonment and neglect, Pelham Parkway is managing to carry on more or less as it always has. Its sturdy brick homes and apartment houses are well-maintained and crime is not a serious problem. And though the population has aged over the last twenty years, as many younger people have moved out of the city, the rising cost of living elsewhere is bringing a new generation of young people into the neighborhood.

"Some of the problems of the big city spill over into Pelham Parkway, of course," said Michael Schmeltzer, who has run the Tryax Realty Company in the neighborhood for a decade. "But basically this is an exceptionally solid middle-class area with fine public services, easy transportation, and some of the best housing opportunities in the city."

Pelham Parkway has been an urban area for only a relatively short time. Until the completion of the Erie Canal in 1825, which made

145

wheat and corn from the Midwest accessible to New Yorkers, the area was a vast farmland that produced a significant amount of those crops.

When the parkway itself was built in 1889, it was the first in the state. The original idea of a "parkway"—an idea that has undergone considerable alteration over time—was to create a way to travel between parks on a bicycle without having to leave a bucolic setting.

The real population and construction boom did not come until the 1920's, when Jewish and Italian immigrants from the crowded confines of lower Manhattan followed the newly completed subway lines to the area. By the 1930's, when most of Pelham Parkway's housing was completed, the area had sprung to life.

The boundaries of the neighborhood differ depending on who draws them. But when most people refer to Pelham Parkway, they are talking about the area between Allerton Avenue on the north, Morris Park Avenue on the south, White Plains Road on the west, and the Hutchinson River Parkway on the east.

There are 64,000 residents, according to 1980 census figures, and the neighborhood has a wide ethnic range. Always a home for immigrants, it recently has experienced an influx of Albanians, Russians, and Asians. In an area whose residents still rely on small shops and markets for their food, delicatessens, Korean markets, and Italian groceries displaying racks of spiced meats and freshly baked breads all seem to compete in relative harmony.

Some of the older apartment houses in the area around White Plains Road show the signs of half a century's wear and tear, but most of the housing stock—divided between single- and two-family homes and large apartment buildings—is in unusually good shape.

"It's a beautiful area, and people are almost always amazed to see that," said Thomas Brown, district manager of Community Board 11. "The public perception of the Bronx is very different from what you find in Pelham Parkway."

Indeed, there is a suburban feeling to many of the shady streets, lined as they are with large brick houses and well-tended lawns. Someone looking to buy a house in New York City will find few neighborhoods that offer more reasonable prices than Pelham Parkway.

"I'm sitting in my den and it seems like I look out into a forest," said Ishwari Rich, who, with her husband, Bernard, recently bought a house on Pelham Parkway North. "I don't know where else we could have gotten this kind of house in such a lovely neighborhood for this price." Their one-family house, which has unusually large rooms, is near easy transportation to Manhattan, where Mr. Rich works for the city as a social-service supervisor in the Human Resources Administration.

The couple paid almost $75,000 for the house in 1982. It would sell today for approximately $100,000, according to local brokers, about average for the area. Property taxes are low in the neighborhood—as they generally are throughout the city—and normally run about $1,500 a year, which is the average for a single-family house in that area.

Two thirds of the residents own homes, but there are also several large apartment complexes, most of which are on the densely populated western edge of Pelham Parkway. As in Manhattan and some other parts of the city, the vacancy rate is low and rental costs are rising. But one-bedroom apartments still rent for about $600 a month.

Community officials make an effort to interest younger couples in Pelham Parkway. "We try to point out the high costs of commuting and mortgages in the suburbs," Mr. Brown said. "When they look around, they see that the schools are fine, and that they can have access to the city without the cost of keeping up a home in Westchester. We have to be competitive, and I think we are."

Most residents buy their groceries in local shops, and many make larger purchases—such as clothing and electrical appliances—at the stores along White Plains Road. But parking there is a major problem, and people with cars often travel to Co-op City or the malls in Westchester to buy more expensive items.

Although public transportation is plentiful in the neighborhood—there are numerous express buses to Manhattan, and two IRT subway lines serve Pelham Parkway—the subway lines are not often used at night by elderly residents because they pass through the most dangerous sections of the South Bronx. The subway run to midtown Manhattan takes about forty-five minutes.

There are many public, private, and parochial schools within the area, and while many are not as well thought of as they used to be—at one time the public schools, along with the Yankees, were the pride of the Bronx—the nine public schools in the area still are among the better schools in the borough in terms of standardized reading tests.

Many Pelham Parkway residents send their children to parochial schools, some of which are outside the neighborhood, and a fair number of Orthodox Jewish children attend schools in the Washington Heights section of Manhattan or the Borough Park section of Brooklyn, where there are large Jewish populations. Most public schools in the area are not nearly full, and city officials attribute this problem in part to the aging population and the national trend for people to postpone having children until they are older.

The close proximity of the Bronx Municipal Hospital Center, on Pelham Parkway and Eastchester Road, is a particularly attractive benefit to living in the community. It offers comprehensive health services at the eastern edge of the neighborhood.

PELHAM PARKWAY

Another asset is the nearby New York Botanical Garden, which is often as close as most outside visitors get to Pelham Parkway. The spacious lawns add an extra feeling of freedom to the community.

For the most part, Pelham Parkway is a happy amalgam of the new and old. It is a small community that still attracts the most recent immigrants, but it also offers a pocket of stability in a city that often seems to thrive on change.

Even the Skate Key Roller Rink, on White Plains Road, has one foot in the future and the other in the past. Its customers can twirl to a throbbing disco beat under syncopated lighting, but the young patrons are far more concerned about wearing the right person's skate key—like the school ring of another time—than with sporting the latest fashion in metallic pants.

—MICHAEL SPECTER

RIVERDALE

To midtown Manhattan: Subway or bus 50 to 60 minutes

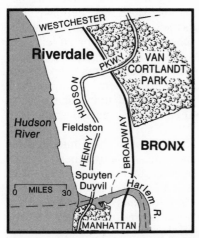

When Laurie Kiefson Gross, a New York City schoolteacher and the mother of a five-year-old girl, decided she wanted to leave Staten Island, she looked for more than a year throughout the city and suburbs before buying a cooperative apartment in Riverdale. "It gave me everything I wanted," she said of the northwest Bronx neighborhood, "a child-oriented place with good schools, relatively clean air, and lots of greenery, and it was close to Manhattan."

When Barry Lipman, a native of Virginia, was named deputy police commissioner for management and budget a few years ago and moved to Riverdale, a major attraction for him and his wife, Paula, was what he called the community's "blend of the urban and suburban."

Ms. Gross and the Lipmans were lucky. She was able to buy her apartment at a price she could afford, and they were able to rent a two-bedroom apartment they liked for $560 a month. Their building later was converted to a cooperative, and they purchased their apartment.

People who want to move to Riverdale now may find it harder. Many plans for cooperative conversion have been submitted to the state attorney general, and apartments in some buildings anticipating conversion are being kept vacant by landlords to be sold later. "The rental market in Riverdale is not good," said June M. Eisland,

149

RIVERDALE

a member of the city council who lives in the community. "A lot of people, especially young families, cannot find apartments to rent and they cannot afford to buy what is available."

Even before this trend began, and for different reasons, some longtime residents were complaining that Riverdale was not the place it used to be. They say that it has become overdeveloped and overcrowded, and that some of the newer residents lack a commitment to the community. But others say that while Riverdale has changed, it is still one of New York's more desirable sections.

Architecturally, some of the high-rises are less than commendable, and double-parked cars often choke the shopping streets. But there also are many stately mansions overlooking the Hudson, smaller but handsome private houses elsewhere, vintage apartment buildings with spacious rooms, and more modern buildings that, while undistinguished in design, provide good living space. And everywhere there are quiet tree-lined streets, parks, and green spaces.

The community has 50,000 residents, most of them middle-class and with a tendency to vote for Democrats. Although there are still members of some old Riverdale families in the community—the Dodges, Delafields, and others whose names have been perpetuated on street signs—Riverdale now is predominantly Jewish, with a growing Orthodox Jewish segment. According to the 1980 census, only 4 percent of the population is black.

Many persons prominent in city life are residents, along with members of United Nations missions. And there also is a large transient population of Japanese businessmen and students. Japanese children account for nearly 20 percent of the enrollment at the community's two public elementary schools.

According to popular belief, Riverdale comprises the high ground along the Hudson River, on both sides of the Henry Hudson Parkway, from the Harlem River to the Yonkers city line. "If you start at 231st Street and Riverdale Avenue and go up the hill, to the left and the right is all Riverdale," said Grace Belkin, district manager of Community Board 8. But the Reverend William A. Tieck, pastor of the Edge Hill Church and author of a two-volume history of Riverdale, said that, properly, only the section north of the World War I monument at 239th Street and Riverdale Avenue is Riverdale.

Until 1874, Riverdale was part of Westchester County. In those days the community was known as Riverdale-on-Hudson, and today there are still some who cling to that name. Many use Riverdale as their address rather than the Bronx, although the section is in the borough.

"Riverdale is one of the safest neighborhoods in the city," said Captain Andrew Dillon, commander of the 50th Precinct. "It is still a place where people can walk their dogs late at night and feel safe."

RIVERDALE

Even so, crime is as much a concern in Riverdale as elsewhere; the police say its affluence makes it a target for car thieves and burglars.

Riverdale is about fifty minutes to an hour away from mid-Manhattan by subway and bus, including normal waiting time. Some residents commute on Metro-North's Hudson line from the Riverdale station to Grand Central Terminal. Others take the Liberty Lines express buses. Still others drive to work. The Henry Hudson Parkway, whose construction in the mid-1930's set the stage for Riverdale's post–World War II growth, and the nearby Major Deegan Expressway offer convenient access to Manhattan.

Riverdale's schools are a major asset. The two public elementary schools—P.S. 24 in Spuyten Duyvil and P.S. 81 in north Riverdale—are considered among the city's best in terms of pupil achievement. At both schools, well over 80 percent of the pupils read at or above grade levels. Junior High School 141, which draws pupils from other areas as well, also is well regarded.

Those Riverdale pupils who remain in the public system and do not go to a specialized high school attend John F. Kennedy High School in the area "down the hill," near Marble Hill. It is a large and overutilized school, with many more students than it is rated to serve.

There also are several independent schools in the area, among them the Riverdale Country School, Horace Mann, and Fieldston. There are parochial schools and schools with religious orientation, among them St. Margaret's, St. Gabriel's, the Salanter Akiba Riverdale Academy, and Kinneret Day School, the latter two Jewish. Manhattan College and the College of Mount St. Vincent also are in Riverdale.

Riverdale Neighborhood House and the Riverdale Y.M.-Y.W.H.A. provide a range of community services, and a weekly newspaper, *The Riverdale Press,* is a valuable source of community news and information. The Wave Hill Center for Environmental Studies sponsors many cultural and other events.

Robert B. Hill, who heads the real-estate concern founded by his father in 1919, said the volume of sales of private homes has rebounded over the last few years and prices are moving up. In the estate area along the Hudson, he stated, houses often sell for prices approaching $1 million. West of the parkway and in Fieldston, the lowest price for a house is about $250,000. In the north end, a small house can sometimes be had for $60,000 to $80,000.

Cooperative apartments are available in a wide price range. A three-bedroom apartment in a fifty-year-old building recently sold for $150,000, but there are apartments for less and also for a great deal more.

The pickings are slimmer in apartment rentals. At Skyview in the north, whose three 22-story towers and 1,309 apartments make it the largest residential complex in Riverdale, there is a waiting list of from a few weeks to several months. Rentals range from $500 to $600 for a studio and from $750 to $1,100 for a three-bedroom apartment.

At the Century in southern Riverdale, there are 588 apartments but vacancies are rare. When they are available, the rents are $800 to $900 for a one-bedroom apartment with a dining room to $1,400 and up for a three-bedroom unit.

Despite the tight rental market, some people manage to find attractive but less expensive apartments in rent-regulated buildings. Verne Vitrofsky, a teacher, found a large one-bedroom apartment in an older building with a river view. "On Riverside Drive, they asked for $850 a month for a sliver of the river. Here, for $350, I've got a whole chunk of the Hudson."

—LEONARD BUDER

THROGS NECK

To midtown Manhattan: Bus 50 minutes

On cold, rainy days in late spring, motorboats, cabin cruisers, and sailboats huddle together in the Locust Point Marina, waiting, like their owners, for warmer weather. Nearby, the white-shingled one- and two-family houses and the tidy streets of Throgs Neck provide a serene backdrop to the windswept waters of Eastchester Bay.

To a visitor, this isolated area of the southeast Bronx seems like a well-kept suburb. "But on a summer day you'd think you were in Florida or California," said Gene Holtzman, who has lived with his wife, Mary, for five years in a two-bedroom condominium on Shore Drive.

From the private beach a few steps from their living room, City Island is visible two miles to the east; to the south is a view of what the area is best known for, the Throgs Neck Bridge. "Friends come to visit," Mr. Holtzman said, "and can't believe we live in the Bronx."

Throgs Neck, a community of about 30,000 residents, mostly of Italian, Irish, and German ancestry, is bounded by Westchester Creek on the west, Eastchester Bay and Long Island Sound on the east, the East River on the south, and the Bruckner Expressway and Layton Avenue on the north.

History has it that it was named after John Throgmorton, who settled there in 1643. A source of pique, however, to Peggy Vega,

153

president of the Throggs Neck Homeowners Association, is that two *g*'s were the norm until 1955, when the bridge was completed, and the city now uses only one *g* for the community name on maps and official documents.

Another complaint, Ms. Vega said, is that funds ran out when the city was paving the streets some years ago and many were paved only in the center, which causes curb flooding in heavy rains.

Ferry Point Park, a largely undeveloped tract of 298 acres in the southwestern corner of the community, until 1983 was just a dumping ground for junked cars. But then the cars were cleaned out and now the park has playing fields for team sports. A couple of miles to the east, on a peninsula stretching under the Throgs Neck Bridge, is the 1,200-cadet Maritime College of the State University of New York.

Few Throgs Neck homes, including three rental apartment buildings, are more than seven blocks from a bay, creek, inlet, or river. Because the waterfront is so accessible, many families belong to one or more of the small beach and fishing clubs along Shore Drive and Clarence Avenue. Some of the clubs are more than seventy-five years old, and, as one member said, if they were not so determined "to hold fast," condominium developers would be buying every inch of waterfront property.

Waterfront condominiums have changed the face of Throgs Neck and, according to developer-builders like Bill Procida and the Ruffalo brothers, changed it for the better. "We believe in this area—it's a beautiful part of the Bronx," said Peter Ruffalo, who lives with his wife and children in Country Club Estates, one of the condominiums built by him and his brother, George.

In 1979 the twelve units in Country Club Estates, at Shore Drive and Layton Avenue, were sold for $74,900 to $99,000. The Ruffalos' most recent condominium project, built almost on the shoreline and affording a dramatic view of the bay, is Bay View Estates. The one- and two-bedroom apartments have fireplaces, decks, and mooring facilities and sell for $150,000 to $225,000.

White Beaches, a fifty-two-unit condominium with a twenty-five-slip marina at Schurz Avenue on the East River, is the project of Mr. Procida, a twenty-one-year-old developer and scion of a three-generation construction family. Situated on the waterfront between the Whitestone and Throgs Neck bridges, the two-bedroom apartments cost $120,000 to $225,000 and three-bedrooms go for $190,000 to $230,000. The slips sell for $12,000.

"We hope to bring back the upper middle class—people, for example, who will spend more money on East Tremont Avenue," Mr. Procida said, as he stood near an Italian-marble fireplace in the carpeted living room of one of the sixteen units in the first phase of White Beaches. "This is one of the last strongholds of the Bronx. If this area goes, then Country Club and Pelham Bay Park will go." He was referring to the two upper-middle-class areas adjacent to Throgs Neck.

"Throgs Neck is a very stable community," stated Joseph Limongelli of Better Homes Realty on East Tremont Avenue. Excluding Edgewater Park and Silver Beach, he said, typical one-family homes go for $75,000 to $80,000, two-families for $90,000 to $100,000.

According to Ms. Vega, houses are often sold within a few weeks. "A person planning to retire to Florida, for example, might tell his neighbor. The next day he gets a phone call or a knock on the door from a relative of his neighbor and a sale is made."

An unusual area within Throgs Neck is Edgewater Park on Eastchester Bay. Starting in the 1920's, it was a summer community of more than 600 cottages for Manhattanites. Later, after renovation and winterizing, the cottages became permanent homes owned by their tenants. But because all the land was owned by one family, the Shaws, the owners could only lease their lots.

Edgewater Park homeowners hope they soon will be able to buy the land in a cooperative arrangement similar to one made in Silver Beach, another waterfront community in Throgs Neck. There, a decade ago, residents formed a cooperative and paid $1.6 million for the eighty-three acres on which their homes were built. The one- and two-family homes now sell for $45,000 to $50,000, subject to approval by the co-op board.

Residents can find most necessities in the small, family-owned stores on East Tremont Avenue, the main thoroughfare. One store, Benny and Joe Mondello's Delicious Kold-Kuts, which specializes in homemade sausages and cheeses and salads, boasts that it is the home of the original "Salami Bread," a rounded loaf of Italian bread with Genoa salami slices baked into it.

For major clothing and household purchases, many residents get in their cars and go to shopping malls. Joan Payne of Silver Beach, points out that the malls in Paramus, New Jersey, are only a half hour away.

Throgs Neck residents who work in Manhattan say transportation is convenient. One route is by city bus to the Westchester Square IRT station, an hour's ride from midtown. Express buses leave every five minutes in rush hours and make several stops along East Tremont Avenue before making their fifty-minute run to midtown.

According to James Vacca, district manager of Community Board 10, reading and math scores in the two public and two parochial elementary schools are above average. And Robert Leder, principal of the neighborhood Herbert H. Lehman High School on East Tremont Avenue, said that 82 percent of the graduates go on to higher education.

THROGS NECK

Among the many residents who have lived a lifetime in Throgs Neck is Anna Randazzo, owner of the Marina del Rey, one of the Bronx's most popular catering establishments. Bookings in the three lavishly decorated dining rooms overlooking the East River are made more than a year in advance. Ms. Randazzo, a small, energetic woman who refuses to divulge her age, puts in a seven-day week supervising her large staff. She shows off her enormous kitchen to visitors and says she is most proud of a separate kitchen she had built for Hasidic weddings. "Because they have to get married under the sky, I had a skylight made in the main dining room. And in good weather, they get married outside with the view of the bridge and the water."

—DOLORES DOLAN

QUEENS
V.

Whitestone

Astoria

Bayside

Douglaston

Jackson Heights

Sunnyside

Forest Hills

Jamaica Estates

Richmond Hill

A S T O R I A

*To midtown Manhattan: Subway
15 minutes*

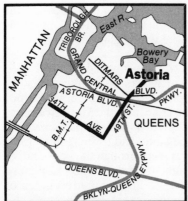

Soft strains of bouzouki music are heard as waiters in the small Nea Hellas cafe on Ditmars Boulevard bring coffee and Greek pastries. John Caviris, eighty-three years old, goes there nearly every day. "He meets his friends and they sit around all day and talk about Greece," said Peter Caviris, his twenty-year-old grandson. "He loves it."

There are many people like John Caviris in Astoria, and sharing the cafe with him are likely to be other residents with briefcases and manila envelopes—people who work in Manhattan and have discovered the pleasures of living in a quiet northwestern Queens neighborhood where residents care about their homes.

Small apartment buildings and two-family houses line the streets, and a short walk in almost any direction will lead to some of the better Greek and Italian restaurants in New York. Newspapers from almost anywhere in the world are on sale on bustling Ditmars Boulevard.

Astoria, which is adjacent to Long Island City, is bordered by Bowery Bay on the north, 34th Avenue on the south, 49th Street on the east, and the East River on the west. It was once the playground of the rich, and at the turn of the century many shipping executives lived in houses with widow's walks and towers along the rural roads that are now part of Shore Boulevard.

The opening of the Queensboro Bridge in 1909 made Astoria easily accessible to those weary of crowded living conditions in Manhattan. As the first bands of Irish and Italian immigrants arrived—many working for the Steinway Piano Company or the Police Department—richer families moved east to Douglaston in Queens and Manhasset, Glen Cove, and Oyster Bay on Long Island.

There has long been an industrial presence in Astoria, beginning with the opening of the Steinway Piano Company in 1857 through the arrival of Standard Motor Products, a manufacturer of auto parts, in 1919 and the opening of Charmer Industries wine and liquor distributorship in 1942.

In 1978, Steinway Piano and Charmer threatened to leave, but stayed after the city spent $12.1 million to rehabilitate the area. Today 19th Avenue, the major industrial thoroughfare, has fifty-two companies employing more than 5,000 people.

In 1920 the Famous Players Lasky Studio opened at 34-31 35th Street. Productions at the studio, which was later taken over by Paramount Pictures, featured such players as Rudolph Valentino, W. C. Fields, Ethel Barrymore, Lillian Gish, and the Marx Brothers, who used it for their first films, *The Cocoanuts* and *Animal Crackers.*

The Army used the studio for propaganda and training films from 1942 to 1972. In 1976 the studio was revived through the cooperative efforts of the city, the federal government, and the motion-picture and television industry and unions. The result was the formation of the nonprofit Astoria Studios Production Center.

Since that time, soundstages at the complex, now known as the Kaufman Astoria Studios, have been used for *The Wiz, All That Jazz, Kramer vs. Kramer,* and, most recently, *The Cotton Club.* The complex, which includes fifteen buildings on a twelve-acre site and employs more than 500 people, is just completing a $50 million expansion.

Of the 100,000 residents of Astoria, an estimated 45,000 are Greek-born or of Greek descent. Once more Irish and German, Astoria still has many Italians and Slavs, along with more recently arrived blacks and Hispanics.

"It's a cozy community," said George Delis, district manager for Community Board 1. "It has that European flair. People are out at night. They go for a beer or coffee."

Property values have increased about 25 percent in the past year, according to Bedros Sarkissian, owner of Aamen Realty on Ditmars Boulevard. "The landlords are never stuck with a vacant apartment. There's such a demand."

Mr. Sarkissian said Manhattan's high cost of living had attracted many young people to Astoria. "Their main concern is the rents. In Manhattan, a one-bedroom apartment can cost $1,500. Here, if I offer one for $450, they love it."

A one-bedroom apartment in Astoria rents for between $400 and

$500. Studio apartments, much in demand, cost between $300 and $400. The few one-family houses in the area sell for around $125,000, two-families between $140,000 and $175,000. A one-family house is taxed at the citywide rate of $9.10 for each $100 of assessed valuation, which is 17.35 percent of market value.

While there is little new construction planned for the area, Mr. Sarkissian said, much rehabilitation of older buildings is under way. "They're not building more, but Astoria is spending a lot of money renovating."

Catherine Heedles, who works in Manhattan as an investment assistant, has lived on Ditmars Boulevard since 1982. She and her college roommate came to Astoria after failing to find an apartment that fit their income in Manhattan. "There was nothing," she stated. "The only thing we could afford was a studio, and it wasn't in a good neighborhood. A friend suggested we look in Astoria." Ms. Heedles said they found a large two-bedroom apartment for $475 a month, and the commute to her job in midtown is quick and convenient. "If I leave my apartment by 8:30, I get to work by 9. It's heaven. There's even a bus into the city if I don't feel like taking the subway."

The BMT RR train makes its long elevated run along 31st Street and ends at Ditmars Boulevard. It runs frequently, and the ride to midtown Manhattan takes about fifteen minutes.

Astoria's children attend one of twenty elementary schools and five intermediate schools in Astoria, Long Island City, and Jackson Heights. High-school students attend Long Island City High School or William C. Bryant High School. The Board of Education rates the elementary schools serving Astoria in the top third of the city's schools in terms of reading scores.

There are eleven Greek Orthodox churches, eight Roman Catholic churches, and four synagogues in the neighborhood. St. Demetrios, a high-domed Byzantine church at 31st Street and 30th Drive that is more than fifty years old, has the largest community of Greek congregants outside Greece, according to the Reverend Demetrios Frangos.

Astoria Park on Ditmars Boulevard has fields for baseball, softball, soccer, and football; a playground; three pools; and fourteen tennis courts. The track facilities were renovated in 1983 at a cost of $1.5 million. The community's shopping area is the largest in Queens: a recent study by the city's Office of Economic Development found that more than 10,000 shoppers visit Steinway Street on Saturdays.

A $2 million redevelopment of Ditmars Boulevard, with the federal government paying half of the total and the city and state each paying a quarter, increased investment in the area and cleaned up the neighborhood. Sidewalks and streets were repaved, trees were planted, streetlights with ornate domes now shine in different colors, benches were placed on the sidewalks, and new green signs went up at street corners.

It is a neighborhood with delis like Kalamata on Ditmars Boulevard, where feta cheese and black olives are sold; with fruit and vegetable stores on almost every street; and with pastry shops selling homemade baklava and bakeries redolent of freshly baked bread.

It is also a neighborhood where the local pizza shop sells gyros and the photography store has a large picture of Miss Greece in the window.

—MARIA EFTIMIADES

BAYSIDE

To midtown Manhattan: Train 25 minutes

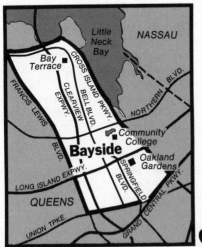

Joe Friscia has vivid recollections of his father selling fish from a three-wheeled pushcart on dusty Bell Boulevard in Bayside, Queens, in the 1930's. Now, the third generation of the Friscia family is selling fish on the same spot, but the pushcart has become Joe's Bayside Fish Market and the dirt road is a paved thoroughfare that has become one of Bayside's main commercial avenues.

There are many more enterprises like Joe's Fish Market—Parker Hardware, Kraus Paint & Wallpaper, and Tanenbaum's clothing store among them—that have been familiar to Bayside residents for more than fifty years. This is not surprising, since many of Bayside's 71,000 residents have lived there most of their lives and many families date back several generations. "Once people come here they usually stay for good," said Edythe Rogozinski, a real-estate agent in the community for twenty-eight years.

For decades Bayside was a small suburb with a one-room schoolhouse, colonial-style homes, and a volunteer fire department—a quiet farming area with a cigar factory as its only industry. But in the early 1900's, Bayside became known as the "Beverly Hills of the East." W. C. Fields and the actresses Norma Talmadge and Marie Dressler lived there to be near the movie studios in Astoria. Another prominent resident was the boxer "Gentleman Jim" Corbett. The rich built homes on the waterfront of Little Neck Bay,

163

B A Y S I D E

where they sailed yachts and partied on broad lawns. So many movie players lived there that Corbett Road was dubbed "Actors Row." Most headed west when Hollywood became the movie capital, but the marina and yacht club they frequented are still there on Little Neck Bay.

After World War II land started becoming scarce in Bayside as plots were quickly bought for one-family homes. The community that once had several golf courses now has just one, and real-estate agents say that just about every patch of available land has been built on. But it retains its small-town character.

The community is bounded by Little Neck Bay on the north, Union Turnpike on the south, the Cross Island Parkway on the east, and Francis Lewis Boulevard on the west.

For commuters, there are several express buses to Manhattan and buses that connect to the end of the Flushing subway line. By the Port Washington line of the Long Island Railroad, the trip to Pennsylvania Station takes twenty-five minutes.

Most of Bayside has been developed with detached one- and two-family houses. In recent years, however, there have been many illegal conversions into three- and four-family houses. Bernard Haber, chairman of Community Planning Board 11, which covers most of Bayside, blames the high cost of housing in the neighborhood for the problem. But community opinion is divided on the issue. Residents who want the one-family character of the neighborhood maintained blame city officials, who they say have been willing to enforce zoning laws strictly. Others say the tolerated violations are a pragmatic compromise that accommodates the needs of people who cannot afford a single-family house.

One-family homes range in price from $85,000 to $270,000. Six years ago, said Charles J. Belanich of Bell Realty, he sold 50- by 100-foot plots for $19,000 to $20,000. Today, the same lots would cost $80,000, but even at that price they would be hard to find.

As in the rest of the city, taxes are low. The tax bill on a new one-family house costing $150,000 would be $2,368 a year.

But in the last two years, much of the market in Bayside has been shifting to condominiums. Five new projects have opened, with more than 2,000 units. At the Bay Club, Bayside's largest condominium community, units were selling for $90 a square foot when the complex opened, after delays and the failure of one developer, in 1981. A one-bedroom apartment of 900 square feet sold for $80,000 to $85,000. Now, the units are selling for about $130 a square foot.

The median family income in Bayside is $29,500, compared with $16,000 citywide and $20,506 for all of Queens, according to Michael Levine, the director of community development at the city's Department of Planning.

Many residents shop in small stores, such as Charmet Dress Shop and Kurtzberg's Commercial Stationers, that line Bell Boulevard. But there are also shopping centers nearby in Bay Terrace and Oakland Gardens.

Activities for old people are offered at the Bayside Senior Center, and the Y.M.C.A. has programs for families. There are day, night, and weekend courses for college or noncollege credit at Queensborough Community College in southern Bayside. The community's three parks have tennis courts and ball fields, and Clearview Park has the remaining golf course.

Eight of the nine elementary schools and both junior high schools in Bayside belong to District 26. The other school belongs to District 25. Stanley Weber, executive assistant of District 26, said more than 80 percent of the students have reading and math scores at or above the norms for their grades.

Older students go to Bayside or Benjamin N. Cardozo high schools, or Francis Lewis High School in Flushing. All three have advanced-placement programs, and more than 80 percent of their students go on to some form of higher education.

Bayside is one of New York's safer communities. The biggest crime is auto theft. "It's a problem because this is an area where most families generally own more than one car," said Officer Wayne Schneider, head of community affairs in the 111th Precinct.

"This is an area where people take crime precautions and follow through on crime-prevention methods recommended by the precinct," Officer Schneider added. There are also three volunteer patrols and a private patrol sponsored by the area's civic associations.

One of the community's persistent problems is a lack of parking space for shoppers on Bell Boulevard. Merchants blame commuters who park near the Long Island Railroad station on the boulevard. The municipal parking lot a few blocks from the station holds only seventy-nine cars.

That kind of congestion still surprises Celia Greenfield, a longtime resident who owns Parker Hardware on Bell Boulevard with her brother, Edward. "The people are the same but the place certainly has changed," she said. "I can remember when a fruit and vegetable truck used to deliver to our homes."

—EVE C. GUILLERGAN

DOUGLASTON

To midtown Manhattan: Train 25 minutes

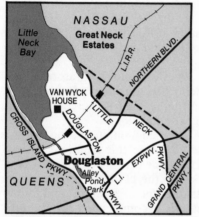

Through the tall grass of a saltwater marsh called Udalls Cove, Herbert and Aurora Gareiss may see the faint outline of Co-op City across Long Island Sound. That sight is a constant reminder that their Douglaston, Queens, home of nearly forty years is in New York City, not the Louisiana bayous. Aurora Gareiss proudly calls herself a New Yorker. But her kind of city life is not of congested Manhattan streets or monolithic skyscrapers. It is, instead, a life close to a tract of unspoiled wilderness inhabited by shorebirds, fish, and shellfish that lies behind her house.

For her, the hundred-acre marsh is too valuable a resource to fall victim to development plans, and she has fought for fifteen years to have New York State acquire the land. The state now owns 94.1 acres and is negotiating to buy the rest.

Ms. Gareiss and her neighbor, Virginia Dent, can remember the days when they swam off the land now occupied by La Guardia Airport, several miles west of Douglaston. "Suddenly the small farms and trees were gone, and the roads came in," said Ms. Dent, who is executive director of New York State's Northeastern Queens Nature and Historical Preserve Commission. "We've only managed to preserve certain areas over here by not allowing New York City planning commissions to bulldoze them out of existence."

The spirit of environmental and neighborhood preservation runs

166

high among Douglaston residents, many of whom would prefer that their community retain its small-town flavor. They have clashed repeatedly with city government to halt highway construction, preserve historic sites, and prevent commercial development alongside Alley Pond Park.

Douglaston is one of a small number of residential neighborhoods in the city where development is limited to one- and two-family houses, although several postwar apartment buildings along Douglaston Parkway and south of the Long Island Expressway were completed before zoning laws were modified in the early 1960's.

The average one-family house in Douglaston costs more than $150,000, according to David Rea, a real-estate broker who has spent most of his life there. Homeowners pay New York City property taxes, which are about one third of those in the Village of Great Neck Estates just east of the Nassau County line. Like houses in the rest of the city, those in Douglaston are assessed at 17.35 percent of market value and are taxed at the rate of $9.10 per $100. Thus the average tax on a $175,000 house would be about $1,300 a year, depending on the age of the house and the date of original assessment.

"People can move in, raise their kids, pack them off to college, and then stay on after they retire," Mr. Rea said. "In Great Neck, people can't afford to keep their homes because of the taxes."

Douglaston is a rectangle just west of Nassau County bounded on the north by Little Neck Bay, on the west by the Cross Island Parkway, and on the south by the Grand Central Parkway. Little Neck Parkway is generally agreed to be the boundary between Douglaston and Little Neck, Queens, just to the east.

Northern Boulevard, the older of Douglaston's two commercial avenues, runs east-west and has a stretch of modern fast-food restaurants. This contrasts with the quaint one- and two-story shops lining Douglaston Parkway, the other commercial artery. Near the Long Island Railroad station, The Weeping Beech, one of Douglaston's most popular restaurants, is housed in an Old English–style cottage alongside the Firewater liquor store.

On the other side of the tracks, Aline's Stationery shop doubles as a post-office branch and the Douglaston Market serves as an old-fashioned general store. Off Douglaston Parkway, along rolling side streets, the constant drone of lawn mowers can be heard on almost any summer afternoon. Traffic is light enough on the roads and narrow sidewalks to allow children to play softball and to volley tennis balls on them.

The population of more than 15,000 is primarily middle-class, according to the 1980 census figures. It is also the oldest in New York City, says Bernard Haber, chairman of Community Board 11, whose jurisdiction includes Douglaston. He cited a recent study showing that 28.2 percent of the residents were between the ages of forty-five and sixty-four.

Most apartment buildings in Douglaston have been converted to cooperatives, causing rental units to become scarce, Mr. Rea said. Two-bedroom apartments are priced at about $70,000 in southern Douglaston, while those closer to Little Neck Bay may cost from $100,000 to $150,000 and in some cases even more.

Douglaston has three public elementary schools and a junior high school and sends many of its older students to Benjamin N. Cardozo High School in Bayside. District 26, which includes Douglaston, has consistently ranked first in the city in reading ability, with 80 percent of students scoring at or above their grade level in citywide tests, according to Irwin Altman, the community superintendent for the district.

The schools offer special programs for gifted and talented children and are providing education "above and beyond the basics of reading, writing, and arithmetic," with a special emphasis on science classes, Mr. Altman said.

The earliest inhabitants of Douglaston were Matinecock Indians, some of whom are buried in the cemetery of Zion Church on Northern Boulevard, which dates from the eighteenth century. One of the community's oldest homes, now occupied by Mr. Rea's family, is a small farmhouse on the corner of West Drive and Alston Place built in 1740 by Cornelius Van Wyck.

The community's founder, William P. Douglas, was a yachtsman who successfully defended the America's Cup in 1871 and often sailed on the Sound with his friend Cornelius Vanderbilt. The area was named for Mr. Douglas by the Long Island Railroad in 1876 after he donated a building for the station.

Most Douglaston residents commute to jobs in Manhattan on the L.I.R.R., a trip that normally takes less than twenty-five minutes. Despite its proximity to the rest of New York, however, Douglaston shares few of the crime problems facing other city neighborhoods.

"It's one of the safer communities in the city," said Officer Wayne Schneider, who is in charge of community affairs for the 111th Precinct. "There is no major-crime problem whatsoever."

The 572 homeowners who belong to the Douglas Manor Association live in an exclusive section on a tract three quarters of a mile long and half a mile wide, formerly owned by Mr. Douglas. Before the association was formed in 1906, the Finlay Realty Company bought the land from Mr. Douglas and developed it as a middle-class suburb with homes in a variety of styles, from Swiss chalet to Spanish villa. Today, Manor homes cost from $240,000 to $800,000.

For annual dues of $220, Manorites get the use of a private dock, access to two private beaches, and additional security and sanitation service from private firms. To prevent the widening of streets and protect several valued trees, the Manor has relieved the city of its obligation to install a sewer system. Residents say the Manor's building codes are far stricter than the city's.

During the 1920's and 1930's, Douglaston was home to many film and theater personalities, among them Ginger Rogers and Arthur Treacher. Among the current residents are Claudio Arrau, the pianist, and Henry R. Fulton, the city's highways commissioner. Until recently, the tennis star John McEnroe and his family lived in a small house near the Douglaston Club, where he learned to play the game.

The club is housed in a white mansion on Douglaston Parkway and Manor Road built in 1813 by Wynant Van Zandt, a New York alderman. Its facilities include bowling alleys, tennis courts, and a pool, and annual fees depend on how many of them a member elects to use. One member who uses all facilities said he pays more than $3,000 a year.

—PETER J. GERARDO

FOREST HILLS

To midtown Manhattan: Subway 30 minutes

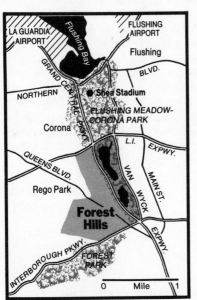

For all but the newest of New Yorkers, mention of Forest Hills evokes one of two images—or sometimes both. One is of star-studded tournaments at the West Side Tennis Club, long the most romantic of the city's sport scenes, where the National Amateur and later the United States Open were played inside the turreted, half-timbered residential colony of Forest Hills Gardens. The other is of a memory now more than a decade old: an embattled middle-income community picketing against an 840-unit, low-income "scatter site" housing project, an experiment to disperse such housing outside ghettos after a special federal commission warned of the danger of "two societies, one black, one white" in its report on the 1967 race riots.

Although the Open moved to Flushing in 1977, tennis tournaments still brighten Forest Hills and its economy. And the community lives peaceably with the Forest Hills Cooperative, the low-income housing on its northern border that, in a compromise solution, was eventually cut to only half its proposed size.

And now the community also is known as the home of Geraldine Ferraro, the first woman to be nominated for vice president by a major party.

But Forest Hills is, and always has been, a great deal more than its public image. It is a cosmopolitan, white-collar, central Queens com-

170

munity of landscaped apartment buildings, seven to twelve stories high, many of them rushing to convert from rental to cooperative, as has the borough's tallest building, the thirty-four-story Kennedy House on Queens Boulevard just east of 108th Street.

It also is Old Forest Hills, the original Forest Hills, a district of handsome one-family houses north of Queens Boulevard and just west of the Corona Park lakes. Begun in 1904, three years after the area (formerly Newtown) was consolidated with New York City, it was built by the Cord Meyer Development Company. The company is still a large Forest Hills landlord—it owns the Continental apartment tower—and it has been adding to the community's stock of two- and three-family houses.

Northward from its Queens Boulevard commercial strip, Forest Hills is also a twenty-four-block business and residential artery along 108th Street to the Long Island Expressway. Here a typical block offers Mario's Restaurant, the Shalom Food Center ("Kosher, Israeli, American"), Tong's Garden Chinese Restaurant, Calabria Hair Cutting, Zion Pizza, a Russian-émigré candy store, and a French dry cleaner with an Oriental proprietor.

Forest Hills is also Austin Street, overflowing its traditional four-block commercial stretch near the former Forest Hills Inn (now a co-op apartment house with a Beefsteak Charlie's in its old dining room). Austin Street, originally known to Gardens residents as "the village," has blossomed with restaurants, movie houses, boutiques, and fancy-food shops into a year-round magnet for much of Queens and Nassau County.

"New York style at Queens prices," is what many residents as well as merchants like to tell outsiders. "It's a very lively scene, quite international, and at its peak on Saturdays," a resident said.

"Despite the traffic crush, we equate ourselves with a small town," said Paul Klotz, president of the Forest Hills Chamber of Commerce. His gift shop on Austin Street offers greeting cards in "sixteen or maybe twenty" languages.

Among the restaurants nearby are the Cafe Continent and My Kitchen, both offering a range of dishes from quiches to steaks; the Irish Cottage, featuring shepherd's pie; the Wine Gallery; and the Stuffed Bagel. On Queens Boulevard, at the 71st Street–Continental Avenue subway stop, is the T-Bone Diner, a favorite with locals if a surprise to visitors; it is an authentic former railroad car offering full bar service with meals.

Among the handcrafted toys and English-style prams at Lewis of London on Austin Street are 24-karat-gold-plated cribs and cradles tagged at $1,000 and more.

"There are a lot of solid-gold babies around here," said Joel Rallo, the proprietor. "And it's not just the high-income families—middle-class people, you know, they get grandma and the relatives involved."

The 1980 census showed the Forest Hills population up only slightly since 1970 to 50,000. The public elementary-school population is 5,000. According to the City Planning Commission's Queens office, the census count was 89 percent white, 7 percent Asian, 2 percent black, and the rest other. Eight percent said they were of Hispanic origin.

Some 5,000 Russians have arrived since the late 1970's. The latest immigrants are Iranians (largely Jewish, but also some Moslems) and Pakistanis. There are also some North Africans. "These 'new Americans' have lent some spice to our community," said Anthony H. Atlas, chairman of Queens Community Board 6 and a lawyer with a Manhattan practice.

Buddhist and Moslem centers have been added to the Forest Hills array of six Protestant churches, two Catholic churches, and nearly a score of Jewish congregations and community centers. There are two yeshivas, two parochial schools, and a private school.

Public schools rank high in a district that is among the city's highest in reading scores, according to Dr. Arnold Raisner, Community School District 28 superintendent. The two junior high schools, he said, are "feeders" for Stuyvesant High School, which accepts students only on the basis of achievement examinations. Forest Hills High School "has perhaps a greater academic emphasis," Dr. Raisner stated, but "Hillcrest High offers a wider variety of courses."

Only a hundred or so Forest Hills commuters regularly travel by Long Island Railroad now—fourteen minutes by timetable to Penn Station from seventy-year-old Station Square. Most go by express or regular buses or the E, F, N, and GG subway trains, which take about a half hour to get to midtown Manhattan.

The "co-op fever" that Mr. Atlas said "has hit Forest Hills harder than any place in Queens or maybe outside Manhattan" is fueled by prospective buyers price-squeezed out of Manhattan or Brooklyn Heights. For co-ops, which outnumber condominiums, Robert M. Hoff of Terrace Realty said the prices range from $15,000 to $25,000 a room, but many luxury apartments in Forest Hills are priced far higher.

Rentals are scarce, with one-bedrooms averaging about $700 per month.

Single-family houses sell for from $150,000 to $250,000, and two-families begin at $175,000. In Forest Hills Gardens and in the area north of Queens Boulevard, however, many houses are listed at $350,000 and more.

Strangers who drive or walk in Forest Hills should not be unsettled by the peculiar illusion that they are only moving in place. The repetitive street grid north of the Long Island Railroad, progressing grudgingly from, for example, 63rd Avenue to 63rd Road to 63rd Drive, resulted from the subdivision of supersized "country" blocks formed by the original layout of the avenues.

—LAURIE JOHNSTON

JACKSON HEIGHTS

*To midtown Manhattan: Subway
20 minutes*

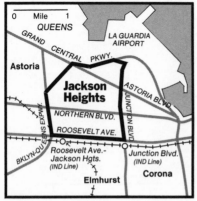

In 1909 the Queensboro Corporation began transforming a hundred blocks of farmland in northern Queens into a neighborhood that could lure residents from Manhattan, seven miles away. Moving people to what were still the cornfields of Queens meant, the company decided, that charm had to be built into its new Jackson Heights community.

The project began with large apartment buildings—among the first cooperatives in the city—featuring courtyard gardens, sun rooms, parking facilities, fireplaces, high ceilings, and peaked roofs, all done in an eclectic mixture of English, Dutch, and Spanish styles that added up to charm for many residents of that day and still does for today's residents. Early in the 1920's, construction of private row and two-family homes was begun. The row houses had private garages but shared gardens.

When the IRT elevated line was built along Roosevelt Avenue on the neighborhood's southern border in 1917, and the Fifth Avenue bus line—now the M-32—was extended over the Queensboro Bridge late in the 1920's, Jackson Heights became an easily accessible part of New York City.

The original scheme called for open spaces and parks to line the avenues and lead into the courtyards of the apartment buildings. During the 1920's, however, the Queensboro Corporation sold some

174

of the open land, and the patterns of clustered houses that now characterize the neighborhood began to develop.

Today the neighborhood, bordered on the west by the Brooklyn-Queens Expressway and on the east by Junction Boulevard, sprawls under the paths of planes from La Guardia Airport on its northern edge. It is a twenty-minute ride into Manhattan on the E, F, GG, and N trains of the IND subway line and by the IRT's No. 7, or Flushing line, trains.

A walk through Jackson Heights is best accompanied by a hearty appetite, a vast curiosity about small shops—there are some 600—and a knowledge of the difference between a griffin and a gargoyle.

Roosevelt Avenue, the border to the south, runs under the long shadows of the el. On this street, it is possible to purchase a house or rent an apartment from a Spanish, Indian, or Chinese real-estate dealer, buy a sari, have a corned beef on rye, strip an abandoned car of its chrome, live with the noise of the train, and see a father, in a sweatshirt bearing George Orwell's picture, pushing a carriage while reading philosophy.

One block north is 37th Avenue, where shops, as small and close as those on its parallel street, seem less active (perhaps because of the distance from the el, whose noise is muffled by trees on the side streets). Here, too, is heaped up variety. Romeo's Pizza is across the street from Julietta's place, but there are also antique stores where owners display sofas on the sidewalk, and dress boutiques, health-food stores, and a suggestion in the facades of the graceful architecture of the homes nearby.

Jackson Heights displays its frequent infusions of ethnicity like badges; from the names of the stores to the choice of holiday lights, the range is wide. With a population of 80,403, it has the largest number of Argentines of any area in New York City. It also has large numbers of Asians, Italians, Irish, and Hispanics.

"There is no racial problem here," said Gloria Porras, a resident for twelve years. "We have Balkans, Himalayans, Jamaicans up the block and Hindus on the corner, and we have some people from Guyana."

Jackson Heights has been in the news in the last few years for drug-related crimes. In 1981 a special law-enforcement task force uncovered a nationwide ring of cocaine smugglers and suppliers linking Colombian drug trafficking to Jackson Heights—a neighborhood that the Colombians were said to call "the colony." At the time, it was believed to be the center of the cocaine trade. But many residents as well as the local police believe that the traffic does not directly affect most people who live in the neighborhood.

Crimes against property, however, are on the minds of the residents. Cars are kept on the streets, as one put it, "only if they are old cars—at least secondhand."

Louis Lopardi and his wife, Margaret Lundin, have lived in Jackson Heights for several years. He is a musical conductor. She works for an investment firm in what they both call "the city." They live in a single-family home on 91st Street for which they paid $60,000 in 1980. A similar house on the block sold recently for $79,500, but most houses in the neighborhood are more costly.

Mr. Lopardi feels that crime in the neighborhood is decreasing. "This is a neighborhood where, when there was a purse-snatching recently, it was the postman who caught the guy," he said, "and where, if somebody gets mugged, it's a big event—which says to me that not everyone gets mugged all the time." A police spokesman at the 110th Precinct confirmed this assessment.

There are five public elementary schools in Jackson Heights, but no public high schools. There are also five parochial schools—three Catholic, one Jewish, and one Protestant. There is one private school, the Garden School, and one vocational school, the Lexington School for the Deaf.

Sports are built into the life of the community. There is an active Elmhurst–Jackson Heights Little League, as well as a soccer program. There are also junior soccer clubs and, on mild Saturdays, stickball on the side streets and pickup handball nearer the shopping area.

The Jackson Heights–Elmhurst Kehilla, or lay council, represents five synagogues and five Jewish civic organizations in the area. Fred Kasner, executive director of Kehilla, calls Jackson Heights "the Upper West Side of Queens, the interesting mosaic of the borough." He said recently that he saw "nothing but positive things for the community, with the significant influx of middle-class people with a commitment to community activities and cultural life."

According to Beatrice Sanchez, who works in the Now and Then antique store on 37th Street, Jackson Heights is one of the areas of Queens that young people are moving into. "I feel safe here," she said, "and the business does well." For the last twelve years, she has lived in a three-and-a-half-room apartment near the store, for which she pays $219 a month rent.

Apartments are available throughout the neighborhood. According to Mathew Kalaburckal at Seema Realty, rents for a one-bedroom apartment average $550 to $600 a month, with two-bedroom units costing $650 to $700. Mr. Kalaburckal said that many of his clients, whom he described as singles or young families, come to Jackson Heights because they "want to live outside the city, but not too far."

Cooperative apartments in the neighborhood are mostly large and range in price from $30,000 to $40,000 for a two-bedroom apartment in a walk-up to $50,000 to $60,000 or more for two bedrooms in a building with an elevator. Apartments are almost without exception in imposing buildings with recessed entrances and names that suggest high style—Boswell, Colton, or Princeton Court.

Many have tile work on the outside. Some have pillars, and others have columns topped with lions or lamps. Most have meticulous shrubbery. There are odd stained-glass touches in some windows and small panes in nearly all the others.

The prices of houses start at $100,000 and go beyond $150,000 on some blocks. They can be found in rows of solid red brick on one street and pastel shingles in the next. But there are design touches—almost all Art Deco—on most.

The Lopardis have a beamed ceiling over the sunken living room in their home. There are thick walls, wide-board floors, and a splendid Art Deco bathroom, which, they maintain, is a common find in the area. "In fact," Mr. Lopardi said, "there is enough lavender tile in Jackson Heights to cover the whole U.S."

—MARION ROACH

JAMAICA ESTATES

*To midtown Manhattan: Subway
45 minutes*

Back in the days when glaciers crawled across the terrain of what would become Queens, a halt occurred at a point later to be appropriately named Hillside Avenue, the southern boundary of the rolling hills of Jamaica Estates. Steep hills and winding roads are characteristic of this compact enclave, almost hidden amid lavish shade trees, many of which line Midland Parkway, the main road. On a clear day, from the highest point—what is now the grandstand of St. John's University—the Manhattan skyline can be seen.

Property values have been increasing rapidly and this is changing the character of the community, according to David H. Brown of Estates Realty. "The prices are getting out of reach. Young couples can't afford to live here, unless they have wealthy parents or in-laws to make the down payment."

Houses that come on the market are listed at a minimum of $150,000 and the prices range up to about $550,000. Nevertheless, the sixteen real-estate brokers in the neighborhood say prospective customers greatly exceed available houses, a factor that keeps prices steep.

The reasons abound. The varied, custom-built, one-family homes are enveloped by lush greenery throughout the area's eighty-three square blocks. The schools nearby are among the best in the city. An assortment of shops is just blocks away. In addition, the crime rate is

178

low and the vocal community organization, the Jamaica Estates Association, works hard to preserve the area. All this makes Jamaica Estates what Assemblyman Saul Weprin, a resident for twenty-two years, calls "the finest neighborhood in the city to live in."

Another attraction is that Jamaica Estates is less than forty-five minutes from Manhattan on the IND E and F trains. The 179th Street subway station on Hillside Avenue is the first stop on the lines. Express buses to Manhattan run frequently during rush hours and once every twenty minutes during off-peak hours. Jamaica Estates is about a forty-minute drive from midtown on the Grand Central Parkway or the Long Island Expressway.

Tudor houses are the hallmark of the area—there is even a street called Tudor—although colonials and ranches are sprinkled here and there, and there are a few Cape Cods on the perimeter. Most were built with expensive materials and they have been well maintained.

The average plot is 60 by 100 feet, although several properties cover up to an acre. Most of the 1,800 houses in the Estates have large lawns tended by gardeners, with many trees.

There are also seven six-story apartment buildings on Wexford Terrace, one block north of Hillside Avenue, and all have long waiting lists. Rents are in the range of $600 for a one-bedroom apartment and $750 and up for two-bedrooms. There are also a few two-family houses.

There are no public schools in Jamaica Estates; local children attend either P.S. 178 in nearby Holliswood, which has 350 students, or P.S. 131 in Jamaica, with 573 students. Both schools rank at the top of the lists in their districts, as measured by scores on standardized reading tests given by the Board of Education.

Estates children go on to Ryan Junior High School in Fresh Meadows, which has about 1,000 students, and also ranks high in citywide tests. High-school students attend Jamaica High School.

There are two Catholic parochial schools in Jamaica Estates, Immaculate Conception and Mary Louis Academy. Three other private high schools—Highland, Hillcrest, and Yeshiva—are within walking distance.

St. John's University forms part of the western border of the community, which is bounded on the south by Hillside Avenue, on the east by 188th Street, and on the north by Union Turnpike. The turnpike's mile-long stretch of shops offers everything from infant-sized tuxedos at a shop called Malawi & The Mighty Mole to $1,000 dresses at Celeste. Quaint shops such as Grandma's Attic and The Happy Homemaker sell the usual and the unusual.

The Hillcrest branch library, which opened in 1980, is on Union Turnpike directly across from Jamaica Estates. The library offers free French and Italian lessons for adults and has frequent guest speakers. It also has special children's programs.

JAMAICA ESTATES

Crime in Jamaica Estates is mostly property-related, usually burglary, according to Officer Michael T. Kelty, operational planning officer of the 107th Precinct, which covers the neighborhood. Violent crime is practically nonexistent, he said.

Officer Kelty cited the Jamaica Estates Association as an effective deterrent to crime. In 1979 the association began a private security patrol that about 1,000 residents support with annual contributions. The association has about 1,400 members.

"It's a community that's aware," said Barry Weinberg, president of the association. "People are willing to devote time and effort into preserving the area." The big winter snowstorm of 1983, he added, was an example. "We paid for our own private snow removal and the tab came to $2,600. We bailed ourselves out when the Sanitation Department forgot where Queens was."

Michael Bookbinder, who writes the monthly bulletin for the association, is raising his children in the house he grew up in. "It's great," he said. "The faces have changed but the neighborhood is as well kept now as it was thirty-seven years ago."

The Estates began as 503 acres of hardwood forest. It was sold by the city in 1904 to Timothy L. Woodruff, lieutenant governor of New York under Theodore Roosevelt. Mr. Woodruff was a partner in the Jamaica Estates Company, along with Edward M. Groat, a onetime state comptroller, and Michael Degnon, a pioneer in the engineering of the city's first subway. They hoped to transform the forest of maples, oaks, elms, and chestnuts into a second Tuxedo Park, a wealthy community in Orange County. The streets of the Estates were given a distinctly English flavor. Among the names are Aberdeen, Cambridge, Hovenden, Wareham, Edgerton, and Kent.

State Senator Frank Padavan remembers growing up south of Hillside Avenue in Hollis. "I used to deliver *The Long Island Press* in Jamaica Estates. I always thought it would be a great place to live, but at the time my family wasn't in the position to afford it." Today the senator owns a large red-brick colonial on Radnor Street.

Donald R. Manes, the Queens borough president, has lived in a sprawling, two-story contemporary-style house atop a hill in Jamaica Estates since 1966. "It's truly a great place to bring up my children," he said. "We've been very happy here and have no intention of moving."

—MARIA EFTIMIADES

RICHMOND HILL

*To midtown Manhattan: Subway
30 minutes or bus 45 minutes*

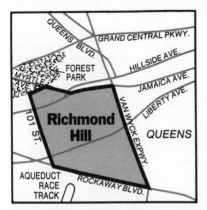

Painted on a 160-square-foot wall in the south wing of the Richmond Hill Public Library in Queens is a Philip Evergood mural depicting the promise of a bucolic life for city dwellers longing to leave urban grime and congestion. On one side, young families dance in fields where the library now stands on Hillside Avenue; on the other, pale children stand dejectedly on a crowded city street. Prominent in the center of the painting is Albon Platt Man, a New York lawyer who teamed up in 1868 with Howard Richmond, a landscape architect, to buy several farms in what was then known as West Jamaica. They subdivided the land and sold suburban lots, naming the new community Richmond Hill after the fashionable London suburb.

Richmond Hill is still a quiet oasis and a haven from the city's hectic pace. Tall shade trees line broad sidewalks, many spacious homes are set behind generous front lawns, and wooded hills stretch for miles through adjoining Forest Park.

The community's generally accepted boundaries are 101st Street to the west; the Van Wyck Expressway to the east; Forest Park, Myrtle, and Jamaica avenues to the north; and Rockaway Boulevard to the south.

Although house prices are on the rise, they are still substantially lower than those in neighboring Kew Gardens and Forest Hills. "Prices here range from $40,000 to $150,000, and they are as rea-

181

sonable as any you'll find in Queens or Nassau," said George A. Clark, who has been selling real estate in the area for forty-six years.

The property tax on a house that sold recently for $130,000 is $958, based on the citywide rate of $9.10 per $100 of the assessed valuation, which was about $11,000.

Brokers attribute the relatively low cost of homes to a perception by many buyers that commuting to Manhattan is difficult and time-consuming. In fact, the community is served by three subway lines, local and express buses, and the Long Island Railroad.

The J train along Jamaica Avenue takes forty-five minutes to reach Broad Street in lower Manhattan, and the Atlantic Avenue A train takes thirty minutes to 34th Street. Express buses reach midtown in forty-five minutes. A ten-minute bus ride to Kew Gardens connects the commuter to an E or F train for a half-hour ride to 34th Street or the Long Island Railroad for a ten-minute ride to Penn Station.

There may be more convenient neighborhoods, but residents say that what Richmond Hill lacks in instant access it makes up for in charm. The large houses that date back to its early days are found primarily in the area stretching from Jamaica Avenue to Forest Park. Their predominant style is Queen Anne Victorian, a type of architecture favored at the turn of the century.

Large and small balconies abound on upper floors. Round, square, three-sided, and even octagonal turrets are prevalent. Spacious open porches, with a rich variety of ornamental columns and gingerbread decorations, are designed to catch summer breezes.

Entry halls tend to be spacious. Often, there is a massive oak staircase brightened by leaded stained-glass windows. Many houses have both front and back parlors separated by massive oak pocket doors. A second, smaller staircase sometimes leads from the kitchen to the attic. A fifteen-room house is not an unusual size.

Many of the large old homes that come on the market are a restorer's delight. "Some of these owners have lived there thirty to forty years, and you find old-fashioned porcelain tubs on legs, bath sinks on pedestals, and enamel stoves in the kitchen," said Anita Johnson, sales associate for the Bite of the Apple realty agency.

But such houses, which now sell for $100,000 and up, are getting harder to find and seldom linger on the market. Buyers with more modest prices in mind should look south of Jamaica Avenue, said Tina Romeo, owner of Lido Home Sales on Jamaica Avenue. There, older homes mingle with narrow row houses, typical of those built by the hundreds around 1920 for blue-collar workers and their families. Local brokers refer to them as "Archie Bunkers" and they sell for around $60,000.

In the early 1970's there was a rapid turnover of homes in the community because young families were lured by cheap new housing on Long Island that promised better schools, larger lawns, and fresher air. At that time, some unscrupulous realty brokers attempted to start a flight of white families, as had been done in other neighborhoods, but community residents fought back. The Richmond Hill Block Association's first action after it was organized in 1972 was to obtain a cease-and-desist order from the New York secretary of state barring brokers from soliciting sales.

With a membership of 270 neighborhood blocks, the association continues to be a powerful and stabilizing force in the community. According to Loraine Paolino, its president, the turnover in homes is now so small that any house coming on the market usually sells quickly by word of mouth.

The community is a mixture of many nationalities and religions. Hispanics and, more recently, Indians are the relative newcomers in an area that was once predominantly German, Italian, and middle European.

Ethnic stores cater to the diverse palates. A concentration of small Italian specialty shops can be found on 101st Avenue between 101st and 105th streets, offering shoppers the opportunity to buy homemade pasta, pastry and sausages, cheeses, and a variety of continental imports.

On Jamaica Avenue and 110th Street, meats and cold cuts at Colonial Foods are popular with Armenian residents. Close by are the old Munich Delicatessen, specializing in German home cooking, and the Triangle Delicatessen, which carries Italian delicacies.

The Triangle Hofbrau on Jamaica Avenue, established in 1867 as a hotel for travelers along the Jamaica Plank Road, was later made into a restaurant. For many years, it was a favorite of some of baseball's greats, including Babe Ruth and Lou Gehrig, and Mae West was also a frequent patron. The cooking is German, with sauerbraten, venison, and game in season the specialties of the house.

The stained-glass windows, the two carved wine barrels in the main dining room dating back to the 1800's, the mahogany bar, and even the elevated trains rattling by outside provide diners with an ambience that has not changed much over the last eighty years.

Virtually at their doorsteps, Richmond Hill residents have Forest Park, with its rich variety of recreational and cultural opportunities. Within walking distance are an eighteen-hole public golf course and fourteen tennis courts, seven clay and seven all-weather. A $10 million renovation of the park is under way.

Richmond Hill also has its own community traditions. A drum-and-fife corps parades along Jamaica Avenue on the second Sunday in June, an event coupled with an arts-and-crafts fair at the grounds of the Richmond Hill Library.

The community has seven public elementary schools, with about

65 percent of their pupils reading at or above grade level. Children attend one of three junior high schools in nearby Ozone Park and South Ozone Park, then, for the most part, return to Richmond Hill to attend Richmond Hill High School. The eighty-seven-year-old school, which has an enrollment of 2,000, has had National Merit Scholarship winners among its recent graduating classes and sends 75 percent of its graduates on to college. There are also many parochial schools within easy reach.

Felix J. Cuervo, a local historian always glad to take a visitor on impromptu tours of locations of interest, noted that Richmond Hill has many historic buildings. One, the Daniel Eldridge mansion on 111th Street south of Jamaica Avenue, now houses a nursery school. Mr. Eldridge, who was a member of the Boss Tweed Ring, reportedly watched from a widow's walk atop the house when the police came to arrest him. The house dates back to 1867.

The Jeremiah Briggs farmhouse, built in 1840, stands on 117th Street south of Jamaica Avenue. Some of the apple trees that were part of the Briggs farm still bear fruit in the backyards of local homes, Mr. Cuervo said.

—DIANA SHAMAN

S U N N Y S I D E

*To midtown Manhattan: Subway
15 minutes*

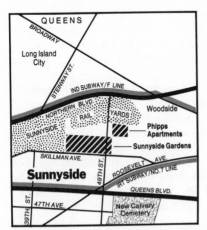

From the heart of Sunny-
side, Queens, the midtown Manhattan skyline is a looming presence, obscured in some places by heavily leafed street trees and at
some times by a soft industrial haze, but close enough to offer a
panoramic view from many apartments. Sunnyside is a community
aptly characterized by its name and setting. Its stocky walk-up
apartment buildings and two-story row houses are built into the
south side of a rolling plateau that is but a fifteen-minute subway ride
to Times Square.

A visitor to the once predominantly blue-collar, Irish-American
neighborhood can now hear Korean, Spanish, German, and Armenian in street-corner conversations. And among its 44,900 residents
are young professionals, too. Their presence has attracted to Skill-
man Avenue specialty shops and restaurants catering to the needs of
young families. Among them are La Marjolaine, a French pastry
shop just over the community's border at 52nd Street, and several
Korean restaurants along Queens Boulevard.

"Sunnyside is almost like being in a little village," said Lorraine
Wallnik, a retired nurse who is a thirty-year resident of Sunnyside
Gardens, a twelve-block planned community within the larger neighborhood. "It's really a warm feeling here, even with the growth and
change." The change she speaks of is one of character rather than
spirit. A lively remnant of the once-dominant Irish-American flavor

SUNNYSIDE

of the neighborhood is the cavernous Donovan's Pub, at 57th Street and Roosevelt Avenue, where the jukebox plays Irish music exclusively. And though many Sunnyside residents are recent arrivals, the community's long-established organizations and churches are booming.

Groups like Sunnyside Community Services, the primary neighborhood volunteer agency, offer many services, among them programs for old people and the handicapped and a community credit union. Sunnyside's several Catholic and Protestant churches are frequent sponsors of get-togethers.

"Most of my friends in New York live within five blocks of here," said Jeff Buyers, an executive producer at WOR-Radio who is also a resident of Sunnyside Gardens. "It's a small-town feeling in a big city."

Over the sixty years of its existence, Sunnyside's unofficial boundaries have varied, but only slightly. Community Board 2 defines them this way: Its western border is 39th Street, lined with heavy industry that long ago settled on the shores of the East River. On the south, it is bounded by 47th Avenue and light industry and warehouses. Woodside, a larger, more commercial neighborhood than Sunnyside, abuts it on the east along 49th Street. To the north, about where 39th Avenue would lie, is the community's northern border—the Sunnyside rail yards, built in 1902 by the Pennsylvania and Long Island railroads.

When subway service was first extended in 1918 to connect the Queens rail yards to Manhattan, the eyes of developers fell on the city's eastern borough, especially on Sunnyside, then an undeveloped tract between Woodside and a now-defunct community called Winfield.

After considering the development possibilities of the area, Clarence S. Stein, chairman of the city's Commission for Housing and Regional Planning, in conjunction with the engineer Henry Wright, undertook in 1924 to build what Lewis Mumford, the urban historian, said was the nation's first planned garden community. The pair, who completed the 400-unit Sunnyside Gardens development in 1928, modeled it on the garden cities developed in Britain in the nineteenth century. Using inexpensive red brick and mortar to build the exteriors of one-, two-, and three-family row houses, the team of Stein and Wright built the community around a private park, complete with clay tennis courts and a series of common, ivy-walled garden areas.

Mr. Mumford, who lived in Sunnyside Gardens for eleven years, once praised the notion and use of the garden community, saying: "It has been framed to the human scale and its gardens and courts kept that friendly air."

In 1930, Mr. Stein and Mr. Wright began work on Phipps Gardens, a complex of rental units built around a small park. The first of the two 4-story apartment complexes was completed that year. The second, Phipps Gardens II, was finished in 1935. In all, there are 472 apartments in the complex.

The community built by Mr. Stein and Mr. Wright today comprises Sunnyside Gardens. Most of the original garden houses and apartments still exist, many of them unchanged. Several of the common garden courts were partitioned into private backyards in 1964 when the development's forty-year easement expired, but the garden concept of living still dominates the area just south of the rail yards.

On average, one house in Sunnyside Gardens becomes available for purchase each month, according to Lois Schenck, an independent real-estate broker who owns her own agency. She specializes in properties in the historic district. Prices ranged from $105,000 to $135,000 for a one-family unit, and from $150,000 to $190,000 for two- and three-family units, depending on their condition.

"The houses are charming," she said, "but no one is charmed by fifty-year-old plumbing, heating, and wiring." Rental housing in Sunnyside Gardens is limited, Ms. Schenck stated, but when available, units vary in rent from $500 to $550 a month for a one-bedroom apartment on up to $700 a month for two- or three-bedroom apartments. Some apartments in Phipps Gardens, which is operated by a nonprofit corporation, rent for as little as $200 a month, and it can take as long as seven years to reach the top of the waiting list.

Much of the remainder of Sunnyside was influenced by the low density style of housing in Sunnyside Gardens. Most apartment buildings in the community have fewer than six stories and many were originally built as walk-ups. Several buildings along 46th and 47th streets north of Queens Boulevard were built in the Art Deco style, and census figures show that 73 percent of all buildings in Sunnyside were built before 1939.

Many apartments in Sunnyside are spacious and offer unobstructed views of the Manhattan skyline. Average rentals outside Sunnyside Gardens are about $100 lower than those in Sunnyside Gardens, Ms. Schenck said. Comparable houses sell for about the same prices throughout the neighborhood.

Most students attend one of the nearby public schools, P.S. 11, P.S. 199, or P.S. 150, which has a special program for children with learning disabilities. About 50 percent of the pupils in the elementary schools and at Junior High School 125 read at or above grade level. There are three Roman Catholic schools in the community covering grades seven through twelve—Queen of Angels, St. Raphael's, and St. Theresa's.

The school-age population is growing fast as families of young professionals move in, attracted in part by the easy access to midtown Manhattan. Crime in the neighborhood is quite low relative to the rest of the city.

The Queensboro Bridge and the Queens-Midtown Tunnel originate within blocks of Sunnyside. Two subway lines, the IRT No. 7 and the IND F, serve the community, and by either one midtown Manhattan is only a quarter of an hour away. Bus service to Manhattan is provided by the Transit Authority's M-32 bus and the No. 60 of the private Green Lines.

Diane Miller, who moved to Sunnyside Gardens when it was still unfinished and now spends her days gardening, recalled the days in the 1940's and 1950's when the community was called the "maternity ward of Greenwich Village" because so many artists and writers moved to Sunnyside to start families. "We never used to lock our doors," she said. "It was so different. But really, it hasn't changed that much."

—MARCUS W. BRAUCHLI

WHITESTONE

To midtown Manhattan: Bus and subway 45 minutes

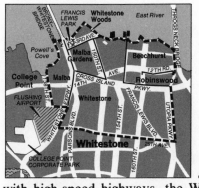

Although it is laced with high-speed highways, the Whitestone section of Queens has retained the flavor of a small suburban town. Its main street is 150th Street between 10th and 14th avenues. There is no large supermarket, but shoppers have their choice of a rich variety of small stores.

Freshly baked breads piled in large baskets in a bakery window entice passersby. Restaurants are small and intimate. The post office is centrally located, and the local library is around the corner, adding to the feeling that everything essential to everyday living is within easy walking distance.

The community is in the northeastern quadrant of Queens and serves as the gateway to the borough for travelers entering by the Whitestone and Throgs Neck bridges. It has a population of about 16,000, and its borders are those of the Whitestone postal zip-code area (11357)—on the west, 138th Street to 20th Avenue and then south on the Whitestone Expressway; on the south, 25th Avenue; on the east, Utopia Parkway; and on the north, the East River. The neighborhood includes sections called Malba, Malba Gardens, Whitestone Woods, Robinswood, and Beechhurst.

Le Havre, a complex of thirty-two 8-story buildings with more than 1,000 apartments, occupies the northeasterly corner of Beechhurst, along with the 328-unit Cryder Point Apartments. Both have been converted into cooperatives, provoking complaints that a lack of rentals is forcing out the younger generation.

The riverfront has two marinas and large houses—some of which sell for more than $1 million. Also on the river is the Crest Haven day camp, owned by the Roman Catholic church, which has three swimming pools and seven clay tennis courts. For a family fee of $400, residents may use two of the camp's pools and its tennis courts on summer evenings and on weekends. The other pool is open to the public seven days a week.

A popular riverfront spot for catching a summer breeze is Francis Lewis Park just east of the Whitestone Bridge.

In the Beechhurst section at 168-11 Powell's Cove Boulevard is a landmark neo-Tudor–style house built in 1924 by Arthur Hammerstein, a theatrical producer who was the uncle of the lyricist Oscar Hammerstein 2d. The structure, which later became a restaurant, was declared a landmark in 1982. It is now empty and its future is uncertain.

Whitestone was settled in 1645 by the Dutch, who named it after a large white boulder that they discovered at the spot where the East River meets Long Island Sound. The boulder served as a major navigation point for passing ships.

The village was originally part of the Town of Flushing until both were incorporated into New York City in 1898.

The discovery of a large clay deposit in Whitestone in 1735 led to the manufacture of pipes and pottery. A century later, the community became noted for a spring discovered on a farm at Old Whitestone Avenue and 14th Street. A local doctor recommended the water to patients who needed extra iron, and it came to be known as Iron Springs. In 1920 the city's Water Department sank wells at the site, but they were abandoned following complaints that the iron in the water ruined clothes.

Very little industry remains in the community. But in a tiny industrial enclave along Powell's Cove Boulevard near Clintonville Street is the Commercial Diving Institute, one of only seven schools in the country that teach commercial deep-sea diving.

Travelers once used ferries and coaches to get to the city. But around the turn of the century, a rail system was completed that wound through Queens and Brooklyn and got commuters to Park Row in Manhattan.

Today, commuters can catch the Transit Authority's Q-14 bus on 150th Street for the twelve-minute run to the Main Street subway station in Flushing. From there, the IRT No. 7 train takes thirty-three minutes to Times Square. Queens Transit also runs express buses to Manhattan, which make several stops in the Whitestone community. Travel time averages forty-five minutes.

Most of the houses in Whitestone date back about thirty years because major development began only after construction of the bridges and highway systems made the area more accessible.

The Malba section is considered to be the most exclusive. Waterfront properties there sell for no less than $500,000, and other houses range in price from $350,000 to $450,000.

Elsewhere, more moderately priced houses may be found. Anthony P. Vincent, a local broker, said that there were three-bedroom houses with one or two bathrooms on 40- by 100-foot plots available for around $160,000 in Whitestone proper.

Older houses in the city are often assessed at a small fraction of market value. Thus a fifty-five-year-old colonial listed for sale last year in Whitestone at $279,000 is assessed at only $11,000 and its owner pays about $1,000 a year in taxes, including water and sewer charges.

There has been little new construction lately, but the Flushing Bay's Ciampa organization recently completed a forty-eight-unit waterfront condominium known as Beechhurst Shores. The two- and three-bedroom town houses sold for $120,000 to $150,000.

With the noneviction conversion of the twenty-five-year-old Le Havre apartments to cooperatives, buyers have been able to purchase one-, two-, and three-bedroom apartments, each with a terrace, for $60,000 to $90,000, with a monthly maintenance ranging from $340 to $560. Amenities include two pools and three tennis courts, but residents are charged for their use.

About a third of the 1,023 units have been sold, but there is a waiting list for purchases, since apartments become available only when tenants move.

Across the street from Le Havre, the Cryder Point Apartments also are being sold as co-ops at prices starting at $75,300 for a one-bedroom unit and going to $203,460 for three-bedrooms. Maintenance costs range from $407 to $847 a month.

Whitestone has at least one store—Stork's Pastry Shop on 150th Street—that has earned more than a local reputation. It was started thirty years ago by Karl and Doris Stork and has become renowned not only for its French and German pastries but also for its chocolates and other candies. The brick colonial-style Stork building houses a bakery downstairs, but upstairs is a chocolate factory that turns out such delicacies as marzipan, almond nougats, and truffles.

Down the street from Stork's is Irene & Sal's Bakery, where Italian baked goods are prepared in front of customers. Along 150th Street and on some of the side blocks are several German and Italian delicatessens that offer a variety of imported as well as homemade delicacies. Mercurio's on 150th Street, for example, specializes in fresh mozzarella cheese and several varieties of homemade Italian sausages.

Also on 150th Street is La Colomba, an Italian restaurant highly regarded for its pastas and veal dishes. For seafood, many residents go to the Lobster King Seafood House on 154th Street.

The Whitestone Mall, off the Cross Island Expressway at 153rd Street, is somewhat of a sore point with 150th Street merchants, since it drew away business and garnered all the community banks. The mall has a large Dan's Supreme Supermarket, a Woolworth's, a movie theater, and many small specialty stores.

Whitestone's public schools are among the best in the city system. Reading scores at the four elementary schools show that well over 85 percent of the pupils read at or above grade level. About 85 percent of the graduates of Bayside and Flushing high schools, to which Whitestone students are zoned, go on to college.

—DIANA SHAMAN

STATEN ISLAND
VI.

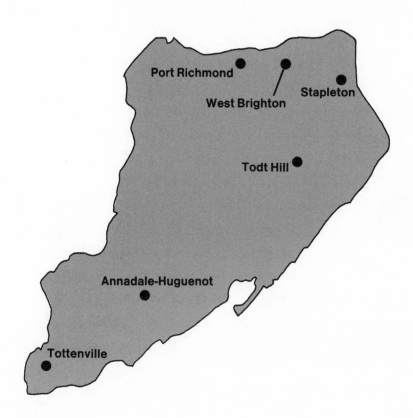

ANNADALE - HUGUENOT

*To midtown Manhattan: Train,
ferry, and subway 75 minutes; bus
45 to 60 minutes*

Nestled together on the South Shore of Staten Island bordering Raritan Bay, the communities of Annadale and Huguenot have many things in common: a tough commute to Manhattan, large tracts of woodland populated by the frequent pheasant, a dearth of sidewalks and sewers, alternately muddy-dusty-muddy roadways, and people putting up houses worth anywhere from $275,000 to $750,000.

The area has come a long way since its settlement in the latter half of the seventeenth century by the Dutch, English, and persecuted Huguenots, who gave their name to one section. (Annadale took its name from the train station, which was named around 1860 in honor of Anna S. Seguine, scion of an old Staten Island family.) But the area has come less of the way than the rest of the island, thanks to some quirks of fate that spared Annadale-Huguenot the matchbox-house development of neighboring towns.

Al Calvanico, an engineer and architect with Calvanico Associates in Willowbrook, which helped build many of the area's spectacular new homes, listed three factors that he said encouraged big houses: a 1968 Health Department ruling on lot sizes for septic tanks, an urban-renewal plan's freeze on new-home construction from 1965 to 1975, and the area's residentially oriented zoning.

Of the three, the freeze, instituted to give the city time to produce a disciplined plan for growth (a plan that was scuttled), may have been the most important. In 1965, 70 percent of Annadale-Huguenot was vacant land. Today, perhaps 50 percent still is. Nearby Eltingville, on the other hand, which was also mostly woodland in the mid-1960's, now has street after street of row houses virtually indistinguishable from one another. But Annadale-Huguenot missed that spurt of frenzied growth.

That does not mean the new developments are the stuff of planners' dreams: much of the construction is undisciplined. But there is room for individuality, especially for the more affluent.

According to William Wolfe, of Wolfe Realty, it is not unusual to find $300,000 homes sitting next to $80,000 bungalows. And while lots in Annadale-Huguenot still are considerably cheaper than their counterparts in Staten Island's more prestigious sections, such as Todt Hill, prices are skyrocketing, even at city auctions. "The auctions get a little wacky," Mr. Wolfe stated. "People overpay. Often they get caught up in the excitement." In a recent private sale, he noted, a 100- by 100-foot unimproved lot went for $55,000, and many city lots are beginning to fetch near that amount even though some of them have creeks meandering through them. Mr. Wolfe said his office was listing everything from a twenty-year-old, three-bedroom ranch for $89,900 to a two-year-old, all-stone mansion with six bedrooms and seven baths for $750,000.

Homes in Annadale-Huguenot, as elsewhere on Staten Island, are assessed at less than 20 percent of market value; the owner of a house costing $100,000 would pay about $1,500 a year in taxes.

Rentals in two-family houses range from $350 a month for a three-room apartment to $750 for a six- or seven-room apartment; house rentals range from $600 to $1,000 a month.

The "old towns" of Annadale and Huguenot are clustered around the Staten Island Rapid Transit system stations, where people go for the morning paper, a haircut, or to shop at the deli. "Downtown" Annadale, with its stores grouped around a pedestrian-oriented village common at Jefferson Boulevard, has an upstate flavor.

"There are lots and lots of trees," said Lois Baird, who lives with her husband and three children in a Cape Cod on Poillon Avenue. "It's great for kids." The Bairds are a rare Staten Island breed: they moved to Annadale twenty-four years ago from Westerleigh on the North Shore, a community with sewers.

"We are in an area that is better off because there are no sewers," Ms. Baird explained. "In areas where there are sewers, they are building on 40- by 100-foot lots. In our area, houses with septics are going up on 100- by 100 lots. It gives us some elbow room."

Like many of her neighbors, Ms. Baird is active in the community. She has worked with others to preserve the local habitat. The results: Claypit Pond State Park, in nearby Bloomingdale, and Blue Heron Park, a 147-acre preserve that, like Claypit, is used for nature walks and other arboreal pursuits.

Liv Pandolfino, a native of Norway who moved to Annadale five years ago from Brooklyn, differs with Ms. Baird on the sewer issue. "I would like to see sewers in my area because of the water problem," she said. "If we didn't have the water problem, Annadale would be ideal to live in."

The "water problem"—flooding after heavy rains—is endemic to the South Shore of Staten Island. Nicholas LaPorte, the city councilman who represents the neighborhood, said the area was beginning to get a larger share of the city's money for storm sewers.

But there are other advantages to life there. The 123rd Precinct in Tottenville, which covers most of southern Staten Island, has one of the lowest crime rates in the city. "House burglaries, car thefts for joy rides, and criminal mischief" are the main problems, said William Murphy, the Staten Island district attorney.

On the other hand, Annadale-Huguenot is not exactly commuter heaven: the most efficient link is the S.I.R.T., whose modern, graffiti-free trains take twenty minutes to reach the ferry terminal in St. George. City buses, the 103 and the 113, to the ferry can take up to an hour. The twenty-five-minute ferry ride puts commuters in Manhattan's financial district, and those who work in the midtown area need twenty minutes more for the subway ride uptown. Even with good connections, the S.I.R.T.-ferry-subway trip adds up to a commute of an hour and a quarter.

City express buses—the 11X, 13X, and 17X—travel to downtown and midtown Manhattan via the Verrazano-Narrows Bridge. They make the trip in forty-five minutes to an hour. There also are private bus and van services that make the run to the Port Authority Bus Terminal, by way of New Jersey highways and the Lincoln Tunnel, in about the same time.

Good restaurants in New Jersey, via the Outerbridge Crossing, are near enough to lure many residents. Luigino's, an Italian restaurant on Annadale Road, the Sleepy Hollow Inn on Bloomingdale Road in nearby Woodrow, and the Dellwood Manor in the South Shore Golf Course that borders the area all have their devotees.

For recreation, there is the golf course. Wolfe's Pond Park in Prince Bay offers fishing and picnicking. Great Kills Harbor and the Gateway National Recreation Area are close by.

The Staten Island Mall is ten minutes away, as are the Hylan Boulevard shopping centers. But in Annadale and Huguenot, shopping is spotty. "There is a new shopping center going in at the corner of Rossville Avenue and Woodrow Road," said Richard Irwin, executive director of the Staten Island Chamber of Commerce. "And you have to figure that with all those expensive homes going up, more will follow."

There is a hodgepodge of civic associations in Annadale-Huguenot, all vocal and protective of what they consider to be the small-town ambience of their communities. "People in Annadale and

Huguenot don't mind the extra commute," Mr. Wolfe stated. "They want to get away from it all. It's one of the last frontiers in New York City."

Annadale-Huguenot's schools are sources of both pride and concern to residents. "They have exceptional schools," remarked Christy Cugini, deputy school superintendent for Staten Island. The two public elementary schools, P.S. 36 in Annadale and P.S. 5 in Huguenot, rank twentieth and eleventh, respectively, of the city's 623 elementary schools in reading scores. Of the children in P.S. 5, 91.9 percent read at or above grade levels; the figure for P.S. 36 is 88.8 percent.

I.S. 7 in Huguenot consistently scores in the top five among the city's 181 intermediate schools, with most of its students reading at high-school levels. Tottenville High, where local children are zoned, is one of the most modern in the city.

But with all the new home building, residents worry about possible overcrowding. Two new schools, I.S. 75 and P.S. 63, are expected to forestall that problem.

—LAWRENCE J. DEMARIA

PORT RICHMOND

To midtown Manhattan: Bus, ferry, and subway 65 minutes

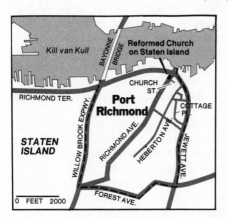

The trees lining Richmond Avenue, the main commercial street of Port Richmond, Staten Island, are scrawny and new, planted in freshly dug plots in the long shadows of the modern street lamps. The granite curbing, too, is new, marking the renovation of the downtown blocks of Richmond Avenue. The new look is the result of a $1.2 million commercial revitalization project paid for by Federal Community Development block grants and planned by the Northfield Community Local Development Corporation, a private, nonprofit organization.

In tandem with these improvements, $150,000 more in federal funds was granted the local corporation in 1983 to make low-interest loans to store owners to spruce up their premises. The development corporation recently allocated another $2 million for commercial street improvements.

But despite the emphasis some community leaders place on the need for commercial growth, Port Richmond remains more than 80 percent residential, according to the 1980 census.

For its 11,000 people, the commercial rejuvenation signals a return to the past, when the community on Staten Island's North Shore, facing New Jersey, was the shopping center of the island. "When I moved to Staten Island twenty-four years ago, I lived on the South Shore," said Ann C. O'Halloran, president of the local

199

development corporation. "Back then, you had to go to Port Richmond to do your shopping."

In the years following World War II, Port Richmond thrived as a commercial center. By the 1970's, however, two new shopping centers—Forest Avenue Shoppers Town, just south of Port Richmond, and the Staten Island Mall in New Springville—had replaced Port Richmond as the primary commercial center and many local businesses relocated, Ms. O'Halloran said.

Although Port Richmond, which is bounded on the east by Jewett Avenue, on the west by the Willow Brook Expressway, on the south by Forest Avenue, and on the north by the Kill van Kull, is easily accessible, construction of the malls in the center of the island made it seem distant, she said.

One of the oldest structures in Port Richmond is the Reformed Church on Staten Island, at Richmond Avenue and Church Street. The present church, which was built in 1844, is the third on the site. The first, erected in 1715 and known as the Dutch Reformed Church, was destroyed by fire during the Revolutionary War. The second was built in 1787. The Reverend Fred W. Diekman, pastor of the church, said the congregation had three graveyards, one of which is Staten Island's oldest "burying place," dating back to 1700.

The red-brick, Greek Revival church has had as its organist for the last fifty-five years John M. Braisted, Jr., a former Staten Island district attorney. The church sits on the western edge of Veterans Park, a small square shaded by several tall trees and the only park in the community. Across the park from the church is the Port Richmond Public Library, where the community's annual Columbus Day parade begins.

The town adopted the name Port Richmond in 1835, when a ferry ran between what was known as Decker's Ferry and Bergen Point, New Jersey. The following year, Aaron Burr died at what was then Winant's Inn, near the intersection of Richmond Avenue and Richmond Terrace. Port Richmond was incorporated in 1866 and became part of New York City along with the rest of Staten Island in 1898.

"Port Richmond's historical background makes it the opposite of a sterile environment," Ms. O'Halloran said. "It's a walking community and people get to know their neighbors."

Houses in Port Richmond vary greatly in size and age. Along Heberton Avenue is a row of spacious Victorian houses built late in the nineteenth century. The strip still is known to some locals as "doctors' row" for the number of physicians who lived there and practiced medicine in their homes.

Along nearby Cottage Place are many small, cottage-style houses with neatly trimmed trees and hedges. Most of Port Richmond's streets are wide, and the lawns of many houses are fronted by curbside trees.

PORT RICHMOND

"These houses were built in the days when people built strong, well-constructed houses," said Linda Black, an urban planner who works with the local development corporation. "And the houses are affordable. If people buy here, we can help them get going."

Prices for houses are relatively low for the New York area, according to Ron Burroughs, executive director of the development corporation. The smaller cottage-style houses sell for about $55,000 while the larger Victorian houses, which are less often available, cost between $85,000 and $100,000, depending on condition, he said. There are only a few rental apartment houses, but some owners of private houses rent rooms.

"Property values here have gone up lately, but they're not yet out of sight," Mr. Burroughs said. "You can still buy a house and maintain it."

The tax rate is $9.10 for each $100 of assessed valuation, and houses are assessed at less than 20 percent of market value. Thus the taxes on a $60,000 home would be about $1,000 a year.

Port Richmond is a quiet community with a low-key nightlife. Gene's and the Casanova, both Italian restaurants on Richmond Avenue, draw moderate crowds. There are no movie theaters in the community.

The crime rate is very low, even compared with other Staten Island communities, according to Detective Clarence Lake of the 120th Precinct, which covers Port Richmond.

Children can attend P.S. 20, which was built in 1898 and enlarged in 1905. More than 1,200 students attend Port Richmond High School, which scores slightly above the citywide average on reading tests. Two parochial schools, St. Mary's and St. Roch's, serve children of all grades.

Port Richmond is easy to reach from Manhattan and New Jersey. It is the terminal point for several Staten Island bus lines and the Bayonne Bridge is nearby. The Staten Island ferries at St. George, which leave every half hour and take twenty-five minutes for the run to the Battery in Manhattan, are a five-minute drive or a twenty-minute bus ride away. From the Battery, midtown is another twenty minutes away by subway.

Because of Port Richmond's accessibility, Ms. O'Halloran said, she believes the community will experience the same sort of resurgence as its commercial district. "I feel strongly about bringing back neighborhoods. It's so mixed and there's so much architectural and social variety that Port Richmond has to be appealing."

—MARCUS W. BRAUCHLI

STAPLETON

To midtown Manhattan: Bus, ferry, and subway 50 minutes

Even on a clear day, you can't see forever from the open back porch of the McAndrew house on a tiny street called Smith Terrace in the Staten Island community of Stapleton. But when the leaves fall from the trees, you can see as far as the World Trade Center, ten miles off across the bay.

No matter. For Mr. and Mrs. McAndrew—Robert, a theatrical designer, and Linda, a dancer, both in their thirties—Stapleton itself is the attraction. They are proud boosters of the neighborhood, and he has served as chairman of the annual house tour of the Mud Lane Society, the neighborhood homeowners' association. He wants the world to know about Stapleton.

And largely because Stapleton and its remarkable blend of old houses—colonial, Italianate, Queen Anne, Spanish, Greek Revival, Victorian—were "discovered" by so many younger families in the middle 1970's, the community has made a strong comeback from the vicissitudes of decline apparent until their arrival.

More or less the same might be said of all the older waterfront communities on Staten Island's North Shore, from New Brighton through St. George, where the Manhattan ferry docks, through Tompkinsville to Stapleton to Clifton. But Stapleton is singular among them not only because of the extent and variety of its housing stock but also because of its large commercial district, clustered around a kind of village square called Tappen Park.

S T A P L E T O N

The stranger is likely to know Stapleton best from the commercial district along Bay Street, with its bustling antique row that the driver cannot miss en route from the ferry terminal to the Verrazano-Narrows Bridge.

But it is the adventurer on the interior streets—notably St. Paul's Avenue and the side streets up the hillside, or on parts of Van Duzer Street—who is likely to see the housing that sends new settlers into rapture. The McAndrews, who came from "off the Island" in 1976, are among them.

They had been working in Virginia and had a chance to come to New York. "I knew New York," Ms. McAndrew said. "I had danced there. I didn't want to go crazy carrying my groceries up three flights of stairs. I said to Bob if we could find a place with grass and trees, I'd come."

So he stayed with a friend in a loft on 19th Street in Manhattan and started to house hunt. He drove forty-five minutes north and was still in the city. He drove west into New Jersey and "saw nothing." Then he drove to Staten Island.

"I wasn't crazy about Staten Island either, on first glance," he said. But a friend pointed him toward Stapleton, and in time the McAndrews bought their fifteen-room pre-1840 Victorian house on two thirds of an acre, with a large garden in which they have since installed a pool and plantings. They paid $55,500 and went to work on a home-improvement program.

Bernadette Donahue, a broker with Rand Properties Inc., said there still are brick ranches and colonials in Stapleton on the market for $45,000 to $60,000. Some cost that little because they are modest and old and need a lot of work; others are newer and in good condition but situated near a large apartment development called Park Hill on Park Hill Avenue.

The tenant makeup of the complex turned from white to black with such rapidity a decade ago that the social stability of the surrounding community was upset. As a result, the values of homes in the neighborhood have not appreciated at a normal rate.

On the finest Stapleton streets, however, there are houses for sale for between $95,000 to $125,000, Ms. Donahue stated. And on the most exclusive streets prices range between $145,000 and $160,000, and sometimes go higher.

Restoration makes a great difference in price. In a few years, some restored houses have appreciated almost 50 percent in value.

As in the rest of New York City, real-estate taxes on homes are low. The owner of a house with a market value of $100,000 would pay approximately $1,000 a year in taxes.

But buildings alone do not a community make. Stapleton has a broad ethnic and social mix, with a low-income population in the large Stapleton Houses public-housing project, a sizable population of longtime residents of Irish and Italian background, and a substantial number of newcomers from the arts and professions.

Commuters may use any of three bus routes that run through Stapleton, linking it to the Staten Island ferry terminal in St. George, five minutes away. The Staten Island Rapid Transit, an island railroad, also stops in Stapleton. This mass-transit access has made the community popular with people who work in lower Manhattan; the ferry ride to the Battery takes about twenty-five minutes. Those continuing to midtown Manhattan add another twenty minutes for the subway ride uptown.

While most would agree that car ownership is a necessity at least for food shopping, the Stapletonian can look in his own backyard for restaurants. The most ambitious of them is a French restaurant called Zazou's at 690 Bay Street. In an unpretentious setting at 381 Van Duzer Street, Browne & Ferri's has been serving unusual continental food for several years. Nearer the waterfront, Grandpa's Place on Water Street and a pub called the Choir Loft on Union Place attract a younger clientele. Another local landmark restaurant particularly popular with the younger crowd is Demyan's on Van Duzer Street, in an old building on a hillside site at one time occupied by a brewery.

That younger crowd consists mostly of couples, many in their thirties, and many only starting to have children. When the children reach preschool age, many may start to attend classes at the Trinity Lutheran Church on St. Paul's Avenue, or travel to a preschool center at the Snug Harbor Cultural Center in West Brighton.

For older children, there are both public and parochial schools. The Immaculate Conception Church's school on Targee Street runs to the eighth grade. Public School 14, near Stapleton Houses, has turned almost entirely black. To advance the prospect for racial balance in Staten Island's high schools, new students from the housing project and Park Hill are bused to New Dorp High School. For other children, Curtis High School in St. George is the public school.

Community activism spills over into social events. There is an annual Stapleton Steeplechase Hometown Race, an annual footrace in April up and down Stapleton's hills. There is a Stapleton Civic Association street festival every year. There is the Serpentine Art and Nature Commons Harvest Festival, the Stapleton Waterfest, and the Holiday Candlelight Caroling.

There is even a Stapleton bard, a photographer and writer named Donald Sutherland. He writes and speaks regularly on the community's history.

Some of the most remarkable restoration activity undoubtedly has occurred in the antique row on Bay Street. Anthony Deorato, an entrepreneur, converted a large building that the Volunteers of

STAPLETON

America had abandoned into the Edgewater Hall Antiques Center, with twelve antique shops inside and a cabaret called Oddsbodkins in the rear.

A dozen other antique shops have opened elsewhere on Bay Street and others are still coming. In some cases established stores have upgraded their merchandise, hoping to benefit from the new arrivals.

"Ten years ago the idea of living anywhere but in Manhattan was horrible to me," said Caroline Hulse, a designer who lives in a secluded cottagelike house on Stone Street. But now she and her husband, who prints and binds books, have studios near their house and work as well as live in the community.

—ALAN S. OSER

TODT HILL

To midtown Manhattan: Bus 60 minutes

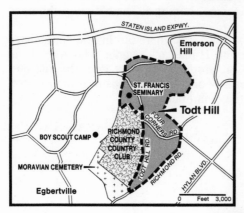

To some people, Todt Hill conjures up feelings of status, wealth, and property. But to its residents, it is just the best, most unspoiled place to live on Staten Island.

Louise Porcelli, who lives in a sprawling ranch house off Todt Hill Road, said she and her family had moved to Todt Hill four years ago from a quiet, near-rural neighborhood in Richmondtown because they wanted a "bigger piece of property, a bigger house," and Todt Hill offered both. But for her, her husband, Peter, and their two children, it offered more. "Do you know the feeling you get when you go someplace and it feels warm?" she asked. "That's how I feel about Todt Hill."

A strictly residential neighborhood, Todt Hill has no delis, restaurants, bus stops, candy stores, or supermarkets. What it does have is a reputation as Staten Island's most exclusive residential neighborhood, with more than 700 homes within a square mile and a history dating back to before the Revolution.

In 1856 *The Staten Islander,* a local paper, traced the origin of the hill's name back to a skirmish between some Indians and the area's original Dutch settlers. Some of the settlers were killed, and as a result the battlefield was named Todt, or Death, Hill. The word is pronounced "tote," and the hill really is a hill. At 409.8 feet, it is said

206

to be the highest point on the East Coast. Residents enjoy commanding views of New York Harbor to the east and New Jersey to the west and south.

Todt Hill is in the north-central part of the island, close to the Staten Island Expressway. It is bordered on the north by Ocean Terrace, on the west by the Richmond County Country Club golf course, and on the south and east by Richmond Road.

Over the last century, this area became the site of many opulent homes built by old-line families who to some extent still are represented there. It always has been an expensive place to live, but since 1964, when the Verrazano-Narrows Bridge was completed and house prices began to rise sharply all over Staten Island, they rose even more precipitously in Todt Hill.

"About $325,000 would be the cheapest house there, and they go up to $1.5 million," reported a broker with the Otto Vitale Real Estate office at the foot of Four Corners Road. The agency handles a majority of the sales on Todt Hill.

The neighborhood offers a selection of homes unrivaled in the borough, and perhaps even the city. With R-1-1 zoning, the minimum building plot is 100 by 100 feet, and many lots are considerably larger.

Some of the estates are on two acres, stated Mr. Vitale, adding that even the minimum-size lots cost between $175,000 to $200,000. "That's $20 a square foot. Elsewhere on Staten Island the norm is more like $6 a square foot."

Todt Hill's homes range from Mediterranean villas to classic colonials to English Tudors to dramatic contemporaries and broadside ranches. The houses tend to be large and have tennis courts. Many streets, such as Buttonwood Road, are canopied with trees. A few homes, especially those off Flagg Place, where there is a sharp, clifflike drop in the topography, offer spectacular views.

Who lives on Todt Hill? A. Timothy Pouch, who heads Pouch Terminal in the Clifton neighborhood on the Narrows, which is being converted into the One Edgewater Plaza waterfront office site, said Todt Hill's residents included many people in the shipping industry because of its proximity to New York's waterfront. Mr. Pouch, whose family has been on Staten Island for four generations, has lived on Todt Hill for fifty years. "Todt Hill is unique," he stated. "It offers all the provinciality and privacy of a small New England town, and yet it is completely cosmopolitan."

Mr. Vitale, who lives in an 1850 farmhouse on Four Corners Road, said many young executives from Brooklyn and Manhattan have bought homes on Todt Hill because it offers them a short commute to work. And, he added, there is a fair sprinkling of doctors, judges, lawyers, and other professionals.

Burglaries are the chief crime problem, although they are few in number, said William L. Murphy, the Staten Island district attorney. "But when there is a burglary, it tends to be a large one," he added.

There is one school, a private institution called Staten Island Academy. Its ten-acre campus at 715 Todt Hill Road accommodates about 450 students from kindergarten through high school. It attracts students from all over Staten Island, in part because it can offer classes with an average size of only fourteen. It also offers two swimming pools, tennis courts, soccer and hockey fields, an arts complex, and a computer laboratory.

"It's a small school and we don't want to have a very narrow socioeconomic spectrum," said J. Stevens Bean, the headmaster. Its tuition, he added, is lower than that of other independent schools such as Collegiate in Manhattan or Brooklyn Polytechnic, but it is higher than that of parochial schools.

The fees start at $2,400 a year in kindergarten and range up to about $4,600 in the senior year in high school. Financial aid is offered to families who need it. The academy graduates about thirty-five seniors a year and "virtually 100 percent go on to a four-year college," Mr. Bean said.

Parents who prefer public or religious-oriented schools for their children find a plethora of choices in the surrounding communities.

Todt Hill is convenient to the rest of the city. There is easy access to the Staten Island Expressway, which connects to the Verrazano-Narrows Bridge, and buses to the ferry run regularly on Richmond Road. Express buses that get passengers to midtown Manhattan in an hour or less can be boarded on the service roads of the expressway, as well as on nearby Victory Boulevard, Richmond Road, Clove Road, and Hylan Boulevard. The Staten Island Rapid Transit has a stop in Dongan Hills, just below Todt Hill.

The shopping areas along Richmond Road in New Dorp are minutes away by car, as is Hylan Boulevard, which has a variety of restaurants, clothing stores, supermarkets, and movie theaters. The nearest hospital is Doctors' Hospital at 1050 Targee Street in the Concord neighborhood.

There are two Catholic seminaries on Todt Hill. The larger of the two, St. Francis Seminary, at 500 Todt Hill Road, is situated on thirty-five rolling acres; it also includes a retreat house. The eight-acre St. Charles Seminary at 209 Flagg Place is also the home of its Center for Migration Studies, which does studies on immigration trends.

The best-known property in the neighborhood is the ninety-five-year-old Richmond County Country Club. The 550 families who are members have access to ten outdoor tennis courts and a swimming pool on the 8.5 shaded acres surrounding the main clubhouse, as well as to a 125-acre golf course, the last private links in New York City.

The club's facilities are often available for private functions, and its restaurant is considered one of the finest in the borough. The club's membership is no longer as exclusive as it once was (it was originally a hunt club). Nicholas Batos, club manager, said an effort had been made to make it more representative of Staten Island's population.

—LAWRENCE J. DEMARIA

T O T T E N V I L L E

To midtown Manhattan: Train, ferry, and subway 90 minutes

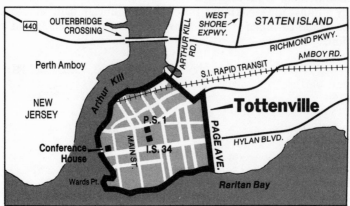

Tottenville: it sounds as if it should have a trolley. This southernmost town in New York State does not, but it does have a train, the Staten Island Rapid Transit (known to locals as the S.I.R.T.), which covers the fourteen miles from Tottenville to St. George in about thirty-seven minutes and costs 75 cents to ride.

Tottenville's residents live mainly in one-family houses, most of them more than fifty years old. The community has the air of a sleepy New Jersey town. Everything moves slowly in Tottenville: in 1982 the Staten Island Chamber of Commerce put its population at 6,969; in 1970 it was 6,379. There is even a Main Street, and there is nothing to do on Saturday night.

Bordered by Raritan Bay on the south, the Arthur Kill on the west and north, and Page Avenue on the east, Tottenville looks across the Arthur Kill at Perth Amboy, New Jersey, to which Staten Island is connected by the Outerbridge Crossing. The town was originally known as Billop's Point, after an English captain who in 1675 built a large house that still commands the bluff overlooking the Arthur Kill.

It was in the Billop House, now called the Conference House, that on September 11, 1776, after the Battle of Long Island, Benjamin Franklin, John Adams, and Edward Rutledge met with Lord Howe in an unsuccessful attempt to end the Revolutionary War. The Conference House is now a Registered National Historic Landmark. It is surrounded by a park that on a recent warm day had a sprinkling of tourists and young lovers walking the grounds.

Tottenville is steeped in history, but its long siesta may be nearing an end. "I can see a tremendous increase in values in that area," said Anthony R. Gaeta, the Staten Island borough president. "A few years ago, you couldn't give land away."

Despite spirited opposition by local residents, who for years had complained about a lack of sewers and other city services, construction has begun on a 900-unit condominium project near the waterfront with units priced at about $85,000 each. Builders are also putting homes on half-acre parcels between Hylan Boulevard and Amboy Road on Satterlee, Connecticut, and Aspinwall streets.

"There is nothing there for under $150,000," said Robert E. Lanning, a partner in J. P. Walsh Real Estate and until recently one of Staten Island's two appraisers for the Veterans and Federal Housing administrations. He noted, however, that "the knowledgeable buyer, the patient buyer" can still find bargains.

"I see a lot of houses that have been sold for $75,000 to $90,000," Mr. Lanning said, adding that such houses, often colonials with large rooms, are "solid" and "mortgageable," with sound heating, plumbing, and electrical systems. "In the $85,000 range, you could get a classic house, a beauty," and there are even "habitable" bungalows near the water in the $45,000 range.

As for crime, Tottenville's residents have little to fear. They have what amounts to their own police precinct, the 123rd, with a station house right on Main Street.

"It's the best place in the city, crimewise," said Officer Joseph Borg, who lives in New Brighton. "You don't have to worry when you walk down the street about getting mugged." The major crime is burglary.

How does he like Tottenville? "It's like being upstate," Officer Borg answered. "There's lots of woods for the kids to enjoy. I take my kids out here to see rabbits and pheasants."

Down Main Street from the station house, just before the S.I.R.T. tracks and the Arthur Kill, is what must be the southernmost bar in the state—Pickles, owned by David ("Pickles") Walters, a retired fireman. He said he was born in Tottenville, as was his mother ("she had twenty-three children, all dead but me") and grandmother, who died at the age of 104 ("just after the talking pictures came in—her name was Totten").

Tottenville "used to be more lively," Mr. Walters said, pointing out the window. "All these homes were paid for by oystermen. They also went clamming and lobstering. But the oil boats came in and sort of drove the fishermen out."

Mr. Walters's tavern is a little different from the typical New York bar. It sells beer for 30 cents and scotch for a dollar. The telephone company took out the pay phone not long ago because it was not generating enough revenue.

Tottenville has other taverns and a roller rink on Main Street called Fantasy Island, but no movie theaters. There also is a community center, paid for by the Tottenville Improvement Council. The center is in Intermediate School 34, the old Tottenville High School building on Yetman Avenue. Just down the street is P.S. 1, which houses a day-care center also paid for by the council. Across the street from P.S. 1 is Our Lady Help of Christians, a Roman Catholic parochial school.

I.S. 34 gets its 1,400 students from Tottenville's P.S. 1, P.S. 36 in Annadale, P.S. 4 in Village Greens, and P.S. 3 in Pleasant Plains. Built in 1896, I.S. 34 has an addition, built in 1907. Despite its age it is an "exceptional" school, according to officials of the public school system, who said a replacement is in their capital budget. P.S. 1 also is highly rated.

The new Tottenville High School, set on a twenty-six-acre tract, is not in Tottenville but 4.5 miles away in Huguenot. Opened in 1972, it draws 4,300 students from southern Staten Island. Its principal, Joseph K. Fisler, was born in Tottenville and still lives there. He said that the school sends 70 percent of its graduates to college, some to Ivy League schools. But it also has strong "career courses" that work closely with large Manhattan companies. The school's word processing and computer laboratories, he said, prepare many graduates for jobs in those companies. "Many of our kids follow in the footsteps of their parents," said Mr. Fisler, whose own daughter is in the school.

En route to Tottenville, the S.I.R.T. stops at twenty-two stations. It has modern cars, ticket sellers, and conductors who know many commuters by name. It lacks both crime and graffiti, and is often on time. "It's probably the most reliable means of transportation we have on Staten Island, and in the city," Mr. Gaeta said.

The S.I.R.T. and the No. 113 and No. 103 buses are direct links to the ferry terminal in St. George. From there it is a twenty-five-minute ride across the harbor to lower Manhattan and about twenty minutes more by subway to midtown. That makes a long commute of about an hour and a half, but the alternative is an only slightly shorter auto trip by way of the Outerbridge Crossing or the Goethals, Bayonne, or Verrazano-Narrows bridges. There also is express bus service to Manhattan.

"It takes me about an hour to get to work," reported Arthur Femenella of Fisher Avenue, who drives in to his stained-glass business in Manhattan by way of the West Shore Expressway, the New Jersey Turnpike, and the Holland Tunnel.

Tottenville has a synagogue and six churches. It also has large expanses of vacant woodland and beach area. The entire south shore of Staten Island is noted for its Little League teams. And while the beaches are unkempt, crabbing and fishing for flounder, bluefish, and stripers have always been good.

There is also a marina for private boats at the foot of Ellis Street. And Tottenville has its own city pool and a racquet club. Golfers tee off at the nearby South Shore Golf Course.

The area has plenty of local shopping, but MJ's, near the Outerbridge, is the only restaurant of note. However, the Sleepy Hollow Inn on Bloomingdale Road, in nearby Woodrow, is locally renowned.

—LAWRENCE J. DEMARIA

WEST BRIGHTON

To midtown Manhattan: Bus, ferry, and subway 50 minutes; bus 45 minutes

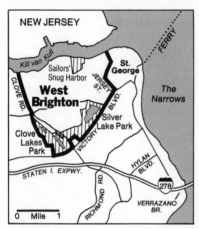

Officially, West Brighton doesn't exist. That's all right with its residents, none of whom care if their corner of Staten Island is ever discovered. To them, West Brighton is the thwack of tennis balls at Walker Park. It is the happy squeals of children sledding at Silver Lake. It is the raucous parade down Forest Avenue the Sunday before St. Patrick's Day. It is the nineteenth-century headstones stumbled upon unexpectedly in the forgotten cemetery in Randall Manor.

The Hagstrom map of Staten Island shows a "West New Brighton," which stretches from Clove Road on the west to Jersey Street on the east, and from the Kill van Kull on the north to Clove Lakes Park and Silver Lake Park on the south. That makes a lot of real-estate people happy, since houses that can be advertised with a "West" anywhere near their "Brighton" can be sold at a premium.

"Originally, there was only New Brighton," recalled Ralph J. Lamberti, the deputy borough president. "Then the western part became West New Brighton. Now it's West Brighton. I was born in West Brighton. I still live in West Brighton. I'm an old West Brighton boy."

If the borough has a political breeding ground, it probably is West Brighton. Many of the people who have held the top borough offices, including the current borough president, Anthony R. Gaeta,

214

are West Brighton–born. Its former United States representative, John M. Murphy, still lives there.

While a statistical guide compiled by the Staten Island Chamber of Commerce shows that West Brighton has had little population growth in the last decade, the section does get infusions of new blood. Many people from "the city" are beginning to realize that West Brighton's proximity to the Staten Island ferry in St. George makes it an easy place from which to commute to Manhattan. The ferry ride takes twenty-five minutes.

Buses plying Forest, Castleton, and Henderson avenues and Richmond Terrace all stop at the ferry terminal. There also is a rather informal taxi service in which people who live in the same neighborhood share rides and split fares.

Another way to go is a forty-five-minute express bus service to midtown Manhattan. One route goes through New Jersey and the Lincoln Tunnel and the other over the Verrazano-Narrows Bridge and through Brooklyn.

Jennifer Straniere, the treasurer of the Staten Island Civic Theater, based at Christ Episcopal Church on 76 Franklin Avenue, said that West Brighton also is attracting people "who make their living in the arts," because it offers both high-quality housing and neighbors who strongly support local theater. The Civic Theater has benefited by an influx of talent from Manhattan.

Many of the people who moved to West Brighton also are attracted by the variety of housing available. Livingston and Randall Manor, two of the half-dozen smaller sections that constitute the community, has turn of the century Victorians that offer large rooms, fireplaces, turrets, and heavily treed lots. Houses designed or inspired by Stanford White are common.

The average price for a house in West Brighton is about $120,000, but in the Randall Manor section the average slides up to about $175,000, according to figures compiled by Otto Vitale Real Estate. Local brokers say house prices have appreciated around 20 percent in the last two years.

But there are many large but run-down houses available for under $50,000 that might tempt buyers unafraid of a big remodeling project. The private, nonprofit Neighborhood Housing Service of West Brighton administers a revolving loan fund available to qualified homeowners who want to make improvements. The service has a staff rehabilitation specialist and also offers workshops and helps set up block associations. Its office is at 1196 Castleton Avenue, and its telephone number is 442-8080.

The area also has garden and other kinds of apartments. A modern two-bedroom apartment in a good neighborhood rents for about $500 a month.

The 120th Precinct, with headquarters in St. George, covers West Brighton. Officers report very little violent crime, but they concede that there is a significant burglary problem, although it is small in comparison to other sections of the city.

"West Brighton is not only safe, but in the rare incidents where crime does occur, the community is supportive of the victims," said William L. Murphy, Staten Island's district attorney, who has lived in West Brighton all his life. "Strangers come to the attention of people here," he said. "I have a feeling the criminal element knows that."

There are five public elementary schools and two intermediate schools serving 4,000 students in West Brighton. All the public schools have small class sizes, "better than anywhere else on Staten Island," said Christy Cugini, deputy superintendent of Community School District 31, which covers all of Staten Island. The majority of students in West Brighton are zoned into Susan E. Wagner High School in Seaview, one of six secondary schools on Staten Island. Wagner officials say about 40 percent of the school's graduates go on to four-year colleges.

Five Roman Catholic elementary schools and one high school, St. Peter's Boys High School, serve about 2,000 students, some from other sections of Staten Island.

The two parks forming the southern boundary of the community are its major recreational resources. Silver Lake Park has two large man-made lakes, an eighteen-hole golf course, tennis courts, and ball fields, and Clove Lakes Park has four lakes, playgrounds, ball fields, riding trails, and an ice rink. Fishing and boating are allowed. In addition, there is Walker Park, off Davis Avenue near Richmond Terrace, which offers tennis and cricket.

Near Clove Lakes is the Staten Island Zoo, which has a widely acclaimed reptile collection and the normal run of lions and tigers, as well as a children's petting zoo.

For cultural events, West Brightonites can turn not only to the Civic Theater but also to the Y.M.C.A., the public library, and the Sailors' Snug Harbor Cultural Center. Snug Harbor used to house retired mariners, but it is now home to the Newhouse Art Gallery, antique fairs, theater groups, and other attractions.

There is a mile-long stretch of taverns along Forest Avenue extending from Hart Boulevard to Clove Road that is known as "the strip." Many cater to the luncheon trade, which includes many of the lawyers, judges, and politicians who work in nearby St. George. Blaine's, on "the strip," and Roscoe's, on nearby Castleton Avenue, are among the most popular spots. Also on Forest Avenue are the Staaten; Pal Joey's, an Italian restaurant noted for its pizza; and Framboise, which serves highly regarded French food.

The Forest and Castleton Avenue areas are also known for their delis and specialty shops, including Edith Susskind's well-known gift shop on Castleton. Even people who move to other parts of Staten Island—other parts of the country, for that matter—come back for cold cuts from Dick's Deli on Castleton Avenue.

If West Brighton is anything, it is stable. Some of its families have been there for two or three generations, and many neighbors have known one another since grammar school. Youngsters are often taught or coached by men and women who grew up with their parents. And it is not unusual for children who get in trouble to wind up with only a stern lecture from a cop or a judge who grew up with, and got into scrapes with, their fathers.

"You go to the stores and you know everyone," said Deborah Thompson, who lives in the Livingston section. "There's a lot to do. You can walk anywhere you want to go. On the South Shore you have to get in your car. Here, you can play tennis at Silver Lake or Walker Park, and the pace is slower."

—LAWRENCE J. DEMARIA

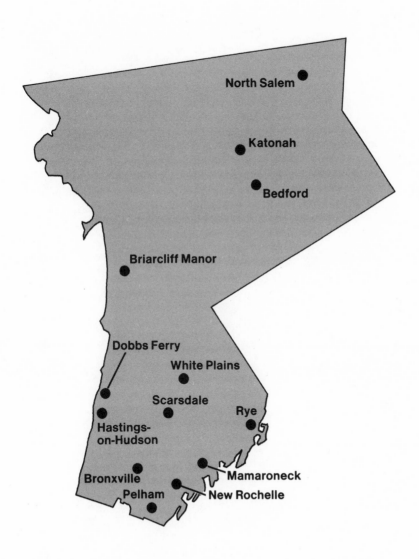

North Salem

Katonah

Bedford

Briarcliff Manor

Dobbs Ferry

White Plains

Scarsdale

Rye

Hastings-
on-Hudson

Bronxville

Mamaroneck

Pelham

New Rochelle

BEDFORD

*To midtown Manhattan: Train 75
minutes*

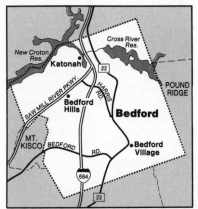

If the town of Bedford in
northern Westchester County has one symbol, it probably is the
Bedford Oak on Route 22, which some say is 400 years old. A few
years ago, a developer sought permission to build a house next to
the open field where the aged tree stands alone. Concern that sew-
age might damage its roots touched off a fund-raising effort that
amassed $51,000 from contributors as far away as California.

With the money, the Bedford Historical Society purchased the
land and had $11,000 left over for what Donald W. Marshall, the
town's historian, calls "the tree's own trust fund" to keep it pruned
and safe. The event tells a good deal about how the 15,100 people in
this 303-year-old community of large estates and horse farms forty
miles north of Manhattan respect their town's past and its rural
character.

It all began in December 1680, the story goes, when twenty-two
men from Connecticut purchased 7,600 acres from the Indians; the
following year they laid out Bedford. In 1700, King William III of
England settled a New York–Connecticut border dispute in New
York's favor, making Bedford part of Westchester.

Today, the town's thirty-six square miles of fields, estates, and
rolling hills contain three hamlets near which most of the population
lives. The offices of town government are in one of them, Bedford
Hills. Rail commuters to New York City board their trains there and

221

at Katonah, a second hamlet, whose Metro-North station parking lot often contains cars with Connecticut license plates. From either station, express service takes about an hour and a quarter to Grand Central Terminal in Manhattan.

The third hamlet is Bedford Village, whose Green and 1787 courthouse in the southerly section of town evoke images of New England. In 1972 the Green, which is surrounded by white clapboard shops and a pre–Revolutionary War cemetery, was listed in the National Register of Historic Places.

With Mount Kisco on the west and Pound Ridge on the east, Bedford is pierced by the Saw Mill River Parkway and Interstate 684, two major north-south thoroughfares that meet at the town's northern border near the Croton and Cross River reservoirs. The reservoirs form part of New York City's water system.

"This is rural, not suburban," said Herbert C. Neumann, the town's highway superintendent, who noted with some satisfaction that of the town's 110 miles of roads, thirty-one miles are unpaved. "Here it's like death to suggest that they be paved," said Town Supervisor Robert D. Hazzard. "A lot of residents work in New York City, and after a pressure day they like to come home and drive down their dirt roads, even though they're dusty."

Most of the town is zoned for residential lots of at least four acres, but estates of twenty acres are common. Farms on which owners graze horses—and even cattle—are often three times that size.

Large estates with barns, other outbuildings, and stone fences often command $350,000 and more. Dan Bixler, a leading real-estate broker with an office on the Green, said that although "we don't see $1 million sales every day," a sprawling house with more than ten acres that was built in the 1920's was listed recently at $1.2 million. More typical, he said, is a new five-bedroom house on 4.5 acres that was listed at $355,000.

Many homeowners allow members of the Bedford Riding Lanes Association to canter across their property on more than 200 miles of trails marked with small, yellow-and-black signs. The 250 members, who pay up to $125 a year in dues, also use the trails for nature walks and snowmobiling.

Shopping is clustered along main streets in the three hamlets. There are A & P supermarkets in Bedford Village and in Katonah, and a Caldor's and Shop-Rite in Bedford Hills, where a large part of the town's commercial and light industrial development has been placed along Bedford Road and Adams Street.

Close to Bedford Hills and Katonah are garden apartment houses varying in density from nine to twelve units an acre and groups of two-family dwellings. The 1980 census showed 1,234 renter-occupied units in the town and 3,451 units occupied by their owners.

BEDFORD

Building development "slowed to a dead halt" during recent periods of high interest rates, said R. Bradlee Boal, chairman of the Town Planning Board. But now, he added, a forty-nine-unit condominium development in Katonah is "going ahead."

Bedford Mews, a 160-unit community on Harris Road in Bedford Hills, is the most recently completed multifamily development, Mr. Boal stated. There, units of one, two, or three bedrooms are selling for between $85,000 and $120,000.

As in other communities, rising costs have made many of the largest estates too heavy a burden, and their owners have split them up over the years. A new zoning code effective in 1983 legitimized accessory apartments such as caretakers' cottages on such estates and also on more modest properties.

What kind of people live in Bedford? "The growth area has been in the middle- and upper-middle-income brackets," Mr. Boal said. "They work for General Foods and I.B.M. in Westchester and at Xerox in Stamford." Mr. Bixler, the real-estate broker, said his figures showed that 62 percent of recent home buyers were in the thirty-one to forty age group, with 16 percent between the ages of forty-one and fifty.

The town's relatively large lots and low density, according to Mr. Boal, make for an atmosphere of relative anonymity. "You can live here and not get involved. But if you don't like the country or are afraid of skunks, that's the wrong attitude."

Although there is a town water system covering a small percentage of homes, most houses have their own wells and septic systems. There are no sewers.

Property tax rates vary between $54 and $60 per $1,000 of assessed valuation, depending on location, according to Lawrence E. Dryer, the receiver of taxes. Houses are assessed at about 45 percent of full value, so the annual taxes on a house worth $100,000 are about $2,600.

The town shares two school districts—Bedford Central and Katonah-Lewisboro. Children in the northern quarter of town attend John Jay High School, in the town of Lewisboro, about a mile east of the Bedford line. John Jay has 900 students in grades ten through twelve, and sends about 70 percent of its graduates to four-year colleges. Children in the southern part go to Fox Lane High School, which has 1,225 students in grades nine through twelve. It sends about 75 percent of its seniors to four-year colleges.

The three hamlets have features in common. Each has a library, a volunteer fire-fighting force, and a town park with a swimming pool, tennis courts, and baseball and soccer fields. On Memorial Day, each has its own service of commemoration and a parade with bands, Boy Scouts, and veterans.

223

BEDFORD

The town provides a thirty-one-member police force, the Highway Department, Tax Assessor, and Town Clerk, among other governmental offices.

Among the town's cultural resources is the John Jay Homestead. Standing on a section of Route 22 called Jay Street, it is a national landmark owned by the state and is open to visitors as a museum from Memorial Day to Labor Day. Built in 1787, the same year the courthouse was put up, the house was the home of John Jay—the first chief justice of the United States and later New York governor—from 1795 to 1801.

The Katonah Gallery exhibits art works lent by museums and artists and allows members to borrow them. The gallery is in the lower level of the library.

At the Caramoor Center for Music and the Arts, once a private home on Route 137, a music festival is held each summer. The house, which is built around a courtyard and is furnished opulently, is open to visitors.

—FRANKLIN WHITEHOUSE

BRIARCLIFF MANOR

To midtown Manhattan: Train 45 minutes

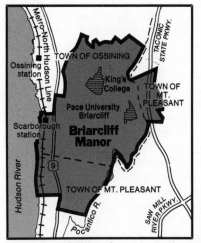

People who live here wouldn't think of living anyplace else," a real-estate agent said of Briarcliff Manor, as she gestured over the tops of chimneys, each bespeaking several hundred thousand dollars of dwellings, toward the Hudson River down the hill. And it is true. It is hard to find residents or officials unhappy with their lot in this Westchester County suburb, from high-school students destroying awe-inspiring sundaes in the soda fountain, to elbows-out white-haired women digging up garden borders, to members driving to the top of the hill to the Sleepy Hollow Country Club, a Stanford White redoubt where one joins only when someone else dies.

Briarcliff Manor is forty-five minutes from Grand Central Terminal on Metro-North's Hudson line, convenient to all of Westchester's major parkways and the Governor Thomas E. Dewey Thruway. The village proper contains 7,100 people living in six well-forested square miles, air-cooled by the river, most of it with no need for baffle walls against humming traffic.

Its modest 1930's-style downtown—with fancy groceries where one can buy Saga cheese and the Images Gallery, which stocks Sovjani watercolors and hand-carved furniture, but where one can still buy a bag of nails—is not being drained dry by any strip-zoning shopping center just out of town. Its 1,800 households are governed by a mayor and trustees, all unpaid, and day-to-day affairs are di-

225

rected by a paid appointed administrator. Politics is thus sober, non-partisan, and zoning-conscious.

The village's premier historic figure, Walter W. Law, at the turn of the century built frame cottages for the townspeople—that is to say, his Briarcliff Farm employees—when he was seeking to have the area incorporated to give him taxing power to provide municipal services.

Law used his own land, built the houses, and sold them to the workers on attractive terms, holding the mortgages himself. In 1902 *The New York Times* recorded the successful vote for incorporation, noting Mr. Law's clubs and saying, "He takes a keen interest in municipal improvement and, it is said, will spend much money to make Briarcliff Manor a model village."

The soda fountain downtown is named the Yellow Brick Road, and it may be that Briarcliff Manor residents consider that Mr. Law succeeded and their village is the one to be found over the rainbow.

There is one catch to it all, and no one makes any bones about it. Briarcliff Manor is not a first-house town. House prices are too high, with $125,000 about the lowest, and turnover is too low. Permits to add another bedroom to small houses are more common than sales, said Anthony Turiano, the village assessor. "People just don't want to move away," he added. "We get people moving up the ladder and they add on or move up and stay." Mr. Turiano estimated the annual number of house sales in the village at fewer than a hundred these days, and he and real-estate agents believe that fifty or sixty of these may be to new people.

The village has 150 or so rental apartments, in three units, plus North Hills, which contains ninety-seven apartments for the elderly. Scarborough Manor, a tall apartment building near the river, now a co-op, is just north of the village, in Ossining. There are waiting lists for these gateways into the village.

Agents say that the houses that do come on the market most often acquire "For Sale" signs as a by-product of a divorce, and these tend to be larger houses. The other reasons people give up Briarcliff Manor, its adherents say, are death in the family and, with decreasing frequency, business transfers. The average price of these larger houses, according to the Carolyn Dwyer agency, ranges from $250,000 to $300,000.

The cottages Law built, on Dalmeny and Poplar roads and other places in the village, have distinctive, steep Hansel and Gretel roofs and are spaced well apart on half an acre. But open porches use up part of the downstairs, and the living space, said to be different in each house, is small. Even these houses, when they come on the market, cost $125,000 to $150,000. Newer homes, under construction in three separate subdivisions in the eastern area of Briarcliff Manor, cost between $300,000 and $495,000. They are on one-half to one-and-a-half acre sites and include luxury amenities, according to Lois Seiden of Lois Seiden Real Estate.

Law's projects fill the village, and the tastes and beliefs of the founder, who was a partner in W. & J. Sloane, the furniture store, before he became a gentleman farmer on a large scale, are demonstrated everywhere. The resort lodge he built as an outlet for the products of his farm is now part of King's College, a state-accredited evangelical college, and his manor house is a dormitory.

Robert Marville, the unpaid head of the village planning board, said Law's concept of developing the town in an orderly fashion while retaining a rural atmosphere has held on. This kind of development, Mr. Marville believes, has attracted people committed to the same ideas and has enabled the town to be governed largely by unpaid residents.

Briarcliff Manor lies in two towns—Ossining and Mount Pleasant—and two public school districts. The records of the latter stack up well against the best in other parts of Westchester. In addition to King's College, the village is also home to a division of Pace University, once known as Briarcliff College. The village also has its protecting border rivers, the Hudson and the Pocantico, and a cozy public library in a former railroad station on the New York Central's Putnam division. Philips Laboratories and the Frank B. Hall insurance company headquarters, employing a total of 250 people, help to keep the tax base solid.

The community also has tough attitudes toward development: there is still land to be built on in the village, and the zoning rule requires one acre or an acre and a half for a house. Much of what keeps the hopefuls pounding on the door in preference to nearby towns with similar blessings and possibly smaller price tags is probably embodied in the recreation network.

The park system began in 1918 with a donation by Law of seven acres that now are part of Law Park, in the middle of town, bordering on the Middle School. It provides a big swimming pool, a pond, tennis courts, platform tennis courts, and baseball diamonds. By the mid-1970's, the village was operating 208 acres of parks, including a sanctuary along the Pocantico.

In the summer, organized programs and lessons are provided in Law Park, the Chilmark Recreation Area, and schools around the village. People paying property taxes of $2,700 to more than $6,000 a year mentally deduct the costs of tennis club membership or a camp for younger children.

The future probably holds change in quantity but not in quality. The Daitch-Shopwell supermarket in the Chilmark Shopping Center is expanding into a Food Emporium. There were letters of complaint to the local paper, but the expansion was approved.

The thirty-four-acre Beechwood Estate has been redeveloped

tastefully with thirty-four town-house condominiums in clusters, while preserving the grounds and the huge mansion, now divided into three condominium units. And the Wilderness, an area of 145 acres on the south end of town, is being developed with 116 condominiums.

But growth will not happen in a rush. "In 1954–55, 115 houses were built," Mr. Turiano recalled. "That was a high-water mark. We won't see that again. We've got a good planning board and they want only the best."

—BETSY WADE

B R O N X V I L L E

To midtown Manhattan: Train 30 minutes

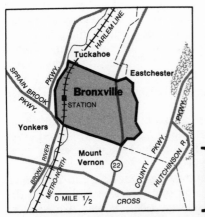

Bronxville started small, a community filling only one square mile, and it has remained that size, maintaining the village atmosphere that has been its hallmark. It is something special and splendid among Westchester suburbs, and it remains as similar to its origin as it is possible to be.

Lewis Mumford has referred to the suburbs that were built between 1850 and 1920 as owing their existence primarily to railroads. In his *The City in History,* he cited Bronxville as one of the new communities that were "discontinous and properly spaced." He wrote that "as long as the railroad stop and walking distances controlled suburban growth, the suburb had a form."

The form that the community has maintained is classic, both in living style and architecture. Although there have been some changes, most notably in the conversion of rental apartments to cooperatives and condominiums, Bronxville looks today much as it did in the 1930's, when three decades of development were all but completed.

This community of 6,200 people is tucked into the south-central portion of the county, and it is just twenty-eight minutes and fifteen miles by train from Grand Central Terminal. It is part of the town of Eastchester, but it has a personality all its own. Gracious houses, many in the Victorian or Tudor style, range beyond the downtown shopping district along roads that often follow the contours of the village's many hills.

It has long held a reputation as a heavily Republican and largely Protestant community, and as an enclave of the wealthy. If that is still the case, it is less so in each category.

For example, Monsignor Patrick J. Sheridan of St. Joseph's Roman Catholic Church, which serves a parish of 3,000 members that extends beyond the village's borders, said he thought Bronxville was "perhaps 20 to 25 percent Catholic." There are several Protestant churches but no synagogue.

As for politics, Republicans outregister Democrats by more than three to one, and few Democrats are ever elected village trustee. However, a heavy crossover vote in Bronxville not long ago helped to elect a Democrat, James Doody, as Eastchester town supervisor.

The 1980 census showed that the largest income category was "$75,000 or more" and the next largest "$50,000 to $75,000." House prices reflect those facts.

Joan Harris Spencer, a real-estate broker, said that of twenty-four houses recently for sale in the village, three were listed over $100,000, eight over $200,000, five over $300,000, seven over $400,000, and one was "quite expensive."

Some of the finest and most interesting houses are in Lawrence Park, Bronxville's oldest section and one that was included in the National Register of Historic Places in 1980. It was named after William Van Duzer Lawrence, who bought much of the hilly farm in 1889 as an investment for his children.

He restored its manor house and, as an experiment, built twelve houses in parklike settings. The residences, some of them clinging to rocky perches, quickly became popular with writers and artists, and then with the professional people commuting to New York City.

Bronxville has a slightly English flavor, with lots of stucco and fieldstone, many houses in the Tudor style, and even some Victorian dowagers, usually on small plots. A "really big house might be on an acre of land," Ms. Spencer stated, "but the typical house is on one half to two thirds of an acre."

Most houses in Bronxville, she reported, sell for $250,000 to $500,000 "and they are everywhere; you can't say there is a $250,000 neighborhood." This is partly because of the village's size. While larger suburbs often experienced waves of development, producing architectural differences section by section, Bronxville's building came in one rolling wave, with varieties of style on each street.

Almost nothing is dramatically modern, and there is little chance of anything becoming so. James E. Gordon, the village administrator, said there had been very little construction in recent years "and there are only fourteen building lots left." Change comes slowly, and that seems to suit most of the village's residents, according to Mayor William Murphy.

A few years ago, he said, an attempt was made to install sodium lights throughout the village, but the plan was abandoned in the face of public pressure. Opponents likened the orange glow to a supermarket parking lot.

"The new lights would have saved an annual $30,000, and more later," Mr. Murphy said, "but people said, 'We'll pay the $5 and $10 a year; keep the old lights.'"

Bronxville's apartment buildings, clustered for the most part near the shopping area and railroad station and containing nearly 40 percent of the village's residents, offer the same elegant atmosphere as many single-family homes, often dating from the same periods.

There are luxury co-ops, including older structures with apartments of up to seven rooms and newer, smaller units with balconies overlooking the Bronx River. There are also two-story, Tudor-style cooperatives, so-called garden apartments of up to three bedrooms.

"The average co-op goes for $130,000 to $225,000," Ms. Spencer said. "The garden apartments range from $95,000 to $250,000."

There are also the community houses, attached town houses in clusters of two to eight. The fifty-year-old structures were originally rental units but are now owned by their residents. Built in English, Norman, colonial, and Mediterranean styles, they resemble elegant little alleys in Manhattan's Murray Hill area and sell for $150,000 to $250,000.

The newest condominium is Hilltop, on the site of the Gramatan Hotel, where thirty-six attached town houses with cathedral ceilings, travertine marble fireplaces, and top-floor studios sell for $250,000 to $325,000. Property taxes there are $6,000 for a two-bedroom unit.

Property taxes in Bronxville are generally high. For a typical house with an assessed valuation of $49,800, which means a market value of about $250,000, the total tax—county, town, and school district—is $6,329, according to John W. Gallaway, Bronxville's assessor and deputy treasurer.

The village has a twenty-three-member police force, twice-weekly garbage pickup from behind the houses, four fall leaf pickups from the curb, a village firehouse, a library, and some tennis and paddle tennis courts, but few ball fields outside the school athletic area. There is no village pool.

Bronxville has an excellent school system. Almost all of the high-school graduates go on to higher education. The system has an enrollment of about 1,100 and a student-teacher ratio of 17 to 1.

Dr. William H. Greenham, the superintendent of schools, said students were "subject oriented" and scored very well on the Scholastic Aptitude Test—well above 500 in verbal ability and about 550 in mathematics. (The national averages are in the 400's.)

Bronxville also has Concordia College, the 281-bed Lawrence Hospital, and a downtown shopping area that serves more than the community itself. There are several worthwhile restaurants, among them Le Bistro, Izumi, Tumbledown Dick's, Town Tavern, The Alps, and The Tap. Sarah Lawrence College, in adjacent Yonkers, is within the Bronxville postal district, which extends beyond the village's border.

—JAMES FERON

D O B B S   F E R R Y

To midtown Manhattan: Train 35 minutes

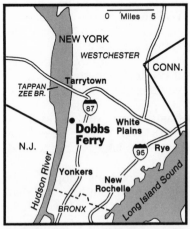

On sunny Saturdays in Dobbs Ferry, girls from the Masters School, dressed by Bean and shod by Bass, stroll down the hill to the Grand Union and shop for snacks alongside matrons in designer jeans who assess the eggplant with practiced fingers.

On autumn weekends, hundreds of residents in this historic Westchester County village of 10,053 attend high-school football games at Gould Park.

After mass on Sundays, descendants of Italians who arrived in this hilly Hudson River village in the 1880's gather in the Caffe Vesuvius on Cedar Street for live broadcasts of soccer games from Rome.

On Thursday nights, the Ferry Inn hires two extra bartenders to accommodate the students from Mercy College who congregate for beer and taped rock music.

On the Fourth of July, everybody gathers in the Hudson breezes for a picnic and entertainment in Waterfront Park.

This is life in Dobbs Ferry, a mix of suburban affluence, ethnic traditions, local pride, and boosterism—in short, an extraordinary diversity for so small a community.

In its housing mix as well, this village, from which William Dobbs's eighteenth-century ferryboat crossed the Hudson to Rock-land County, is a testimonial to diversity. Within its borders—the

Hudson on the west and the Saw Mill River Parkway on the east—
are represented nearly every style of American architecture, according to Karen Kennedy, an architectural historian who lives in Rye.
Washington once made his headquarters in the now-vanished Hyatt-
Livingston estate, which, in the nineteenth century, became one of
the large private properties that arriving Italian immigrants helped to
maintain, she said.

Houses of the 1920's, 1930's, and 1940's were built on the twist-
ing, narrow roads 400 feet above the village's old stone railroad
station, where former Mayor Colon W. Reed, a Manhattan lawyer,
and 450 other regular commuters board Metro-North's Hudson line
trains for the thirty-six-minute trip to jobs in New York City. Commuters complain of insufficient seating, lack of air-conditioning in
the summer, and late trains. By car, it is a forty-minute drive from
midtown Manhattan, by way of the Saw Mill River Parkway to the
Ashford Avenue exit.

Frederick W. Streb, a leading real-estate broker, said the average
price of a single-family house is about $185,000. "We've lacked the
public relations that the Bronxvilles and Scarsdales have gotten so
we have better dollar values."

Several well-known doctors and "United Nations people" who
"want their seclusion" live here, Mr. Streb noted. But he added that
"carpenters, plumbers, and electricians who work in the lower Hudson Valley" live here, too.

Tudor and Mediterranean Revival mansions built early in this century with vistas of Ardsley Country Club fairways are set back from
the river. Some of the newer houses on Villard Hill have spectacular
views through oak and elm to the river and its Palisades beyond.

Halfway down the hillside, along Main and Palisade streets in the
middle of town, many houses are framed in wood with their original
clapboards stuccoed over by immigrant owners filled with nostalgia
for the south of Italy. Many Main Street dwellings contain ground-
floor shops—hardware and shoe stores, a beauty parlor, a pharmacy,
a pizzeria, and other enterprises.

Six-story apartment houses, the earliest built in the late 1920's,
stand along Broadway (Route 9), which links the village with Hast-
ings-on-Hudson to the south and Irvington to the north. Many of the
apartments have been converted to cooperative ownership in recent
years with prices of $55,000 to $95,000. When rental apartments are
available, they range in cost from $350 for studios to $800 for three-
bedroom suites.

The village is one of six incorporated communities in the town of
Greenburgh. Former Mayor Reed acknowledged that the village
needs more private industry to produce tax ratables. Mr. Streb estimated that with The Masters School, Mercy College, Children's
Village, and seven religious institutions, about 35 percent of the as-

sessable property in the 2.4-square-mile village is exempt from taxes. Taxes are $213.32 per $1,000 assessed valuation, based on village, town, school district, county, and sewer district levies. The taxes on a typical $150,000 home in Dobbs Ferry, depending on location and age of the structure, would be approximately $4,000.

Children's Village employs 350 psychiatrists, psychologists, and others who care for 300 emotionally disturbed boys in the government-supported institution. About 80 percent of the boys, who range in age from six to fifteen, are black and Hispanic, mostly from New York City. Children's Village moved from the city to its woods-surrounded, 200-acre campus here in 1905. The boys live in twenty-one cottages built after World War I in Tudor and chalet style and attend remedial classes at the George S. Leisure School on the site.

Mercy College opened in 1961 on a campus that slopes gently toward the river from its entrance on Broadway. Run by the Sisters of Mercy, the four-year college is a nonsectarian, commuter school that confers associate degrees in the arts and sciences. There are 4,000 students, 62 percent of whom are over twenty-five, according to a spokesman, John Modzelewski. Many are attracted by the school's criminal justice and accounting programs.

At The Masters School, a 108-year-old prep school on Clinton Avenue, many of the students who once went off to eastern women's colleges such as Vassar and Smith, now matriculate at Harvard, Duke, and Sweetbriar as well, according to the headmaster, John H. Wright, Jr. Of the 150 Masters students who come from Westchester homes, fewer than a dozen live in Dobbs Ferry, Mr. Wright said. "It's not a very rich little town," he added.

More than 300 persons are employed by the largest private-sector business in town, the Stauffer Chemical Company, according to William Williams, the village administrator. Stauffer owns a research and engineering building on Livingston Avenue, part of which it leases to I.B.M.

Two other major employers, with sixty workers each, are Oceana Publications, Inc., which publishes books on international law, and Morgan Press, Inc., which prints fine museum and art books as well as technical photographic volumes.

Several Hudson River towns have lost population since the 1970 census. This village showed a 2.9 percent drop, according to the 1980 figures. One reflection of the decline is found in the public schools. In 1969–70 the school system had 1,694 students. Now there are about a thousand, according to Dr. Raymond J. Gerson, the superintendent. Well over half the graduating classes enter four-year colleges.

Crime is not limited to traffic violations. Burglary is "a sore spot" and vandalism "a problem," according to Police Chief James F. Neal.

D O B B S   F E R R Y

News of Dobbs Ferry appears in *The Enterprise,* which also covers Hastings and Ardsley. The weekly has fifteen reporters and a circulation of about 3,000. The village's only movie theater, the Pickwick on Cedar Street, shows first-run films, but only on weekends. The public library, with 34,000 volumes and a stock of for-loan toys, is in a small Tudor-style building at the corner of Cedar and Main. The staff cheerfully answers reference questions.

—FRANKLIN WHITEHOUSE

HASTINGS-ON-HUDSON

To midtown Manhattan: Train 40 minutes

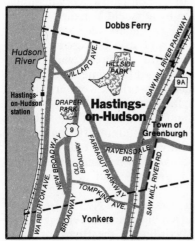

Hastings-on-Hudson was named after Hastings, England, or so the story goes, because the hilly nature of the Westchester County village reminded an early settler of the cliffs of the British coastal town. More than a century later, those features remain an important part of the community's personality.

Arthur O. Riolo, a real-estate broker, said that Hastings consists mainly of three hills and a valley. The steeper slopes, laced by winding roads, provide settings for homes that seem comfortably nestled behind stone walls or shrubs. And for those with westward vistas, there are the magnificent Palisades on the opposite shore of the Hudson River.

The shopping district below, with its small-town atmosphere, stretches along Warburton Avenue parallel to the river. It is part of a downtown section that almost seems part of a separate community, containing shops, offices, apartments, and condominiums, and, along the Hudson, vestiges of a once-thriving industrial waterfront.

Diversity, in fact, may be Hastings' hallmark—in its geographical features, types of housing and architectural styles, and, most significantly for many of its residents, in the population itself. Hastings is more than a bedroom community; it is a suburb that virtually defies definition.

The village's first industry, a century and a half ago, was the quarrying of sandstone and marble, an operation that drew Irish immigrants to a community of mostly tenant farmers. In the late 1800's it became the site of sugar refining, which attracted German immigrants. Later, a deep-water port added more industry and jobs.

But others were coming to this riverside community—"city people of medium wealth who established country estates," according to Karolyn Wrightson, past president of the Hastings Historical Society. They were afraid to incorporate as a village, she said, because of the "rabble vote" that could prove to be politically overwhelming, but did so in 1879 to resist annexation by adjacent Yonkers.

This parallel development of Hastings, meanwhile, was to continue well into this century. On the one hand, estates were being sold off for housing. University professors, for example, were buying land for suburban homes as early as 1906. At the same time, Polish, Ukrainian, Czech, Italian, and Hungarian workers were arriving to work in chemical and manufacturing facilities.

By 1920, Ms. Wrightson said, about 70 percent of the village's population was foreign born, with "thirty different first languages" spoken in the high school. That is hardly the case today, but the diversity in this village of 8,573 remains. Mayor Frances MacEachron stated "we've never had an 'in' group, or an 'in' section of town."

"Hastings was Republican for many years," said Neil B. Hess, the village manager, "but the mayor is a Democrat and the village board now has a Democratic majority." According to the Board of Elections, there are 1,965 Democrats, 1,768 Republicans, and 892 independents among registered voters in the village.

Hastings is forty minutes and nineteen miles from Grand Central Terminal by way of Metro-North commuter trains, with nearly 900 riders using the line each way on weekdays.

Mr. Riolo said that of twenty-two single-family homes listed for sale recently in the village, ten were offered for more than $100,000, eight were for more than $200,000, and four more were for between $300,000 and $400,000. He added that there were "no ultra-exclusive areas" and that prices of homes were determined more by size, style, and location—a view of the river being crucial—than by neighborhoods.

But there are differences. The Pine Crest section in the southwest corner of the village, for example, includes older homes with some small estates of up to two acres. Prices range from $115,000 to $400,000. Just to the east, on the village's southern hill, prices start lower, at least in the Uniontown area.

Uniontown first housed tenant farmers and later attracted industrial workers. The section contains small cottage-style homes worth $85,000 and slightly larger structures zoned for two-family occupancy. Wood-frame structures, some of them with a Revolutionary-period look, dot the neighborhood.

The hill also includes the heavily wooded Park Knoll section, a twenty-five-year-old development of ranch and split-level styles that has a rural quality to it, right down to the stone walls. And there is the Shadow Lawn portion of the hill, with many English Tudor-style homes built a half century ago.

Hudson Heights, the village's central hill, is the location of Hastings' single elementary school, the municipality's three-pool complex, some of its tennis courts, and a great variety of homes, from contemporary to older, classical styles ranging in price from $175,000 to $325,000.

River View Manor, in the northwest quadrant next to Dobbs Ferry, is on the village's third hill. It, too, boasts a great variety of homes, selling from $175,000 to $400,000. Like other sections of Hastings, homes at either end of that price range can be situated next to each other, although the most expansive are clustered atop the hill.

According to Mayor MacEachron, of 3,000 households in Hastings, 1,200 were in multifamily dwellings. There are seven major apartment complexes, four of them cooperatives with apartments ranging in price from $55,000 for a one-bedroom to $115,000 for a two-bedroom. Rents start at $650 and go to $1,100 a month for river views.

But there are smaller apartment buildings as well, the mayor said, representing "a variety that a lot of people are not aware of." This housing is closest to the river and is in great demand.

The total annual tax bill for a typical house with a market value of $200,000—which would mean an assessed valuation of $20,000—is about $4,300. The payments are shared among the school district, the village, the county, and the Town of Greenburgh.

Hastings has no shopping malls and only one supermarket, but residents are adequately served by a cluster of retail stores in the downtown area. Ranging from the traditional to new ventures such as Moviehouse Mews, a theater converted into boutiques, it is a business district "where people know each other, or at least recognize you," Ms. MacEachron remarked.

Hastings has a "small but outstanding school district," according to Mary Lou Dickenson, the superintendent. The 1,170 students include 500 in the high school. Since the school district is only two square miles in size, students above grade six walk to school. Only those who are younger and live more than a mile away have access to school buses.

The Hillside School, a postwar building nestled against the community's vast Hillside Park, is the single elementary school structure, while the Farragut Middle School, for grades six through eight, is part of the high-school complex. Ms. Dickenson said that students score above national averages on the Scholastic Aptitude Test and nearly 90 percent of the graduates go on to college.

But Hastings' enrollment has been falling, and there has been talk of merger with the similarly small Dobbs Ferry school system. Hastings decided in 1983 not to put the issue to a referendum, choosing instead to share two administrators with Dobbs Ferry.

Hastings has had some illustrious residents, from the actress Billie Burke and her producer-husband, Florenz Ziegfeld, to Jacques Lipchitz, the sculptor, and Jasper F. Cropsey, a noted painter. A Lipchitz sculpture, "Heaven and Earth," graces the lawn of the library. There is also a flourishing Creative Arts Council, with a gallery atop Village Hall.

And common to all is the village's ample recreational space, from the well-used path for joggers and bikers atop the Croton Aqueduct to Hillside Park, with dozens of acres laced by nature trails and paths—a woodsy retreat in a busy suburb, and another example of diversity.

—JAMES FERON

KATONAH

To midtown Manhattan: Train 75 minutes

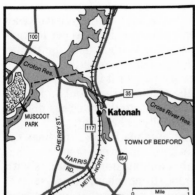

At the turn of the cen-
tury, when Katonah quite literally picked itself up and started over,
great care was taken to ensure that the small hamlet would get off,
again, on the right foot. Breweries and distilleries were prohibited,
as were slaughterhouses and soap factories, and anyone planning to
build a new house had to agree to spend at least $2,500.

Ever since residents were forced to move their village lock, stock,
and barrel a mile to the south because New York City needed the
land for reservoirs, this northeastern Westchester County community—one of three hamlets in the town of Bedford—has taken pains
to see that its original charm and quality of life remain intact. Its
main residential streets, with wide, landscaped greens, have been
declared historic areas by the state, and local citizens and officials
are now seeking federal recognition.

With mixed zoning down to a quarter acre, Katonah does not
much resemble the surrounding countryside of horse farms, country
clubs, and rambling estates. Its housing is a mélange of Victorians,
colonials, and ranches, and its 4,300 residents are a blend of commuters, professionals, and local store owners. It is neighborhood
oriented, and many residents seem to have a vested interest in keeping it that way.

"We had toyed with the idea of moving to Providence a few years
ago, but we finally decided we get so much more for our money

241

here, with the schools and recreation," said Joan Arnold, president of the Katonah Neighborhood Preservation Area Advisory Group. "I guess I'm high on Katonah." The four-year-old group pinpoints areas in need of help and acts as a conduit for government aid.

Although there are no official boundaries (except, of course, on tax-district maps), Katonah is generally described as a rough oval with the Metro-North commuter rail tracks on the east; Cherry Street, a main thoroughfare, on the west; Route 35 on the north; and Route 117 and Harris Road on the south. Real-estate advertisements tend to take a much more liberal view and sometimes lead the prospective home buyer far afield.

The hamlet has easy access to both the Saw Mill River Parkway and Interstate Route 684, and it takes about an hour to get to midtown Manhattan by car. By Metro-North's Harlem line, the trip to Grand Central Terminal takes an hour and fifteen minutes.

Part of Katonah's allure is that every part of it is within walking distance of every other part—from the elementary school on Huntsville Road, to the Memorial Park on the hill, to the business district and the rail station. Street crime is virtually unheard of.

The business district along Katonah Avenue follows the lines established in 1897, with small shops where the owner is apt to call a customer by his first name. There are clothing stores, markets with fresh vegetables and fish, five banks, three pharmacies, several hardware stores, a gourmet food shop, a bakery, two bookstores, and some other specialty stores. There is a medical group office in the hamlet, and the nearest hospital, the Northern Westchester Hospital Center, is in Mount Kisco, about ten minutes away.

The library, with 60,000 items, was established by the Katonah Village Improvement Society. Next door, the Katonah Gallery presents lively exhibits, occasionally with the works of local artists. And just five minutes from the center of the hamlet is Caramoor Center for Music and the Arts, which stages outdoor music festivals each summer.

"Katonah is a very strong village," said Suzy Ewing, a sales agent for the Renwick & Winterling real-estate agency in nearby Bedford Hills. "It looks like the central part of the United States picked up and put down on the East Coast." The attractiveness of the hamlet has kept resale values "marching ahead," she added.

And Donna Reimer, an agent at the Katonah office of the Houlihan-Lawrence agency, said "this is not a transient community; people live here and die here and add on here." Her agency puts the average price of a house at $180,000, with some selling for as little as $120,000 and others selling for as much as $200,000.

Houses are assessed at 45 percent of market value, according to Conrad Veenstra, the town assessor, with local taxes averaging about $23 for each $1,000 of assessed value. That includes the county tax with the town and Katonah assessments, which cover town water, a park with a swimming pool, tennis and paddle courts and playground, as well as street lighting and other services. With the school district tax rate of $33.11 per $1,000 of assessed valuation added on, the tax on a $150,000 house would come to about $3,800 a year.

The local school district is a big selling point for Katonah. Joseph M. Fletcher, assistant superintendent of the Katonah-Lewisboro School District—which covers Katonah, the Town of Lewisboro, and portions of Pound Ridge, Bedford, and North Salem—said the community's "ability to pay and desire to pay" for quality education has a lot to do with students' high test scores and the good reputation of the district.

He also cited the quality of the district's staff, its low turnover rate, and the area's "demographics," meaning that the district is affluent and that the children have something of a head start.

More than 80 percent of the graduates of the high school go on to college. The ratio of students to instructional staff is about 17 to 1.

Katonah's park has a summer day camp for children. Nearby, there are two county parks. The Ward Pound Ridge Reservation, in nearby Cross River, has 4,000 acres of woods, streams, and hiking trails. In the winter, the trails are opened to cross-country skiers. The other is Muscoot Park on Route 100 in Somers, a working farm with nature trails and exhibits.

Fishing is allowed by permit in the nearby Croton, Muscoot, and Cross River reservoirs, owned by New York City. It was because of these reservoirs that the residents of old Katonah, named for a local Indian chief, had to pull up stakes. Many of the Victorian houses in the hamlet are among those that were picked up off their foundations beginning in 1897 and pulled south on wooden skids lubricated with laundry soap.

Plans for the new hamlet put emphasis on a country esthetic, with wide streets and wide greens up the middle. Robert Postel, who lives in the historic district, said he found his 1896 Queen Anne–style house about two years ago while visiting family in Katonah. The house, one of the first actually built in the hamlet, has been faithfully restored.

It is the type of restoration town officials envisioned when they sought state historic-district designation, which does not restrict a property owner from making changes, however dramatic.

"Victorian is gaudy," said Mr. Postel, a carpenter who did most of the work on the house himself. "This house and this town should be preserved. It's what the machine age did. With all those little pieces of turned wood, Victorian is the height of the industrial age. That's the heritage here. We should preserve it."

—STEVEN J. RAGO

M A M A R O N E C K

To midtown Manhattan: Train 35 minutes

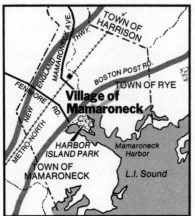

Time was when a wealthy Boston merchant could buy "three necks of land" on Long Island Sound for a handful of wampum and some stockings, gunpowder, and kettles. But that was 300 years ago, and home buyers who want waterfront property in the Village of Mamaroneck today have to dig a lot deeper into their pockets.

It is the waterfront that lures newcomers, mesmerizes residents, and virtually doubles the value of property on it. Indeed, Mamaroneck's waterfront houses range in price from $550,000 up to nearly $3 million. Houses within walking distance of the shore cost $125,000 to $375,000.

The waterfront's appeal is most evident on a sparkling winter's day, when sea gulls' wings glint in the sun and cattails stand tall in the neighboring marshes. The gleaming white spire of the United Methodist Church, built in 1771, is as picturesque as the masts standing in the harbor and boatyards.

Primarily a residential community with a central business district and a small area zoned for light industry, the Village of Mamaroneck comprises 3.5 square miles set twenty-three miles northeast of New York City. It is bounded on the north by the Town of Harrison, on the south by the Sound, on the east by the Town of Rye, and on the west by the unincorporated area of the Town of Mamaroneck. About a

244

third of the village lies in the Town of Rye, while the Town of Mamaroneck also includes the village of Larchmont.

"What attracts people to Mamaroneck is its heterogeneity and the fact that its recreational facilities are exceptional," said Mayor Suzi Oppenheimer.

Indeed, "Mamaroneck the Friendly Village" (as it is known on official stationery) boasts a long-standing ethnic mix that residents credit with fostering stability and cohesion in the eighty-eight years since the village was incorporated. More than half of its 17,600 residents are Catholic, according to Mayor Oppenheimer; 20 percent are Jewish and 20 percent Protestant.

Many residents, Ms. Oppenheimer said, are descendants of Italians who immigrated at the turn of the century to build roads and dams. "They were the construction people, the tradespeople, as they are today. They helped build southern Westchester." Much of Mamaroneck's work force today, in fact, consists of plasterers, builders, and plumbers. Many others work in local light industry, for service companies, or in boatyards, one of which, Robert E. Derecktor, Inc., has produced two America's Cup contenders.

Fewer than half the residents commute to work, real-estate agents say, a far lower proportion than in most of the rest of the county. Grand Central Terminal is thirty-five minutes away by Metro-North.

The 1980 census put the median annual family income in the village at $30,959, with 434 families at $50,000 or more. Many of these live in spacious, sprawling dwellings in the prestigious Orienta and Shore Acres sections, which hug the coast and offer views of the Sound. Lower-income and younger residents tend to live in well-maintained, two-story frame houses worth up to $175,000 north of the Boston Post Road, a major commercial strip paralleling the shoreline.

Mamaroneck has an all-volunteer, 325-man fire department and no fewer than twelve volunteer boards, committees, and commissions that furnish the mayor and the other four salaried members of the Board of Trustees with expertise on everything from dredging the harbor to activities for the disabled.

Another unifying feature of the village, according to the mayor, is that "a whole cross section of the community" takes advantage of Mamaroneck's recreational facilities. One focal point is Harbor Island Park, a forty-four-acre recreational area jutting into the harbor with eight tennis courts, numerous ball fields, boating docks and moorings, swimming floats, and a municipal beach manned in the summer by lifeguards. Throughout the summer, some 1,500 boats bob offshore, half belonging to members of the village's half-dozen private clubs and the rest sailing out of the municipal marina.

"Mamaroneck is unique," said Mona Faye Harris, president of

Marion Halstead Cremin, a local real-estate agency. "People are attracted to all the allure the water offers and they just don't leave." Turnover in property is, consequently, lower than in neighboring communities like Larchmont and Rye.

Houses for rent are much harder to find than houses for sale. The rents range from $1,100 a month for a small three-bedroom colonial up to $3,300 for a three-bedroom ranch, with the average about $1,600 a month. There is a limited selection of cooperatives and condominiums, with one-bedrooms for about $50,000 and town houses for around $350,000.

Houses in the village of Mamaroneck are assessed at about 11 percent of full-market value, according to Lloyd Wright, the village assessor, and the rate is $265 per $1,000 of assessed valuation. The owner of a house with a market value of $100,000 would pay taxes of about $2,900 a year.

Some new construction is going on. Diane Millstein, a property developer, has built thirteen modern-style town houses in fashionable Orienta, with prices ranging from $275,000 to $395,000. Ms. Millstein, a long-term resident of the area, said her six-year struggle to get village approval for the development reflects the somewhat conservative nature of the community. "Mamaroneck does not like dramatic changes," she noted, "but it is progressive culturally."

Indeed, the Emelin Theatre for the Performing Arts, part of the village's Free Library, is a magnet not only for Mamaroneck's residents but also for neighboring towns. Seating up to 300 people, it offers concerts, children's theater, plays, films, musicals, and dance programs.

Among other establishments in the area, two restaurants on the Boston Post Road—the recently opened Charlie Brown's and the James Fenimore Cooper Inn—afford family-style evening fare. The Unicorn Restaurant-Diner and the Mamaroneck Inn, two lively diners also on Boston Post Road, serve faster, less formal meals.

Arts programs are also emphasized in Mamaroneck's schools, which are highly respected in the area. Three years ago, said Thomas Tiktin, principal of Mamaroneck High School—which attracts more than 1,600 students from the Larchmont-Mamaroneck area—the school was awarded a $10,000 Rockefeller Brothers Fund grant as having one of the nation's ten outstanding fine- and performing-arts programs.

According to Mr. Tiktin, around 80 percent of the graduates go on to college and more than half of those taking advanced placement examinations score 4's or 5's, the highest ratings.

Citing a range of arts courses and languages from Russian to Japanese and Chinese, Mr. Tiktin said the school provided "not variety in terms of a smorgasbord but rather of tailor-made courses."

The Mamaroneck School System comprises four elementary

schools, one middle and one high school, serving half of Mamaroneck Village and all of neighboring Larchmont. Many other Mamaroneck students attend the much smaller Rye Neck school system, which also serves an affluent section of Rye called Green Haven. Mamaroneck has several parochial schools as well.

"There's a real feeling of pride about this village," Ms. Millstein stated. "It's not just the people—it's the unique waterfront we all enjoy."

Mamaroneck has set up a five-member Coastal Zone Management Commission to create a marine zone that would preserve public access to the village's nine miles of waterfront. The establishment of the commission reflects fears that the character of much of this land may change under development pressures. "All along the coast, traditional waterfront marine activities are being displaced by major office complexes and condominium developments," said Kathryn Clarke, the commission chairman. "We believe certain places should be preserved so access is available for more people."

—MERIDA WELLES

NEW ROCHELLE

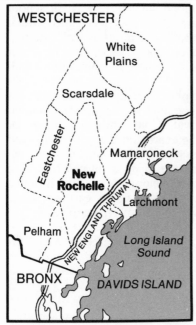

WESTCHESTER
White Plains
Scarsdale
Eastchester
Mamaroneck
New Rochelle
NEW ENGLAND THRUWAY
Larchmont
Pelham
Long Island Sound
BRONX
DAVIDS ISLAND

To midtown Manhattan: Train 35 minutes

Ask City Manager C. Samuel Kissinger about the character of New Rochelle and he will say it is a community that cherishes the values and ambience of the American small town. "Here there is clearly a priority on maintaining the residential life-style. This is what makes New Rochelle." Then he proudly cited the economic development that is reviving a once-decaying downtown business district.

New Rochelle was established on the southernmost tip of what is now Westchester County nearly 300 years ago by Huguenots and named after a community in their native France. It has a housing stock made up mostly of single-family homes built in a variety of styles, from stately Norman-Tudor to more modest American wood-shingled. Most of the houses sit on clean, tree-shaded streets of the kind that exemplified middle-class suburbia before the advent of the development tract.

The town's homey charm is captured in the works of Norman Rockwell, the illustrator, who lived here early in his life. Among the city's current celebrities are E. L. Doctorow, the author of *Ragtime;* Robert Merrill, the opera singer; and Ruby Dee and Ossie Davis, the actors.

"Some of us never realized those Rockwell bird cages and kitchen tables we thought came from Iowa were all right here," said Thea

248

Eichler, who with her husband, an accountant, moved here from Manhattan in 1964. The Eichlers have since raised a family of five children in a baronial three-story house with ten rooms situated on more than a third of an acre. The parcel is in a section called Paine Heights, once part of a farm owned by Thomas Paine, the leading pamphleteer of the Revolutionary War.

According to Fran Eisner, principal broker in the real-estate concern of Oshlag-Eisner, a house similar to the Eichlers' today might range in price between $235,000 and $260,000, and its annual taxes would range between $3,500 and $4,500. In the city's less affluent areas, older houses cost around $115,000 to $150,000. Rentals are $650 and up for a one-bedroom apartment but finding one is difficult. The vacancy rate is low.

For rentals, "people are going into second-floor taxpayers or the older multiple-dwelling walk-ups over stores in the southern end of the city," Ms. Eisner said. "There are no apartments in the residential areas," she added. "The shortage is one of our problems."

The city is close enough to New York to make commuting relatively easy. Traveling by auto on the New England Thruway, which slices diagonally across its lower half, New Rochelle is a seventeen-mile drive to Manhattan. By Metro-North's New Haven division, Grand Central Terminal is about thirty-two minutes away.

With a 1980 population of 70,794, the town is large enough to support two radio stations, a cable-television station, and its own daily newspaper, *The Standard Star,* with a circulation of about 14,000.

A pervasive spirit of voluntarism knits the city together. There are forty religious institutions and 500 community organizations, among them such groups as the New Rochelle Art Association, the Boys' Club, Communications Club, the Huguenot–Thomas Paine Historical Society, the Rotary Club, and the North Italy Society.

Students, educators, and parents all speak highly of the quality of the schools. Average class size for both elementary and secondary school is about twenty-four students. There are six elementary schools, two junior highs, and one high school, as well as several parochial schools. The city also is home to two institutions of higher learning, the College of New Rochelle and Iona College.

New Rochelle Hospital Medical Center, a 470-bed voluntary facility, has more than 225 physicians, surgeons, and dentists affiliated with it, and its services extend to the surrounding communities of Larchmont, the Pelhams, Mamaroneck, Eastchester, and Scarsdale.

The city also has abundant public amenities: nine miles of Long Island Sound shoreline, sandy beaches, a dozen marinas, and nearly 400 acres of parkland.

During the 1950's and 1960's, public controversy over school desegregation led to the nation's first urban conflict over the busing issue. That dispute was resolved amicably, however, and now there is little evidence of racial troubles. About 20 percent of the population is black and Hispanic.

Jaquetta Cole, who heads the New Rochelle Task Force for a Better Community, cited one situation as an example of the current state of intergroup relations. "When we tried to get a hundred units of federally subsidized housing for the poor, mostly blacks, who live along Lincoln Avenue, we went to the mayor and the Development Council for help. We're getting our housinig units and we credit Mayor Leonard Paduano for the support we needed."

Melvin Sirner, chief rabbi at Beth-El Synagogue in New Rochelle's affluent north end, said: "We have a truly pluralistic community with Catholics, Jews, blacks, and Hispanics all living and working alongside each other in a tradition of good feelings."

Ossie Davis, who moved to New Rochelle in 1963, recalled: "New Rochelle had some minor civil disorder over the Vietnam War and the death of Martin Luther King. But we never had the violence or the sense of rot you felt elsewhere."

During the 1960's and 1970's, however, there were fears of economic rot, prompted by shrinking commerce in the downtown area and the depletion of the city's tax base. Much of New Rochelle's nineteenth-century stock of buildings was in need of renovation. Two major stores—Arnold Constable and W. T. Grant's—had closed and other commercial enterprises were about to follow, leaving vacant buildings with boarded windows and graffiti-scarred facades.

In 1974 the New Rochelle Development Council, a sixty-five-member consortium of business leaders from the city's financial, industrial, and retail sectors, was formed. Lewis Fechter, executive director of the council, said it has helped bring fifteen companies to New Rochelle that have taken a half-million square feet of space for offices and light industry and employed more than 1,000 workers. "We help companies with every facet of establishing themselves here, from site selection through the placement of loans."

The council also has helped in the renovation of 60,000 square feet of commercial space in the three-story Constable building downtown and 120,000 additional square feet in what was formerly a Bloomingdale's store.

Under a $20 million renovation program, the city provided the downtown area with broader sidewalks, trees, plantings, and facade improvements, restoring ninety Victorian and Art Deco buildings.

The city also has completed a $6.3 million library and a $1 million plaza. A total of $2.3 million has been spent on a semi-mall and street drainage project, and $3.5 million on a multipurpose community center, replacing what formerly was the Southside Boys' Club.

By far the most promising venture ahead for the city is a proposal

NEW ROCHELLE

by Xanadu Properties Associates of Honolulu to erect 3,000 luxury condominium units on Davids Island, an unused eighty-acre parcel in the Sound, just off the mainland. Feasibility studies have not yet been completed, and one of the still-unresolved questions is how to link the island with the mainland.

—GEORGE W. GOODMAN

N O R T H   S A L E M

To midtown Manhattan: Train 90 minutes

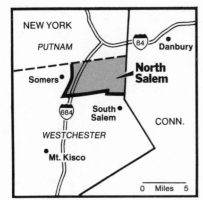

NEW YORK
PUTNAM
84 • Danbury
North Salem
Somers •
684
South • Salem
CONN.
WESTCHESTER
• Mt. Kisco
0   Miles   5

There are no traffic lights on the hundred miles of roads that wind through the hills and fields of North Salem. The nearest supermarket and movie theater are in neighboring towns. And cable television has yet to be hooked up.

This sparsely settled town in northern Westchester County exults in its rural setting. Macouns and Cortlands are harvested each fall from the apple orchards along Hardscrabble Road, and the frosts of autumn add an early-morning sparkle to the fields of the town's horse farms.

Some people say in jest that there are more horses than people in this town of 4,563, which was settled early in the 1700's. There are, in fact, a score of farms on which horses are bred, jumped, and shown. Many private houses have their own barns out back. And the town has more than sixty miles of bridle paths, many of which cross the rolling meadows and stone walls of estates whose owners grant permission for riders to pass.

About a hundred families belong to the Goldens Bridge Hounds, whose mounted members, clad in pinks and swooping after baying hounds, hunt foxes twice a week in the fall and winter.

The houses that dot North Salem's forty-two square miles represent nearly all styles of American architecture, from Federal and Georgian colonial to Greek and Italianate Revival. Some of the large estates in the eastern part of town occupy more than a hundred acres and have sold recently for as much as $600,000.

More modest three-bedroom ranch houses that were built on two acres for $30,000 in the Lake Hawthorne section in the 1960's and 1970's sell now for $150,000, according to the town historian, Richard de Frances, who lives there.

North Salem is bounded on the east by Ridgefield, Connecticut, on the north by Putnam County, on the south by the Town of Lewisboro, and on the west by the Town of Somers. North Salem's two principal hamlets, Croton Falls and Purdys, lie close to the western boundary along Interstate 684, which runs roughly north and south.

Salem Center, where municipal offices occupy a white clapboard house with a Dutch gambrel roof built about 1770, is some fifty-five miles north of Manhattan by car on I-684 and the Hutchinson River Parkway.

"If you want elbow room, you've got to come this far north," said Jerome Billingsley, a real-estate broker whose family has land investments here. About 300 residents make the ninety-minute commute to New York City from Metro-North stations at the two hamlets. Others commute by car to corporate offices in the region, such as I.B.M. in Armonk, Pepsico in Purchase, Texaco in Harrison, and Union Carbide in Danbury, Connecticut.

Change has come slowly to North Salem. One section of Route 121, a local thoroughfare, appears to be unchanged when compared to an 1895 photograph, Mr. de Frances said, save for paving. Yet, with several residential, commercial, and industrial developments either under way or in planning stages, the pace of development is quickening.

Mr. Billingsley, the real-estate agent who began selling the land in 1979, said that the first lots had sold for between $30,000 and $50,000 and now go for "more than $100,000." They range from three to twenty-three acres, with the average about ten acres.

Multiple dwellings, which now exist only in small numbers in Purdys and Croton Falls, are scarce but more may be on the way. In 1982 the town lost its final appeal of a State Supreme Court finding that its zoning was "exclusionary." Robert Marsecca, an investor from New York City who brought the suit on the zoning ordinances, is expected to seek approval of a plan to build about eighty-four units on a twenty-one-acre site between Route 22 and I-684. But until a new master plan is approved, all major construction in North Salem has been halted.

According to local realtors, the owner of a house in North Salem with a market value of $150,000 would pay about $2,950 in annual taxes. New York City has been the largest single payer of property taxes here since the Titicus Reservoir was built in 1900 as part of the city's water supply.

Socially, North Salem is "sort of a low-key town," stated Gail Pantezzi, president of its Improvement Society. "Once they meet you, they're very friendly," she said of the residents. "It's not a pseudosophisticated town. They're not always going to cocktail parties."

Many, however, take advantage of the Italian and French cuisines that can be found at the Mona Trattoria Bolognese on Route 22 in Croton Falls, the Box Tree at the intersection of Routes 116 and 22 in Purdys, and the Auberge Maxime Restaurant on Route 116.

More than 200 residents gather for the annual Christmas Eve carol sing and bonfire across Route 116 from the post office. And basketball games at the North Salem High School—the school has no football team—sometimes draw a hundred spectators, according to Stanley Toll, superintendent of schools.

The high school, with about 350 students and an average class size of less than twenty, sends about 75 percent of its graduates to college. Soccer is perhaps second to horseback riding in popularity among the young. More than 300 boys and girls between the ages of five and fifteen participate in an American Youth Soccer Organization program of games against neighboring communities. The program of Sunday games in the fall and spring is run by residents independently of the school athletic programs.

The town also runs a baseball program for young people and has built two outdoor tennis courts. Two other courts, renovated, are available at the high school for public use. Joggers frequently run the hilly roads, and, in July, distance runners from a wide area participate in the Titicus Seven, a seven-mile race around the reservoir.

The North Salem Free Library was completed in the spring of 1980, with its $300,000 cost entirely defrayed by community donations. For more than a decade, the Committee for Music in North Salem has been sponsoring instrumental programs twice a year at the Hammond Museum on Deveau Road.

The twenty-five-year-old museum, with a hilltop view of North Salem fields, describes itself as a "museum of the humanities." It has a tranquil Japanese "stroll garden" with reflecting pools, and its exhibitions include rare books, engravings of sixteenth- and seventeenth-century London, and needlepoint by its founder, Natalie Hays Hammond.

There are a variety of religious congregations that appear to be supportive of each other. Almost everyone contributes to the smorgasbord of the Purdys Methodist Church, the auction at St. James's Episcopal Church, the chicken dinner at the Croton Falls Presbyterian Church, bingo at St. Joseph's Roman Catholic Church, and periodic fund-raising events of the Croton Falls Baptist Church.

—FRANKLIN WHITEHOUSE

PELHAM

To midtown Manhattan: Train 30 minutes

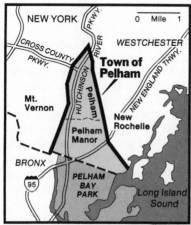

We're a small, sleepy town," said Anthony J. Noto, the Pelham town supervisor.

Small, yes, for the town—which actually consists of two villages, Pelham and Pelham Manor—is only 2.4 square miles in area. Sleepy, yes, with cul-de-sacs and winding roads that make motorists slow down to see the fine old trees and some of the most elegant homes in southeastern Westchester County.

Pelham's size, its residents say, is one of its attractions. It is small enough so that anyone can walk to the railroad station (it takes about a half hour by train to get to Grand Central Terminal), the movies, or the stores. The schools have been placed so that any child in the Pelhams may walk to school.

Pelham Manor is among the most affluent sections in the state, with a median annual family income of about $35,000. The Town of Pelham is bounded by New Rochelle, Mount Vernon, the northern boundary of the Bronx, and Long Island Sound.

The zoning laws in Pelham Manor are geared to keep the sense of spaciousness, with building permitted only on lots of at least 100 by 100 feet; in Pelham, the zoning is less stringent, with building allowed on lots of 50 by 100 feet. About 130 houses change hands yearly, with older residents sometimes trading larger homes for smaller ones. Many of the town's children have returned to raise

255

their own families, but when they do, they find they need two incomes.

The town, with a combined population of nearly 13,000, has a cosmopolitan air about it, in part because it attracts residents who like its proximity to Manhattan. They come from the worlds of publishing, television, and the arts, from the United Nations, and from major corporations. Pelham Manor is home to the Finnish and British West Indies United Nations representatives and to scores of lawyers and nearly a hundred physicians, none of whom practice in Pelham. Republicans outnumber Democrats three to one.

Several Bronx politicians, including City Councilman Jerry L. Crispino, State Senator John D. Calandra, and Surrogate Bertram R. Gelfand, technically live in the Bronx, but on streets that border Pelham Manor. Their homes are on a narrow strip of land that is cut off from the rest of the city by a park and thruway. Under an agreement with the city's Board of Education and the Pelham schools, twenty-one city children may attend the Pelham Manor schools.

To live in Pelham requires a substantial income, according to Jean Hardy, a broker with Stiefvater Real Estate. Houses—Tudors, clapboards, ranches, gingerbreads, and carriage houses—generally sell for between $150,000 and $350,000, with some costing as much as $800,000. Taxes are high and, according to town officials, going higher. Nonetheless, brokers report that demand is strong. In recent listings, the average price is about $215,000.

Residents pay five taxes—county, town, sewer, school, and village—and together they add up to an average bill of $4,800 a year. Unlike Pelham Manor, which has a large industrial park, the village of Pelham has no industry. Most of the 500 commercial businesses are in Pelham.

For such a tiny place, Pelham has a lot of government. Each of the two jurisdictions has its own village board, consisting of a mayor and trustees, that is empowered to handle police, fire, public works, property assessment, and taxation.

Each village also has its own fire department with paid fire fighters, but each also relies heavily on volunteers. The town government, which oversees county and state fiscal matters, is under the direction of Town Supervisor Noto and four councilmen.

In attempting to keep businesses in Pelham, the town fathers undertook a revitalization of Fifth Avenue, the main street, and new stores and restaurants, antique and ice-cream shops have opened in recent years. There are minimalls in Pelham Manor and in towns nearby.

In recent years Pelham, which has a well-regarded school system and good recreational facilities, has attracted many younger people. Often these are families who want to keep strong ties to New York

P E L H A M

City, and many visit the Bronx, particularly to see the Zoo and the Botanical Garden. Travel is easy; the Hutchinson River Parkway and Interstate 95 are a stone's throw from the town's main streets.

With an annual income of about $2.5 million, Pelham Manor spends roughly half its budget on police protection. It employs twenty-six police officers, giving it a ratio of 4.1 officers per 1,000 population, the highest in the county. There are twenty-four police officers in the village of Pelham, with a ratio of 3.5 per 1,000 population.

To read about the police in a booklet published by the League of Women Voters in Pelham is to be transported to the mythical village of Brigadoon, where crime does not exist.

"The Pelham police answer countless calls for help—children lock themselves in bathrooms; adults lock themselves out of houses or cars; and cats stubbornly sit atop trees. Police meet evening trains at the railroad station. They provide escort service and special traffic control, maintain a lost and found department, and can advise you on road conditions."

The reality is a bit different: after some coaxing, Peter Zambernardi, the police chief of Pelham Manor, acknowledged that house burglaries were his biggest headache, with roughly five reported every month. "Mostly petty stuff," he said. "We consider $5,000 a big one." The townsfolk, he added, take precautions, and the burglars generally turn out to be youths who live outside the Pelhams. The more serious crimes, shoplifting and robberies, occur in a nearby industrial and retail plaza off Boston Post Road.

The public school system, like the systems of many older towns, is enrolling fewer students. Enrollment is slightly more than 2,000 in kindergarten through high school. There are four elementary schools, from kindergarten through sixth grade. The two-year junior high school and the four-year high school are housed in a single building. The average class size in the elementary school is twenty-one pupils and in junior and senior high about twenty-five pupils.

Pelham Memorial High School sends many of its children to college, and some to the very best in the nation. It has long had advanced college-level courses in English, history, and other subjects, and its students score more than a hundred points higher than the national average on the College Board Achievement Examinations in every subject area except mathematics.

Much of the village's energy is spent on children, with a Spring Festival, children's theater, and Little League games. The town has several tennis courts and recently opened a minipark on the Sound. There is a Pelham Community Orchestra and a Pelham Arts Center that puts on shows during the year.

In summer Pelham provides a day camp at a small fee for its

young residents. There is also a summer program for the disabled. The county provides five beaches, two golf courses, swimming pools, and acres of woodland for hiking, fishing, and camping.

Public recreation, say residents, is adequate, but some maintain there is not enough parkland in the village. The major stretch of green is a golf course that is privately operated by the Pelham Country Club.

The Pelhams have two Roman Catholic churches, as well as Congregational, Presbyterian, and Episcopal churches and one Jewish Center.

—MARCIA CHAMBERS

RYE

To midtown Manhattan: Train 40 minutes

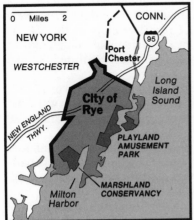

Rye City is a small, tranquil community on Long Island Sound with a wealth of trees, open spaces, marine vistas, and residents who are aware of the town's advantages and are quick to point them out. "It's a wonderful place to raise a family," said Nancy Steed, a lifelong resident who is active in church and civic organizations. "Everything parents could want for their children in the way of quality education, social activity, safety, and a cross section of life can be found right here."

Rye City is situated in the Town of Rye, in Westchester County, on the New England Thruway near Connecticut. Thirty-eight minutes away from Manhattan by train and twenty-five minutes by car, it has an abundance of recreational facilities and a blend of housing styles from Victorian to modern.

"Rye residents have to thank their forefathers for having the foresight to keep so much land available for recreational purposes," said Frank J. Culross, the city manager. Recreational facilities cover 184 acres, one-fifth of the town's land.

Rye dates to 1660, when English settlers from what is now Greenwich, Connecticut, moved several miles west along the coast to establish the farming community they named after their ancestral home. Rye Village was established in 1904 as an incorporated section of the town, but it seceded in 1944 to become Rye City.

Rye Towners have long maintained that the move had more to do with fiscal matters and the villagers' desire to separate themselves from their less-affluent neighbors in Port Chester than with a wish to control their own government. Whatever the motive, no one seems to regret the decision.

The city is completely independent of the town, has separate taxing authority, and provides all essential services, from police and fire protection to highway maintenance and garbage collection. An elected mayor and a six-member council form the policymaking body, which appoints a city manager, the chief administrative officer.

Rye's quiet, woodsy character, along with its proximity to New York City, made it a popular summer resort as early as the 1880's. Over the years, it has developed into a residential community of single-family homes that have attracted generations of middle- and upper-class families.

The 1980 census showed that Rye City had a population of 15,083; the median age was 36.2. Of 5,206 housing units, 5,060 were occupied, and of those, 3,480 units were occupied by owners and 1,580 by renters.

House prices cover a broad range, from $100,000 to $3 million, and rentals are scarce. Rye Colony, one of two luxury rental apartment complexes, where one-bedroom apartments rent for a minimum of $500 a month, has a waiting list of up to two years.

As has happened in many suburbs in the metropolitan area, rental apartments in Rye have been converted into cooperatives and condominiums, and new multifamily housing is created for sale rather than rental. At Waters Edge, a condominium overlooking the Sound that opened in 1979, two-bedroom units that are offered for resale carry prices of $275,000 to $300,000, according to Nancy Neuman, who heads the Country Properties real-estate agency.

Rye's accessibility by highway and train—it is served by the Metro-North line—and its two miles of coastline have made it attractive for residential development. But there has been very little commercial or industrial development, with the exception of Avon Products, which has a warehouse-distribution and office center on Midland Avenue. In addition, the Dictaphone Corporation and the Continental Baking Company have offices in the community.

The city's tax rate is $204.38 for each $1,000 of assessed valuation, up from $172.77 in 1982. Although city leaders acknowledge the need for an improved tax base, they, along with residents, have for the most part resisted commercial development. Strict zoning laws have kept out motels, most manufacturing establishments, and shopping centers.

Rye's coastline provides superb fishing and boating. The Rye City marina, on Milton Harbor, has space for 350 boats. Docking fees are nominal. Nature lovers can enjoy strolls through Rye Nature Center,

R Y E

with forty-six acres of hidden trails for field trips, a bird sanctuary, and a nature museum. A Westchester County–owned Marshland Conservancy of more than a hundred acres is also within the city limits.

Among the city's better-known resources is the Playland Amusement Park, a facility on seventy-eight waterfront acres that includes a beach, ice-skating rink, pool, and boardwalk.

The city also has a municipal country club with an eighteen-hole golf course, indoor and outdoor restaurants, and a swimming pool. Club memberships for Rye residents cost $795 a year for a family and $435 a year for individuals.

The Rye School District has three elementary schools and a combined middle school and high school. There are about twenty students for each teacher in the district. Nearly 80 percent of the high-school graduates go on to college.

The city also has two parochial schools—one elementary and one for grades nine through twelve—and the Rye Country Day School. The latter teaches kindergarten through twelfth grade. There are four nursery schools—one operated by the city and three by churches and a synagogue.

"Everything you want is right here," said Anne Pastor, president of the Chamber of Commerce, which has twenty-five merchants among its members. The chamber's slogan, "Try Rye First," appears to have caught on, judging by the weekend shopping traffic in the village—the nickname for the main shopping area around Purchase Street.

The city's library, which is still called the Rye Free Reading Room, contains more than 50,000 volumes and has separate areas for young people and adults.

While the city is not as rich in historic landmarks as some other Westchester communities, the Square House on Purchase Street, built around 1672, is on the National Register of Historic Places. It has been restored by the Rye Historical Society as a museum and is open to the public. The Rye Arts Center and the Rye Performing Arts Center also enrich the community's cultural life.

Many Rye residents say they remember a time when they never locked their doors. Most now do, but the city has one of the lowest crime rates in Westchester County and New York State. And many derive a sense of security from the Police Department patrols of neighborhoods, especially during the summer months when many residents are away on vacation.

The Police Department has thirty-five uniformed officers and a police commissioner. The fore is assisted by forty trained volunteers. The city Fire Department has sixteen paid fire fighters and over 200 trained volunteers.

R Y E

The major medical facility in the area is United Hospital, a nonprofit, voluntary institution in Port Chester, less than a quarter of a mile from the Rye City border.

Many residents believe that the city has prospered because its people are committed to the community. "We're never at a loss for volunteers," said Mr. Culross, the city manager. "Whether we need financial support for a community project or to raise money for food baskets, the townspeople are there. Our citizens play an active role in governing the city and we welcome their help."

—LENA WILLIAMS

SCARSDALE

To midtown Manhattan: Train 40 minutes

everal years ago, a *New Yorker* cartoon showed a middle-aged couple with suitcases walking down a road marked Scarsdale. They had rejected two other routes, one marked Sodom and the other Gomorrah. "Let's hope," the man was saying to his wife, "that our decision hasn't been too hasty."

Hasty or not, the choice is made by a few hundred families a year—some renting their homes, the majority buying. And they learn, according to long-term residents, school officials, and others, that Scarsdale is a somewhat more varied community than its national reputation as a cohesively affluent suburb suggests.

Once, Scarsdale was a stronghold of wealthy Protestant executives and their families who voted Republican and ran the community almost by consensus. Today it is a more heterogeneous mixture of the rich and hardly rich who tend to support Democrats by a slight edge and participate heavily—often noisily—in local matters.

The demographic changes, with Catholic and Jewish families having grown in numbers, took place after World War II; the political changes appear to date from the 1960's. A nonpartisan form of elected government is coming under more intense challenge each year, and Village Board meetings now, according to old-timers, border occasionally on the rancorous.

But Scarsdale remains conservative in terms of how it should look and function, fiercely resisting most proposed changes. It has held fast, since its origins as a suburb in the latter part of the nineteenth century, to the concept of planned development. Estates of several acres may still be sold and broken up, but single-family homes, rather than the more contemporary clustered town houses, tend to rise on those sites.

Scarsdale's elected leaders—Seymour E. Sims, the mayor, and a six-member Village Board—serve without pay, leaving the day-to-day operation to Lowell J. Tooley, a professional manager who has administered the town for two decades.

"I'd describe Scarsdale as semirural," Mr. Tooley said. "It has no sidewalks, for the most part, and narrow winding roads, the majority only twenty-four-feet wide, and they are not heavily lighted. And I'll tell you what else it's not—it's not manicured." It is heavily treed, however, and punctuated generously with parks and playgrounds.

Scarsdale is both a town and a village, the latter designation being added in 1914 as protection against proposed annexation by White Plains; state law says that a town can be divided, but not a village. The suburb sits in the center of Westchester's populous southern region, surrounded by the towns of Eastchester, Greenburgh, and Mamaroneck and the cities of New Rochelle and White Plains.

The Lordship and Manor of Scarsdale was established by royal edict of William III of England in 1701 and was granted to Caleb Heathcote, who found the "scars," or crags, and dales reminiscent of his home, the Hundred of Scarsdale in Derbyshire. The Westchester version was populated largely by farmers until the mid-1800's, when a commuter rail line linked it to Manhattan twenty-one miles south. (The run now takes about forty minutes.)

City residents began to move to Scarsdale and to other communities served by the railroad, and the trend was accelerated by the heavy turn-of-the-century immigration that added to Manhattan's turbulence. To maintain neighborhood character in some communities, including Scarsdale, officials began to establish limitations on construction.

In Scarsdale, the subdivisions differed according to lot size, and those differences have been maintained, producing a mosaic of five neighborhoods that give the community its internal differences, from the modest homes of Edgewood to the estates of Heathcote.

"There is little to be had in Scarsdale for under $200,000," said Dudley D. Doernberg, Jr., a real-estate broker, and those homes can be found mostly in Edgewood, the town's southernmost portion, zoned for fifty-foot-wide frontages. Edgewood was the village's first community, attracting Scarsdale's first trades people, teachers, and white-collar employees.

The Greenacres section, closest to the Hartsdale railroad station in the northwest section, is "a well-mixed neighborhood," according to Mr. Doernberg, with fifty- and sixty-year-old houses with seventy-foot fronts selling for $200,000 to $350,000 and up. A decade ago, those same residences sold for $75,000 to $100,000.

Fox Meadow, between Greenacres and Edgewood, is somewhat newer and more expensive, with many houses dating from the 1930's and selling for $350,000 to $900,000. Much of the Quaker Ridge section, bordering on Mamaroneck, is newer still, and there the prices range widely, from $200,000 to $500,000 and up.

Heathcote, in the center of Scarsdale, was developed around a station for the New York, Westchester, and Boston Railway, which failed in the Depression. Although Heathcote today contains seventy- and hundred-foot-wide fronts typical of Scarsdale, it also has the village's largest estates, some of them with 250-foot fronts. They are zoned for one and two acres, and sell for $500,000 to $1 million and more.

Vincent Pagliaro, the town assessor, said the average tax bill, covering town, village, and school levies, is $6,300. The tax rate is $300 per $1,000 of valuation, but Scarsdale uses partial valuation, so a house worth $90,000 a decade ago and perhaps $230,000 today would still be assessed at only $21,000.

The Scarsdale school system, characterized by residents as the village's major industry, has a reputation for excellence, and for internal competitiveness. "Most of what we do," said Dr. Thomas Sobol, superintendent of schools, "is prepare students academically and intellectually for college, where they can replicate their parents' success.

"This is a community of achievement-oriented people who have high educational aspirations for their children," he added, "and the kids tend to reflect those values." Roughly 95 percent of high-school graduates are continuing their education, with about 90 percent in four-year colleges.

Enrollment has been declining, Dr. Sobol said, "although less steeply than in other suburban school districts where they have been forced to close elementary schools." In addition to the high school, which has about 1,600 students, there are a junior high school and five elementary schools, one in each of the neighborhoods. The community tends to keep close to the schools, largely through the activities of parent-support groups. Their interests reflect today's family patterns, dealing with single-parenting, divorce, drugs, and school behavior. In 1983 a nonprofit parent cooperative began providing an after-school day-care program in the elementary schools.

The 1980 census put Scarsdale's population at 17,650, with a median age of thirty-seven. Once 60 to 70 percent Protestant, it is now estimated to be about 40 percent Jewish and 30 percent Catholic. The number of Japanese (309) nearly equaled the number of blacks (314).

Of roughly 5,400 households, nearly 500 are single-person households, most of them widows and widowers who are "frozen in place," as the former mayor Jean Stone put it. Some are unable to move and many are unwilling to leave a community of friends. Scarsdale has few rental or cooperative apartments to offer them.

Roughly a fourth of the village's 4,300 acres is controlled open land. The community has twenty parks and playing fields, nineteen public tennis and nine paddle tennis courts, three golf courses within its borders (one county-owned and two private), and a handsome outdoor complex of three swimming pools and one diving pool.

The Police and Fire departments each have about fifty paid employees, and roughly 1,500 of Scarsdale's homes have burglar alarms linked to police headquarters. Ms. Stone said the alarms are helping to cut the number of burglaries.

—JAMES FERON

WHITE PLAINS

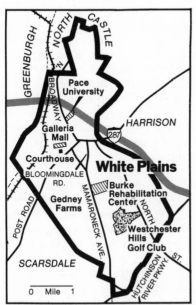

To midtown Manhattan: Train 35 minutes

While it sleeps, White Plains is a city of 47,000 residents. Then, as the sun rises on weekday mornings, office workers and shoppers stream into town by bus, train, and car, transforming the Westchester County seat into a bustling city of about 300,000.

Commerce, government, and development are triple themes in this 300-year-old city. A.T.&T., General Foods, and Nestlé occupy their own buildings here. Branches of Bloomingdale's, Neiman-Marcus, and Saks Fifth Avenue cluster on or near Bloomingdale Road.

The twenty-story County Courthouse, opened in 1975 and joined to the older County Office Building, towers over a 120-acre downtown urban-renewal area under development for the last twenty years. Tall cranes still puncture the skyline over rising office structures.

Shoppers come from as far away as Poughkeepsie and Kingston to spend an estimated $900 million a year in the city's department stores, its shops along Mamaroneck Avenue and the Post Road, and its three-level Galleria mall, which opened in 1980.

There is a daily outflow of people, too, but it is much smaller than the influx. About 7,000 commuters board trains and buses for New York City, twenty-two miles to the south, or drive east or west along I-287 to jobs in corporate office campuses that have given the thoroughfare its nickname, "The Platinum Mile."

WHITE PLAINS

The trip to Grand Central Station on the Metro-North line takes thirty-five minutes by express trains, forty-eight by locals. County express buses also take passengers to and from Manhattan (as far south as the Wall Street area) six days a week. Passengers board at Central Park Avenue and Tarrytown Road.

Settled in 1683, White Plains was designated the county seat in 1778, two years after the British engaged George Washington's troops in the Battle of White Plains and retired to Dobbs Ferry. It is bounded roughly by Route I-287 on the north, Scarsdale on the south, Greenburgh on the west, and the Hutchinson River Parkway on the east.

"It's a very strong commercial and retail city, but when they leave at five o'clock, we still have a very strong small-town community," said Constance S. De Filippis, a real-estate broker who was born and reared in White Plains.

A wide tax base resulting from the concentrations of commercial development is one of the reasons that real-estate taxes are among the lowest in Westchester County. The White Plains assessor, Elliot Glaser, said that taxes on a $150,000 house would average about $3,000 a year. He added that assessment levels have remained the same for many years.

Three office buildings planned or under construction in the urban-renewal area between the Galleria and the city's railroad station will eventually contribute about $1.8 million in taxes to the city, according to Edward C. Steinberg, director of the city's Urban Renewal Agency. He estimated that the buildings, to be completed within the next two years, could lower the tax rate by $3 to $4 per $1,000 of assessed valuation.

Yet, the city is not encouraging commercial development, believing that residential building is a greater present need. "Nobody gets rezoning from residential to offices," said Mayor Alfred Del Vecchio of applicants who come for permission before the city's six-member Common Council.

A wide variety of new housing—from single-family subdivisions to condominiums—is being planned and built both in the business district and in the southern areas of the city where most of the open space remains.

More than 450 condominium units are under construction in the business district, with 720 more condominiums and rental units planned, according to the city's planning commissioner, David C. Ornstein. South of the Westchester Hills Golf Club, between Mamaroneck Avenue and North Street, 413 condominiums and single-family homes are under construction or planned, Mr. Ornstein said. They include two-, three-, and four-family clustered condominiums priced at $160,000 and up.

High costs have made rental apartments so risky for builders that no rental building has been put up in Westchester County without government subsidy since the early 1970's. But a 120-unit, ten-story rental building in the heart of the city's downtown urban-renewal district is going forward, subsidized, in effect, by its developer, the Robert Martin Company. A one-bedroom apartment will rent for about $800 a month.

"This is going to lose money," said Mr. Steinberg, the director of urban renewal. A trade-off was negotiated between the agency and the developers, who agreed to drop plans for 292 condominiums and substitute the rental units in return for permission to build 262,000 square feet of adjacent office space.

Just south of the sprawling lawns of the Burke Rehabilitation Center is Gedney Farms, a neighborhood in the south-central part of the city that took its name from a family of Loyalist farmers who bought a large tract early in the 1700's. The 300-room Gedney Farm Hotel with tennis courts, golf course, and swimming pool, was built there about 1913.

The hotel was a popular place with such movie stars as Mary Pickford and Douglas Fairbanks, Sr., according to the city historian, Renoda Hoffman, who added that Eddie Cantor was there in 1924 on the night it burned down.

Houses built in the 1920's in the Gedney Farms area are primarily stately Tudors or stucco center-hall colonials on half-acre plots. They have been selling for $300,000 and up.

In Rosedale to the south, three-bedroom split-levels and ranches sell for about $200,000, Ms. De Filippis said, while Hillair Circle houses on larger lots south and west of Mamaroneck Avenue go for $450,000 and more.

Six elementary and intermediate public schools in the ten-square-mile city prepare students to enter White Plains High School, which has 1,850 students and about 160 teachers. More than 80 percent of the graduates go on to some form of higher education, according to Dr. Saul M. Yanofsky, special assistant to the superintendent.

About a hundred students in the seventh to twelfth grades "who are willing to take the responsibility for defining their own programs" are enrolled in the Community School, which allows time for internships in community activities and for taking college courses.

White Plains has three movie theaters, one on the Main Street level of the bustling Galleria shopping mall. Fast-food stores on the mall's Grove Street level offer tacos, sushi, and souvlaki, which shoppers can eat at tables in a sunken dining area at the bottom of the three-story atrium.

Foreign cuisine abounds. Indian tandoori cooking is featured at the Bengal Tiger Restaurant, across East Post Road from the Spanish Meson Castellano, and French cuisine is featured at Le Gai Pinguin on Westchester Avenue.

269

American cooking prevails at such restaurants as Victoria Station on Water Street, Sassafras on Mamaroneck Avenue, and Oliver's on South Broadway, where a youthful singles crowd gathers in the evening.

One of the county's five public golf courses, Maple Moor, lies along the Hutchinson River Parkway. In addition, the city maintains 190 acres of recreation land, including two outdoor swimming pools, twenty-eight tennis courts, five platform tennis courts, an artificial ice rink, and a center for the elderly.

—FRANKLIN WHITEHOUSE

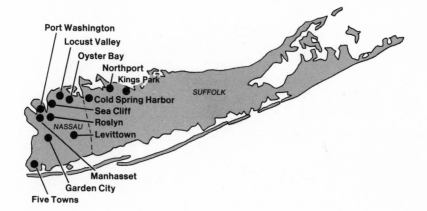

Port Washington
Locust Valley
Oyster Bay
Northport
Kings Park
Cold Spring Harbor
SUFFOLK
Sea Cliff
Roslyn
NASSAU
Levittown
Manhasset
Garden City
Five Towns

COLD SPRING HARBOR

To midtown Manhattan: Train 50 minutes

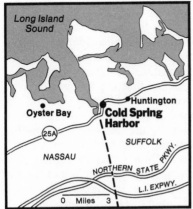

old Spring Harbor, a natural inlet on Long Island Sound fed by underground springs from the surrounding hills, has been serving as safe harbor for new residents since the seventeenth century.

Among the more recent settlers is Ruth Walker. She arrived with her family in 1974 and, like many before them, became attached to the harbor's deep blue water and the lush greenery of the surrounding hills. "I've got a lot of fishermen," she said, referring to her four children and her husband, Richard, a management consultant. The Walkers also were attracted by the school system, one that soon involved not only the Walker children but Ruth Walker herself. She has been serving on the Board of Education. "It kind of snowballed," she explained. "I just started out helping, and one job led to another."

The earliest settlers of Cold Spring Harbor were Dutch, but by the end of the seventeenth century, the English had firmly established themselves. The first settlers built a dirt road north and south on the east side of the harbor and then eastward as the town grew. By the early years of the nineteenth century, the road had become Main Street, and the harbor had grown into a bustling whaling port, its deep waters and new docks filled with tall-masted ships.

Cold Spring Harbor was a home base for whaling captains. One of them, Manuel Enos, a native of Fayal in the Azores, married a local

273

woman and around 1860 built an imposing white house at 298 Main Street. He and his crew later disappeared at sea, but the house still stands, as do other sturdy buildings built by ship carpenters.

Perhaps the oldest building in town is the Conklin-Seaman House, erected about 1720 as the home of Richard M. Conklin, a Suffolk County judge who was sponsor of a whaling company. In the nineteenth century, the house became Seaman's Railroad House. Ezra Seaman, its proprietor, provided lodgings for sailors and travelers making connections with sailing ships or the local stagecoach at the Cold Spring railroad station.

But when kerosene replaced whale oil as the favored fuel for lighting, the whaling era ended for Cold Spring Harbor. The inlet was then discovered by wealthy New York families, who began to buy up large tracts for summer homes. Among them was Louis Comfort Tiffany, the artist and decorative designer whose glass vases, lamps, and windows depict scenes that are thought to have been inspired by the view from his home in Cold Spring Harbor. The flowering wisteria that frames scenes of water and rolling hills in Tiffany stained-glass panels that now hang in the Metropolitan Museum of Art in New York is a recurring pattern in Tiffany's work. Wisteria abounds in the wooded hills of Cold Spring Harbor.

Though the whaling industry has long since gone, much of the old harborside character of the hamlet remains, encouraged by landmark status approved in 1976 by the Town of Huntington.

Cold Spring Harbor residents pay taxes to Huntington and are served by that town's elected officials. Some residents are annoyed that the village has not incorporated, as have several neighboring communities of similar size, and resent the fact that the village does not have government that is purely its own.

Brick sidewalks edged with picket fences line Main Street, where restaurants, antique shops, boutiques, and galleries attract residents as well as visitors from other North Shore communities.

Typical of the nineteenth-century commercial structures that border Main Street is the Burr-Gardiner House. The building, with two halves built separately, was occupied in 1858 by Elbert Burr, a shoemaker who rented some of his rooms to guests. Later, Townsend Gardiner, who is listed in census records as a fisherman, laborer, and shoemaker, used the building as a boarding house.

Now, the shops along Main Street vary from Talbots clothing store to Lexie's Clothes for Kids, Inc., to Valdemar F. Jacobsen Antiques at Bedlam Corner. Among Main Street restaurants are Gourmet's Delights, Prescott's, Country Kitchen, and the Ice Cream Parlor. Another is the Whaler's Inn on Harbor Road, or Route 25A.

While crowds of visitors who regularly stroll through the village provide business for shopowners, some residents have expressed concern that the shopping district attracts too many tourists and that the Main Street and waterside areas are in danger of being over-developed.

The predominant style of home architecture in the 2.5-square-mile hamlet is the colonial with a cedar shake exterior. But there also are clapboards, split-ranches, and brick Tudors.

According to Carol Tintle of the Daniel Gale Agency, houses range upward in price from about $250,000, with some exceptional properties costing almost $600,000. Most homeowners pay from $4,000 to $5,000 annually in taxes. The zoning in the hamlet is predominantly two-acre, with smaller lots near commercial areas.

Suffolk County provides police protection and Huntington maintains the hamlet's roads. Garbage is collected by Huntington and private contractors.

The Cold Spring Harbor Laboratories, which conducts extensive marine and biological research, employs a few residents, but most work outside the hamlet. Many of the 5,200 residents are newcomers, transferred executives and managers employed by large companies.

Mr. Walker, like many commuters to New York City, rides the Long Island Railroad. "It takes him fifty minutes to reach the city from the Cold Spring Harbor station," said Ms. Walker, "and thirty-five minutes to either La Guardia or Kennedy." Although she had few kind words for the L.I.R.R., she said, "We've lived in a lot of places, and I don't think there is any place with an easy commute."

There is also the Huntington Area Rapid Transit, known as HART, which operates buses in Huntington, Cold Spring Harbor, and several other villages. The buses stop at all L.I.R.R. stations in the town.

More than a score of religious denominations are active in the area, with sixty-four houses of worship. Among them is the Methodist Meeting House, a white clapboard structure built in 1842 on Main Street.

In 1852 a group of residents formed the Eagle Engine Fire Company and purchased a hand pumper, now on view in the Suffolk Museum and Carriage House in Stony Brook. The volunteer Cold Spring Harbor Company of today operates seven pieces of modern equipment.

Across the street from the present firehouse, which was built in 1930, is the Cold Spring Harbor Library, built in 1913 and run by Laura Farwell. Her husband, Robert, is director of the Cold Spring Harbor Whaling Museum. The library, at the west end of Main Street, or the museum, at the east end, is a good place from which to begin a tour of the hamlet.

Dr. Martin Davis, who has served as superintendent of schools since 1960, said he has seen the system grow "from three little elementary schools into a highly academic and structurally strong school district." He noted that more than 95 percent of high-school graduates go on to higher education. There also are sixteen private schools in the area.

"It's one of the nicest places I know on Long Island," Mr. Farwell, the museum director, said of his hometown. "It's close enough to New York City for cultural activities, but, at the same time, it's far enough away from the city to be a fairly quiet residential area."

—JOHN T. MCQUISTON

FIVE TOWNS

To midtown Manhattan: Train 35 to 45 minutes

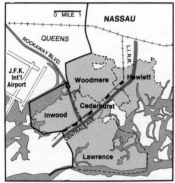

ount carefully and you will find more than five towns in the Five Towns, an area in the wetlands of southwestern Nassau County that has estates worthy of barons, striking contemporary palaces, and smaller suburban split-levels. The basic five are Lawrence, Cedarhurst, Woodmere, Hewlett, and Inwood. But the area also includes some unincorporated communities and two tiny villages, Hewlett Bay Park and Woodsburgh, that are not added to the final total.

Whatever the actual number, the Five Towns contain some of the wealthiest neighborhoods in the metropolitan area, some of the poorest, and some of the noisiest. The area is under the Kennedy International Airport flight paths, and depending on the weather and on the runways in use, windows may rattle and shoppers on street corners may have to shout to be heard.

Outsiders wonder how Five Towns residents cope with the whining of the jets, but cope they do. "Even for those of us who live directly under the flight path, it just becomes part of life," said Maryann Sutel, director of admissions and development at Lawrence Country Day School. "After you've lived here a while, you're not particularly aware of them, but they do break up your barbecues."

Each community has its own identity. Cedarhurst, for example, has Central Avenue, where the fashion-conscious say they find dress

277

shops that offer far more than standard suburban shopping centers. Within a ten-minute drive are major shopping centers in neighboring Valley Stream, and within a five-minute drive are department stores and discount shops on the border between Queens and Woodmere. In Hewlett—the oldest of the Five Towns—Trinity Church, a stunning example of the American stick style, stands out among many architectural treasures. And in Hewlett Bay Park, there are houses designed by Stanford White and Marcel Breuer.

The homes in Inwood are more modest, and its median income is one of Long Island's lowest. Woodmere is a mixture of large custom-designed houses and smaller suburban split-levels. Lawrence was once described as "the most aristocratic of the Five Towns," and many Five Towners say it still is, what with its rambling, hundred-year-old houses that are still called "cottages" because they were built for summer people and winterized later.

Ms. Sutel, who lives in one of the Lawrence "cottages," said hers is the smallest on the block (it has nine bedrooms, the others have twelve). But although hers was big enough for her six children and five cats, it was not without its problems. "These houses are a bit short on structure, and we all share data on lolly columns," she noted, referring to posts that are added in the basements to provide extra structural support. "If you don't shore them up, they won't support mortar-tile bathrooms. The originals had freestanding fixtures. If you put in a modern bathroom, that's what happened to me. My living room sagged three inches."

For Five Towners, the commute to Manhattan on the Long Island Railroad takes thirty-five to forty-five minutes, depending on where they board. Each of the Five Towns has its own station, and some trains also stop at the Gibson station between Hewlett and Valley Stream.

The Five Towns are incorporated villages within the Town of Hempstead. The Nassau County police protect them, and there is some pooling of educational resources.

According to Hayward Cirker, publisher and local historian, the Five Towns were not called by that name until the 1930's. The term caught on after Far Rockaway, the original hub of the area, became part of New York City. A 1917 history refers to the area as "the peninsula" or "the branch," Mr. Cirker said. "Five Towns is a meaningless term because there is no government that controls just those five towns. I think it began to be used because these towns all had about the same income level."

With the exception of Inwood, they still do. Federal census reports show that Hewlett Bay Park is the richest of the five communities, with an average income of more than $22,000—well above the state average.

House prices in the area tend to be well above average, too.

Brokers say they have few listings for less than $150,000, except in Inwood. In Woodmere a four-bedroom split-level typically sells for $200,000 to $250,000, according to brokers there, and in Lawrence colonials with five bedrooms and five baths are listed at $275,000 to $300,000. Tax bills, which are based on the age of the structure and include village, town, county, school, and water district levies, vary within the area. On average throughout the Five Towns, the owner of a $200,000 house would pay between $3,500 to $4,000 in annual taxes.

In recent years condominiums have been developed and more are being planned. The prices range upward from about $145,000 for a two-bedroom unit.

Hewlett was settled first, in the 1750's. Its first family was a branch of the Hewlett clan, which settled throughout the island. According to Mr. Cirker, the most famous of the Five Towns Hewletts was Richard, a Tory sympathizer who fled to Canada and did not return until after the Revolution. Local legend has it that he tried to poison George Washington.

In colonial days Rock Hall in Lawrence was a major plantation. It is now a museum, with its outbuildings and slave quarters open to visitors. The Hewletts bought the house in the middle of the nineteenth century. In the 1920's, R. Buckminster Fuller, the futurist and inventor of the geodesic dome, was married in Rock Hall. His wife, Anne, who died a few days after he did in 1983, was a Hewlett.

When the Fullers exchanged their vows, the Five Towns were just beginning to boom. "Until the railroad came through after the Civil War, the population was minimal and Far Rockaway was the fashionable place," Mr. Cirker said. "But the railroad opened it up to suburban development, although there were a number of real estate developers who failed badly."

One was Samuel Wood, who gave his name to Woodmere, but his hotel there was a flop, Mr. Cirker said. In the 1890's, Abraham Lawrence gave his name to another Five Towns community. These days the Five Towns are not as much of a resort area as they once were. But many summer renters still go there because it is close enough to Manhattan for working parents to have the pleasures of the shorefront; a variety of tennis, beach, and yacht clubs; and an easy commute.

The public schools in the Five Towns are generally regarded as among the best on the island, in part because the area's substantial property-tax base makes possible smaller-than-average class sizes and higher-than-average instructional expenditures. There are also a substantial number of private schools. Two of the best known are Lawrence Country Day School, in Hewlett, and the Woodmere Academy.

All these schools fit in comfortably, and the proximity of the Five

F I V E   T O W N S

Towns to the city is one of the things that people who live there say they appreciate. "If you lived farther out, you'd have traffic problems on the Long Island Expressway," Ms. Sutel said. "I like to be able to live in the woods and still get in the car and go to the opera."

—JAMES BARRON

GARDEN CITY

To midtown Manhattan: Train 30 to 40 minutes

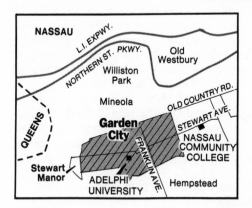

Garden City began as the dream of a wealthy man and became a subject for dreams in the heads of house hunters. It is the kind of village that really does have tree-lined streets and lush green lawns and gardens that do justice to its name. That Garden City turned out that way is something of a surprise, considering what it originally looked like.

Early in the nineteenth century, Timothy Dwight, the president of Yale College, wandered across Long Island's treeless midsection and called it "the easternmost of the American Prairies." "Its vegetation," he wrote, "is nothing but a coarse wild grass, which supplies indifferent pasturage for a great number of cattle."

These days cattle are banned in the Garden City area, and the neighboring community of Stewart Manor, named after Garden City's founder, goes so far in its restrictions on animals as to prohibit the ownership of more than three cats.

Garden City is in the middle of Long Island, more or less midway between the Sound and the Atlantic Ocean. Its 25,000 residents live in an area of approximately 4.3 square miles, more than two thirds the size of Manhattan.

The community was the dream of Alexander Turney Stewart, an Irish-born multimillionaire who founded, built, and operated the entire village from 1869 until his death seven years later. He bought the land for $55 an acre—about 30 percent more than previous offers—

and one of his first tasks was to convince the people who owned farms adjacent to his planned community that he did not intend to develop what Mildred Smith, the village historian, calls "tenements and public charities."

He did so by unveiling ambitious architectural plans and, according to Ms. Smith's book, *History of Garden City,* by hauling in and planting thousands of trees and shrubs from a nursery in Flushing, Queens. He built a dozen huge Victorian houses at a cost of $17,000 apiece and rented them for $100 a month. They quickly became known around the village as the "Twelve Apostles"; smaller houses that were somewhat similar were dubbed "The Disciples."

Within weeks of Stewart's death in 1876, his widow decided to give money for a cathedral that would be the seat of the Episcopal Diocese of Brooklyn, which then included Long Island. When the ornate neo-Gothic structure was completed, it was the tallest building on the Island, and sailors said they could see it from the East River, miles away.

In the gay 90's, the architect Stanford White, husband of one of Stewart's heirs, was commissioned to design a 200-room hotel. The idea was to cater to wealthy New Yorkers who had begun flocking to Long Island resorts, and the hotel was what put Garden City on the map.

From its opening the guest list carried the signatures of Harrimans, Morgans, Astors, Cushings, and Vanderbilts. And although White's original hotel burned only four years after its completion, his firm, McKim, Mead & White, was immediately hired to design a fireproof replacement. That hotel lasted until 1973, when it was demolished; a new luxury establishment went up on the same site and it opened in 1983.

Residents who had grown fond of the cupola atop the old hotel were delighted to see that it had been retained on the new one. They also were pleased to have the hotel's three new restaurants in town.

Living in Garden City is expensive. Houses sell for an average of $300,000 to $350,000, and one-bedroom cooperative apartments for an average of $140,000, according to Elaine Nolan of Nolan Realty. But prices can range from as low as $120,000 to $150,000 for a three-bedroom, one-bath, brick colonial-style home to $1 million for a six-bedroom, four-bath house on several acres. Taxes on a $250,000 home, depending on age and size, average about $2,700.

Real-estate brokers say that Garden City houses hold their value in part because of the village's proximity to New York City. For commuters who want to be up, up, and away in a matter of minutes, a helipad is a five-minute drive from the heart of the village, and midtown is a seven-minute flight from the helipad.

For earthbound commuters, the trip to Pennsylvania Station on the Long Island Railroad takes between thirty and forty minutes.

GARDEN CITY

Midtown Manhattan is about twenty miles away via the Long Island Expressway or the Northern State Parkway, and outside rush hours the trip can take as little as forty minutes.

In a way, Garden City is a village of schools. For 105 years the Episcopal Diocese has run St. Paul's and St. Mary's, separate boys' and girls' schools, near the cathedral. The public school system is praised by residents for its quality and small size; the senior high-school class has about 450 students. Almost 90 percent of the graduates go on to college or other forms of education.

Some Garden City graduates can go to college right at home: Adelphi University, a four-year liberal arts institution, left Brooklyn in 1929 for its seventy-four-acre campus, which is not far from the cathedral. Adelphi now has an enrollment of 11,000 studying every-thing from arts and sciences to banking and money management to nursing to social work. Garden City's other campus belongs to Nassau Community College, which has almost twice as many students as Adelphi. Not only is Nassau the largest school in Garden City, but it is also the largest two-year institution in New York State.

Garden City is also the home of the Adelphi Festival Theater, which operates under the university's aegis. Thought to be one of the finest summer-stock theaters in the New York metropolitan area, it often plays to capacity houses. The artistic director is Jean Marsh, better known outside the village for her role in *Upstairs, Downstairs.*

The New York Arrows practice at Nassau Community College, and the Nassau Veterans Memorial Coliseum, where the New York Islanders play, and Hofstra University, where the New York Jets hold their training camp, are in Uniondale, less than ten minutes from the heart of the village.

In recent years new office buildings have filled in the space be-tween the courthouses that straddle the Garden City-Mineola line and the Nassau County Police Headquarters on Franklin Avenue, which is lined with branches of the major New York department stores. But despite the new construction and the comings and goings of shoppers and new tenants, the traffic and the atmosphere are hardly hectic.

"Garden City reminds me of Switzerland," said Jean-Robert Cauvin, general manager of the Garden City Hotel, who was born in France and educated in Switzerland. "It's very, very clean. I would even compare Garden City to Monte Carlo, but we don't have the mountains."

—JAMES BARRON

KINGS PARK

To midtown Manhattan: Train 90 minutes

In 1982 the school board of Kings Park, Long Island, voted to close one of its four elementary schools, signaling a new phase in the history of this small North Shore village. Kings Park was graying—again.

The rapid growth of the 1960's and 1970's that transformed a small, aging hospital village into a bustling young suburban community of some 22,000 has slowed. The young couples with the large families are now middle-aged and their children are leaving.

But the stabilization of the population will not drastically change a community that stands out from many others on Long Island because of several distinctions—some good, some bad, some mixed.

With its main street a mixture of old and new, its core the old, well-kept village ringed on the outskirts by medium-size suburban developments, Kings Park does not fit the stereotype of suburban sprawl.

Forty-eight miles from Times Square and fifteen miles inside Suffolk County, between larger and wealthier Northport and Smithtown, it is best known for its state mental hospital. Founded ninety-five years ago, the hospital was originally for residents of Kings County, hence its name and that of the village, which in 1887 was little more than a railroad station and farms.

It was known then as Brooklyn East, and in some ways it still is. The onetime hotel at the main intersection was known as the Brook-

284

lyn until it was transformed at a cost of $300,000—many times its original price—into the Baker Street Inn, with offices above. Even today, a considerable number of Kings Park residents are natives of Brooklyn.

The ride to Manhattan takes ninety minutes on the Long Island Railroad when the trains are running on time, one to two hours by car depending on the time of day. During rush hour, traffic is heavy almost all the way, testimony to the eastward population shift.

There are other distinctions: Kings Park has five miles of shoreline, almost all publicly owned, and more parkland, open space, and recreation area than most Long Island communities. It borders on one of the few rivers on Long Island, the Nissequogue, ideal for canoeing.

A suburb itself, it has two distinct suburbs of its own, wealthy Fort Salonga, with one- and two-acre zoning, and middle-class San Remo, which began as a summer community for mostly Italian-Americans.

Houses are generally cheaper and taxes lower than in most other communities in northwestern Suffolk. Larry Flynn, a local broker, puts the median price of Kings Park houses at $140,000. Property taxes on such a house would be about $3,500 a year.

Predominantly Catholic, it also has one of the island's oldest Jewish communities. Rabbi Gordon Papert of the Kings Park Jewish Center said the first temple was built shortly after the turn of the century.

Kings Park High School has acquired a reputation as a training ground for the service academies, with twenty-six of its alumni now in the five academies. This is at least partly because the school—and particularly an English teacher, Leo Ostebo—has made a point over the last fourteen years of seeking out prospects. Another secondary school, St. Anthony's High School, run by the Franciscan Brothers, is at the eastern edge of town.

On the negative side, Kings Park has landfills at both its southern and western borders—one of the prices of having open spaces and being at the edge of the Towns of Smithtown and Huntington, which meet at the borders of Kings Park. The village itself is in Smithtown.

The hospital is the dominant feature of the community, although its influence has been diluted in the last twenty-five years. It is an economic fact of life as well as a geographic landmark, providing thousands of jobs over the last century for its first Irish immigrants, their descendants, and other lower- to middle-income workers.

"That hospital enabled many of us to stay in the community," said William Richards, the presiding officer of the Suffolk County Legislature, who was born and raised in Kings Park and began work in the hospital.

The hospital, which once had its own farm, is in a parklike setting on the Sound that contributes substantially to the greening of Kings Park. Its grounds have shrunk over the years from 870 to 600 acres, with its valuable land going at low cost for a Catholic church, a Jewish center, a modern library, the public high school and athletic fields, and a new government complex east of the old community. The complex includes a water district building and a Parks Department headquarters.

"There is a tiny bit of stigma attached to the hospital, but it has been a major employer in the town," said the Smithtown supervisor, Patrick R. Vecchio, a Kings Park resident.

If the hospital is a mixed blessing to some, few would question the advantage of the 1,266-acre Sunken Meadow State Park, with its mile-long beach, three-quarter-mile boardwalk, picnic areas, cross-country track, and the Sunken Meadow Parkway, which provides an easy connection to the Long Island Expressway and parkways as well as a lightly traveled greenbelt to further separate housing developments.

Flanking the state park on the west is the Smithtown beach and picnic area, restricted to town residents. It is called Callahan's Beach, another sign of the original Irish cast of Kings Park. East of Sunken Meadow is "the Bluff" and the town marina where the Nissequogue River empties into the Sound.

Across the small "harbor" is another town beach, Short Beach, which includes a small camping area on a peninsula jutting into the Sound. Two town parks, the extensive high-school and junior high-school playing fields, and a privately operated indoor tennis facility and an indoor ice-skating rink complete the Kings Park greenery and recreation facilities.

These natural resources are complemented by what some call the cozy atmosphere of Kings Park. "What I like is the small-town air about it, the considerable community feeling," said Walter R. Arnold, the superintendent of schools, who presides over a high school, a junior high school, four (soon to be three) elementary schools, and a student population of about 4,800, down nearly 2,000 from the 1974 high.

There are two medium-size shopping centers, one just south of Main Street in Kings Park and the other in Fort Salonga. The one movie in town still features "ladies' night" on Monday, when women are admitted free.

The heart of the community is Main Street, with its mixture of buildings, some newly renovated and others still dating back to the turn of the century. Just south of Main Street and the railroad station is Reddy's grocery store, where many of the town's tradesmen and Republican politicians gather for morning coffee and conversation in the back room.

Main Street (actually Route 25A, which stretches east from the

East River) has only two lanes in Kings Park. Unlike most such roads that become gasoline alleys in other communities, it is tree-lined and residential except for the four-block business area of the village itself.

The housing in the community, almost exclusively one-family, is as varied as Main Street. It ranges from waterfront estates in Fort Salonga through typical suburban development houses, substantial older homes in the village, and summer bungalows converted for year-round use in parts of San Remo and the village.

The variations in housing are reflected in a friendly rivalry between the "townies," or old-timers, and the newcomers. When he ran for fire commissioner, Edward J. Collins was needled by several old-timers for running against a townie, Joseph Teigue, who was born in Kings Park more than half a century ago and has lived there all his life. Mr. Collins—a resident for a mere quarter-century—won handily.

—FRANK LYNN

L E V I T T O W N

To midtown Manhattan: Train 60 minutes

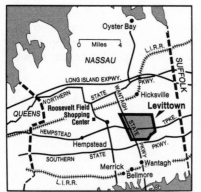

Almost four decades after the first William J. Levitt house appeared in the potato fields of Nassau County as an innovative refuge for returning World War II veterans and their families, Levittown is again serving as a community where young married couples may find affordable housing and a pleasant environment in which to begin raising a family.

As retired homeowners move out, new young families are moving in, continuing the transformation of Levittown. "It's a perfect starter house," said Barbara Tufano, who in 1983 bought a six-room "handyman's special" on Hunter Lane. She said her husband, Carmine, a carpenter, has added four more rooms, and they expect the house to last another thirty years. "The Levitt house is a good buy," she said. "It's well laid out and you can do so much with it." She noted that she and her husband recently have bought two other Levittown houses as income properties for themselves and their eight-month-old son, Carmine, Jr.

Leslie Campbell, who lives with her husband and two young children on Elm Tree Lane, said that to find similar prices they would have had to move to Suffolk County. "And since my husband works at two jobs near Levittown, and the price was right, we bought here," she added. "If we lived in Suffolk, we'd never see him."

Many of the Levitt Cape Cods and modified ranch homes have been remodeled, reshingled, or expanded, as the community con-

288

tinues to confound those who nearly four decades ago predicted that Levittown would become a slum.

The first residents paid $65 a month rent with an option to buy for $6,990 (no down payment for veterans). By the time the last new "ranch" was sold on Tardy Lane in November 1951, the basic house built by Mr. Levitt cost $9,500. Now the houses cost $90,000 to $120,000 and sometimes more.

The owner of a typical $100,000 house would have a tax bill of $2,400 a year for school, county, town, and fire district levies.

The first 300 families moved into the uniform, four-room Cape Cod houses in September 1947. Nearly 17,500 houses were constructed. The original Levitt house was 750 square feet, with a living room, two bedrooms, a kitchen, bathroom, and "expansion" attic, according to John Pergola, one of the original Cape Cod residents who has operated a real-estate agency in Levittown for twenty-five years. He noted that many of the houses have been doubled in size as owners raised their roofs, added dormers, and pushed out their walls to include new bedrooms, dens, sun rooms, and garages.

The initial low cost of the Levitt houses was made possible by mass-construction techniques as innovative in their time as the Model T Ford assembly line was in its time. More than thirty houses were going up each day at the peak of production, all basically of the same design, but with some variations.

The Cape Cods were offered in three models, and the ranches in five variations. But in each, the floor plan was the same. The construction was deliberately designed so that additions or other alterations could be made.

The developer encouraged change by placing the homes at different distances from the street and at different angles on each plot, which averaged 60 by 100 feet.

To facilitate development as a garden community, ornamental trees and shrubs, as well as four fruit trees, went with each house. There were also nine community swimming pools, half a dozen "village greens" that included a few shops, such as groceries and coin laundries, and more than 116 parklike playfields.

The community sprawls across some 7.3 square miles in an unincorporated area almost entirely within the Town of Hempstead, with a tiny bulge in the Town of Oyster Bay.

For many of its 65,000 residents, Levittown is still a stepping-stone, still the first house in the suburbs, a factor demonstrated by its annual turnover rate of around 10 percent.

Situated just south of the center of Long Island in Nassau County, Levittown identifies with neither the South nor the North shore. It sees itself as a midisland community, with concerns that reflect those of the county in general.

Levittown residents have long led the battle to hold down property taxes on the Island and have dealt with such problems as providing working parents with day-care centers at neighborhood schools and creating programs for the growing population of elderly.

The graying of the population in Levittown has been the most recent concern of officials worried about a declining school population. However, they note that generally lower mortgage interest rates are enabling younger couples to move in. Still, shrinking school enrollments have led Levittown officials to close a high school and convert it into a district adult- and special-education headquarters.

Levittown's school system began in a three-room country schoolhouse in 1947. By the 1960's it was one of the largest in the state, with more than 16,000 students and a budget of $9 million. Total enrollment now is about 8,000 students. The budget of more than $40 million operates two high schools, two middle schools, and six elementary schools.

The high schools graduate about 700 students each June, and well over 80 percent of them go on to higher education, according to Gerald Lauber, superintendent of schools. He noted that test scores in the district had "gone up dramatically" as the result of a new reading program that matches the reading level of each student with a variety of textbooks. As for changes in student enrollment, Mr. Lauber observed: "We are still losing about three hundred students a year from the system, but we expect that to stabilize as home sales increase. We are looking forward to a rebirth of the school district."

Residents say one of the attractions of the community is its relative safety. The Nassau County Police say their biggest problem in Levittown has been simple criminal mischief and residential burglaries, primarily by youths, but that both had been decreasing with the aging of the population.

Hempstead Turnpike, which runs east-west through the center of Levittown, is the main street for business and entertainment. The Roosevelt Field Shopping Center, the largest mall on the Island, is in nearby Uniondale.

There are six Protestant churches in Levittown, along with two Roman Catholic churches, one of which is undergoing a $1.8 million renovation, and two Jewish congregations, Reformed and Orthodox.

Fred Neist is chairman of the Levittown–Island Trees Youth Council, which provides a program of athletics, art, and music for 14,000 children. He moved to Levittown thirty-three years ago, and three of his five children now own houses there and are raising families. "We find many of our children coming back to town as professionals—teachers, lawyers, doctors—and setting up business here," Mr. Neist said, "and that pleases us."

Although the Levitt organization built Levittown, complete with sewers and roads, part of its infrastructure is now in the process of being replaced. New sewer and major repaving projects have been completed.

Residents who make the one-hour commute to New York City have a choice of traveling several miles north to the Long Island Railroad station in Hicksville, or several miles south to the Merrick, Bellmore, or Wantagh station.

Bus service to the railroad stations and along the major roads— Hempstead Turnpike, Newbridge Road, Jerusalem Avenue, and Hicksville Road—is provided by the Metropolitan Suburban Bus Authority.

Motorists can reach Levittown by several major routes: the Long Island Expressway to Exit 41, then south on Route 107; Northern State Parkway to Exit 33, south on Wantagh Parkway, then east on Hempstead Turnpike; or Southern State Parkway to Exit 27, north on Wantagh Parkway, then east on Hempstead Turnpike.

—JOHN T. MCQUISTON

LOCUST VALLEY

To midtown Manhattan: Train 70 minutes

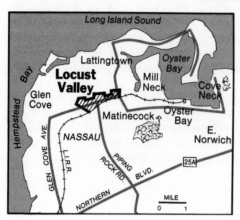

According to the Long Island Railroad, Locust Valley is only an hour and ten minutes from Pennsylvania Station. But it seems a world away.

In this rolling green enclave in the Island's North Shore area, the car-repair shop is a coach and motor works, and the drugstore is a chemist. The shopping center is a cluster of French Provincial cottages, and there is even La Barbichette, a pet-care salon tucked behind a beauty shop. Tall trees line gently curving roads, marked not by street signs but discreet wooden mileposts. Rambling houses sit on wide, lush lawns, and there is a feeling of spaciousness and unhurried ease.

Yet, Locust Valley proper, an unincorporated village of the Town of Oyster Bay, covers only 1.0421 square miles along the L.I.R.R.'s Oyster Bay line, part of its southern boundary. Much of the scenery and many of the mansions that give the area its exclusive reputation are actually in the adjacent villages of Matinecock to the south, Mill Neck to the east, and Lattingtown to the north. (Its neighbor to the west and south is Glen Cove.)

Still, Locust Valley's luster is such that people often use its name when referring to the surrounding villages as well. The social register is sprinkled with names of those who live in the area—such as Frances Morgan Pennoyer, daughter of J. P. Morgan, Jr.—most of whom pay dearly for the privilege.

292

LOCUST VALLEY

"It's hard to say what the price of an average house is, because we hardly ever have any average houses," said Janice Deegan of Coach Realty–Janice Deegan Inc., a local real-estate brokerage. "They're all sort of extraordinary. About the lowest we have now is a three-bedroom Cape Cod for $139,500, and from there they go up to a million and more."

Even for those who can afford the prices, the market is tight. "We have lots and lots of customers and not enough houses," observed Ms. Deegan, who has been selling property in the area for twelve years.

Patrick Mackay, a broker with Piping Rock Associates, agreed. "I wish we had a lot of people who could spend $250,000 to $300,000 for a house and we had lots of houses like that, but they just don't exist. Small village houses that were selling for $40,000 and $50,000 in the mid-70's now go for $200,000 or more. And it's almost impossible to find anything for less than $150,000."

Part of what makes living in Locust Valley and environs so appealing for many, and so expensive for all, are zoning ordinances that require minimum plots of two to five acres. There are a few exceptions like the Mill Neck Estates development in Mill Neck, with one-eighth-acre plots, although the rest of that village has three- and five-acre minimums. But in general, properties in the area have not seen the division and subdivision that swept so many parts of the Island after World War II. If the large estates of the 1920's and 1930's are no longer completely intact, they often seem to be no more than quartered.

And the variations in zoning can mean even higher prices. "A house in one village, a brick Georgian on nine acres, for instance, could bring $950,000 where the minimum zoning is five acres," Mr. Mackay said. "You could have the same house across the road on nine acres in another village with two-acre zoning and it would bring much less." But buyers can find something, he added, if they are persistent "and have the wherewithal."

For those who do find something in Locust Valley, the rewards can be substantial. Within the swath of several thousand acres are two arboretums, two wildlife preserves, and several golf courses and country clubs, the most exclusive of which is probably Piping Rock. The Locust Valley Tennis Association, on the grounds of the Locust Valley Library on Buckram Road, has five clay courts. The village's gray-stucco colonial firehouse—its biggest municipal structure—sits next door.

The schools, public and private, have solid reputations. The Locust Valley Central School District serves 2,128 students in the villages of Locust Valley, Bayville, and Brookville. It has four grade schools—two in Bayville, a few miles north of Locust Valley, and two in Locust Valley itself—and a combined junior-senior high school in Locust Valley.

LOCUST VALLEY

"The schools are outstanding," said Dr. Donald Cande, the district's superintendent, who cited National Merit Scholarship finalists in the high school. The average score last year for the verbal Scholastic Aptitude Test was 426, one point above the national average. The average mathematics score was 492, well above the national average. Dr. Eric Berger, the high-school principal, said that more than 80 percent of the school's graduates went on to higher education.

About 600 students in the district attend private schools, according to Dr. Cande, most at either the Portledge School or Friends Academy, local coeducational day schools. Portledge has a college preparatory program, with 280 students from nursery school to the twelfth grade. Founded in 1933 as the Stoddart's School, it was exclusively a nursery school until 1965, when it began adding one grade each year. The first high-school class was graduated in 1975.

Friends Academy was founded in 1877 by Quaker farmers. It is a selective college prep school for 656 students from nursery through senior high. All of its graduates go on to college, according to the headmaster, Frederic Withington.

The combined tax rate for the unincorporated village of Locust Valley, including school, town, and county taxes, is $33.48 per $100 of assessed valuation, with the average valuation at $13,300, well above the county average of $7,050, according to Thomas J. Preston, Jr., assistant to the chairman of the Nassau County Board of Assessors. Thus total taxes on an average house in the district last year were $4,452.70, Mr. Preston said.

The first European settlers came to Locust Valley in the 1660's, and in 1667 Captain John Underhill negotiated land deals with the Matinecock Indians and founded the community of Buckram. In 1725, Quakers established the Matinecock Meeting House, and the area began to grow. In colonial days it was part of a region known as the North Riding, which also encompassed Westchester County and parts of Queens. In 1856 the hamlet, by then a railroad stop, was renamed Locust Valley.

For residents and outsiders, Locust Valley's biggest attraction is probably its elegant shopping district, centered in the Country Shops on the Plaza mall near the railroad station. La Shack, a chic women's dress shop, shares quarters there with La Bonne Vie (linens and housewares) and Le Joaillier (fine jewels). Antique stores, a custom cabinet shop, a rare-book store, and a florist are nearby.

But Locust Valley is not all ritzy stores and big houses. The 1980 census found 4.3 percent of the population on welfare. Single women head 15 percent of the 963 households.

Woody Lewis, executive director of the Grenville Baker Boys' and Girls' Club in Locust Valley, said his organization tries to help families by serving the needs of youth in the community. "A lot of people say, 'Why do you need a boys' club in Locust Valley? It's so rich.' But it's clear that we fill a real need for the 650 kids involved in our programs." For $8 a year in dues, the club, founded in 1950 for boys only and coed since 1981, offers counseling, summer job placement, educational programs, athletics, and social activities.

The Locust Valley Library, one of the newest centers of village life, is also one of the oldest. The gray-shingled structure, which hugs a wooded hillside along Buckram Road, was renovated and expanded in 1983. Built as a recreation center in the 1920's by the Matinecock Neighborhood Association, it proved too expensive for the group to maintain during the Depression and was donated to the community. The renovation preserved the original dark wood beams and hanging cast-iron lanterns while making more room for the library's 45,000 volumes.

—TODD PURDUM

MANHASSET

To midtown Manhattan: Train 35 minutes

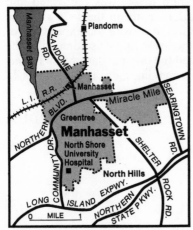

he Matinecock Indians who lived in what is now Manhasset, on Long Island's North Shore, called the area "Sint Sink"—and with reason, for the name meant "the place of many stones." Although Ice Age glaciers flattened the rest of the Island, this area was left with an uncharacteristically steep terrain and a forty-foot-long boulder weighing 1,800 tons. According to legend, Captain Kidd lifted the enormous rock, dug a hole, and stored some of his booty beneath it.

The Kidd tale may have been the first time that wealth, a well-known name, and Manhasset were all knit together, but by the twentieth century Manhasset was synonymous with grandeur and money. It had become the home of families who bred horses, played polo, and spent the winter somewhere else.

Manhasset, which consists of fifteen villages spread over more than five square miles, is a loosely defined community. One-family houses are the norm except for North Hills, the village closest to the Long Island Expressway, where the construction of condominiums has sharpened concern about whether tighter zoning regulations are needed.

North Hills enforced a moratorium on new construction from 1978 until 1980, when local officials adopted new zoning regulations intended to encourage a mix of condominium units and detached single-family houses. The new code permits up to six units an acre, less than what was allowed before the moratorium. Manhasset's other

296

villages bar condominium construction, but unlike some North Shore communities, Manhasset has not adopted a one-acre minimum for new single-family houses.

Perhaps the most famous Manhasset estate is Greentree, the 500-acre property between Shelter Rock Road and Community Drive that belonged to John Hay Whitney, master of one of this country's great fortunes. E. J. Kahn, Jr., Whitney's biographer, said that Whitney's adopted daughter, Kate, who was Franklin D. Roosevelt's grandchild, once took her children through the White House. "After inspecting it," Mr. Kahn wrote, "they pronounced it nice enough, but hardly on a par with Greentree."

Today single-family homes are hidden behind heavily tree-lined avenues. And two-bedroom condominiums with a vaguely California look and prices of $175,000 are clustered along Searingtown Road. Brokers say a typical four-bedroom house in Manhasset sells for $250,000 to $300,000.

Property taxes on a house with a market value of $200,000 are about $3,500 a year, held down by the tax base of department stores on the Miracle Mile, on Northern Boulevard between Searingtown Road and Community Drive.

The Miracle Mile, built mainly in the 1940's and 1950's, offers branches of four major department stores—B. Altman, Lord & Taylor, Abraham & Straus, and Bonwit Teller—and a Brooks Brothers branch that sold more than $80,000 worth of suits on its opening day in 1983, a record for the chain. It also offers restaurant patrons everything from traditional European dishes at the Brasserie St. Germain to Chinese at the First Wok to standard Americanized fare at the International House of Pancakes.

Off the Miracle Mile, there are smaller shops along Plandome Road. Local laws forbid self-service gas stations, and solid-metal security gates on storefronts were banned in 1983 by lawmakers worried about the impression they created of an embattled, high-crime inner-city neighborhood. Businessmen had said the gates were needed for protection against teenage vandalism, but Town Councilman Gerard Cunningham said he saw no reason for a "siege mentality."

The Long Island Railroad provides daily, thirty-five-minute train service to Manhattan on its Port Washington branch. Manhasset is two stops from the end of the line, which means that commuters have a good chance of getting seats in the morning.

The four public schools in Manhasset teach about 2,200 students (there were 2,867 in 1970) on a $12.8 million budget, or about $5,800 a pupil. That is $300 a pupil higher than the average for North Hempstead, and school officials use the extra money to keep class sizes small and buy new equipment for individualized instruction, such as computers.

School officials say that more than 75 percent of the graduates of

Manhasset High School go on to college. There is also a parochial high school—St. Mary's—which opened in 1949 on Northern Boulevard at Plandome Road.

The 1980 census showed that there were nearly 21,000 people living in Manhasset, slightly fewer than in 1970. It also showed that the median family income was $34,415 and that 2,116 of the 2,832 housing units in the unincorporated sections were owner-occupied.

Manhasset is protected by the Nassau County Police and by the volunteer Manhasset-Lakeville Fire Department, which maintains six firehouses. The public library has more than 72,000 books, including 18,000 children's titles, and the library building on Onderdonk Avenue just north of Northern Boulevard is being enlarged.

There are three churches at Northern Boulevard and Plandome Road—Christ Episcopal, built in 1932 on the site of earlier sanctuaries; the Community Reformed Church of Manhasset, whose white frame building and bell tower are older; and St. Mary's Roman Catholic Church, the largest, with some 2,500 families in its parish. There are also Baptist, Lutheran, and Unitarian sanctuaries. Temple Judea of Manhasset, on Searingtown Road, was dedicated in 1960.

History buffs can drive by the Plandome Mill, which local historians say was built between 1693 and 1720. Used to grind grain until 1903, it is now a private home. For natural history there is the Science Museum of Long Island, across from the mill on Plandome Road, about a mile north of the railroad station.

There are two hospitals in Manhasset—the Manhasset division of Long Island Jewish–Hillside Medical Center on Northern Boulevard, with 126 beds, and North Shore University Hospital, with 553.

North Shore's expansion plans have triggered a debate about land use that began in 1982, when the hospital—situated on fifty-six acres on the east side of Community Drive, midway between the Long Island Expressway and Northern Boulevard—made public a five-year plan for growth. Although the proposal has since been scaled down, it still calls for new offices and research labs, a six-story staff residence, and parking garages.

Since Mr. Whitney's death in 1982, there have been persistent rumors that the Greentree estate is to be sold, but family representatives have denied them. Still, the Council of Greater Manhasset Civic Associations, among others, favors designating the Whitney property a protected area as a way of preserving the underground aquifers from which the area draws its drinking water.

Elsewhere in Manhasset, construction continues. Between 1970 and 1980, according to the Census Bureau, the number of houses rose 9.5 percent. And officials say the figures—and the new condominiums—are still going up.

—JAMES BARRON

NORTHPORT

To midtown Manhattan: Train 75 minutes

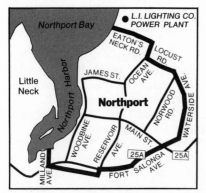

When it was founded in 1656 on land purchased from the Matinecock Indians, the village of Northport was known as Cowharbor. The name is revived each year on Cowharbor Day, the last Sunday in September, when thousands of visitors pour in, a good many of them in running shoes to compete in a 6.5-mile race.

Cowharbor Day, and a summertime trolley drawn by horses named Frick and Frack, are two of the things that have made this village of 7,600 residents a tourist attraction. What attracts prospective homeowners as well as longtime residents is the village's small-town atmosphere just an hour and fifteen minutes by the Long Island Railroad from the bustle of New York City, a heterogeneous population, some of the best scenery on either side of Long Island Sound, and the convenience of shops and services that can be reached on foot by a large portion of those who live there.

Its Main Street follows the original Indian path to the Northport Bay inlet and comes to a dead end there. Along the way there is a fifty-year-old ice-cream parlor with a decor that does not appear to have changed over the decades, a wood-floored five-and-ten where some items can still be had for a quarter, an old movie house that charges $1 for admission, and a barber who gets $2 for a routine haircut and, in a modern concession, cuts the hair of both sexes and any age.

The most compelling attraction, however, is, now as always, Northport Bay. "Nautical Northport," a recent retrospective exhibit at the Northport Historical Society and Museum, looked back to the shipbuilding and fishing industries that flourished here in the nineteenth century. It also told of Northport as a pre–World War I summer place for New York City residents, who arrived by regularly scheduled ferries.

The harbor and inlets still support local crabbing and oystering, but they offer primarily a recreational and esthetic resource that is available to all residents regardless of income. Boat moorings are free on a first-come, first-served basis. A village park at the foot of Main Street and a pier that reaches well out into the water offer places to stroll, fish, watch the sunset, play games, and, in summer, listen to old-fashioned concerts played by bands on a circular bandstand.

Even the four enormous smokestacks belonging to the Long Island Lighting Company's main oil-fired power plant, to the northeast of Main Street and just over the village border, can be seen through rose-colored glasses here. For Lilco pays nearly $11.5 million a year in taxes to the Northport School District, which has a reputation for innovation and programs for the gifted.

Lilco's payment helps keep residential property taxes substantially below those of other Long Island communities. Taxes on a $100,000 home are between $2,300 and $2,500. Owners of comparable houses in other North Shore communities pay as much as $1,000 more.

The average range of house prices in Northport runs from $150,000 to $165,000, according to Barbara Hinton of Sammis Real Estate. She said that houses in the village—bounded on the south by Route 25A, on the west by Milland Avenue, on the north by Eaton's Neck Road, and on the east by Waterside Avenue—have been selling recently for a minimum of $130,000. Most are modest-size colonials set on city-size lots of 40 by 100 or 60 by 100 feet. But many are old, and that apparently has enormous appeal.

"We can't set prices on a house that comes on the market by looking at comparable recent sales," Ms. Hinton stated. "We suggest a figure to the sellers, and they say we should add between $10,000 and $30,000. We do, and if the house is old, it sells."

William Stein, a teacher who lives on Grove Street, less than a five-minute walk from Main Street and the harbor, said the knowledge that his home—which he bought about ten years ago for less than $40,000—is now worth more than $180,000 has made him think about moving. "But then I think, where could I go to improve my circumstances? And the answer is no place," he added. "It's a kid's paradise and an adult's, too, where you can walk everywhere, launch a boat only ten minutes from the house without getting your feet wet, where you know everybody and where you are part of an active, viable community that has its roots in the earliest days of America."

"Here there is no 'buy me, schlep me, bring me, do me,' because the kids can do all that for themselves," said Paula Stein, repeating the litany of demands that most suburban parents hear from their children. Ms. Stein, a teacher and writer on crafts, also emphasized the benefits of having a community of people of different ages, such as an elderly neighbor who taught them about gardening and gave them some unusual plants.

Although real-estate agents now put Northport at or near the top of the list of the most desirable communities on the North Shore, the village's cachet is relatively recent. "When I first came to Northport, many of the shops on Main Street were boarded up and many of the homes were dilapidated," said Ursula Bach, who runs a women's clothing boutique on Main Street. "But the people who moved in here at about that time could see the fabulous possibilities. We'd all get together on a Saturday night and talk about what we had done to our homes. Now the tourists come and take pictures of Bayview Avenue."

Bayview is a waterfront street with some of the best examples of the mixed architecture that characterizes Northport. Ms. Bach paid $41,000 for her large, 153-year-old house on the water side of Bayview seventeen years ago, and real-estate agents now agree it would sell for about $600,000.

Ms. Bach's merchandise, which started out as modestly priced clothing a few years ago, now has a much more upscale look and price tags to match. Indeed, the newer shops on Main Street reflect the fact that Northport, though still home to many people of modest means, is fast becoming an affluent community.

To cater to this affluence, new establishments have opened along Main Street, such as the Wire Wisk, a gourmet cookware shop; Katsura, a gallery that sells Japanese art; Northport Feed and Grain, whose proprietor tries to keep up with the latest trends in food for two-legged beasts; and the Village Blacksmith, an old-fashioned gift shop that also houses a bakery where warm croissants and fancy cakes can be purchased.

Bernard Reickert runs the shop with his wife, Anna, and his two sons, one of whom operates a forge in the back. "This village is like something out of an old Andy Hardy movie, but it's not hicky," Mr. Reickert said. The stage set that is his store includes the letter-sorting area from an old Long Island post office and an Orchestrion, an automated piano whose insides include other instruments like drums and a triangle that are all activated by a perforated paper roll.

301

NORTHPORT

"The fact is that for ten months of the year this is the greatest place in the world to live," said Malcolm Tillim, one of two partners who developed sixty-six clustered town houses in a colony called Harbour Point at Northport. "The other two months? That's the winter, and what can I say?"

—FRANCES CERRA

OYSTER BAY

To midtown Manhattan: Train 75 minutes

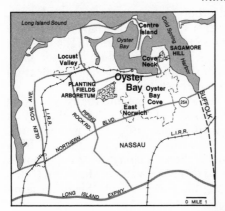

Oyster Bay is the town Theodore Roosevelt called home. Although he was born in New York City, he spent most of his summers there, sailing, hunting, and fishing along the North Shore and raising his family at Sagamore Hill, a rambling, twenty-two-room Victorian mansion.

Like many Long Islanders of today, Roosevelt commuted to and from his office in Manhattan. As the twenty-sixth President of the United States, he welcomed visitors from around the world into Sagamore Hill's broad piazzas.

The calm, sheltered waters of the bay on which Roosevelt often sailed and rowed have long served as a safe haven for both weekend sailors and the serious yachtsmen who set sail from the Sagamore Yacht Club and the Sewanhaka Corinthian Yacht Club on Centre Island in the middle of Oyster Bay.

The deep-water bay is a natural setting for sailing, power-boating, cruising, waterskiing, and fishing. Along the waterfront are several sandy beaches maintained by the town and Nassau County.

"If you like boating, this is the place to live," said Edward Martin, as he sanded the hull of his twenty-eight-foot-long sloop. "You've got all of Oyster Bay, and for rougher, tricky water, there's always Long Island Sound."

During the winter months, when their sailboats are in drydock, some members of the Sagamore Yacht Club put on stage makeup

303

and perform Agatha Christie mystery plays at the Planting Fields Arboretum. The horticultural showplace, which is operated by the Long Island State Park Commission, was formerly the private estate of the late William Robertson Coe, who donated it to the state in 1949.

In April and May, spring bulbs burst into a succession of blooms, along with azaleas, rhododendrons, dogwoods, Japanese cherry trees, magnolias, and other flowering trees and shrubs. The grounds and greenhouses, which contain what the arboretum director, Gordon Jones, describes as the oldest and largest camellia collection under glass in the Northeast, are all open to the public.

Dutch traders were the first settlers to come into the bay, seeking shelter from stormy weather in 1639. A decade later, the Dutch governor, Peter Stuyvesant, joined English officials in agreeing that Oyster Bay was the dividing line between the province of New Netherland to the west and land to the east being settled by English families moving across the Sound from Connecticut. Both the Dutch and English cleared the hills along the Island's North Shore for farming.

English rule soon became dominant, however, after England's King Charles II gave his brother, James, Duke of York, a vast territory in North America in 1664, including all of Long Island. A fleet of ships sent by the Duke arrived in New York Harbor and the Dutch, more interested in trading than soldiering, surrendered without firing a shot.

During the Revolutionary War most of the residents of Oyster Bay were Loyalists. But a group of rebel sympathizers known as the Culper spy ring was also based there. It included a local resident, Robert Townsend of Raynham Hall, who served as Washington's chief spy in New York City. Robert, with the help of his sister, Sally, helped in the disclosure of Benedict Arnold's plot to surrender West Point to the British.

Raynham Hall is today a museum on West Main Street in the center of the business district of the hamlet, surrounded by antique shops, restaurants, and professional offices. The Foodtown supermarket, the biggest in town, is nearby on South Street, next door to Bernstein's department store, the Old Homestead restaurant, the Oyster Bay Sweet Shop, and Nobman's hardware.

And Sagamore Hill still stands on its site overlooking the bay, drawing about 150,000 visitors a year. The Queen Anne–style house, completed in 1885, is crammed with large-scale furniture, western paintings, bronze cowboy sculptures, stuffed buffalo and elk heads, elephant tusks, and other Roosevelt memorabilia. It is maintained and operated by the National Park Service and is open seven days a week.

O Y S T E R   B A Y

Eleanor Perkins, a broker with Douglas Elliman–Jane Hayes in neighboring Locust Valley, said that except for little village plots in the hamlet of Oyster Bay, most of the area, including Cove Neck and Oyster Bay Cove, was zoned two-acre residential. This helps to retain a rural atmosphere, she noted.

White clapboard farmhouses and former taverns serve as year-round homes along East Main Street, which winds through Oyster Bay Cove, then north to Cove Neck and Sagamore Hill.

"We have a broad range of housing, from very grand manor houses to older smaller homes," Ms. Perkins said. Houses in the hamlet, she added, range upward in cost from $120,000, with the price depending on how much land the house sits on and how near the water it is.

New houses are still being built in the two-acre residential areas surrounding the hamlet, particularly in a section of Oyster Bay Cove, near Route 25A. They are listed for about $650,000. Older homes, some with more acreage, are selling for "up to a million dollars," according to Ms. Perkins.

Taxes in the two-acre zone are a minimum of $6,000 a year; in the hamlet, some older homes on smaller plots are taxed at under $2,000 a year. Taxes vary from property to property, depending on age, location, and other factors. The rate is 87.1 cents per $100 of assessed valuation.

Nearly 9,000 residents live in the hamlets of Oyster Bay, Oyster Bay Cove, Cove Neck, and Centre Island. Fifty-seven percent of their taxes supports the public school system; 26 percent goes to Nassau County, which provides a variety of services, including policing and major road maintenance; 12 percent goes for such services as water, fire protection, parks, and libraries; and 5 percent goes to the town.

The Long Island Railroad provides daily, seventy-five-minute train service on its Oyster Bay line to New York City. The hamlet is the line's eastern terminus.

The three public schools in the Oyster Bay area are operated jointly with neighboring East Norwich. Enrollment is about 1,500 students. There are an elementary school and a high school in Oyster Bay, and an intermediary, or middle, school in East Norwich. "Our student population has traditionally come from a wide variety of economic backgrounds," said Dr. Daniel F. Stevens, superintendent of schools. "The students from the village come from moderate economic circumstances, some of them from black families who have lived here longer than most of any of us. There are also students from extremely wealthy families who live outside the village." He said that approximately 65 percent of the public school students continue their education after graduation from high school.

OYSTER BAY

Some students attend private schools. There are the East Woods School in Oyster Bay Cove, Friends Academy and the Portledge School in Locust Valley, and the Greenvale School in Greenvale.

"Since we haven't been a large school district," said Dr. Stevens, who began as a teacher in the district thirty-one years ago, "we have been able to take a personalized interest in each student. Many of our teachers have grown up in Oyster Bay, and they know the students and their families.

"It's that kind of town," he stated. "Even if you move out, there is something about being born in Oyster Bay that makes you come back."

—JOHN T. MCQUISTON

PORT WASHINGTON

To midtown Manhattan: Train 40 minutes

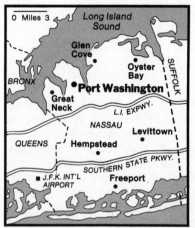

The white palaces of fashionable East Egg glittered along the water," F. Scott Fitzgerald wrote in *The Great Gatsby*. Literary sleuths were quick to figure out that Fitzgerald's East Egg landscape was on the eastern shore of Manhasset Bay, in the area of Port Washington, Long Island, and that the mansions there lined what Fitzgerald called "the most domesticated body of salt water in the Western Hemisphere, the great wet barnyard of Long Island Sound."

Port Washington also was the place where Sinclair Lewis wrote his first novel, where John Philip Sousa wrote his marches, and where Pan American World Airways kept the airplanes used in the first regularly scheduled flights to Bermuda and Europe.

Situated on a peninsula seventeen miles east of Manhattan, Port Washington lies in the northwest corner of the Town of North Hempstead, one of Nassau County's three towns. But Port Washington is not actually a town or a village. It is a five-square-mile area comprising four villages, a large unincorporated area, and part of another village—Flower Hill.

The other villages are Baxter Estates, Port Washington North, Manorhaven, and Sands Point, each of which has its own mayor. The profusion of governmental jurisdictions sometimes causes confusion among Port Washington's 33,000 residents, especially when conversation turns to taxes.

PORT WASHINGTON

More than a decade ago, the different and overlapping tax jurisdictions—for schools, police, and other municipal services—were the basis for a widely read analysis of the "balkanization of suburbia." Things have changed little since then.

The villages collect their own property taxes, which can differ from the taxes on homes in the unincorporated areas. The tax bill on a Victorian house in Baxter Estates, on the market for $174,000, would be $2,600. Another house in the same price range, in an unincorporated section of Port Washington, would have a tax bill of $3,100. The taxes on a third house of the same value, but in the unincorporated Beacon Hill neighborhood, would be $4,000.

One of the pluses of life in Port Washington is its public school system, which generally gets high marks from parents. More than 85 percent of the high school graduates go on to four-year or two-year colleges.

Another benefit is its relationship to the Long Island Railroad. Trains on the Port Washington branch of the L.I.R.R. bypass the railroad's bottleneck at Jamaica, Queens, which frequently delays service on the other branches, and make their run to Pennsylvania Station in about forty minutes. As a result, the level of frustration of Port Washington commuters never quite reaches that of those on the other branches.

"One of the marvels of living in Port Washington is that it's three stops to the city," said Errol Brett, a real-estate lawyer who works in Manhattan. "And we can always get a seat."

The comparative ease of commuting helps keep property values high, according to real-estate agents. So does the water that surrounds the community—Manhasset Bay to the west, Long Island Sound to the north, and Hempstead Harbor to the east.

"It's got the best of the city and the Hamptons in one," said Mickey Friedman, an agent with the Town & Country Real Estate Agency. "I come home and see the boats and don't need Cape Cod. One year my husband said, 'Why'd we go away?'"

In fact, late in the nineteenth century, Port Washington was a summer resort, complete with hotels and "city people" who migrated from Manhattan on weekends. The L.I.R.R. had reached Great Neck in 1867 and a stagecoach carried passengers farther eastward to Port Washington until 1898, when the rail line was extended.

One of Port Washington's first settlers was Richard Cornwall, who, over the objections of his prospective neighbors, was granted title to 1,500 acres in 1674. The Sands family—James, Samuel, and Captain John Sands—arrived from Block Island in 1695 and bought 500 acres from Cornwall. They named it Sands Point, and their houses are still standing.

In the nineteenth century, Port Washington provided the sand and gravel needed in Manhattan. "Whole hills vanished as the companies dug out the sand and shipped it west to New York City, to be made into concrete for construction," according to a history of the community edited by Karyn C. Browne of the Port Washington League of Women Voters.

Real-estate agents say that property values have generally risen in the last few years. New two-family homes have been built on vacant lots in Manorhaven, traditionally the least expensive of the Port Washington villages. The houses sell for $275,000 to $325,000, and rents for the second unit range from $900 to $1,250 a month.

Elsewhere, asking prices for a split-level with three or four bedrooms are typically in the $230,000 to $350,000 range. Homes in Sands Point are situated on larger lots, and so prices are higher; some have been sold for more than $3 million. Waterfront parcels—land only—occasionally come on the market in Sands Point. A two-acre site was offered recently for $1.3 million.

The architectural styles in Port Washington vary. There are large, boxy frame houses in the center of town that were built near the turn of the century. Some of these houses, including many on Locust Avenue near the Port Washington Library, originally stood nearer the center of town. They were moved to make way for newer commercial buildings.

The split-level made its debut in Port Washington, as it did in much of the rest of the nation, after World War II. It was then that developers begin creating subdivisions here with names like Eastern Crest, Salem, and New Salem. Later development added rectangular red-brick garden apartment buildings to the landscape. There are two such complexes facing Manhasset Bay.

Some of the most desirable accommodations in Port Washington do not provide a roof over the tenants' heads. They are at the marinas where boaters rent dock spaces. The demand is bigger than the supply, and the supply is shrinking as marina owners sell their property to developers. As a result, boat space is expensive, ranging up to $3,000 for a forty-foot boat.

Along Main Street are Greek and Mexican restaurants, with Chinese and Italian restaurants not far away. And there is the venerable Louie's, a seafood restaurant next to the town dock that has been owned by one family for generations. Boaters can moor at the restaurant's private dock, while landlubbers must vie for the limited number of parking spaces in the hilly lot across the street.

Appropriately enough for a town where Sousa once lived, there is a bandshell on the bay. Bands perform there weekly during the summer. The Polish American Museum Foundation, established five years ago, recently bought its own building on Bayview Avenue to house its displays and bilingual research library.

Some Port Washington residents, especially those who live on the eastern edge of the community, are concerned about the effect of the Town of North Hempstead's landfill. In 1981 methane gas apparently drifted underground from the landfill to homes nearby. It touched off small explosions, known as "puffbacks," in half a dozen houses in one subdivision abutting the landfill.

Of more concern was a charge by the New York Public Interest Research Group that other dangerous chemicals were seeping from the landfill into the soil. The federal Environmental Protection Agency tested the area in 1982 and later asserted that it was safe.

More than sixty summers after Fitzgerald wrote his novel, some of the glamour may have faded, but the Sound still glitters as the boats glide past Port Washington.

—JAMES BARRON

ROSLYN

To midtown Manhattan: Train 55 minutes

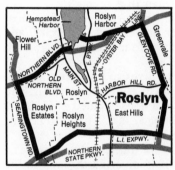

William Cullen Bryant, the nineteenth-century essayist, poet, and *New York Post* editor, was also one of Long Island's first commuters to Manhattan. An 1842 advertisement for the property in Roslyn he was to buy boasted "public conveyances to and from the city," which meant travel by rail, stage, and steamboat, depending on the season.

The trip was three hours each way, but Bryant took it on bravely over his remaining thirty-five years, demonstrating his love for Roslyn and providing a heartening example for the present-day commuter. The peaceful harbor, lakes, and thickly wooded hills that an early Long Island Railroad brochure described as "the Switzerland of Long Island" still give its residents a taste of country life twenty miles from midtown Manhattan.

First settled in 1643, Roslyn Village is a source of pride for many residents and a model of historic preservation for Long Island. Main Street, between East Broadway and Old Northern Boulevard, has thirty-eight pre–Civil War structures, with the earliest, the Van Nostrand-Starkins house, dating from around 1680. Of the dozen or so buildings that constituted the village in the 1790's, eight still stand.

"There are villages farther out on the island that are architecturally as significant," said Dr. Roger Gerry, president of the Roslyn Landmark Society, "but I can't think of any place as close to New York that has the same quality."

R O S L Y N

The village's passion for historical preservation was ignited by a 1961 Nassau County plan to turn Roslyn into a traffic circle that would have involved demolition of many of its old buildings.

"By preserving our older buildings," Dr. Gerry said, "we felt that people on a countrywide basis would be interested in the survival of the village. Without the early buildings, Roslyn didn't stand a chance."

About one fourth of Roslyn's area of one square mile is in a historic district. Landmark homes, which sell for about $250,000, are closely monitored by the Roslyn Village Historic District Board to maintain an appearance of authenticity. There also is a commercial district in the village with a total of about 30,000 square feet of retail space and a turnover rate of less than 10 percent.

Some parts of Roslyn are zoned for one-eighth acre, but most houses have quarter-acre plots. Starter homes go for $175,000 and the prices range upward to $400,000 for a four-bedroom, two-bath colonial or contemporary.

Roslyn's 2,500 residents pay property taxes to a variety of jurisdictions, including the village itself, North Hempstead Town, and Nassau County; generally, the owner of a house valued at $100,000 would pay a total annual tax bill of about $2,000. The 1980 census reported the village's average family income as $35,447.

The issues of greatest concern locally are traffic and parking. The construction of the Roslyn bypass in 1949 diverted through traffic and successfully unclogged the village. But the problem has reappeared as the southbound flow toward expanding areas nearby, particularly Port Washington, sometimes turns the village streets into a winding anaconda of cars. "We are continually asking the county to study the traffic problem and come up with a solution," said Vincent Pastor, the Roslyn village clerk. "Another problem is parking. Our Planning Board is working on a set of recommendations, but there just isn't any more space."

The incorporated villages of East Hills, Roslyn Estates, and Roslyn, plus parts of Roslyn Harbor and Flower Hill, make up most of what is informally referred to as greater Roslyn. The unincorporated areas of Roslyn Heights and Greenvale, administered by the Town of North Hempstead, are also a part of the area.

Before the Depression greater Roslyn was dominated by large estates. The surrounding villages served primarily as supply centers for the maintenance of the estates and their farms.

The Depression ended the Gatsby era, and after World War II the demand for housing spread eastward. With the rise in property values, many estate owners sold their land to suburban housing developers and the area changed from a working-class to an upper-middle-class bedroom community.

312

R O S L Y N

Greater Roslyn has a population of about 25,000 in an area of about six square miles at the head of Hempstead Harbor, an indentation of the Long Island Sound shoreline. Its boundaries are a meandering line above Northern Boulevard on the north, the Long Island Expressway on the south, Glen Cove Road on the east, and Searingtown Road on the west.

The community is predominantly residential and is composed almost entirely of single-family homes. The turnover rate is low; most families remain in the same home at least ten years or longer to raise children. Once on the market, houses usually sell in sixty to ninety days.

Housing prices across greater Roslyn range from $90,000 in a section of Roslyn Heights to $500,000 in Roslyn Estates. Prices rise to $200,000 in parts of East Hills and average $330,000 for a home on at least half an acre in the prime areas of East Hills, Roslyn Estates, and Roslyn Harbor. Property-tax rates are generally comparable to those of Roslyn village.

Demand, brokers say, far exceeds supply. "We just don't have enough houses to sell," said Claire Sobel, whose real-estate brokerage bears her name. "Things will always look good here. For a family looking for a home close to the city with top schools, the Roslyn area offers the most for your money. Still, even I'm shocked at what people are getting for their homes."

A common concern of greater Roslyn residents is crime. Roslyn Estates and East Hills have hired part-time private security patrols to reinforce the protection given by the Nassau County Police. The crime rate for the greater Roslyn community is down this year, which the police attribute more to a general overall decline rather than the effects of additional patrols.

Roslyn residents can choose from several restaurants offering moderately priced foods, the most popular being The Jolly Fisherman, on Main Street, and Heads & Tails, on Northern Boulevard. Folk artists perform at My Father's Place, another Main Street restaurant.

The village also has a movie theater, several parks, tennis courts, and public swimming pools. For something less strenuous, residents can feed the ducks at the duck pond in the center of town.

The Bryant Library contains a large collection of its namesake's writings and memorabilia. The Nassau County Fine Arts Museum in the former Childs Frick Estate in Roslyn Harbor is another cultural attraction.

Commuters to Manhattan have a few options. Many take the Long Island Railroad's Port Washington line from nearby Manhasset, which takes thirty-five to forty minutes. Roslyn itself is on the Oyster Bay line, a route that involves an extra ten to fifteen minutes because of a transfer at Jamaica. Traveling by car to the city on the Long Island Expressway takes thirty-five minutes to an hour, depending on traffic.

Enrollment in Roslyn's schools has declined by 500 in recent years to 2,700 students. As a result, four elementary schools have been closed. In the same period, however, the overall proportion of property taxes channeled to the school district has risen to 60 percent, an increase of 6 percent.

High-school students have average scores about fifty points higher than the national averages on the verbal and math sections of the Scholastic Aptitude Test. About 90 percent of the graduates go on to higher education.

—BRADEN PHILLIPS

SEA CLIFF

To midtown Manhattan: Train 60 minutes

In the weeks before Christmas, artists and craftsmen in the Long Island village of Sea Cliff open their studios and workshops to visitors and shoppers. Maps for self-guided tours are handed out along with a list of numbered locations along the village's hilly and winding streets that overlook Hempstead Harbor and Long Island Sound. The tours, which began in 1975, start at the Village Gift Shop at Sea Cliff and Central avenues, in the heart of the one-square-mile village and its antique row.

The tours are not only a chance to view ceramics, stained glass, and newly crafted furniture and toys but are also an opportunity to take in Sea Cliff's rich architectural heritage, which represents nearly all the styles of home building from the nineteenth century to the present.

While multicolored gingerbread Victorian houses appear to dominate the tightly packed landscape, there also are silver-gray Cape Cod saltboxes, Russian dachas, brick and stucco Tudors, cantilevered contemporaries, and carefully refurbished seaside shanties.

They all cling tenaciously to the ragged, wooded cliff that gives the town its name. It is a glacial deposit created 30,000 years ago by a mountain of ice that, in melting, formed the Sound as well as the harbor. These days, that harbor is a haven for sailors and swimmers and a rich source of sea bass, bluefish, and shellfish.

Many of the 5,346 residents of Sea Cliff have lived in the community all their lives, among them a former mayor, Francis W. Deegan, a lawyer who helped plan the village's centennial in 1983. Sea Cliff became an incorporated village on October 10, 1883, which makes it the fourth oldest on Long Island and among the oldest in New York State.

While the age of a village may provide part of its charm, it also produces problems. For example, Mr. Deegan noted that underground wiring and lighting fixtures had to be replaced in 1983 on Sea Cliff Avenue, one of the village's major roads, and in recent years the sidewalks on that avenue had to be repaved.

The village also has upgraded its beachfront facilities and has built a $180,000 beach pavilion on Hempstead Harbor. It has restrooms, a snack bar, showers, an office, and a first-aid room.

The beach is a narrow strip at the foot of the cliff, which is crisscrossed by winding footpaths that lead down to the sandy shore and nearby wetlands and boatyards. The waterfront and village are dotted with seven well-used miniparks, wedged between outcroppings of smooth granite and along the winding roads that climb the steep cliff and run inland.

Along the cliff, there are many places where time seems to stand still. Local records show that the land, originally referred to by settlers as Muskeeta Cove, meaning "cove of grassy flats" in the local Indian language, was purchased from the Indians by Joseph Carpenter, an Englishman, in the seventeenth century.

Except for the waterfront, the land was little used until the 1870's, when it was developed as a religious retreat by Methodists from New York City. They constructed a huge tabernacle and camp meeting ground atop the cliff, attracting thousands of worshipers to services on summer weekends.

The weekenders would arrive by paddle-driven steamship and ride a cable car straight up the side of the cliff on narrow-gauge tracks. Some of the visitors became all-summer residents and later they built year-round homes, large gingerbread Victorian mansions that remain today, still overlooking the harbor through tall oak and beech trees.

In a few years, Sea Cliff was an established community with a rapidly growing population. Real growth, however, did not come until the arrival of the Long Island Railroad. By the turn of the century, commuters were already lined up at the Sea Cliff station, a classic Victorian structure that still serves the village. The trip to Manhattan takes about an hour.

Sea Cliff is linked to other parts of Nassau County by the Metropolitan Suburban Bus Authority, which, like the L.I.R.R., is a subsidiary of the Metropolitan Transportation Authority.

Several decades ago, Sea Cliff again became a religious retreat, this time for members of the Russian Orthodox Church who fled the

Soviet Union during and after the revolution. They brought with them not only their religion but also their architecture, adding yet another building style to the varied community. As a result, there are two Russian Orthodox churches in Sea Cliff, along with Methodist, Episcopalian, and Catholic churches.

The Sea Cliff Library, organized in 1891, was among the first in Nassau County. Begun with the donation of 1,000 books from private citizens, it remains dependent on public contributions.

Children in the village attend schools in the North Shore Central School District, which includes, besides Sea Cliff, the neighboring villages of Glen Head and Glenwood Landing and parts of Old Brookville, Greenvale, and Roslyn Harbor. There is one public elementary school in Sea Cliff as well as a Roman Catholic grade school.

According to Dr. Christopher J. Warrell, the former superintendent of schools, the average class size in the district is 15.5 students, the lowest in Nassau County. The district high school in Glen Head graduates about 250 seniors a year, about 60 percent of whom go on to four-year colleges. An additional 20 percent go to two-year colleges.

The schools and other services are sustained by a group of local taxes. For a property owner with a $200,000 house, the combined levies would range from $2,600 to $3,300. The rate is determined by the age and location of the property.

Dr. Warrell noted that the average school tax, which accounts for nearly 60 percent of tax bills, is lower than in nearby districts because of tax income from a large Long Island Lighting Company generating facility on Hempstead Harbor.

The village is served by the Nassau County Police Department but has its own auxiliary police force. Formed three years ago, it now has twenty-two members. It also has a twenty-four-hour volunteer fire department.

"This is a unique, mixed community," said Gloria Howard, a Sea Cliff resident and broker for MacCrate Realty Ltd. "We've got something for everyone." She noted that most houses in Sea Cliff cost a minimum of $165,000, although there were some for as little as $125,000. The cheapest ones, however, "need an awful lot of work. We have a lot of younger people moving in and taking over the older houses," she observed, "and they are making them beautiful again."

—JOHN T. MCQUISTON

ROCKLAND AND ORANGE COUNTIES
IX.

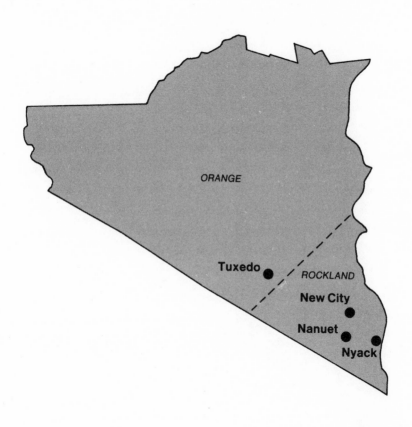

ORANGE

Tuxedo ●

ROCKLAND

New City
●

Nanuet ●

● Nyack

N A N U E T

To midtown Manhattan: Bus or train 60 minutes

here heavily con-
gested Route 59 passes through Nanuet, this Rockland County community seems to be made up entirely of modern, bustling shopping
centers. But just a few blocks away, it becomes an older, less
crowded, almost rural community, with tree-lined streets, well-kept
lawns, and wooded country roads.

"No one will deny that some areas have undergone a transformation," said Catherine Nowicki, a longtime resident. "But if you
ask around, you will find most people here still regard Nanuet as a
small town. It's this rural-urban dichotomy that makes this such an
interesting place to live."

Ms. Nowicki, an English teacher at Nanuet High School and
mother of six children, moved to a landmark pre-Revolutionary house
on Middletown Road in 1960. She remembers a time before the
shopping malls, and before the building boom that followed the completion of the 113-store Nanuet Mall, which includes Sears Roebuck
and Bamberger's department stores, in 1969. "We used to have to go
to Spring Valley or Nyack to shop," said Ms. Nowicki, who is also a
member of the Town of Clarkstown Planning Board, "and in town, it
seemed everyone knew everyone else. But even with the influx of
newcomers in recent years, it is still pretty much the same."

Nanuet was a logical choice for retail development. It is one of the
most accessible communities in Rockland County, twenty miles

northwest of the George Washington Bridge, at the crossroads of the Governor Thomas E. Dewey Thruway, the Palisades Interstate Parkway, and the thruway extension to the Garden State Parkway.

"We call it the hub," said Patricia Sheridan, town clerk of Clarkstown, which provides municipal services for most of the hamlet's 13,000 residents (a small section in the southern part of Nanuet is in the Town of Orangetown). "It is centrally located, with good road access to everything in Rockland County. Lately, it seems that every time you look around, something new is being built."

The boom has not been confined to retail development. Condominium projects and other residential complexes have taken a firm foothold in what once was a community of single-family homes.

The most ambitious such project is Treetops, with 250 cluster units already occupied atop a heavily wooded hill overlooking the hamlet. Plans call for 1,200 more units. Another project, on Main Street just a few hundred yards from the Nanuet Mall, is Normandy Village, with 114 condominium units and 164 rental apartments.

"There is a broad real-estate market in Nanuet," said Ferdinand Horn, head of the Rockland County Multiple Listing Service and the United Real Estate Brokers of Rockland County. Mr. Horn, a former state legislator and county clerk, has lived in Nanuet since 1909, when his father bought a forty-acre farm where the present middle school and high school now stand. In the town's varied housing stock, he said, "you have everything from single-family homes on 100- by 150-foot lots to luxury condominiums."

The typical newer home in Nanuet is on a one-third-acre site. Prices range from $80,000 for older Cape Cods to $200,000 for larger high-ranch and split-level homes. Condominiums range from $85,000 to $100,000 and rental units from $500 to $600 per month.

The 5.3-square-mile unincorporated hamlet is bordered on the north by Bardonia and New City, on the south by Pearl River, on the east by West Nyack, and on the west by Spring Valley.

Most municipal services, including policing, roads, recreation, health, and sanitation, are provided by the town, whose offices are in New City, about five miles away. But Nanuet has its own volunteer ambulance corps and fire department.

The county and town tax rate is $2.63, and school district tax is $3.20 per $100 of assessed valuation. Properties are assessed at 50 percent of full-market value, so the owner of a house valued at $100,000 would pay about $3,000 in taxes.

The hamlet takes its name from Nannaitt, a chief of the Leni-Lenape Indians who occupied the heavily forested area through most of the sixteenth and early seventeenth centuries. The first Dutch and English settlers were trappers and farmers, although there are records of some settlers operating gristmills along the banks of the Hackensack River.

NANUET

Nanuet received a brief economic boost when the main branch of the Erie Railroad was completed in 1839 and later when the New York and New Jersey Railroad formed a junction with the Erie in 1871. But the area remained primarily agricultural until early in this century.

With the completion of the Tappan Zee Bridge in 1955, connecting Rockland County to Westchester and to roads to New York City, the area underwent significant residential growth as newcomers took up residence in developments of single-family homes. Today it is a bedroom suburb, with a median family income of $27,852, according to 1980 census figures.

Most newer residents are business executives who chose Nanuet because of its convenience to major retail areas and its excellent road network to New York and northern New Jersey.

"Another incentive to young families," Ms. Nowicki stated, "is a fine school system." The Nanuet Union Free School District includes an elementary, middle, and senior high school. More than 91 percent of the 137 faculty members hold graduate degrees and more than 75 percent of the high-school graduates go on to some form of higher education. Average Scholastic Aptitude Test scores for the class of 1983 were 472 verbal and 522 mathematics, well above national averages.

"The secret to our success is a very involved and supportive community," said Laura R. Fliegner, school superintendent. "We haven't had one school budget proposal turned down by the voters since 1974, which must be some sort of record."

Nanuet's commuters are served by Red & Tan Bus Lines express service to midtown Manhattan via the New Jersey Turnpike and Lincoln Tunnel. N. J. Transit provides rush-hour train service along the Pascack Valley line of the old Erie-Lackawanna to the PATH station in Hoboken and connections to midtown and downtown Manhattan. Bus or train to the city takes about an hour.

Clarkstown provides free parking facilities for commuters and operates five bus routes from Nanuet to New City and other areas of the county. This service uses nine specially designed school buses.

Nanuet made national headlines on October 20, 1981, with the Brink's armored-car robbery at the Nanuet Mall, but the hamlet is hardly an area of major crime. In fact, Clarkstown police officials say that despite the presence of major shopping centers, the crime rate is quite low compared with other parts of the county.

Among Nanuet's many handsome churches is the fieldstone-faced Roman Catholic Shrine Church of St. Anthony's, which was built in 1920. The hamlet's recreational facilities include the man-made Nanuet Lake, with picnic areas and swimming in a 33.5-acre preserve.

Arts and crafts exhibitions are on display at the Nanuet Mall throughout the year. A few minutes away by car are the Rockland Center for the Arts in West Nyack and cultural programs sponsored by Rockland Community College in Suffern.

There are five movie theaters and a large number of moderately priced restaurants in the community. Some say the most notable one is the Nanuet Restaurant on Middletown Road, which features an Italian-American menu. The Sopwith Camel Pub on Middletown Road and Casablanca on Route 59 are gathering places for singles.

—GENE RONDINARO

NEW CITY

To midtown Manhattan: Bus 65 minutes

N ew City emerged as a suburb late in the 1950's, when two major highways—the Palisades Interstate Parkway and the Governor Thomas E. Dewey Thruway—were cut through Rockland County, putting it within an hour's drive of New York City. Until then, it had been a sleepy, semirural hamlet on the west shore of the Hudson River, in one of the state's smallest counties, Rockland, which people often mistook for part of New Jersey.

The old County Courthouse, across Main Street from a row of small stores in the center of town, symbolizes the past, with its marble trim and lawn with shade trees. But suburbanization has brought big changes to the county seat.

Shopping centers, banks, fast-food outlets, and real-estate offices line Main Street for a mile in each direction, and there are a half-dozen office buildings. Yet, from that bustling downtown area, the South Mountain Range still is visible in the distance with its cele-brated peak, High Tor, made famous by the play of that name by the late Maxwell Anderson, a onetime New City resident.

There are still single-family houses on lots of a third of an acre or more, but close to New City's center are several hundred garden apartments, both rentals and condominiums. The condominiums change hands for $90,000 to $100,000 and more, and a forty-five-unit

325

luxury condominium development is now in the planning stages. Rentals go for $550 to $600 for a one-bedroom apartment.

New City, which is an unincorporated hamlet of the Town of Clarkstown, is one of Rockland's more desirable communities, said Aaron Fried, head of the County Planning Department. "It's like northern Westchester, but not as far, nor as expensive."

Many of the people who have moved in over the last twenty-five years are former New York City residents, mostly from the Bronx and northern Manhattan, who decided to raise their families "out in the country." A good local school system, the Clarkstown School District, helped sell them on the idea. Among the first to come were New York City employees, many of them policemen and firemen, but the more recent arrivals are professionals and business people.

According to brokers, houses range in price from about $120,000 to $400,000, with the average about $150,000. New houses start at $150,000, said a broker with Coyle & Coyle Realty.

Property taxes are roughly comparable to Westchester's, say officials, ranging from about $3,000 to $5,500 a year.

The community covers roughly seventeen square miles and is, loosely speaking, bounded by South Mountain, part of the Palisades, on the north; the town of Ramapo on the west; the picturesque Lake DeForest, a reservoir, on the east; and Nanuet, Bardonia, and West Nyack on the south.

New City, despite its name, is not new. It goes back to the county's earliest period. Rockland County was formed in 1798, when it was separated from Orange County because of communications problems caused by the intervening Ramapo Mountains. Later, the county seat was moved from Tappan to New City, which at the time was said to be "free of commercialism and social distractions."

During the nineteenth century New City was the scene of agricultural fairs, but it also had an industrial base—a clothing factory, three shoe factories, a silver plating concern, and a brewery, which gave its name to Brewery Road.

With the advent of the two major arteries, development of New City accelerated. "We needed everything all at once—government, schools, libraries, shopping," said Mr. Fried. Sewers came late in the 1960's.

New City depends on a volunteer fire department and a full-time police force, the 106-member Clarkstown Police Department. The chief, Robert Schnakenberg, reported there is little violent crime but that burglaries and vandalism, "a lot of it youth-related," are problems.

Some parents say there is not much for teenagers to do in New City unless they belong to a church or synagogue. But according to Theodore R. Dusanenko, the Clarkstown supervisor, the town spends a million dollars a year on parks and recreation programs, including three swimming areas—Congers Lake, Germonds Pool, and Lake Nanuet. "It depends on whether they want to be entertained or be participants," said Mr. Dusanenko, who is also a teacher. Outdoor activities abound in the county, which is small enough for just about any part of it to be within easy reach by car. It has five golf courses and many sites for camping, fishing, boating, swimming, biking, and hiking. In the winter, there are cross-country ski trails in Bear Mountain and Harriman state parks, which both spill over into Rockland.

The county is proud of its Suburban Symphony Orchestra, and a variety of other cultural institutions are near at hand, including the Rockland Center for the Arts in West Nyack, with its two galleries and music and dance programs.

The Clarkstown School District, with more than 11,000 students, has two senior high schools, three junior highs, and ten elementary schools. Dr. Donald Van Wagenen, the school superintendent, said that about 85 percent of the graduates go on to higher education.

There is a Roman Catholic school in the center of New City, St. Augustine's, and a parochial high school, Albertus Magnus, in nearby Bardonia.

Most commuters drive to work, but there are both bus and rail services for those who do not. For train service to Manhattan, there is the Pascack Valley line of N. J. Transit from nearby Nanuet to Hoboken, connecting with PATH trains there. This is basically a rush-hour service. Red & Tan Lines runs frequent buses. Its best and fastest is the No. 49 Parkway Express, which operates in the rush hours between New City and the Port Authority Bus Terminal on West 41st Street. The scheduled time is an hour and five minutes.

New city's population increased from 26,398 in 1970 to 35,800 in 1980, a 29 percent gain, and a further 12 percent increase is forecast by the year 2000.

"New City is generally a wealthier area than the rest of the county, give or take a few communities," said Mr. Fried of the Planning Department. Compared to Westchester, he added, "Rockland tends to have a more homogeneous population. I don't think you'd find either the wealth or the poverty you'd find in Westchester. Westchester was already a suburb back at the turn of the century. There is nothing like a Yonkers here."

The population of New City is mostly middle class, consisting for the most part of families living in their own homes on lots of from a third of an acre to two acres. The census shows about 10,000 homes, nearly 9,000 of them owner-occupied. The average household, according to the 1980 census, has 3.6 persons.

Bradlees discount store is the closest to a department store in New City. Sears and Bamberger's are in the Nanuet Mall, the regional shopping center about five miles away. The mall is a magnet for young people. Some ride the Clarkstown minibuses, which run along major arteries in Clarkstown, at 25 cents a trip.

For food shopping there are several large supermarkets in the center of New City and Cropsey Farm, on Little Tor Road, where produce is sold.

New City has a modern library, two movie houses, nineteen restaurants, twenty-five real-estate offices, eighteen beauty parlors, ten delicatessens, five drugstores, ten churches, two synagogues, forty-nine doctor's offices, and, reflecting its status as seat of government for the county and for Clarkstown, sixty-three law firms. They all help generate traffic, which clusters increasingly at the lights on Main Street.

Besides the Courthouse, New City has several other public buildings, among them the three-story County Office Building and a six-story annex across the street, the old County Jail, behind the Courthouse, and the Sheriff's Offices farther up New Hempstead Road. County employees plus employees in the town offices on Maple Avenue make the city a busy place during the day.

—EDWARD HUDSON

N Y A C K

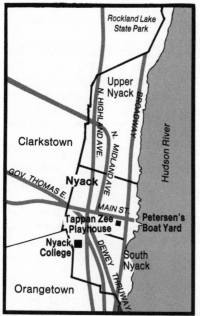

To midtown Manhattan: Bus and subway 75 minutes

A decade ago, the center of Nyack was in decay, and a lack of business was emptying many of its storefronts. But since then this once-shabby and desolate-looking village on the west bank of the Hudson River has sprung back to life.

The revival, according to local officials, is the direct result of an infusion of federal funds used to spruce up the downtown area, where a spectacularly successful center for antiques and arts and crafts has been established. These officials also attribute the revival to the villagers' high level of enthusiasm for the change.

Gabriel Hausner, director of community development for the village, said about $7 million in federal funds had gone into rebuilding Nyack. Ten acres of substandard buildings were cleared under urban renewal, and since then private developers have built a small shopping mall, a large parking area, and 176 units of low- and moderate-income apartments on the site.

Many of the nineteenth-century brick buildings along Main Street and Broadway—the main thoroughfares of this Rockland County village thirty miles north of midtown Manhattan—have been restored and now serve as antique and arts and crafts shops, and stylish restaurants. Among the popular eating places are the Cafe Provençal, Raoul's, and the Gazebo. With thirty-two restaurants and bars, the village now has a thriving nightlife.

NYACK

Nyack and the adjacent villages of Upper Nyack and South Nyack offer an atmosphere unlike that of most suburbs. Nyack itself has some fine old houses, including large Victorians, and many residents of all three communities have excellent views of the river and the Tappan Zee Bridge.

"Diversity" is the word Jo Baer, a Nyack real-estate broker, uses to characterize the village. "There are people from the poor to the upper middle class," she noted. "We have lots of people who teach in the colleges of New York. Some are on the faculties of the medical schools. We have our fair share of creative people, both theatrical and painters and that sort of thing. And then there are people like my husband, who works for I.B.M."

Some residents say Nyack could use more specialty shops and perhaps a supermarket to replace one that closed a few years ago. As it is, they now buy many of their groceries, clothes, and appliances at nearby shopping centers such as the Nanuet Mall.

Nyack has a popular open-air farmers' market in the center of town each Wednesday until Thanksgiving, and several times a year the Art, Craft and Antiques Dealers Association sponsors a street fair. For those wanting to take in a movie, there are the local Cinema East and other nearby theaters.

Each of the three Nyacks has a separate village government. Broadway, a ribbon running parallel to the river, ties all three together. Upper Nyack, with its handsome riverside mansions, is considered the most prestigious. South Nyack is the most varied architecturally, with many fine old houses set back from the streets on deep lots. Nyack has 6,700 residents, Upper Nyack 2,200, and South Nyack 3,000.

Real-estate agents say prices of homes in all three communities are appreciating by as much as 20 percent a year. A simple two-family stucco house might be listed for $110,000 and a three-story house with a deep yard, a two-car garage, and a river view for $150,000.

Houses may still be found for around $85,000 in South Nyack, but they usually need a good deal of work, according to brokers. "For a fairly substantial house with a fairly nice yard, you really have to think of $180,000 to $200,000," Ms. Baer said.

The property taxes on a house with a market value of $100,000 would be about $2,700, with portions of that sum going to the village, the school district, the Town of Orangetown, and Rockland County.

Nyack also has apartments, but brokers report that the market is tight. The rent for a one-bedroom unit ranges upward from $500 a month and from $700 for a larger one. The apartments are in older buildings as well as in several newer ones by the river.

The 162-unit West Shore Towers charges rents of $475 to $1,000 a month, and there is a waiting list for units. Next door, at the ninety-

NYACK

five-unit River Crest Apartments, a cooperative with its own marina, apartments are for sale for $65,000 to $105,000.

Nyack, on a low section of the Palisades cliff that it shares with the Governor Thomas E. Dewey Thruway, traces its name to an Indian tribe that legend says came from Brooklyn and Staten Island. Dowe Harnensen Tallman established the first permanent settlement for the Dutch in 1684. In its early years, the village was a boat-building center, and Petersen's Boat Yard in Nyack carries on that tradition. The village also has a boat club and a public boat-launching facility.

After the Erie Railroad arrived in 1870, shoe manufacturing became the main industry, but in 1893 the village experienced a major depression and development stopped. Most of the buildings in the business district date from 1870 to 1890, the period of its most intensive development.

The railroad brought Nyack within commuting distance of New York City. When the Erie-Lackawanna Railroad went out of business in 1965, Red & Tan buses took over. They connect with the New York City subway system at the George Washington Bridge Bus Terminal in a trip that takes about forty-five minutes. From there, it takes about thirty minutes more to get to midtown Manhattan. Driving to midtown takes about an hour.

Nyack has a strong arts community. There are an amateur playhouse and at least a half-dozen art galleries in the village, and efforts are under way to revive the Tappan Zee Playhouse. The boyhood home of Edward Hopper, the artist, is an art exhibition and community cultural center. Nyack's best-known resident is Helen Hayes, the actress.

On the heights of South Nyack is Nyack College, run by the Christian Missionary Alliance, which offers both professional ministerial and liberal arts programs. The community's health needs are served by the 370-bed Nyack Hospital, and expansion is planned.

Parks in the area include nearby Rockland Lake and Hook Mountain, where families picnic and hikers and joggers enjoy nature along the river.

The Nyack School District, which includes the Nyacks, Upper Grandview, and Valley Cottage, has three elementary schools, a middle school, a junior high, and a high school. The total enrollment is about 3,000 and it is growing. About 80 percent of the high-school graduates go on to further education.

"What we are known for is warmth and individuality," said a spokesman for the school district, Bunny Crumpacker. "We're strong on school spirit."

—EDWARD HUDSON

T U X E D O

To midtown Manhattan: Bus or train 60 minutes

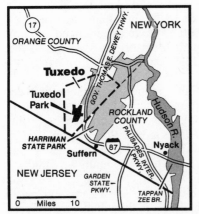

At dusk, when a light fog unfurls across Tuxedo Lake and fishermen cast their lines from small boats dwarfed by the surrounding hills, Tuxedo Park in Orange County resembles a quiet Scottish loch a century ago. That scene has changed little since 1885, when Pierre Lorillard, scion of the wealthy tobacco family, decided to fence in 4,000 acres of hilly, wooded land in Orange County, New York, and build an elegant hunting and gaming retreat for his family and friends. Today Tuxedo Park remains quiet, sporty, and most of all secure, its famous guarded front gates still barring all but those who either live inside or have been invited.

Because of its reputation as a playground for millionaires from New York—just forty miles away—Tuxedo Park scares away many prospective home buyers who assume that high prices exclude them. In truth, however, although some mansions and estates are on the market for $1 million or more, many of the 300 houses in the village are more reasonably priced and are in line with the rest of the New York–Northern New Jersey market.

"There's a real misconception that you have to be loaded to live in Tuxedo Park," said Andrea Bierce, a management consultant in New York City. Ms. Bierce and her husband, Alexander, who has a seat on the New York Stock Exchange, purchased a 1.4-acre lot near one of Tuxedo Park's three lakes in 1979 for $25,000, and built their own Georgian-style, solar-enhanced house on it. The Bierces are typical of a number of professional couples in their mid-thirties who have moved into the village over the last few years, either building their own houses or purchasing smaller ones, former servants' quarters and carriage houses.

When Frank S. Bell, the mayor, moved in from New York City in 1966, the atmosphere was quite different, with roughly half of the homes either abandoned or vacant. "When we first looked at Tuxedo Park, the realtor showed us thirty houses for under $30,000, and not one of them had fewer than ten rooms," said Mr. Bell, the president of an engineering company in Mahwah. "It doesn't sound like it today, but buying in Tuxedo Park then was a gutsy thing to do."

The colorful past of the community—now listed on the National Register of Historic Places—reflects the ups and downs of the American economy over the last century. During its heyday, roughly from the turn of the century to the Depression, it reigned as one of America's most prestigious private enclaves. Tucked away in the woods and with the powerful presence of the Tuxedo Club—an exclusive social spa restricted to residents—Tuxedo Park was a bit less stiff-necked than Newport but no less elegant. In fact, it was at the community's first annual Spring Ball in 1886 that a tailless formal jacket—the tuxedo—was first worn.

The Depression hit Tuxedo Park harder than other places and recovery was slow. By 1905, many families were gone and some of the larger mansions had been abandoned or deliberately burned. In 1953, no longer able to sustain its services—including its own school, police force, and crews for thirty miles of roads—Tuxedo Park incorporated as a self-governing village within the township of Tuxedo.

Restrictions determining who can purchase a home in Tuxedo Park have been abolished. The admissions criteria for the Tuxedo Club also have been loosened. Although membership is still by invitation only, it is no longer limited to residents, and only half of Tuxedo Park's population belongs to the club.

Homeowners in Tuxedo Park pay four sets of taxes—school, village, town, and county—a combined rate of about $43 per $1,000 of assessed value. On a house with a market value of $200,000, the taxes, assessed at roughly 53 percent of value, would be about $5,000. Roughly 1,000 people live in the village, constituting about one quarter of the population of the township of Tuxedo, which surrounds it. Taxes in other Tuxedo communities range from $32 to $42 per $1,000, depending on school district.

Local brokers say that usually no more than twenty-five houses are available in the village at any one time. According to Terry

Szendoy of Tuxedo Park Properties, the prices range from $175,000 to $1 million, reflecting a substantial appreciation over the past few years.

A contemporary five-bedroom house on a two-acre lot, built on part of the stone foundation of a much larger one that burned years ago, sold recently for $230,000. Also sold recently was a converted stone carriage house on seven acres on Lookout Road for $275,000.

One curious feature of many of the grand homes in the village is that they lack the sweeping front lawns that might have been expected had they been built on flat ground rather than the ridges of the Ramapo Mountains.

Tuxedo Park is considered one of the first planned communities in the United States. As laid out by Lorillard and Bruce Price, his architect, it had its own water supply, hospital, prison, and even fish hatchery.

The Tuxedo Park School, kindergarten through the ninth grade, is now a private academy of 130 students that charges up to $3,500 a year in tuition and accepts students from outside the community. Residents also have the option of sending their children to the 450-student Tuxedo Union Free School District, which has a high school and an elementary school on Route 17 just south of the Tuxedo Park gates.

The township of Tuxedo covers 31,000 acres stretching from the Rockland County border to Monroe and encompasses large sections of Harriman State Park and Palisades Interstate Park. The residents of Tuxedo and Tuxedo Park rarely mingle. The one exception comes during the summer, when township residents can buy passes to swim at the beach on Wee Wah, one of the village's lakes.

There are several older hamlets in Tuxedo Township, such as Southfields, Arden, and Eagle Valley, along with newer enclaves in the Sterling Forest Corporation developments of Laurel Ridge and Clinton Woods. Brokers say house prices in these areas range from $90,000 to $175,000.

This area of Orange County is more rural than neighboring Rockland County, but it still is within easy reach of New York. The train ride on the former Erie Railroad—now N. J. Transit's Bergen/Main Line—from Tuxedo Park to Hoboken takes about an hour. From there, it is a short ride on the PATH line to lower or midtown Manhattan. The Short Line Bus Company route, through the Lincoln Tunnel into the Port Authority Bus Terminal, also takes about an hour.

A small shopping area on Route 17 near the Tuxedo Park entrance offers a variety of small stores, but many residents travel into Bergen County to shop. No stores of any kind are allowed in the village, which has remained strictly single-family residential (with just a few two-family exceptions) since 1885.

T U X E D O

Tuxedo Park Associates, a general partnership that owns about 2,800 acres in and around Tuxedo Park, plans some development outside the village, but maintains that there are no plans to build inside. So as the village celebrates its hundredth anniversary, it seems that the tranquil woods, the abundant deer, and the aura of a bygone age will continue to predominate.

—ANTHONY DEPALMA

NEW JERSEY
X.

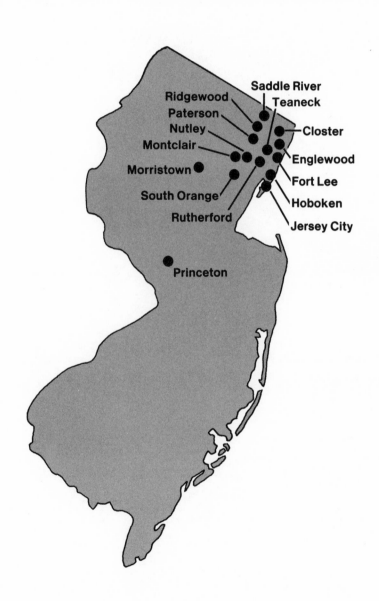

Saddle River
Ridgewood
Teaneck
Paterson
Nutley
Closter
Montclair
Englewood
Morristown
Fort Lee
South Orange
Hoboken
Rutherford
Jersey City

Princeton

C L O S T E R

*To midtown Manhattan: Bus 60
minutes*

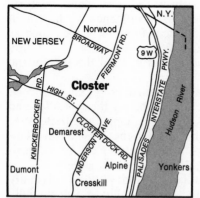

By the time the first
Northern Railroad Company train chugged through in 1859, Closter
was already, in a modest way, a commercial center for the small
suburban communities of northeastern New Jersey. Several general
stores were operating on Closter's main street, and blacksmiths,
gristmills, and lumberyards provided essential services for the
area's businesses and residents.

Today, Closter still serves as "the hub of the northern valley," a
broad plain about two miles west of the Hudson River stretching
from Demarest to the New York State border. And though the commuter trains have stopped running, Closter still supports within its
3.31 square miles a lively mixture of housing, industry, and commercial activity that make it an anomaly in this suburban, station-
wagon-driving corner of Bergen County.

Rich in history, Closter bears the textured, variegated counte-
nance of a community that has evolved over three centuries. It has a
train station converted into a music shop, a curtain factory that now
houses fourteen stores, a bowling alley that was once a theater, and
a score of handsome Revolutionary War–era homes. But it also has
a Kmart shopping plaza and row after row of boxy ranch houses.

The borough—a self-governing municipality—comes close to being what its mayor, Joseph Bianco, called "a cross section of

339

America." It certainly is that in the Oriental grocery that Hyun Sook Park opened on Closter Dock Road a year ago to cater to the large number of Asian-Americans moving into the town. "Very good people come," said Ms. Park in halting but precisely enunciated English. "We have Americans, Japanese, Koreans, Philippines, all coming in here. This is a good area."

This latest migration is leaving other marks on the old community. Next to Ms. Park's store, a beauty salon and a real-estate office have small signs in their windows identifying their businesses in Korean symbols.

When Closter was first settled early in the seventeenth century, Dutch was the language of business. The influence of the Dutch burghers who settled there is still evident in street names such as Lindemann, Naugle, Vervalen, and Westervelt, and in the tidy homes built of local red sandstone that still stand throughout the community.

The borough grew out from the old settlement along Closter Dock Road, which led from a riverfront landing below the Palisades and today is the community's main business and shopping district. After the railroads came (first the Northern, later the West Shore Railroad, connecting in Weehawken with the ferry to New York), businessmen built homes in the borough's quiet country streets.

Those old Victorian houses are still sturdy today and add diversity to Closter's housing market. Many are available at substantially lower prices than the newer, larger houses built in later years.

It was the old houses that attracted Daria Lebduska and her husband, Stephen, who bought a three-bedroom Victorian in 1982 for $79,000. Ms. Lebduska said she and her husband moved from an apartment in Bergenfield to Closter because it was a "good, solid area," surrounded by affluent communities like Alpine on the east and Demarest to the south. "And we liked it because of the zoning— each house has more property," she added. Their house sits on a 100- by 150-foot lot, slightly larger than the borough's 100- by 125-foot minimum lot size.

Most of the homes in Closter, however, are more expensive. According to Marie Lupoli of Doris Larsen real estate, the average price is between $145,000 and $175,000. In the East Hill section, bordering Alpine above the borough, larger homes around twenty years old start at $175,000, and the most recent houses have been priced at around $350,000.

Taxes tend to be high, as they are in all of Bergen County. On a house with a market value of $200,000, the yearly tax bill would come to about $3,350.

Nearly all the houses in Closter are single-family dwellings on individual lots. There are some older two-family homes and a few apartments over stores on Closter Dock Road. A former school building known as "The Elms" has been converted into four rental apartments.

In 1973 developers planned to build a 296-unit garden apartment complex on vacant land near the railroad tracks on the western edge of the borough. The Closter Borough Council, which had final approval power over the project, turned it down because, it said, it would put too great a strain on borough services, and it successfully fought a court challenge filed by the developers.

According to Mayor Bianco, a Republican, Closter has about 200 developable acres out of the 2,500 within its boundaries. The site for the proposed garden apartment complex is still vacant, and several other parcels are zoned for light industry, which some officials hope will produce ratables and lower tax rates.

The largest factory in Closter is the Weyerhaeuser Company plant, which produces cardboard packing boxes. There are a few smaller plants, and more are coming, in a light industrial park that has been established on a ten-acre tract on Ruckman Road. One of the tenants is Inmac, a computer software company.

"There was a violent storm of protest," said Charles H. Windeknecht, the borough administrator. "There was a fear that the new businesses would bring a tremendous amount of truck traffic, but it really hasn't materialized."

Many of Closter's 8,200 residents commute to offices and businesses in New York. Some travel by bus to either the George Washington Bridge terminal or the Port Authority terminal in midtown; the longer ride takes an hour and the shorter forty minutes. Others drive over the George Washington Bridge, nine miles down Route 9W, or through the Lincoln Tunnel into midtown, taking an hour either way.

The community takes pride in its schools. Closter's students attend classes in two grade schools (kindergarten through sixth grade) and one intermediate school before graduating to the Northern Valley Regional High School in Demarest.

In one of the elementary schools, a less-structured optional program is offered in grades one through five. William R. Hanley, superintendent of schools, said the program integrates children from various grades so they can work together.

Closter residents say they can do most of their shopping right in the borough, and there are quite a few restaurants, including several that serve Chinese and Japanese cuisine.

Closter Plaza, a medium-size open shopping center built about twenty years ago, contains a Kmart, a supermarket, a movie theater, and many small specialty shops. It brings with it the unwelcome traffic and crime problems that accompany large gathering places. Police Chief James M. DiLuzio said the biggest crime problems are the passing of fraudulent checks and shoplifting.

C L O S T E R

The Closter police headquarters acts as a communications center for the Interboro Radio Network, a system linking the police departments of seven surrounding municipalities. If one of the other towns has dispatched all its men, incoming calls are routed to the Closter Operations Room, where messages are relayed to officers in the field or, if necessary, additional units can be dispatched.

The role of messenger is a fitting one for this community at the hub of Bergen County's northern valley. On a cold November morning in 1776, as the legend goes, a Closter farmer spied Lord Cornwallis landing at Closter Dock with 4,000 British and Hessian troops. The lone horseman, memorialized on Closter's borough seal and in a monument on Closter Dock Road, warned General Nathanael Greene at Fort Lee, giving the Continental Army time to evacuate and join the rest of Washington's army in Hackensack.

—ANTHONY DEPALMA

ENGLEWOOD

To midtown Manhattan: Bus 30 minutes

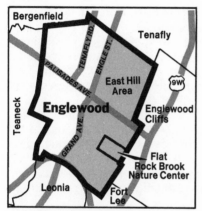

For nearly a century, the spacious mansions on Englewood's East Hill have set the standard for affluent living Bergen County. Yet this multiracial city of 23,700 also has modern, efficient low-income housing units for the poor and many attractive sections for middle-income families as well. What it all adds up to is diversity rather than the one-class makeup that characterizes so many other suburban communities in the county.

"Englewood is a cosmopolitan suburb, just a few minutes from Manhattan, offering all the amenities of a beautiful tree-lined environment," said Mayor Steven Rothman.

"More important," added the city manager, William Sommers, "it is a city with a deep sense of social responsibility, as evidenced by our dedication to the poor, the elderly, and the environment."

Englewood has an unusually large number of churches, private and parochial schools, cultural institutions, and parks. Nearly 25 percent of all property is tax-exempt. This has lowered the tax base and recently prompted an effort to consolidate services and sell off unused and underutilized city properties.

Nearly 12 percent of Englewood's housing is federally subsidized, built expressly for low- and moderate-income residents. The city also provides nearly 300 units of housing for the elderly.

There are 175 acres of parks, including the thirty-eight-acre Flat

343

ENGLEWOOD

Rock Brook Nature Center, one of the last undeveloped tracts of land on the western slope of the Palisades. The Englewood Hospital was recently expanded, and the Public Library contains 124,000 volumes.

Although it maintains a budget surplus, the city has made a strong effort recently to increase tax revenues. In 1984 the City Council gave a green light for 341 town-house condominiums on thirty-six acres of the abandoned Englewood Golf and Country Club. The developer, Charles Reid of Reid Equities, has agreed to retain 71 percent of the property in its natural state. The city has also rezoned several streets and a major parcel of its industrial area, near Route 4, to accommodate high-rise office development.

Englewood is three miles north-northwest of the George Washington Bridge and is bordered on the north by Tenafly and Bergenfield, on the west by Teaneck, on the east by Englewood Cliffs and Fort Lee, and on the south by Leonia. It is one of only a few New Jersey communities with a city-manager form of government.

Englewood, which was primarily an agricultural area until the late 1800's, has a median family income of $24,307, according to the 1980 census, low compared with income levels in neighboring communities with fewer poor residents. Its newer residents, however, are primarily business executives who chose Englewood for its wide assortment of cultural and recreational facilities and its proximity to New York.

The tax rate of $5.15 per $100 of assessed valuation, based on 68 percent of full-market value, is a little higher than average for the area; annual taxes on a $100,000 home would be $3,502. "We have a diverse and very active real-estate market," said Leonard Hansen, a longtime resident who owns Hansen and Hansen Realty of Englewood. "We have sold single-family properties from as low as $46,000 to as high as $1.5 million. There is also a broad section of single-family housing in the $85,000 to $150,000 range."

There is also an active rental market, he added, but many units have been converted to cooperative ownership in the last several years. Prices for rental and cooperative units are also diverse. Rents can be as low as $250 a month for a one-bedroom apartment in some areas and up to $800 elsewhere, with most in the $500 to $600 range. Cooperative units can be bought for from $40,000 to $300,000, also depending on area, but most sell for from $150,000 to $200,000.

There are several condominium projects under way, among them Oak Trail Road near the Fort Lee border, where ninety-three units of cathedral-style two-, three-, and four-bedroom units are under construction.

Although originally settled by the Dutch early in the 1600's, the area was commonly referred to as the "English neighborhood" well into the nineteenth century. Sympathies during the Revolution were sharply divided, but General Washington led his tattered troops through Englewood without incident during his retreat to Trenton in November 1776 and encamped there again briefly later in the war.

The Erie Railroad arrived in 1859, providing connections to Jersey City and New York. It also brought financial and industrial leaders who were lured by the spacious lots, attractive homes, and easy commute to the city and led to an influx of the rich and famous. In the 1890's mansions were built by the novelist Upton Sinclair and industrialists Thomas Lamont and Dwight Morrow. Later Gloria Swanson and other film stars built homes along the winding tree-lined streets in the East Hill area.

Each fall the John Harms Englewood Plaza Theater on North Van Brunt Street, a tastefully renovated vaudeville theater, brings in a season of concerts and other performances. Under the direction of its founder, the late impresario John Harms, and his successors, the theater has presented Itzhak Perlman, Isaac Stern, the Joffrey Ballet, and the Vienna Boys Choir, among others.

Englewood is the site of the Actors' Fund Home for retired actors, and the city has been used as a setting for several motion pictures, among them Woody Allen's *Manhattan* and *Broadway Danny Rose, The In-Laws,* and *Falling in Love.*

Although Englewood residents are within a short drive of the major shopping malls in nearby Paramus, many prefer the convenience of their own 250-store central business district. The district, along Palisade Avenue between Grand Avenue and Tenafly Road, has a wide variety of shops offering clothing, household goods, food, and specialty items.

In an effort to revitalize the area, city officials have in recent years provided merchants with design assistance and low-interest loans to renovate their properties under the Downtown Facade Improvement Program. They also propose to revitalize the area with the sale of municipal properties in the business district for office development.

Englewood, which is well endowed with private and religious schools, has a fully integrated, comprehensive school system. Of the 2,825 students enrolled at the four elementary, middle, and senior high schools, more than half are black or Hispanic, reflecting the city's minority population of 10,000. Nearly 69 percent of the 265 faculty members hold postgraduate degrees and more than 74 percent of the 1982–83 senior class went on to some form of higher education.

There were three National Merit Scholarship finalists in the 1984 senior class. Because enrollment has declined 15 percent in the last ten years, a citizens' advisory panel has proposed the closing of at least one and perhaps two elementary schools. Although the proposal has stirred a debate, education officials maintain that the remaining schools have room for expansion if enrollments begin to grow again.

Commuter service on the railroad ended in 1966, but Englewood is served by N. J. Transit and the Red & Tan Bus Lines. Commuting time to mid-Manhattan by bus is about thirty minutes.

In addition to cultural offerings at the Harms Theater, there are ten art galleries and thirteen antique dealers. Although the nightlife is limited, there are several restaurants, including La Dolce Vita on Grand Avenue, with an Italian menu, and the Club Car on North Van Brunt Street, formerly the Railroad Cafe, which offers seafood specialties. Bennigan's, near Route 4, has become a gathering spot for singles.

—GENE RONDINARO

FORT LEE

To midtown Manhattan: Bus and subway 35 minutes

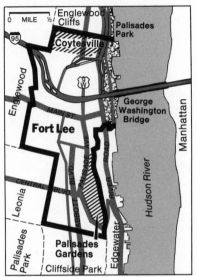

Like the spires of some titanic steel cathedral, the support towers of the George Washington Bridge dominate Fort Lee and the community of 32,000 people who live there. The bridge's superstructure—so close that in some sections it is possible to count both rivets and rust spots from ground level—pierces the sky from nearly every street corner and open window. Paintings of the bridge hang in banks, offices, restaurants, and the library. The borough's championship football team goes by the name the Bridgemen. Streets are dotted with signs that read, simply: "To the Bridge."

There was a Fort Lee before the bridge opened in 1931, a historic and picturesque hamlet atop the 300-foot-high Palisades that had been both a Revolutionary War turning point and the cradle of another revolution: the motion-picture industry.

There was a fort, too—originally called Fort Constitution and later renamed after General Charles Lee—built by Washington's troops and outflanked in November 1776 by Cornwallis as he chased the ragtag Revolutionary Army across New Jersey. A historic park operated by the Palisades Interstate Park Commission re-creates the fortifications and encampment.

But without the bridge, Fort Lee, incorporated as a borough in 1904, would not be the community it is today, and for that, many residents both admire and dislike the 3,500-foot-long steel span.

FORT LEE

"Fort Lee's biggest burden today is the bridge," said Mayor Nicholas Corbiscello. "If anybody was talking about building that bridge here today, I'd tell them to forget about it."

The reasons for this are clear. The grid of seven major highways leading to the bridge dumps a total of 80 million to 100 million cars into Fort Lee a year. Long lines of commuters, trying to avoid toll-plaza backups as they head for the bridge, snake through already congested local streets, freezing whole sections of Main Street in a gridlock. Residents say it can take an hour to cross town in the morning rush hour.

Still, despite the traffic, the tie-ups, and the accompanying pollution from auto emissions, Fort Lee remains one of Bergen County's most desirable locations. It has managed to keep one foot in its small-town past while striding aggressively into the high-tech, high-rise future.

Developers have claimed most of the community's high ground on the Palisades for a squadron of high-rise apartment buildings. Some of them stand side by side with small, wooden, single-family houses that date from the 1920's.

Most of Fort Lee's apartment towers were built as rentals, but in just the last three years practically all of them—and a great number of mid-rise buildings besides—have been converted to condominiums and cooperatives. The more luxurious units can sell for a half-million dollars or more, and local brokers say the apartments sold as investments can be rented for as much as $2,600 a month.

To anyone viewing Fort Lee from Manhattan or passing through on the bridge cut, it seems to be composed entirely of high-rises. But according to the 1980 census, about 30 percent of its housing consists of one- and two-family houses spread comfortably over much of the community's 2.5 square miles. Many are well-built brick structures put up after World War II. They command prices starting at $120,000, but most sell for $200,000 or more.

Prices vary across the borough. The most exclusive neighborhood is Palisades Gardens, where many of the houses perch on the edge of the Palisades and have striking views of the Manhattan skyline. The area was developed in the late 1920's by speculators who expected a real-estate boom to accompany completion of the bridge.

They were right: Marie B. Marshall of the Arthur C. Bruni Agency said a five-bedroom colonial in Palisades Gardens would sell for around $300,000 today, with taxes of roughly $3,500.

Because these homes are so sought after, they rarely are available. The market is not as tight slightly west of the Palisades along Abbott Boulevard, where three- and four-bedroom colonials usually sell for around $200,000.

In Coytesville, the northernmost section of Fort Lee along the Englewood Cliffs border, the houses are older and more closely packed together and thus may sometimes sell for less than $150,000. In recent years many of these older buildings have been demolished and replaced with lavish two-family houses that sell for more than $200,000.

The tax rate in Fort Lee, at $2.33 per $100 of assessed valuation, is one of the lowest in Bergen County—even though the Port Authority of New York and New Jersey, which owns the bridge, pays no taxes. Louis R. Montenegro, the Fort Lee tax assessor, estimated the annual taxes on a $150,000 single-family house in the borough to be about $2,300.

One reason for the low rate is the recent construction of more than a million square feet of first-class office space in several high-rise commercial buildings lining the bridge entrance. As a result, many Fort Lee residents can now work in town. But many also work in the city, and the commuting is easy.

There are more than a half-dozen different buses that pick up passengers in Fort Lee and discharge them at the Port Authority Bus Terminal at the Manhattan end of the bridge. The ride takes about five minutes, and from the Manhattan side, the subway trip to midtown Manhattan on the IND's A train takes a half hour. There are alternate routes through the Lincoln Tunnel to the Port Authority Bus Terminal at 41st Street.

Fort Lee's 2,515 students attend four elementary schools, one middle school, and Fort Lee High School, an imposing Georgian-style building practically in the shadow of the bridge. Dr. Alan W. Sugarman, superintendent of schools, said 85 percent of the graduates go on to further education.

Class size is relatively small, averaging twenty in the high school, eighteen in the elementary and middle schools. Every student from kindergarten through twelfth grade receives several hours' instruction a week on one of the school system's seventy-five computer terminals.

All of Fort Lee's riverfront below the Palisades has been preserved as parkland since the Palisades Interstate Park Commission was established in 1900. Fort Lee's section of the park contains scenic trails, picnic groves, and a small-boat launch, and has a spectacular view of the bridge overhead.

There are several municipal parks in Fort Lee, and the borough operates a recreation center and several tennis courts. The Palisades Interstate Park Commission also runs an ice-skating rink behind the high school.

The oldest of the several shopping districts is along Main Street in the center of town. Restaurants are in abundance, and the international selection is impressive. On one stretch of Main Street stand Japanese, Korean, Italian, and Armenian restaurants and a Jewish delicatessen.

F O R T   L E E

In recent years a large number of Japanese professionals have settled in Fort Lee during their temporary assignments at nearby corporate headquarters. Large numbers of Korean families also have moved in, and the 80,000-volume Fort Lee Library holds an extensive collection of Asian-language books.

Also in the library's collection are films and artifacts from Fort Lee's years as the movie capital of the United States. Hundreds of films were made in the half-dozen studios that flourished in the borough from 1909 until the late 1920's.

Today, a film distribution and storage company is the only link to that era. But before the filmmakers departed for Hollywood's year-round sunshine, directors such as D. W. Griffith and Hal Roach used the rugged cliffs and the willing residents of Fort Lee to start an industry. The many shots of dainty heroines clinging to the dangerous edges of the Palisades even added a new word to the American lexicon: the cliff-hanger.

—ANTHONY DEPALMA

HOBOKEN

To midtown Manhattan: Bus 20 minutes

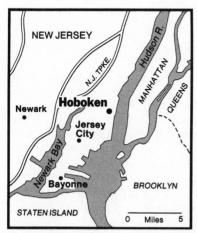

Hoboken has for some time enjoyed a reputation—especially among those wishing to escape New York—as being a close-in, comparatively inexpensive alternative. But time and the unremitting pressures of the Manhattan real-estate market have caused this city to take on some of the characteristics of its neighbor across the Hudson.

Small, older apartments, when available, now rent for $600 and $800 a month, with recently renovated units bringing up to $1,000 a month. One-family brownstones that ten years ago would have sold for $20,000 to $25,000 now sell for $150,000 but "would need work," said Ray McCarthy, a broker with Hoboken Realty. Renovated brownstones bring much higher prices. And one-bedroom condominiums, some of which have been carved out of old tenement buildings, have been selling for from $60,000 to $135,000.

The owner of a renovated $200,000 one-family brownstone, depending on the date of the original assessment, would pay between $4,500 and $5,000 a year in property taxes.

Rising prices and rents reflect the city's growing attractiveness: relatively safe streets, a sense of neighborhood, a cosmopolitan atmosphere, and an ease of commuting—ten minutes to the financial district and fifteen minutes to midtown via the PATH trains or twenty minutes by bus to the Port Authority Bus Terminal at 41st Street.

When Henry Hudson first saw the low-lying tract that now is

HOBOKEN

Hoboken in 1609, it was known to the Leni-Lenape Indians, its first inhabitants, as "Hopoghan Hackingh," the Land of the Tobacco Pipe. The Indians sold the land to the Dutch in 1658.

In 1784, John Stevens, treasurer of New Jersey during the Revolution and later the state's surveyor general, bought it for about $90,000 and began a period of intensive development. By the turn of the twentieth century, Hoboken had become one of the Northeast's main rail- and water-transportation centers. It was the main port of embarkation for American troops in World War I.

Although it remains something of a hub of rail transportation, crossed by the Erie-Lackawanna Railroad and the PATH trains, it is no longer a major port.

Hoboken was settled by successive waves of immigrants. Near the end of the nineteenth century, the number of German immigrants was so great that the minutes of the Board of Education meetings were recorded in German. The Germans were followed by the Irish, Italians, Yugoslavs, and, more recently, by Puerto Ricans, Indians, and Vietnamese.

Each wave of immigrants brought a new culture and language, and the multiplicity is still evident in such shops and restaurants as Van Holland's delicatessen, the Irish House, the Clam Broth House, Marie's Italian bakery, El Quijote restaurant, and the India Bazaar.

Hoboken is relatively compact: one square mile in area, it is eighteen blocks long and sixteen blocks wide. It is bounded on the east by the Hudson River and comes up hard against the Jersey City Heights on the west. Hoboken draws its water from Jersey City, so its residents were among the 300,000 who had to rely on water trucks for drinking and sanitation purposes when the Jersey City aqueduct ruptured in 1982.

The southern end is anchored by the PATH terminal and New Jersey Transit rail yard, while roadways leading to the Lincoln Tunnel form the northern boundary. The main thoroughfare, Washington Street, "The Avenue" as it is known to longtime residents, is lined with shops and specialty stores.

Hoboken's population of 42,460 represents a drop of about 3,000 from the 1970 population, according to officials of the city's Community Development Agency. The decline, agency officials said, reflects a shift from families to singles and young married couples with no children.

Although Hoboken has served as a mecca for people looking for lower-cost housing, it has also offered a respite from higher food, parking, and clothing prices. Residents of Manhattan have been lured through the tunnels to its parking garages by low fees and by PATH trains to food and specialty shops, where prices and sales taxes are generally lower.

Ten years ago, at about the time the character of the population

352

began to change, Hoboken embarked on a major push to upgrade its housing stock. The Community Development Agency, through a variety of neighborhood improvement and loan programs, has assisted in the rehabilitation of about a quarter of the city's 16,000 housing units.

But Hoboken's upgrading has not been problem-free. Tenant groups in the past have charged that arson has been used to displace low-income residents. Cold-water flats with low rents can be converted into luxury apartments.

The city's school system has been another source of concern. The Reverend Geoffrey Curtiss, rector of Holy Innocents Episcopal Church, said, "The educational system is going to have to undergo some major changes for people to stay." Mr. Curtiss, who has a young son, stated that many residents had already turned to parochial schools, which have a combined enrollment of about 2,000.

But Dr. George R. Maier, superintendent of schools, said the school system had improved dramatically in recent years. The reading and mathematics scores of the 6,000 students enrolled in the seven elementary schools and one high school, he said, now compare favorably to other urban school districts in the state.

About 23 percent of public school graduates go on to four-year colleges, Dr. Maier said, and 5 percent to two-year colleges. Stevens Institute of Technology, founded in 1870 by scions of some of the early settlers, sits on the highest point in the city and encompasses some fifty-five acres. About 2,800 graduate and undergraduate students attend its courses in engineering, science, and systems planning, while its library houses frequent art exhibits and its auditorium offers space for dramatic presentations.

Hoboken also offers a variety of poetry readings and dance and music programs. Periodic religious festivals, with statues of saints paraded through the streets, reflect the city's ethnic roots. And the formation of the Hoboken Chamber Orchestra in 1982 was a revival of the musical tradition that abounded when the German Club and the Quartet Club were in their heyday.

Old-time residents boast of having had Frank Sinatra among their neighbors, while newcomers point to John Sayles, the writer and movie director; Glenn Morrow, the singer; and Richard Barone, principal songwriter for the musical group the Bongos.

The city's politics has long been dominated by the Hudson County Democratic machine, and the influx of newcomers has caused concern in some circles that they will try to revise the way things have been traditionally done. "We welcome their getting involved in the governmental process," Mayor Steve Capiello said. "Some people don't like it, but it's for the good."

—ALFONSO A. NARVAEZ

JERSEY CITY

To midtown Manhattan: Train 15 minutes

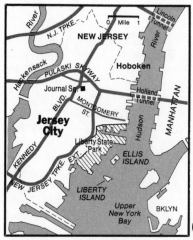

Jersey City has been around for a long time—long enough to acquire a reputation as a gritty manufacturing center that reached its peak in another century. But visitors these days sometimes talk about it as if a team of urban archeologists had just crossed the Hudson River and uncovered the lost city of Atlantis.

There is something distinctly historic, even anachronistic, about New Jersey's second largest city, with its robust collection of nineteenth-century housing still in fine shape and its tangle of un-used railroad tracks and decaying piers acting as a reminder that it once served as a major transportation center.

But it is not really the historic flavor of its many neighborhoods, ranging from the elegant Greek Revival architecture of Hamilton Park to the classic row houses of Bergen Hill, that has suddenly turned this fifteen-square-mile city into a boom town where development and restoration are ubiquitous. It is housing that people can afford, only minutes from Manhattan.

"We could just never afford this space across the river," said Elizabeth Saffir, who with her husband, Ralph, purchased a five-story brownstone in the Van Vorst section in 1982. "We looked pretty hard, but you have to sacrifice too much to remain in Manhattan."

The Saffirs paid $110,000 for their house and plan to spend almost that much to restore it. While bargains are not as plentiful now as

354

they were five years ago, space in Jersey City is far less costly than in Manhattan, or even in the brownstone communities of Brooklyn that offer similar types of housing. When Hoboken—the first close-in New Jersey town to be overrun by New Yorkers looking for cheap urban housing—got too expensive, people looked to neighboring Jersey City for the next good deal.

"In the downtown area, where we concentrate, you can still buy a two-family home in one of the historic districts for less than $160,000, although it would probably need substantial renovation," said Toni Boyne of Boyne Realty, adding that a refurbished brownstone would cost at least $240,000. Property taxes are high. At $130 for each $1,000 of assessed valuation and with property assessed at 35 percent of full-market value, the owner of a $200,000 brownstone would pay over $9,000 a year in taxes.

Rental apartments vary greatly in cost, but local real-estate agents say the average two-bedroom in one of the city's better neighborhoods rents for $800 to $1,200 a month.

"We've always been in the right location," said Mayor Gerald McCann, "but until recently there was a huge psychological barrier called the Hudson River." Although the river is still there, opposition to crossing it each day has eroded at about the same pace as the cost of housing in New York City has escalated.

Jersey City bills itself as a city of neighborhoods, and there is wide diversity, both of type and quality. For the most part, however, it is in the historic communities downtown that the signs of a renaissance are truly evident.

The city was first settled by the Dutch in the 1600's and some of its sections reflect that heritage, among them Paulus Hook, the city's oldest neighborhood and the site of a Revolutionary War battle, and Van Vorst, where hints of past opulence are imprinted on the facades of many elegant town houses. In those sections, and in Bergen Hill and Hamilton Park, homes are being restored at a rapid pace.

Apart from their grace and grandeur, these neighborhoods share several enticing qualities. The first is easy access to PATH trains, which take commuters to the end of the line in midtown Manhattan at 33rd Street and Avenue of the Americas in about fifteen minutes. The second is proximity to the waterfront, where Harbour City, a futuristic $2 billion urban-development project, is under construction. The project, which combines residential and commercial structures, is scheduled to rise over the next fifteen years.

The waterfront is also the home of Liberty State Park, New Jersey's most heavily used urban recreational facility. It is a wonderful place to take in the arresting vista of Manhattan or to gaze up at the nearby Statue of Liberty. Park visitors can take ferries to Liberty Island or to nearby Ellis Island.

Jersey City has the reputation of being a dangerous place to live, but the image may be worse than the reality. The incidence of crime varies widely within the city. It is not as serious a problem downtown, where several large corporations—most notably Colgate-Palmolive, the largest private employer in Jersey City—have many employees. Some of the less densely populated areas of the city, however, are not nearly as safe.

"Things are happening so quickly in many parts of the city that even the recent census figures don't begin to tell the whole story," said Arthur Hatzopoulos, deputy director of the city's Department of Housing and Economic Development.

Despite the large influx of young professionals and managers from Manhattan over the last several years, Jersey City still is basically a working-class town. Of its 223,532 residents, 57.1 percent are white, 27.7 percent are black, 6 percent are Asian (mostly Filipino), and the remainder—most of them Hispanics—identified themselves in the census only as "other."

Among ethnic groups, there are, besides Hispanics, Russians, Greeks, and Poles. Residents point with pride to the house in Hamilton Park where Lech Walesa's late father lived.

Nightlife in the city runs to gatherings at the local taverns, which are in abundance almost everywhere. There are some good restaurants, most notably Casa Dante, a noisy Italian place on Newark Avenue with solid food at moderate prices, and the Summit House in Journal Square, a pleasant, converted colonial farmhouse. There are also many fine ethnic specialty shops for food.

But essentially Jersey City remains a quiet place that shuts down rather early each night, and many residents seek their pleasures across the river in New York. "Our nightlife is still not as active as it might be," Mayor McCann said, "but the development of the waterfront will change all that." City officials are betting heavily on the waterfront project to upgrade the quality of life. Some people even dare to hope that downtown's 4,700-seat Stanley Theater, the second largest theater in the country after Radio City Music Hall, will one day be able to reopen. The fifty-five-year-old movie palace has been dark for several years because it did not draw enough people to make it profitable.

Although Jersey City has a promising future to offer newcomers, it is not without serious problems that will be difficult to resolve. Foremost among them may be its public school system. The strongly Roman Catholic city has traditionally relied on parochial schools to educate its children. Even today it still has almost as many Catholic as public grade schools, although the thirty public grade schools have 23,418 students and the twenty-nine Catholic grade schools have 9,039.

The five public high schools in the city have been plagued by violence and severe budget restrictions. There are nine Catholic high schools and several other private educational institutions.

Another problem is that much of the city is still overgrown lots, rotting piers, and empty rail yards, giving it an air of seediness and decay.

The city still suffers, as well, from an image problem associated largely with an aging Democratic political machine that kept working long after most of the other machinery the city depended on for its livelihood became obsolete. The machine was finally defeated by Mayor McCann, a Republican who ran on a good-government platform.

People say all these problems will lessen now. The spate of new construction, the growth of some specialized trades like the film industry, and a surge in corporate investment in the city seem to suggest that they will. While Jersey City is not quite ready to challenge Hollywood as the nation's film capital, many movies and commercials are being shot there. Among the directors who have been shooting parts of their films in the city are Woody Allen and Sidney Lumet.

For the moment, despite the strong promise of coming vitality, moving to Jersey City remains largely a gesture of hope for the future: hope that Harbour City will work, that residential renovation will expand to communities outside the downtown core, that the city's infrastructure problems will be eliminated, that crime will decrease, and that public education will improve significantly. If all these problems continue to turn around, then Jersey City is probably an idea whose time has finally come—again.

—MICHAEL SPECTER

To midtown Manhattan: Bus or train 40 to 45 minutes

You might think that a town that has one mature shade tree for every two residents and has within its six square miles fourteen parks and playgrounds brimming with swimming pools and skating rinks, as well as a college with a stadium, a professional theater troupe, three general hospitals, forty-two churches, and a Katharine Gibbs School would be content to sit back and smugly contemplate its advantages.

Not Montclair, New Jersey. It is not enough for Montclair to be one of the metropolitan area's more affluent and physically attractive suburbs, nor for it to be a regular tour stop for the Joffrey Ballet and the Boston and Cleveland symphony orchestras, nor for it to house both a traditional and an alternative weekly newspaper. It even has two zip codes (07042 and 07043).

Yet Montclair manages to keep itself in continual and generally amiable ferment. When an issue arises—whether it is a proposal to eliminate forty-four shade trees to widen a road, raise real-estate taxes above the current level of $8.81 per $100 of assessed value, desegregate the schools, create a shopping mall, grant a liquor license, leash dogs, show an X-rated movie, or even decide whether Montclair should be called a town or a township—committees for both sides will form instantly, followed shortly by a third group bent on middle-ground conciliation, thereafter by a call from the League of Women Voters for further study. That is what gives this Essex County township of 38,321 people its vibrancy and spice.

Montclair is seldom dull, even to those who suggest it is occasionally stuffy. Those who complain about its constant state of contention say they would not dream of living anywhere else. Montclairians care about their town and almost never fail to react to an assault on its basic character.

"It's easier to buy a ranch house in Bergen County than it is to live here," said Rey Redington, former head of Montclair's Chamber of Commerce. "In Montclair, you've got to be a little bit different."

Montclair is laid out as a long, irregular rectangle, roughly three miles long by two miles wide, and is dominated by its twin prides, its trees and its private homes. Only a handful of apartments exist within the township's borders, and its 97.7 miles of streets are lined and sheltered by 17,000 trees, most of them towering oaks.

In its eastern lowlands houses are smaller and sit on small lots. To the west, in the foothills of the Watchung Mountains, are huge homes—colonials, Tudors, and Italianate Victorians—that at the turn of the century were the summer homes for some of New York's wealthy.

Vestiges of that Montclair remain. Most of those striking homes, many dutifully maintained, are still on "the Hill," as the slopes up to Montclair's western border, the Mills and South Mountain reservations, are called. They sit along streets called Upper Mountain and Highland avenues, Lloyd and Undercliff roads. No diligent real-estate agent fails to take prospects along these streets, where many houses sell for between $200,000 and $400,000 and some for as much as $1 million.

Down on Valley Road and in the area east of it are the developments of later years, somewhat typical, traditional suburban homes in the $100,000 to $125,000 price range. Many of these have attracted urban newcomers; others are occupied by descendants of the servants to the rich on the Hill. Most residents of the racially integrated developments are upwardly mobile middle-class people who generally support rising school expenditures.

Taxes on a house selling for $150,000, depending on size, age, and location, range from about $3,500 to $4,000 a year.

The community's population is 68.8 percent white, 28.9 percent black, and the remainder other minority groups. The minority-group residents are concentrated in the southeast part of town, and Montclair for years resisted efforts to achieve racial balance in its schools.

Once it made up its mind to work toward that goal, however, the town employed a variety of ways to accomplish it. Busing, so-called magnet schools, offering all manner of esthetic enrichments, and alternate school programs all were employed, largely successfully: though the town was divided, the social fabric did not tear.

In standardized reading tests, Montclair's public school students score higher than 85 percent of all students in the country. About 60 percent of the high-school graduates go on to four-year colleges and another 20 percent go on to two-year colleges or nonacademic training.

Dr. Mary Lee Fitzgerald, who is Montclair's first woman school superintendent, has declared that though the system should continue to produce high reading scores and send graduates to the best colleges, it also must "challenge the most errant of minds."

Montclair elected a black mayor more than a decade ago, and James Ramsey, the present holder of that office, a largely ceremonial post, also is black.

The township is noteworthy in its dedication to the upkeep and preservation of its housing stock. Montclair is a town of single-family homes, the taxes on which pay for 85 percent of its municipal expenses. The prospects for expansion are limited because there are fewer than fifty undeveloped building lots within the township's borders.

Some residents, however, believe that the township is selective. They note that in the zeal for renewal, whole blocks in the poorer sections of town have been leveled to make way for multiple housing units. They remark as well that while low-cost housing was once planned for that area on the eastern border of the township, there now is talk that middle- and upper-income housing will be developed there.

Along Bloomfield Avenue lies Montclair's largest commercial area, which mixes small food shops and boutiques with most of the town's antique shops and a branch of Hahne's Department Store. Two other shopping areas, one called the "South End," along Orange Road, the other in midtown along Watchung Avenue, are smaller and offer basic goods and services. The Upper Montclair shopping area, along Valley Road, like that on Bloomfield Avenue, contains many more clothing shops, jewelers, and crafts outlets.

The town is a bedroom community for executives and white-collar workers who commute to New York and Newark by bus or by N. J. Transit and PATH trains. By train the commute takes forty-five minutes; by bus, forty minutes. And Montclair may be the only suburb with an organized car pool for ministers, to transport them each day to the Interchurch Center in Manhattan.

Montclair's character is rooted in its history. Its predecessors were Cranetown, settled by the English in 1694 roughly in Montclair's present location, and Speertown, a few years later, slightly to the north on land Dutch settlers traded from the Leni-Lenape Indians of New Jersey.

MONTCLAIR

In 1812 the combined settlements became known as West Bloomfield, and in 1868 it became the separate Township of Montclair. In 1894 it was incorporated into a town with a commission form of government, and in 1980 it switched by popular vote to a council-manager form and became a township.

Much of Montclair is fond of its nineteenth-century, and earlier, history. In fact, during Montclair's 1968 centennial celebration, a booklet was published entitled "A Goodly Heritage, A Commemorative History of Montclair, New Jersey." In it, the authors, David Nelson Alloway and Mary Travis Arny, wrote:

"Founded by the venturesome, it has never become provincial; built by the successful, it has never become stuffy. In spite of being one of the wealthiest towns in the world, it has never become ostentatious.

"We do not think our town is perfect. We are very much aware of the fact that it has some tender areas which need attention badly, and we are trying hard to clean them up. Some of these things we will probably have to leave to another generation."

In Montclair these days, most people would rather now wait for the next generation. That may be the most significant recent alteration of the township's basic character.

—FRED FERRETTI

MORRISTOWN

To midtown Manhattan: Bus or train 60 minutes

In its two and a half cen-
turies, Morristown has been a mining town, a Revolutionary War
capital, a playground for millionaires, and a suburban home for corporations. For at least the last twenty years, housing in its three
square miles has been scarce, with reasonably priced homes and
rental units as hard to find as taxis in the rain. Much of the housing
demand in the area has been met by Morris Township, seventeen
square miles of sophisticated country charm that abuts Morristown.

Over the last two decades, Morris Township has grown to 18,400
residents, surpassing Morristown's 16,600. The two municipalities
have merged their school systems, libraries, and other services but
have maintained separate governments.

As the county seat, Morristown continues to be the center of
commercial activity, entertainment, and business in Morris County
and, increasingly, for the entire suburban region of northwestern
New Jersey. It had been that way from the beginning. The first
settlers came to the mountains in search of iron ore, and by the time
of the Revolutionary War, the Morristown mines were among the
few regular sources of iron in the colonies. That attracted George
Washington in the winter of 1777, after he had humiliated the British
at Trenton.

Washington brought his troops back two years later. They camped
at Jockey Hollow, while he and Martha stayed at the home of

362

MORRISTOWN

Theodocia Ford, the wealthy widow of a local merchant. The house is now part of the Morristown National Historical Park.

After the war, the iron in the hills gave out. Morristown struggled for a while, but the Vail family and their manufacturing complex at Speedwell Village (now listed in the National Register of Historic Places), George P. Macculloch, an engineer who planned the Morris Canal, and others kept the town going.

The railroad came to Morristown in 1838, and in the ensuing years some of America's capitalist elite discovered that the community was an attractive place to relax and raise their families while giving them relatively easy access to the bustling commerce of New York City. From 1875 through the beginning of the Great Depression, Morristown and its environs attracted dozens of millionaires who erected opulent estates and transformed the quiet town into an "inland Newport."

The great estates have been razed to make way for, among other things, corporate headquarters like that of the Allied Chemical Corporation, which was built on the grounds of the estate of Otto Kahn, the New York banker. Morristown Memorial Hospital sits where the Charles H. Mellon residence used to be.

The strange marble-and-granite box housing Morristown Town Hall was built as the home of Theodore Vail, who founded what eventually became the American Telephone & Telegraph Company. The Morris Museum, in Morris Township, occupies the mansion of Peter H. B. Frelinghuysen and his sister Matilda's house now serves as the Morris County Park Commission headquarters.

Some smaller old properties remain, and local real-estate agents say these historic homes, still big when compared to contemporary houses, sometimes go for as little as $150,000. But because of the high demand for homes by executives and employees of expanding companies in the area, there are few houses for sale in Morristown.

Homes are easier to find in neighboring Morris Township. Generally, they are newer, more expensive, and built on larger lots. A typical listing—a four- to five-bedroom custom-built colonial with in-ground pool on a 140- by 200-foot lot—is for $249,900 with taxes of $3,637, according to Mary Beth Pappas of Weickert Co. Realtors.

Morristown's downtown area centers on the community's historic Green, fringed by churches, department stores, and smaller shops. South of the Green is South Street, the main commercial thoroughfare, where residents shop at King's supermarket and dine at such restaurants as Society Hill and The Office. North of the Green, on Washington Street, is the Grand Cafe, which features an ambitious menu.

Young families moving into the area are concerned about the school system, which went through a painful merger in 1974. The consolidation was fought by Morristown residents and eventually the State Department of Education had to step in and order the merger. The situation has calmed down since, the high school is now undergoing a $12 million expansion and renovation, and residents now say they are happy with the merger.

"I'm very satisfied with the elementary school system," said Kent Manahan, anchorwoman on New Jersey Public Television's nightly newscast. She has had six children, including a set of triplets, enrolled in the public school system. "The merger has worked out very well for me personally," she said. "With the larger enrollment we have more classes, and that has meant that my triplets can all be in different classes."

About 4,800 students are enrolled in the six elementary schools, one junior high school, and one high school in the merged Morris School District.

There are several private elementary and prep schools in and around Morristown, and three institutions of higher education—the College of St. Elizabeth and Drew and Fairleigh Dickinson universities—are within a few minutes' drive. In addition, the Rabbinical College of America is situated in Morristown.

For young people seeking recreation, there are several large parks in the less-developed sections of Morris Township, including Loantaka and Lewis Morris parks. The township has two municipal pools and Morristown has one.

There are several historic parks in the area, the largest of which is Jockey Hollow. A working farm known as Fosterfields, where visitors may see how farming was done a century ago, sits in the township just north of the Morristown boundary.

People moving into this area weigh commuting facilities nearly as carefully as they do the schools. The completed interstate highways make the thirty-five-mile trip to New York relatively painless. Frequent interstate bus service is available, and the N. J. Transit Morris and Essex line carries trainloads of commuters to Newark and Hoboken each morning. Although the line's railroad cars pale in comparison to the elegance of the "millionaire express" that used to whisk Theodore Vail and other executives to New York City at the turn of the century, they are usually on time. Commuting to midtown Manhattan by whatever mode of travel takes about an hour.

—ANTHONY DEPALMA

NUTLEY

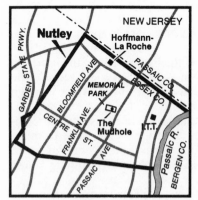

A century ago, a magazine editor living in what is now known as Nutley Town urged his friend Samuel L. Clemens to pay him a visit. "There isn't much that is prettier than this end of New Jersey," he wrote. "It is all upland, tumbling into shallow valleys and bright sunny reaches along the Passaic River, and hillsides white as snow with daisies, and everywhere trees."

Today, the Empire State Building is clearly visible from some of Nutley's highest points, but its pastoral serenity is preserved in the town's hundred-acre park system that polka-dots this suburban community in the northeast corner of Essex County. Visitors walking through the town's eleven parks see willow trees dangling thin branches into brooks that meander through the town, and children fishing in a modest algae-filled pond in Memorial Park that the locals call "the mudhole."

Nutley's bucolic atmosphere has kept many residents from moving away, contributing to its stability, said Carl Orechio, a former assemblyman and town commissioner who is now a real-estate broker. Like many families in the area, Mr. Orechio's has been there for several generations, and his daughter has married and settled there, too.

"The families here are very much rooted in the town," said Michael C. Gabriele, editor of the local newspaper, *The Nutley Sun,* and a resident for nineteen years. "It's an attractive place to live."

NUTLEY

With about 98 percent of the community's 3.5 square miles already developed, very little new construction takes place. Local real-estate brokers sell, on average, fewer than twenty houses a month. Typically, a two-bedroom home on less than a quarter acre costs $90,000 to $100,000, according to Marion Peters, who has lived in town since 1946 and owns Records Realty Company.

But in the wealthy Nutley Park section in the northeastern corner of town there are stately three- and four-bedroom Tudor- and colonial-style houses with at least half an acre of land, many of which sell for more than $200,000.

Most buyers are either people who want to live near New York City or former Nutley residents who just want to move back, Ms. Peters said.

The community's eastern border is the Passaic River, the northern is Kingsland Street, and the western is East Passaic Avenue. The southern border ignores all streets and angles to the river through Reinheimer and Louden parks.

The main commercial street, Franklin Avenue, bisects the community north to south and provides all of life's essentials, from art supplies to intimate nighttime apparel. It passes the center of town, which is dominated by Nutley High School and its athletic fields. Just to the east is the red-brick Town Hall.

For entertainment, the community has one small movie house, the Franklin Theater on Franklin Avenue, and the popular Nutley Manor Restaurant, on Bloomfield Avenue near Kingsland Street, which offers live music and dancing on weekends. A jumble of shady lanes and quaint side streets forms the remainder of the town.

Most of Nutley is residentially zoned, said Joseph Reilly, the town tax assessor, and most of the 7,200 houses are owner-occupied. Industry is allowed only in the fringe areas, including part of Kingsland Street, the headquarters of Hoffmann–La Roche, Inc., the pharmaceutical corporation, where the drugs Valium and Librium were developed.

Nutley's taxes are in the middle range of rates for the twenty-two municipalities in Essex County, and homes have not been reassessed since 1977. The annual tax bill of a house selling for $100,000 would be about $2,500.

Hoffmann–La Roche and the I.T.T. Corporation, which together occupy almost 150 acres of land in Nutley, pay a total of $3.1 million a year in taxes, lightening the burden on residents.

There also are more than 70 apartment buildings, some with up to 200 units, scattered through the town, mostly in the northern half along the main streets, including Franklin Avenue and Warren Street. The apartments rent for about $100 a room a month.

The population is 30,000, according to the 1980 census, and a quarter of the residents are under eighteen years of age.

N U T L E Y

Many residents work in New York City, which is less than half an hour away by car by way of nearby Route 3 and the Lincoln Tunnel. The No. 192 bus of N. J. Transit makes stops along Kingsland Street and also takes about half an hour for its trip into the city.

Parents send their children to one of five public elementary schools in the town, the junior high, and Nutley High School. In recent years students' scores on state competency tests given in grades six, nine, and eleven have risen well above the 90th percentile, said Dr. James J. Fadule, Jr., the superintendent. And more than 70 percent of the high school's graduates go on to college or technical school, he added.

The Nutley Free Public Library, near the corner of Booth Drive and Vincent Place, has 95,000 books and 4,500 records and tapes. Three computers are available for home use, and regular story hours are held for the town's preschoolers. The library's building is almost seventy years old, a mere youngster in a community with a history of more than 300 years.

The settlement of Nutley Town began in 1666, when two men, dissatisfied with the theocratic government of New Haven Colony, bought a large swath of the Passaic River valley from local Indians for a few old clothes and a lot of liquor to form a new secular community.

By the 1700's, Dutch settlers had turned the area into a thriving community. Two legacies of that era are the John M. Vreeland Homestead on Chestnut Street and Kingsland Manor on Kingsland Street; both date to the eighteenth century.

By the 1800's, part of the area now known as Nutley lay within the Township of Belleville. Around the middle of the century, the northern half of Belleville rebelled against the southern half, which it felt was unjustly receiving more than its share of municipal improvements. Eventually, the northern half seceded, and in 1874 formed the separate community of Franklin.

Nutley is named for a turn-of-the-century artists' community centered around a peaceful enclave known as The Enclosure, which bordered Franklin and still exists by the same name in the center of town. It was the home of Reginald Marsh, who painted many New York scenes, and Frederic Dorr Steele, who illustrated many of the Sherlock Holmes short stories. Franklin and Nutley joined together and, after much debate, took the name of Nutley Town in 1902.

More than a dozen years ago, the book *Safe Places,* by David and Holly Franke, named Nutley one of the country's fifty safest communities. "We're far below neighboring communities in crime, especially crimes like burglary," said Detective Robert DeBello, who has been with the department since 1970. Detective Ed Guerino, a lifelong resident, said a major problem in the community was teenage drinking in the parks, which close at sundown.

N U T L E Y

The recreation supervisor for Nutley's Department of Parks, Loretta Kwapniewski, said the town offered year-round activities for its youngsters. More than 1,000 children take part in baseball and softball leagues, which hundreds of parents help to organize. "They just want to see the children have a good time," she remarked.

—MARK B. ROMAN

PATERSON

To midtown Manhattan: Bus or train 60 minutes

For more than a century, Paterson's history paralleled the course of America's industrial expansion. Its mills, powered by the Great Falls of the Passaic River, made it a leading textile center, and its inventors created the Colt Revolver and the Holland submarine.

Like many industrial cities, Paterson was eventually afflicted by urban decay. But city officials say that because of its relatively small size—its population of 138,000 ranks it third in size in New Jersey, after Newark and Jersey City—its problems are manageable.

"This is the oldest industrial city in the United States and it's still alive and breathing," said Mayor Frank X. Graves. He and other officials cited signs of a resurgence: construction of luxury housing and office space and restoration of Paterson's old manufacturing center.

Much of Paterson is actually suburban in character, with quiet streets of one-family houses and neatly kept lawns. But because of its image as an inner city in decline, it often is overlooked by home buyers. As a result, large, attractive houses are available at bargain-basement prices.

The city, the seat of Passaic County, occupies 8.4 square miles straddling the Passaic River. It is ethnically diverse, according to the 1980 census, with whites making up 35 percent of the population, blacks 33 percent, Hispanics 29 percent, and the remainder Orientals, American Indians, and others.

369

PATERSON

It is a forty-minute drive from Paterson to midtown Manhattan by way of Route 80 and the George Washington Bridge. N. J. Transit provides bus service to the Port Authority Bus Terminal at 41st Street and N. J. Transit trains connect to PATH in Hoboken. From there passengers can take trains to 33rd Street or the Wall Street area. Average commutation time is about one hour on either bus or train.

The city was named for William Paterson, a late eighteenth-century governor of New Jersey. Its industrial heart is the Passaic River, whose seventy-seven-foot Great Falls "animate a thousand automatons," wrote William Carlos Williams in his poem "Paterson." In 1791, Alexander Hamilton helped create the Society for Establishing Useful Manufactures to harness the power of the falls for industrial use.

By 1825, the city was known as "the Cotton Town of the United States." It also was a center of labor unrest: the first factory strike in American history took place there in 1828.

In the 1830's the Paterson and Hudson River Railroad laid tracks to the city and a canal was opened linking it with the Pennsylvania coalfields. Samuel Colt established a plant for making revolvers, and in 1837, the first of thousands of locomotives assembled there was made in John Clark's machine shop.

By 1850, Paterson had a new label: the "Silk City." At its peak, the industry produced 30 percent of the country's silk products. European immigrants brought cheap labor and radical ideas: in 1913 workers led by John Reed and William ("Big Bill") Haywood of the Industrial Workers of the World led the picket lines for months in a strike that ultimately failed.

In an effort to transform its industrial past into a more promising future, Paterson's hopes are again centered on the nineteenth-century red-brick mills and factories of the Great Falls Historic District, a 119-acre tract along the banks of the Passaic a few blocks from downtown. "In the district, we have the potential for a recreation area, a business area, and a residential area, all in one," said William Mason, director of the Department of Community Development.

Two mills, the Phoenix and Essex, are being converted to housing for artists. Another mill houses an elementary school and an electronics company. The Paterson Museum's collection of industrial memorabilia has been moved to the former Rogers Locomotive building, with office space in the floors above. Across the river is Raceway Park, a reconstruction of the country's earliest water-power system.

The Great Falls Development Company is trying to encourage the renovation of six other mills for use as office space or factory outlets. The first of the six, the Franklin Mill, is nearing completion and will have approximately 18,000 square feet of office space.

Some parts of the city are blemished by abandoned buildings or sagging frame dwellings, but many areas remain vital. In Riverside, multifamily houses are found side by side with chemical concerns, textile mills, and warehouses. Hillcrest, Lakeview, and the Eastside are among the areas zoned for single-family homes, which vary in style from colonial and Cape Cod to ranch and Tudor.

"In comparison to other areas, the houses are magnificent homes for the price," said Richard Hajjar, owner of Hajjar Associates. In Eastside, houses that would sell for twice as much in neighboring Bergen County cost as little as $40,000, Mr. Hajjar stated. In the Riverside area, two-family homes are available for about $60,000.

Louis Gilmore of Gilmore & Sons Realtors said that homes in the Eastside section, an area that has been successfully integrated, sell for $70,000 to $85,000, while similar homes in Lakeview or Hillcrest, which are still predominantly white, might cost $10,000 more. Apartments also are relatively inexpensive—a two- or three-bedroom usually rents for less than $500, but vacancies are few and waiting lists are long.

Jack and Dawn McLaughlin moved to Paterson in 1982 after the house they rented in Montclair, New Jersey, was put up for sale. Mr. McLaughlin, who works for a Paterson job-training foundation, and his wife, who does paralegal work in Newark, first looked for a house in Montclair but gave up when they realized all they could afford there was "a garage." They eventually turned to Paterson and bought a large three-bedroom house with finished basement and attic in the Eastside section for $65,000.

The tax rate has risen steadily in recent years and now is $8.93 for each $100 in assessed valuation, while services have been curtailed. Paterson's main library and seven branches were shut for lack of funds, and though the main library is again offering a full range of services, the branches are operating at reduced hours.

Paterson's crime rate is high in relation to urban areas of comparable size in New Jersey, but according to the State Police Uniform Crime Report, most crimes are not violent. Asked to characterize the situation, James Hannan, the police chief, said "things have improved tremendously" and gave part of the credit to neighborhood groups that have become active in crime-prevention efforts.

The school system has thirty elementary schools and two comprehensive high schools, Eastside and John F. Kennedy. In the elementary schools, about 85 percent of the students meet the state's minimum standards of achievement. About 45 percent of high-school graduates go on to higher education, according to Frank Arnot, director of the Office of Pupil Personnel Services.

But many parents have little confidence in the public school system and send their children to parochial schools or private preparatory schools in nearby towns. Paterson also has two vocational schools—one private, one run by the county.

Downtown stores provide most shopping needs not met by the many neighborhood shops and groceries. The city's bakeries, restaurants, and cafes suit just about every palate. Among many eating places are several offering the cuisines of Argentina, Italy, and the Middle East. There is also a local dish—the Hot Texas wiener with chili sauce.

On 21st Avenue, there are several Italian stores, such as Gianella Brothers Bakery and Delicatessen. The Farmers' Market on Railroad Avenue, with butchers and vegetable stands, attracts shoppers from around North Jersey. For the overstuffed, the Garrett Mountain Reservation offers opportunities for exercise in its 570 wooded acres on the heights overlooking the city.

Newcomers to Paterson are often surprised by what the city has to offer, both in its suburban and urban incarnations. "When my husband first suggested that we live in Paterson, I said, 'No way,'" Ms. McLaughlin recalled. "I never knew it was this nice."

—CHRISTOPHER WELLISZ

PRINCETON

To midtown Manhattan: Train 60 minutes or bus 90 minutes

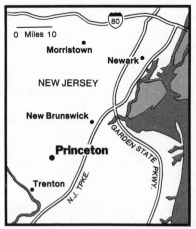

A stroll through the busy center of Princeton, amid all the chinos, plaid skirts, and boating loafers, provides a pretty good idea of what this fabled community is like. At the congested intersection of Witherspoon and Nassau streets stand a bank, a bus station, and the front gates of the university—three privately owned institutions that reflect three of Princeton's most distinctive and appealing characteristics: it has money, it is well educated, and it is just a short trip (by bus, train, car, or plane) from either New York or Philadelphia.

Although Nassau Hall, the university's oldest building, served as the seat of the Continental Congress only through the summer and fall of 1783, Princeton has retained its position as a capital of sorts—of culture, education, and the preppy life-style.

Part of Princeton today still speaks with the moneyed voices heard by F. Scott Fitzgerald during his days as an undergraduate. But the halls of its high school resound with chatter in a variety of languages, and the borough's 12,035 residents represent nearly every rung on the socioeconomic ladder.

Surrounding the old town is suburban Princeton Township, a separate, more commodious municipality of newer houses and a slightly larger population. The borough and township share a school system but have separate municipal services.

Princeton is a small town with cosmopolitan tastes, a peculiarity

373

most residents seem to find attractive and downright endearing. "It's big enough so people don't know everything about you," said Barbara J. Hill, former president of the Borough Council. "But shopkeepers and the people you pass on the street know who you are, and they care about you."

Those people spend a lot of time on Princeton's streets. Nassau Street, which begins in front of historic Morven, home to New Jersey's governors, is always crowded during the daylight hours when its amalgam of shops—from Landau's Icelandic Wools to Woolworth's—are open. And at night, people can always be seen popping into PJ's Pancake House or coming out of the Garden movie theater. Something is always happening either on campus, at the Y.M.-Y.W.C.A., or at the McCarter Theater.

Because of strict zoning laws and a caring community that attends public meetings religiously, the face of Princeton has not changed much in the last twenty years. The Gothic towers of the university buildings set the predominant tone, though many other styles of architecture have melded comfortably.

The Princeton area has enjoyed an economic boom of late. New office complexes and research parks built along Route 1 have brought an influx of executives and scientists who are buying homes in Princeton for $300,00 to $350,000.

House prices in Princeton are among the highest in New Jersey, but Peggy Hughes, a real-estate agent for John T. Henderson Real Estate, said the range is quite broad. It goes from $99,000 to $575,000, she reported, and even more for some select parcels.

Library Place, where Woodrow Wilson lived, and Hodge Road are lined with large estates. Close by is the forty-seven-acre compound of J. P. Morgan's heirs called Constitution Hill, which has been carved into sixty condominiums, ranging in price from $258,000 to $375,000. Taxes are on the high side, too. The owner of a $250,000 house would pay about $3,800 in annual taxes.

Most houses in Princeton, though, tend to be small and are situated on lots of rather limited size. Renting in Princeton is not impossible, but it is difficult, with rents ranging from $600 and up.

Getting to and from New York is a relatively painless fifty-minute train ride from Penn Station to Princeton Junction, and from there just a ten-minute hop on the "dinky"—a tiny train that shuttles between the junction and Princeton proper. The bus from Nassau Street takes a bit longer—about ninety minutes—and the trip by car takes a bit more than an hour. The times are roughly the same to Philadelphia.

What also makes the area attractive is the availability of cultural activities. On campus, the university's art museum and museum of natural history are open to the public as is the campus itself, full of historic buildings and outdoor sculptures by Picasso and others.

PRINCETON

Religious services and musical events are held in the university chapel, which is as big as some cathedrals.

The Princeton schedule of football, basketball, and other sports is played at Jadwin Gym and Palmer Stadium. When the facilities are not being used by the school's athletes, they are sometimes made available to the community.

Local high-school sports, while competitive, have a no-cut policy, which means that anyone who wants to play gets a chance to. But sports are not the main attractions at Princeton High School. Members of the school's three musical groups—the concert choir, the jazz band, and the orchestra—get the hero's welcome when they return from national tournaments with first-place trophies.

Performances in the classroom and on tests also produce winners. Princeton High, with more than a thousand students, has National Merit Scholars among its graduates each year, in most years more than any other school, private or public, in New Jersey.

The three elementary schools and one middle school in the district maintain a similarly high standard. Dr. Paul D. Houston, the superintendent, pointed out that computer-education programs begin in the lowest grades.

It has been said that despite all its elegance, Princeton lacks a first-class restaurant. Lahiere's, a French restaurant on Witherspoon Street, is considered to be, if not the best in town, at least the place to be seen. Another popular place is the Tap Room of the Nassau Inn on Palmer Square, with a Norman Rockwell mural providing a homey atmosphere for its American cuisine.

As civil a community as Princeton is, it still has hundreds of thefts and burglaries each year. They keep the thirty-two-member Princeton Police Department hopping. Ms. Hill, the former Borough Council president, who also serves as police commissioner, said that Princeton is a target because it is known that well-to-do people live there.

Her former home, on a quiet street, had been burglarized twice. Still, she said, Princeton is a very safe place to live. "You just need to not be silly and leave the front door unlocked like I did."

Princetonians have a way of resolving conflicts like this by accepting the danger but not worrying about it. F. Scott Fitzgerald, one of Princeton's most famous nonworriers, once wrote that "the test of a first-rate intelligence is the ability to hold two opposed ideas in the mind at the same time, and still retain the ability to function."

More than two opposed ideas circulate in Princeton on every issue from zoning to cutting down a tree. Yet Princeton has retained the ability to function quite well indeed.

—ANTHONY DEPALMA

R I D G E W O O D

To midtown Manhattan: Bus or train 60 minutes

The Dutch farmers who settled Ridgewood in the 1660's paid both royal agents and the Leni-Lenape Indians for deeds to their properties, with the idea that this would buy them security from problems plaguing other settlers of the New World. It worked.

Three centuries later, the strategy is still working in the Bergen County community, where residents pay a little more for retreats from the troubles of the outside world. Throughout the suburbs, many who fled from crime, congestion, pollution, and school problems in the city now find those troubles following them.

Not so in Ridgewood, where violent crime is rare, where industry has not been invited in with its congestion and pollution to offset high taxes, and where the school system maintains a tradition of excellence. The cost has been high taxes and relatively high housing prices.

Ridgewood has a traditional, small-town appearance and atmosphere remarkably unchanged from decades past. Although it sounds as though it might have been named by a rather unimaginative real-estate developer, the name is descriptive of this extraordinarily leafy village set in the foothills of the Ramapo Mountains. From their expensive homes on Crest Road residents can enjoy a panoramic view of the skyline of Manhattan about fifteen miles away.

RIDGEWOOD

The village, which has had just one housing development, is known for its selection of unusual homes. Developers began carving up the strawberry fields for homesites shortly after the railroad came through in 1848. Growth of the village has been slow and continual.

Although it accelerated after the George Washington Bridge opened in 1931 and in the years after World War II, no growth tide ever washed over Ridgewood as it did other suburban areas in those periods. Most of Ridgewood's housing stock was already there.

Ridgewood—named one of the nation's ten "best suburbs" in a 1975 *Ladies' Home Journal* poll of public officials and business, civic, labor, and religious leaders—is something of a fashionable address, although the very rich choose suburbs such as Franklin Lakes or Saddle River, where they can have more property.

Real-estate agents say the range of house prices in Ridgewood is from about $110,000 to about $700,000. As elsewhere in suburbia, home values appreciate year by year. Because Ridgewood is thought of as a suburb of white-collar professionals, it gets a fair number of corporate transferees, who help to boost the turnover rate of homes to about 20 percent each year.

According to the 1980 census, Ridgewood's population of 25,208 is about 96 percent white and about 2 percent black, with a growing population of Chinese, Japanese, and other Orientals. Religious affiliations are reflected by seventeen Protestant churches, one Roman Catholic church, and one Jewish temple. One of the few complaints about the village is that it is too homogeneous.

There are complaints, too, about high taxes. The rate is $3.67 per $100 of assessed valuation. Real-estate agents say that an "average" three-bedroom home with one and a half baths selling for about $140,000 would have a tax bill in excess of $3,000 a year.

Schools are the major factor in the tax rate, but most residents agree they are getting value for their money. Ridgewood's students score in the top 4 percent nationally on the California Achievement Tests. On the Scholastic Aptitude Test, high-school students score well above the national averages, and more than 80 percent of them go on to college.

Few parents see the necessity for sending their children to private preparatory schools. Our Lady of Mount Carmel is the Catholic elementary school in Ridgewood and there are Catholic high schools in adjacent communities.

The school population is declining, as it is in most of Bergen County, but there have been no school closings, according to Dr. Samuel B. Stewart, the superintendent. There also have been no program cuts. The three-year high school, which has an open campus, offers 257 courses to its 1,450 students. The system is placing a strong emphasis on writing as well as on a new computer program that begins in kindergarten.

RIDGEWOOD

"Ridgewood is a good family town," said Janet Fricke, who lives there with her husband, Richard, and their daughter, Brooke. "The taxes are high, but the services are excellent. It's a good commute to New York. It is an attractive town with a real downtown, a main street, a focal point rather than just all of the malls."

Many residents cite the complete downtown shopping district within walking distance of most homes as a factor in choosing to live in Ridgewood. The shopping area, too, is something of an anachronism. Somehow, the boutiquing of America has passed Ridgewood by, the shops tending more to be named Woolworth's and Buster Brown than something trendier. Merchants feature service and low prices rather than image.

But massive malls and seemingly endless shopping strips are not far away. A five-minute drive puts Ridgewood residents at the intersection of Routes 4 and 17 in Paramus, sometimes referred to as the "Shopping Center Capital of the World." The area has five shopping malls connected by continuous strips of shops, all a discreet distance from Ridgewood.

The consensus of commuters is that service to Ridgewood is swift and reliable when compared with other areas of suburban New York. Train commuters take N. J. Transit to the Hoboken PATH trains, which carry them to midtown or downtown, a rush-hour commute estimated by most at about one hour door-to-door. Others take Short Line buses from Ridgewood to the Port Authority Bus Terminal at Eighth Avenue and 41st Street. An increasing number drive to the corporate offices moving out to such places as Montvale and Saddle Brook.

Most families live in single-family houses; the condo craze, like so many other trends, has not hit Ridgewood.

The community has several nursing homes and a facility for old people with moderate incomes. The Parks and Recreation Department provides a growing number of programs for the elderly, as well as for handicapped people. Many of those programs take place in the Lester Stable, part of Ridgewood's last farm, which was restored in 1982 with donated labor, money, and materials and now also serves as offices for the Parks Department.

On Tuesday and Thursday evenings during the summer, families gather on blankets in front of the village bandshell to view ballet, barbershop quartets, "family films," and other attractions. They buy ice-cream cones and stroll around the duck pond.

Children fill the village greens and the Graydon municipal swimming pool, a two-and-a-half-acre spring-fed lake with a sand bottom and its own island. Surrounded by lawns, tall shade trees, and parents in repose, it seems a picture of days gone by.

—WILLIAM E. GEIST

RUTHERFORD

To midtown Manhattan: Bus 30 minutes

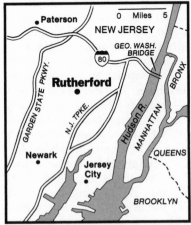

att and Tom Shannon were sitting in a fast-food outlet on Meadow Road talking with their uncle about growing up in Rutherford. "There's a lot of sports," Matt said, "but to tell you the truth, if it weren't for athletics, there wouldn't be much for kids to do."

Tom finished his hamburger. "Nobody goes out at night anymore," he said, "since cable television." Matt and Tom, who are teenagers, spoke of Rutherford in a way that was not much different from what their uncle had felt decades earlier.

The place has changed, of course. Nine out of ten members of the midcentury class at Rutherford High School went on to college. The current rate, according to Barbara Jones, the high-school guidance director, is about two thirds.

William Kraus, the police chief, said he expected as many as 200 breaking-and-entering cases a year. "Twenty years ago, there would have been, maybe, seventy or eighty."

But there are still weekly summertime band concerts in Lincoln Park, the triangular stretch of grass and trees across from the Borough Hall. The No. 30 buses still run every few minutes to New York through the day and into the early evening. It is only a half-hour ride even in the morning rush hour now that there is the express lane through the Lincoln Tunnel. Or commuters can take N. J.

379

Transit trains to Hoboken and PATH service from there to get to Pennsylvania Station in Manhattan in about forty-five minutes.

Every other lawn glows with azaleas in the spring. And, said Barbara Chadwick, a Republican former mayor who presided over an unruly Democratic majority in the early 1980's, "it's a nice town to live in."

Rutherford still has almost no industrial or business area except for the slice of meadowland safely away on the other side of Route 17, where some commercial buildings have risen around the site of the old Bonnie Dell Dairy, and on Route 3 near Giants Stadium.

Rutherford always had a sense of being special—whether or not it was—of being a bit more white-collar and Protestant than its municipal neighbors along the Bergen County ridge between the Hackensack and Passaic rivers, nine miles west of midtown Manhattan, but it is less different than it once was. The population is more blue-collar and the politics a good deal more basic than they used to be.

But the periodic crises that the old-timers warned would destroy Rutherford as we know it have passed without significant impact. "It's still a rose among thorns," said Chief Kraus, whose status as a lifelong Rutherfordian entitles him to serve as a municipal booster.

When Fairleigh Dickinson Junior College spread out from its modest beginnings in the Ivison "castle" on Montross Avenue and expanded into a university after World War II, the neighbors were certain it would overwhelm them. That has not happened. Some students board in town, many shop there, and far too many park their cars there. But the school has proven an amiable neighbor, bringing a bit of cultural enrichment and a minimum of disruption.

When the sports complex opened a few years ago in the Meadowlands a couple of miles away across Berry's Creek in East Rutherford, everyone agreed that crime, clutter, noise, and misbehavior would inevitably invade Rutherford's tree-shaded 2.6 square miles. That has not happened either. "It wasn't supposed to be a plus," said Ms. Chadwick, "but it hasn't had a negative impact at all, as far as I can tell."

The sports complex did not bring the influx of business predicted for the stretch of stores along Park Avenue, but neither did it crowd local streets with traffic and local sidewalks with undesirable visitors. And those who wish to visit the racetrack, Giants Stadium, or the Brendan Byrne Arena can get to them in minutes by regular buses along Paterson Plank Road in East Rutherford.

Convenience of travel has always been a big thing for Rutherford. The community's most famous resident, the poet William Carlos Williams, wrote in his trilogy of novels about his wife's family how they had taken the Erie Railroad out from Jersey City to make their home at the first stop, a leafy slice of suburbia. The old frame home at 9 Ridge Road, where Dr. Williams practiced pediatrics for many years, still has a pediatrician's shingle outside, belonging to his son.

As late as the 1950's, a railroad strike could prompt John Thomas Wilson, Sr., editor of the weekly *Rutherford Republican* (a community resource that is now extinct), to spread across page one pictures of doleful shoulder-to-shoulder commuters waiting on the platform for the trains that would not come.

"Now you've got people going to work in all directions," Chief Kraus said. "Some go out to Morris County, a lot to the new businesses in Secaucus. So they drive." Others take the buses, to New York, Newark, Hackensack, and Passaic.

At night, they come back to a community that, to the surprise of its officials, has slipped slightly in population since the 1970 census. Just 19,068 residents were counted in 1980, compared with 20,802 a decade before, and the mix has shown some changes.

The shopping center along Union Avenue in the west end now includes some bank branches, apparently a reflection of the settling-in of private homes and garden apartments in the uneven triangle between Jackson Avenue and the Passaic River—which, when Chief Kraus and his friends used to go sleigh-riding there years ago, was a scruffy sort of wooded area.

Housing prices in Rutherford are not modest. But in the main, except along prosperous Ridge Road from the grounds of the First Presbyterian Church to the Lyndhurst border about a half mile away, prices do not reach the stratospheric levels that prevail in more upscale places like Ridgewood or Montclair.

Still, real-estate brokers say that a typical home bought in Rutherford for $20,000 in the 1960's would sell for $105,000 to $108,000 today. Real-estate taxes would come to $4.95 for each $100 of assessed valuation.

Another sort of housing purchase—conversion of apartment houses into co-ops or condominiums—has stirred local concern. With rents kept low by local ordinance, owners of the sprawl of garden apartments along the Passaic River and some of the apartment buildings along Union Avenue and Orient Way have converted the buildings into co-ops. The prices range from $61,000 to $75,000, according to John T. Ehrhardt, president of the Ellwood S. New agency, while rentals range from $400 to $600 a month.

Downtown Rutherford is hardly the liveliest spot in the Garden State. Most restaurants close early, and because the community continues to ban consumption of liquor in restaurants, those who want a drink with dinner must go to East Rutherford or go south across Route 3 to Lyndhurst.

But residents have an impressive range of other diversions in town, even without heading out to the Meadowlands. The Recreation

Department puts out a twenty-eight page booklet listing events alphabetically from aerobics to yoga and including programs for handicapped children, trips to Broadway shows, shopping visits for the elderly to malls, classes in magic and in cheerleading, parades and parties, and lots of sports.

There is—despite what Matt Shannon noted—a lot to do.

—MAURICE CARROLL

SADDLE RIVER

To midtown Manhattan: Bus 45 minutes

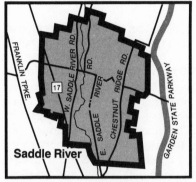

Residents of Saddle River, New Jersey, don't mind saying that theirs is a dull little town. They note that there are no movie theaters or places to buy a beer or anything of that sort. Former Mayor Duncan Cameron said, only partly in jest, that the greatest excitement in town may be filling bird feeders.

Disdaining publicity and believing that there are enough people living here already, residents are pleased to further point out Saddle River's lack of amenities: no food store, train station, library, hospital, high school, sidewalks, streetlights, sewers—not even running water. You dig a well if you'd like some.

With so little to offer, some people are surprised to learn that it would cost them $210,000 to $350,000 to buy a place to live here—and that they'd still need a house. These are the going rates for two acres of land, the minimum lot requirement.

In a densely populated metropolitan area, such tranquil, semirural areas with woodlands and meadows are at a premium. Although less than a one-hour commute from Manhattan, this 4.9-square-mile borough of about 2,900 people is a place where one can still keep horses—one per acre—see a deer, listen to the birds, and catch a fish in the trout stream that gives the town its name. You may even spot a former President of the United States on a morning stroll near his home.

SADDLE RIVER

Richard M. Nixon moved to this Bergen County community in 1981. With the financial wherewithal to live anyplace he pleased, why did he choose Saddle River? Mr. Nixon answered, through one of his aides, that he moved here for the privacy, the tranquillity, and the country atmosphere convenient to New York. He said that the desire to live in such a place that is less than an hour from his downtown Manhattan office precluded his moving to similar communities in Connecticut, northern Westchester County, or on Long Island. Many local residents give the same reasons for moving here.

The price of tranquillity is steep. Saddle River is the wealthiest community in New Jersey, according to 1980 census statistics, with a per capita income of $21,536, compared with a national figure of $7,313.

Mr. Nixon spent $1.025 million for his modern, fifteen-room house on more than four acres with lighted tennis courts, a swimming pool, and a 1,000-bottle wine cellar.

New houses are priced from $625,000 to $1.5 million, according to Joseph J. Murphy of Murphy Realty–Better Homes and Gardens in Saddle River. He said older houses, meaning those built about thirty years ago, are generally smaller, have less acreage, and cost less, in the $200,000 to $295,000 range. The least expensive house his agency has listed recently was a thirty-year-old, three-bedroom ranch on less than an acre—having been built before the two-acre zoning requirement—with an asking price of $259,900 and taxes of $1,053. The least expensive house on a two-acre lot was priced at $335,000, with taxes of $2,959.

With few public services rendered, the village is able to keep its property taxes low. The rate is 98 cents per $100 of assessed valuation, and the borough assesses houses at 100 percent of market value, which means a $500,000 house would pay $4,650 a year.

"No one really cares," said Murphy, who is a builder as well as a real-estate agent. At his Burning Hollow development, he is building ninety-four homes priced from $625,000 to $1.2 million—the latter with an indoor racquetball court. Walking through the "Great Room" of a 6,000-square-foot house with a thirty-foot cathedral ceiling, he stated: "If you have to ask about heating bills and taxes, you can't afford to live here." Several purchasers were moving from expensive co-ops in New York, he added, "and think all this space is a bargain for the price."

Mr. Cameron, the former mayor, speaks with a note of pride about the thwarting of efforts by some residents and the county government to install sidewalks, streetlights, and traffic lights and to widen the narrow roads. During his tenure he saw himself as "a caretaker of what people moved here for."

Many people say Mr. Cameron performed that function well. The downtown, such as it is, is reminiscent of a New England village, and advertising agencies frequently ask to use the white clapboard Zion Evangelical Lutheran Church as a backdrop. It is one of two churches here, along with St. Gabriel's Roman Catholic Church. There is no multifamily housing or industry in Saddle River, just a few small businesses and no industry.

A new professional office building called The Commons stirred controversy, with numerous calls to local officials from residents fearful that it might be an apartment building. Mr. Cameron said the building was constructed only "because there was nothing we could do—the zoning was there." Space in the 24,000-square-foot building, which was built in a clapboard style appropriate to the village, rents for $17.50 a square foot.

The borough has restrictive ordinances and an architectural-review panel regulating such things as signs and landscaping, making sure that homeowners don't let their paint peel, and ensuring that no developer comes in to build dozens of what officials call "look-alike" houses or anything "radical." New residents and those seeking building permits are asked not to cut down trees.

A hyperbolic press release for a housing development describes Saddle River as a twenty-five-minute commute from New York City, but this seems to presuppose that one works on the city line and rides to work in Mario Andretti's car pool. Commuters said it was about a fifty-minute drive to midtown, with no traffic.

According to the 1980 census, 87.2 percent of Saddle River's employed residents take automobiles to work—more than a few in chauffeur-driven limousines. Many residents work in corporate headquarters and office complexes in nearby suburbs. But residents also can travel to New York via the Short Line bus (a forty-five minute ride) or catch the N. J. Transit train from Allendale or Ho-Ho-Kus (an hour's ride to Hoboken).

With new houses being built, the population is growing, but enrollment at Wandell School, the only public school, has been declining since 1974. The school, kindergarten through eighth-grade, has slightly more than 200 pupils, with class sizes averaging less than fifteen. Most students go on to Ramsey High School, although Robert Collins, the school superintendent, said about 35 to 40 percent of Saddle River students opt for parochial high schools, with a few attending private schools.

Mr. Collins attributed declining enrollment here to the high cost of housing: "People who can afford to move here often arrive when their children are in high school or college." But Mr. Murphy said well-heeled younger couples with school-age children were moving into town.

A common complaint among parents is that there is little for the children to do, and they must chauffeur them to movies in Ramsey, skating in Montvale, or bowling in Paramus. This dependence on the car also extends to their own shopping and entertainment and is indicated by the three gas stations in the small downtown. There is a twenty-three-acre park in Saddle River, however, equipped with playgrounds and tennis courts, and there are recreation programs. As for shopping, easy access to Route 17 gives residents all they need in the concentration of malls just a few miles to the south.

The biggest threat to Saddle River, Mr. Cameron said, is the Mount Laurel court ruling by the New Jersey Supreme Court holding that all communities must work actively to provide housing for the poor. "We are working to see that Saddle River is an exception," he stated. "Saddle River is exceptional."

Charles Blessing, a real-estate salesman, said, "If people come here looking for high society, they won't find it. Residents are very low-keyed and unpretentious."

—WILLIAM E. GEIST

SOUTH ORANGE

To midtown Manhattan: Bus or train 45 to 60 minutes

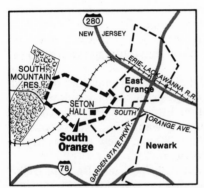

The village of South Orange, which spills down the steep side of South Mountain in a corner of Essex County, once advertised itself as the "Switzerland of America." Houses built into the mountainside have such steeply raked front lawns that mowing is a strenuous battle with gravity.

Today, South Orange does not much resemble a quaint alpine village, but it is a comfortable and convenient commuter suburb with fine views of the New York skyline eighteen miles away, reasonably priced and architecturally diverse homes, and good educational and recreational facilities.

First settled by Puritan farmers soon after Newark was founded in 1666, South Orange experienced a spurt of growth late in the nineteenth century that transformed much of its open farmland at the foot of South Mountain into broad streets lined with mansions and in-town estates.

The population is just under 16,000, with a per capita income of $12,469 and a number of residents who easily fall into the category of millionaire. The village's 2.8 square miles are split unofficially into three sections: the older, Victorian homes in the southeast corner; a large neighborhood of comfortable, middle-class residences filling in the valley from Seton Hall University through the busy village center and train station area up to the foot of South Moun-

387

tain; and the mountain itself, where newer, larger, and more expensive homes have been terraced into the mountain's side.

According to Joy Straub of Raymond Connolly Realtors, the neighborhoods of South Orange offer houses in a broad range of prices. A five-bedroom colonial near Seton Hall recently sold for $110,000, with taxes just above $2,800. A six-bedroom colonial in the Montrose Street section went for $175,000, with taxes of $4,100, and another six-bedroom colonial on the mountain, with a skyline view, went for $250,000 and had a $5,500 tax bill. Other houses sell for as much as $650,000.

South Orange has relatively few rental apartments and no subsidized housing.

Bertrand Spiotta, village president, said many South Orange residents moved into the community from the mostly Jewish Weequahic section of Newark just after World War II. Families moving in today tend to be young, many of them coming from outlying suburbs to be closer to their jobs.

A fifteen-minute ride on the old Erie-Lackawanna line operated by N. J. Transit connects South Orange with Newark's downtown Broad Street station. It takes another fifteen minutes to get to the Hoboken terminal and PATH trains into Manhattan. Auto commuting also is convenient, with Interstate 280 just a few minutes away, and there is regular bus service to New York.

"For us it is perfect—it really and truly is," said Rhonda Balk, who in 1980 moved with her husband, Louis, a New York laywer, and their two sons into an eighty-five-year-old, fourteen-room English Tudor.

Ms. Balk's neighborhood is just a few blocks from East Orange and the slender neck of Newark's Vailsburg section that comes up to meet it. The population of those two cities has shifted in recent years, and crime, along with the perception of being an unsafe place, has become a significant problem there. Many outsiders believe that South Orange, too, has changed and become dangerous, but local residents disagree.

"I'm not concerned about walking around here," Ms. Balk said, "and I don't think any of my friends are either." Driving through the area offers a different perspective than looking at a map. The section of East Orange along South Harrison Street leading to the village is lined with new, high-rise apartment buildings and condominiums, which mingle with older buildings that seem to be well maintained. On the village's other side, Vailsburg is a mostly Italian-American section of single-family frame buildings, a still-thriving business strip, with a small-town cohesiveness foreign to the rest of Newark.

Police Chief Frederick E. Gayder said that some of the crime outsiders associate with South Orange really is centered in Seton

Hall University, which is situated completely within South Orange. "Seton Hall has a lot of functions going on all the time, and with a student population of around 10,000 things are bound to happen."

Chief Gayder considers South Orange a safe community. "Our greatest problems are shoplifting and juvenile crime—malicious mischief. And most of the juveniles involved come from outside the village."

Though by its charter South Orange is considered a village, there is little about it that resembles a village except the old Municipal Hall, a wood-and-stucco barn of a building with a three-sided clock tower and an aging interior that, on hot summer days, is said to smell of manure from the police horses once stabled there.

Still, village streets—excepting busy South Orange Avenue, a county road—are broad and uncluttered, an image fostered by the absence of garbage cans, on-street parking, and overhead wires. Utility lines are strung through the backyards, and private trash collectors walk to the back of the houses to pick up the garbage.

Enhancing the serene, turn-of-the-century picture are South Orange's gas street lamps. Some 1,500 of them glow dimly in front of older homes. Lamplighters are a common sight in the village, walking from lamppost to lamppost checking pilot lights and adjusting timers.

The small shopping district offers most necessities, including a supermarket. An abundance of trinket stores and party planning shops serve the wealthy clientele. There are several restaurants just off the village center, including Alex Eng, along with casual lunching places and Gruning's Ice Cream Parlor.

Village residents are active in civic affairs and demand a high level of municipal services in return for their substantial taxes. The public library contains 91,000 volumes, and the Consolidated School District, which South Orange shares with neighboring Maplewood, is well regarded around the state for its faculty.

There are nine schools in the district, including the 2,000-student Columbia High School in Maplewood. About 80 percent of the graduates continue their education in college.

South Orange is rich in cultural and recreational opportunities. There are a symphony orchestra and a theater group, and village residents may participate in all events at Seton Hall. On the west, the village borders the South Mountain Reservation, a 2,000-acre park of trees, trails, and escape.

There are more than sixty acres of parkland in the village itself. The village-owned community center contains three swimming pools, fifteen lighted tennis courts, and several sports fields.

Paul B. Connolly, a real-estate man who lives in South Orange, said residents receive an abundance of services in return for their high taxes, but the exchange is fair. "To a large extent, we pay taxes for facilities we would otherwise have to pay for, like the pool membership. For a young family with kids in the school system, it really turns out to be inexpensive."

—ANTHONY DEPALMA

TEANECK

To midtown Manhattan: Bus 30 to
40 minutes

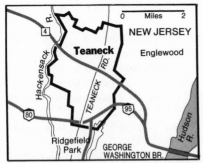

"Teenakut" to its ancestral
Minsi Indian tribe, "Tiene Neck" to its Dutch settlers, "Tee Neck"
to Robert Erskine, George Washington's cartographer, who mapped
it in 1778, is a small town on the high ground of Bergen County four
miles west of the George Washington Bridge. Route 4 cuts through
its center and the newer Route 80 runs along its southern rim.

Its racial and ethnic diversity, a source of almost excessive community pride as well as occasional friction, has long been a deter-
minant in Teaneck's development.

Once an insular, Christians-only town of real-estate restrictions
and covenants, it became after World War II a haven for Jews who
left the urban atmospheres of Jersey City, Hoboken, Manhattan, and
the Bronx. Now, Jews make up slightly more than 20 percent of the
population.

Teaneck anticipated the national thrust for school desegregation.
Well before busing and other educational devices became mandated
tools for school desegregation, Teaneck, with a black population of
about 25 percent of the total, created a magnet school system and
alternative educational programs in a largely successful effort to
avoid racial friction.

As the township's population mix changed, many of its institutions accommodated themselves to those changes. Thus Teaneck's
major Roman Catholic church, St. Anastasia's, opened its doors to

391

the Moslem Congregation Dar-Ul-Islah while that group's mosque was being built. It also housed the Chinese Community School for some of Teaneck's newer Asian residents.

"We have been enriched by all of these new people," said Mildred Taylor, author of *The History of Teaneck*. She has lived in a small frame house on Palisade Avenue for thirty-seven years and is a member of the Bergen County Historic Sites Committee, which is currently involved in identifying and cataloguing many of Teaneck's 10,000 single-family homes.

Another longtime resident is Robert D. Gruen, a lawyer who practices in nearby Hackensack and who for eight years was municipal judge of Teaneck. He described the town, where he has lived for thirty-five years, as "well-run by pros" and "as good as you'll find anywhere."

Alfred P. Levin, whose real-estate office has been on Cedar Lane, the main shopping avenue, for more than three decades, said years ago residential zoning called for large lots, many more than a half acre. "Then, as more people from cities came in, permissible lot size dropped to 50 by 100. Later, to prevent too much density, gradually the size has grown to 60 by 100, then 75 by 100."

In 1982 friction developed between liberal-minded Jews who settled in Teaneck in the years after World War II and other Jews, virtually all Orthodox, who arrived more recently. Most of the latter group send their children to yeshivas in New York City and in Passaic County rather than to the township's fourteen public schools. A controversy arose over the Orthodox group's desire to construct a mikvah, or ritual bath, a move that the older Jewish residents opposed as divisive. It was eventually built and the issue was settled amicably.

Conflicts such as this have not torn the community's fabric, however, and for the people who live in the bucolic six-square-mile township, Teaneck is a good place in which to live, a convenient thirty-minute commute to midtown Manhattan by both N. J. Transit and private bus lines.

Much of its housing stock was built late in the 1920's, when the George Washington Bridge was under construction. There are vast stone Tudors, Normans, and colonials with rolling frontages along Winthrop Road; English stuccos and brick Dutch colonials on curving, maple-lined Standish Road; and smaller frame and brick houses, the most numerous type, throughout the town. Prices range as high as $350,000 along Winthrop, to about $150,000 along Standish, and as low as $80,000 for the smaller, older frame houses on small lots.

Teaneck's tax rate of $3.28 per $100 of assessed valuation supports a variety of municipal services and amenities and the township's share of the county's maintenance. Its system of eleven elementary schools, two junior high schools, and one high school sends about 75 percent of its graduates on to higher education. Town services are overseen by Werner H. Schmid, the township manager.

The community's main shopping area, Cedar Lane, is a wide boulevard of service shops, food stores, restaurants, and boutiques, with such names as Pickwick Village, Jade Spoon, Tabatchnick's, Look & Cook, The Judaica House, and Stitches. According to Mr. Schmid, a bit of a merchant-inspired renaissance has seen storefronts refurbished and new businesses moving into the shops along Cedar Lane. The reason? In Mr. Schmid's view, many residents, weary of shopping in the malls scattered about Bergen County, are "shopping at home."

Teaneck has municipal police and fire departments, but its trash removal is done by private carters whose services are paid for by individual residents. It has a general hospital, Holy Name, is home to Fairleigh Dickinson University, and, where the town meets Interstate Route 80, a $120 million development called Glenpointe. The fifty-acre complex, when completed, will include two 7-story office buildings, a 14-story luxury hotel, 292 condominium units, a two-level mall of shops and movie theaters, and a four-story parking garage for 2,400 cars.

Teaneck's nine-member school board is elected, three each year. Its legislature, a seven-member council, is elected on a nonpartisan basis and chooses a mayor, a largely ceremonial position.

The mayor, Bernard Brooks, is the first black to hold the office. To some, he is a symbol of Teaneck's continuing boast of its ability to be a place that can accommodate people's differences.

The Hellers are another example. Chuck Heller, a vocational counselor to the State of New Jersey, is white and Jewish. His wife, Marcia Pinkett-Heller, who teaches health administration at Columbia University, is black. "We are not an oddity in this community," said Mr. Heller. He added that he and his wife had lived in North Bergen, East Orange, and Hackensack before moving to Teaneck a few years ago, and that "either she or I felt uncomfortable in those towns." He said he had been raised in Teaneck, had "fond memories" of it, and knew it to be a "town that tries to deal with all sorts of situations."

Ms. Heller agreed. "There is a sense of community here. It is a town that has focused on itself. Neighbors are amiable, friendly, interested in one another."

Another couple, John and Janet Graham, both black, have also lived in Teaneck for two years. Why Teaneck? "We looked and looked," Mr. Graham replied. "Basically, we were interested in cost, nearness to the city, and population mix. The house we found suited our budget, and Teaneck had the reputation for being a community where we would not be uncomfortable. We're not at all disappointed. People here are willing to recognize you and respect you."

—FRED FERRETTI

CONNECTICUT
X I.

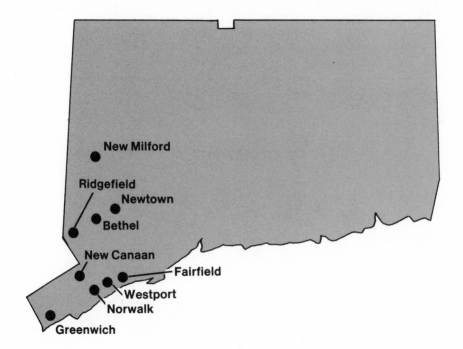

New Milford

Ridgefield

Newtown

Bethel

New Canaan

Fairfield

Westport

Norwalk

Greenwich

BETHEL

To midtown Manhattan: Bus and train 105 to 120 minutes

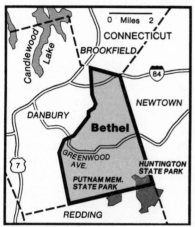

Back in the early 1970's, Robert M. Gilchrest used to tell potential newcomers that Bethel had features some neighboring Connecticut towns lacked, such as municipal sewers and water, a full-time police force, and downtown shopping. "There was no question—for your dollar, you got your money's worth here," said Mr. Gilchrest, now superintendent of schools of the northern Fairfield County community.

A lot of people apparently felt the same way, for between 1970 and 1980, Bethel's population jumped by 46 percent, one of the larger increases in Fairfield County. The influx has transformed it from a small New England town that a few old-timers described as a bit provincial into a diverse, active community of more than 16,000 residents, where houses dating from the 1700's and turn-of-the-century Victorians blend with suburban ranch houses and even a few apartment complexes and condominiums.

In part, Bethel's growth was caused by its location. It is within auto commuting distance of the corporate office centers in Stamford and Greenwich in southern Fairfield and White Plains in New York, yet far enough away so that its housing is cheaper than in towns nearer Long Island Sound. It also is next door to Danbury, which has been attracting corporate headquarters of its own, such as the Union Carbide Corporation.

"We've found that many of those interested in Bethel were people

397

who had looked in southern Fairfield County areas and found that they get a lot of good value here—a lot better value for the money, and still have all the amenities," said George J. Shaker, the owner of a Bethel real-estate firm bearing his name.

"It's a transient town," stated Edward J. Mills, former first select-man, or chief executive. "We do have a lot of people who commute to Hartford, Stamford, White Plains, even those who commute to New York City."

In its early days, Bethel (pronounced BETH-el) was part of Danbury, which was founded in about 1700. It acquired its name in 1759 when the Connecticut General Assembly authorized a new parish, the First Ecclesiastical Society of Bethel, and it became a separate town in 1855.

The square in the center of town, with its statue of a World War I doughboy, is named for P. T. Barnum, who was born there in 1810. Bethel still honors its native son each fall with a Carnival of Clowns, which features a parade, floats, and clowns of all ages.

The showman, who later settled in Bridgeport, presented his birthplace with a bronze fountain in 1881, according to the town history books, and said of Bethel: "I have invariably cherished with most affectionate remembrance the place of my birth, and the old village Meeting House, without steeple or bell, where in the square family pew, I sweltered in summer and shivered through my Sunday School lessons in winter."

Barnum's fountain and the hat factories that once stood near it are long gone now, and the most prominent features of Greenwood Avenue, the main thoroughfare, are antique and craft shops, boutiques, and restaurants, including some in the town's old opera house.

Old-timers say that, despite the name, the opera house never staged an opera—just some local productions, choruses, and silent movies. Over the years, the white brick building has housed a variety of businesses.

The downtown stores attract out-of-town visitors, especially on Saturdays, but they also provide residents with most of the essentials, ranging from shoes and furniture to food and laundromat service. More extensive shopping, or a first-run movie, requires a trip to neighboring Danbury.

Town officials are working on a new ten-year plan of development that they hope will allow the renovation of the older buildings along Greenwood Avenue without destroying the community's old New England flavor. Many of the buildings in the business district are sixty to eighty years old, said Mr. Mills, "part of the history of Bethel."

Bethel, which is about sixty miles from New York, covers seventeen square miles and is surrounded by Danbury, Brookfield, Newtown, and Redding. Its residents are slightly younger than those of neighboring towns, according to the 1980 census, with a median age of 29.7 and 15.5 percent of the population 9 years old or younger. Its per capita income of $8,623 is higher than Danbury's but lower than Brookfield's, Newtown's, or Redding's.

The 1980 census put the median value of an owner-occupied single-family house in Bethel at $78,800, making it thirty-second among Connecticut's 169 towns and cities in the ranking of housing values.

Bethel's zoning laws have permitted the development of a more diverse housing stock than that of some of its neighbors, such as Newtown and Redding, where the single-family house is the norm. According to the 1980 census, almost 20 percent of Bethel's housing is multifamily, ranging from two-family houses to apartment projects. There are more than 400 condominiums. The mean value of owner-occupied condominiums was put at $65,673. Of the town's 1,100 rental units, the mean rent was $337.

The major condominium projects are Chestnut Hill Village, Mountain View Estates, Plumtrees Heights, and Hudson Glen. Prices range from $67,000 to about $95,000, according to local brokers.

As for single-family houses, Mr. Shaker, who has lived in Bethel since the early 1930's, cited as typical a two-bedroom Cape Cod his agency sold recently for $85,000. Depending on the size of a lot, which can range from a quarter acre to two or more acres, he said that prices range from $85,000 to $130,000 for a three-bedroom house and $90,000 to $190,000 for a four-bedroom house. "Bethel is very much in demand," he added.

Property is taxed at $36 for each $1,000 of assessed valuation, according to the assessor's office. The assessment level is 44 percent of market value, so the annual bill for a $100,000 house would be about $1,500.

Bethel has three elementary schools, one middle school for grades seven and eight, and one high school. The middle school is near Town Hall downtown; the others, all built in the last decade, are clustered in a 165-acre campuslike setting.

The enrollment, now about 3,200, has been declining about 2 percent a year, which Superintendent Gilchrest attributed to relatively high housing prices that prevent some young families from moving in.

On the Scholastic Aptitude Test, Bethel students score a few points higher than the Connecticut average, and about 70 percent of them go on to some form of higher education.

Bethel has a twenty-nine-member police force, twenty-two auxiliary members, and a neighborhood crime-watch program that town officials credit with keeping the burglary rate down. There are two volunteer fire departments and an active park and recreation program that includes everything from "tiny tot" dancing and tumbling to mixed volleyball and roller skating. Two state parks—Putnam Memorial and Huntington State—straddle the Bethel-Redding town line.

There also is public transportation: buses of the Housatonic Area Regional Transit agency (HART) run a regular schedule between Bethel and Danbury, and seven weekday Metro-North commuter trains connect Bethel to New York City by way of the Danbury branch line, which joins the New Haven division main line at South Norwalk. The trip takes from an hour and forty-five minutes to more than two hours each way.

"Overall, Bethel is a likable town," said Mr. Mills, the former first selectman, who came to Bethel a decade ago by way of Brooklyn and Long Island. "You have the old-timers who have been here for many, many years. They seem to be the stem of the town. The newer people look to the old-timers for a sense of history."

—RICHARD L. MADDEN

F A I R F I E L D

To midtown Manhattan: Train 70 minutes

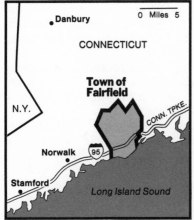

It is neither an exaggeration nor a matter of chauvinism to say that the Town of Fairfield has a rather strong sense of itself. Because the British burned the village in 1779, for instance, Fairfield refused to celebrate the American Centennial with everyone else in 1876. It held its own festivities in 1879.

A century later, Fairfield deigned to mark the Bicentennial with the rest of the nation, but by that time the town was showing its individuality in another way. Connecticut towns from Greenwich to Westport were being transformed by the influx of major businesses, but Fairfield never really joined in the courtship of the corporations.

"We seem determined to keep out anything that will build up the place," said a nineteenth-century writer in the local newspaper, *The Southport Chronicle,* and the words still have the ring of truth. Fairfield has not been anti-industry, and it certainly has not been antigrowth—the population doubled to 60,000 in the last thirty years. But it has basically remained more residential, more oriented toward small family businesses, and more affordable than many of its neighboring towns down the coast.

"It's the first true Connecticut town along the shore," said Ronald Henry, Sr., owner of a real-estate agency and a longtime resident. "It's the first town that doesn't just look to New York."

Sylvia Hayes, who moved to Fairfield from Colorado recently

401

with her husband and two children, agreed. "We had pretty well settled on living in Connecticut, and we started looking in Greenwich and moved up the train line from there. We stopped here. Fairfield was the first place that looked like it had a life of its own besides being a commuter stop."

Rather, Fairfield is a town composed of many small and distinct neighborhoods. There are the cottages and newer, larger homes along the beach, the historic Federals on Old Post Road, the former farmhouses on Greenfield Hill, and the Cape Cods within walking distance of downtown. The terrain rises from the salt marshes on Long Island Sound to the pine-covered hills in the northern part of town, from which one can gaze over the Sound to Port Jefferson, Long Island.

Life can be a bit old-fashioned here, without apology. The American Legion post has a billboard with the Pledge of Allegiance written in foot-high letters. A sign outside the Du Pont factory reminds workers to buckle their safety belts while driving.

Fairfield likes its habits, too. John J. Sullivan served for twenty-four years as first selectman before retiring in 1983. The school superintendent, Charles W. Fowler, has served nine years, a relatively long tenure. And many of the townspeople's favorite institutions still inhabit the downtown area. There are signs of change—a sun-tanning parlor, computer and video stores—but a favorite night out remains a hot fudge sundae with homemade ice cream at Allington's and a movie at the Community Theater, where an R-rated film is the exception.

The Breakaway restaurant is a standard spot for lunch and dinner. Tommy's has long been the epicenter of singles life, and Mike's Pizza draws college students and "townies" alike.

Fairfield celebrates its own holiday, called, unsurprisingly, "Fairfield Day," with a foot race, a scuba-diving treasure hunt, and a carnival. Church fairs and tag sales abound.

When summer arrives, activities proliferate both at the public beach and in the private domains along Fairfield Beach Road—the land of margaritas and catamarans. "It's the whole Noel Coward scene," said John J. Geoghegan, 3rd, a writer and editor for several Connecticut publications, who lives in the town. " 'Let's go to the country for the weekend. Have elegant conversations. Smoke Monte Cristo cigars." But Fairfield, he added, is also "the kind of town where you can go into the post office and expect to see someone you know."

The price of living in Fairfield can vary greatly. Homes sell for an average of about $150,000, and condominiums for a minimum of $95,000, according to several local real-estate brokers. At the lower end of the range are two-bedroom, one-bath brick houses built shortly after World War II for $95,000 to $110,000, and at the upper end are new four-bedroom, two-and-one-half bath colonials for as much as $350,000.

History and location often raise house prices, although they still tend to be lower than the prices of comparable properties ten or twenty miles closer to New York. Perhaps the biggest boom in Fairfield has occurred in the beachfront properties that stretch for about a mile east and west of Shoal Point. Many of the houses originally served as summer cottages and had neither the heat nor the other amenities needed for year-round comfort. But in the last decade, a spate of rehabilitation and new construction has pushed the prices of such properties up by as much as 500 percent.

A townwide property reassessment was completed in 1983, but the average tax bill of about $2,000 a year compares favorably with those of other municipalities in Fairfield County.

Among the biggest draws for newcomers are the public and private school systems. The two public high schools, Ludlow and Warde, send 70 percent of their graduates on to higher education. Their students achieve higher average scores on the Scholastic Aptitude Test than the national norms, said Ann Black, the director of pupil and psychological services for the school system. But declining enrollment has forced Fairfield to close four of twelve elementary schools, and it remains uncertain whether both high schools can continue to operate separate and complete programs.

Fairfield Prep is one of the most highly regarded private schools in the state. More than 95 percent of its graduates attend college. The school has a strong athletic program, and it requires students to participate in community service projects.

Two colleges—Fairfield University and Sacred Heart University—are in nearby Bridgeport, and the University of Bridgeport is about ten minutes from downtown Fairfield. The town of Fairfield also operates adult-education programs.

Although Fairfield is not known as a commuter town in the way, say, adjacent Westport is, about 600 residents do travel daily to New York by Metro-North's New Haven line. There are three round-trip expresses daily to Grand Central Terminal, taking about seventy minutes each way. Midtown Manhattan is about fifty-five miles from Fairfield via the Connecticut Turnpike or Merritt Parkway, but traffic jams are to be counted on in rush hours.

An increasing number of Fairfield residents commute to jobs in the corporate belt of Stamford and Greenwich, about twenty-five minutes away by car or train.

Fairfield is quintessentially suburban in its crime as well as its commuting. Property loss, not violence, is the problem. The Police Department's statistics show few murders or assaults but a sizable number of motor vehicle thefts and burglaries. The police say that Fairfield's reputation as a well-to-do community, its location on two major expressways, and its proximity to Bridgeport, a city with 12 percent unemployment, account for much of the crime.

And, for better or for worse, Fairfield seems reluctant to change an image that has lasted a century. The town, colonial origins notwithstanding, became known as a cottage colony for city-dwellers. With the advent of local trolley service in 1894, it developed as the bedroom community for industrial Bridgeport. The trolley is long gone, but the bedrooms have stayed, only multiplying with time.

—SAMUEL G. FREEDMAN

GREENWICH

*To midtown Manhattan: Train 45
minutes*

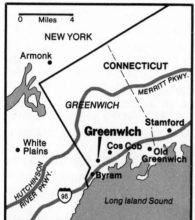

ar beyond its borders, the
name Greenwich connotes not only affluence but old-money affluence. It can seem like something out of a *New Yorker* cartoon.
"Greenwich is a lot of good land, well guarded—the affluent society," said Beth Henry, a sculptor who has lived in the town for a
quarter of a century.

It still has the yacht, golf, and hunt clubs; the Junior League and
the Social Review; the Festival of Trees and the Preview of Spring
for all who want them—and thousands do.

But for all its continuity of image, Greenwich also is a place of
change. It is a town growing into a city, more populous, more industrial, more diverse than in its earlier incarnations. Its population
grew by 50 percent between 1940 and 1970, and so many corporations have come to Greenwich in the last decade that ten times as
many people now commute there to work—25,000—as Greenwich
residents commute to New York City.

The metamorphosis has troubled many residents. Change does
not come easily here. People have fought a shift in legal status from
"town" to "city," 60,000 population or not, and some longtime residents no longer shop downtown because of heavy traffic. When
Greenwich Time, the local newspaper, streamlined its design under
new ownership in 1981, some readers howled. "Whatever made you
upset our customs of ages and force us to rearrange our habits?"

405

wrote an eighty-year-old reader. She could have been speaking about more than the newspaper.

But younger residents and newcomers seem to like the new Greenwich, finding it bustling, vital, and more welcoming than they had anticipated.

"I enjoyed it much more than I thought I would," said Tanya Clark, who moved to Greenwich in 1982. "The people are different than they are in a smaller town like New Canaan because the town is larger and more diverse."

"It's a very stimulating place," said Jacqueline Bashian, who came to the town in 1980 with her husband, Gary, a lawyer. "I feel I could never get bored here. There are so many different types of people, so many things to do. It's very sophisticated, yet very countrylike. You can have the nicest things imaginable to buy in town and still be riding horses in the backcountry."

The difficulty is that it costs more than a little to live in Greenwich. The average family income is $53,878 and the average house is worth $172,210, according to the 1980 census. And that figure is, if anything, too low to use as a benchmark for the current market. Houses sold in 1984 fetched an average of $384,000, condominiums $206,000, accoring to Stanley Klein, president of Empire Realty. Rents rarely dip below $650 to $700 a month for a one-bedroom apartment and the vacancy rate hovers around 1 percent.

"It's very difficult for a young person—unless he's independently wealthy or has made it quickly—to live here," said Robert Hansen, a longtime resident. "It's getting out of the range of all but the wealthy."

Nevertheless, cheaper houses are available. In contrast to the $750,000 manses on two to four acres in the "backcountry" of Greenwich's 50.6 square miles are more affordable houses for $150,000 or a bit less on smaller lots that can be found near downtown or in the neighborhoods of Cos Cob, Byram, and Old Greenwich. Despite its moneyed reputation, Greenwich never has been a town solely for the rich.

The property-tax rate is $22.70 per $1,000 of assessed valuation, with houses assessed at 45 percent of market value.

The town was the tenth founded in Connecticut by families from Massachusetts Bay Colony. Robert Feake and Daniel Patrick— Patrick was kicked out of Massachusetts for "crude and unbecoming behavior"—bought the land from Indians in 1640 for twenty-five English coats.

The now genteel Greenwich was downright raucous at the start. A claim in the General Court in New Haven in 1650 alleged that Greenwich residents "live in a disorderly and riotous fashion, sell intoxicating liquors to the Indians, receive and harbor servants who have fled from their masters and join persons unlawfully in marriage."

GREENWICH

In time, however, Greenwich settled down. The Post Road's mail couriers, the stagecoach, and finally the railroad tied it to Boston and New York. Mills, smokehouses, a motor works, a felt factory, and a shellfish industry primed the local economy.

But by the early 1900's, affluent New Yorkers had begun building or buying summer cottages here on Long Island Sound. William Marcy Tweed, the "boss" of New York's Tammany Hall machine, built a mansion and family bathhouse in town and a hotel, the Americus, on an island offshore. And, as a sign of the Greenwich to come, the first Cadillac arrived in town on January 29, 1915.

Money has lured many amenities to Greenwich since then. The town boasts a bounty of restaurants—Cinquante-cinq for French cuisine, Lotus East for Chinese, the Colonial Inn for Greek food, and Love & Serve for vegetarian.

Nor does Greenwich lack for cultural opportunities; it has the Bruce Museum for art, the Greenwich Philharmonia for music, and the well-regarded town library. With midtown Manhattan less than an hour away by train or car, all of New York City's theaters, museums, and nightclubs are within reach.

The community has many beaches, an entire island with ferry service to the mainland, a skating rink named after Dorothy Hamill, the local Olympic medalist, and a recreation center in Old Greenwich for pickup basketball.

Excellent public and private schools serve Greenwich. About 73 percent of pupils attend the public system, which culminates in Greenwich High School. A *Money* magazine survey of college admissions counselors found that they rated the high school among the dozen best in the nation in preparing students for college. Sixty-four percent of its graduates attend four-year colleges and students score well above national averages on the Scholastic Aptitude Test.

Some parents prefer private schools for reasons varying from family tradition to the small class sizes. The favorites are Greenwich Country Day School, a coeducational school that goes through eighth grade; Brunswick School, an all-boys school for all grades through high school; and the Greenwich Academy, an all-girls school for all grades through high school.

One problem with affluence, however, is that burglars, too, know all about it. For all Greenwich's "small-town" mystique, people not only lock their doors but pay hundreds and even thousands of dollars for security systems. The police have received as many false alarms in a month as there are thefts in four months, and they record many auto thefts, burglaries, and incidents of vandalism, according to Police Chief Thomas Keegan.

Parents, too, must maintain a certain wariness of Greenwich's wealth. It can provide a child with an excellent education and a worldliness, but it also can spoil a child. "It can be tough on kids," said Arlene Hansen, who, with her husband, Robert, and their three children has lived in the community for thirteen years. "Greenwich is a town with tunnel vision. You want your children to have all the privileges of Greenwich, but not to think the whole world is like this."

—SAMUEL G. FREEDMAN

NEW CANAAN

To midtown Manhattan: Train 65 minutes

Decades ago, and not in a moment of humility, the town fathers of New Canaan christened the Connecticut village the "next station to heaven." Even now, the homeowners who can afford to move in and the businessmen who can seize the sparse commercial space show no signs of disagreeing with that description.

The nickname derived from New Canaan's hilltop railroad station. But to many residents the name applies to the village's fine public school system, spacious lots for homes, quaint shopping district, and solid municipal finance—taxes of $26.60 per $1,000 of assessed valuation and $1 million in annual budget surpluses.

Residents gloat, too, about the physical setting: twenty-three square miles of wooded land, creased by hills and threaded by streams, in the southwest corner of Connecticut. The approximate borders are Pound Ridge, New York, on the north, the Merritt Parkway on the south, Stamford on the east, and Wilton on the west.

"The town, quite bluntly, is in love with itself," the writer Anne Longley has observed. Charles P. Morton, the first selectman, said: "Don't tell people we're such a good place to live. We'd be just as happy if they didn't move in."

Prices and zoning take care of much of his concern. Houses range in cost from $150,000 to $2.25 million; the average home on less than ten acres of land sells for $300,000 to $400,000 and the average condominium for $250,000 to $275,000.

N E W   C A N A A N

Commercial space rents for $22 to $28 a square foot, comparable to or lower than the rates in adjacent Greenwich and Stamford, brokers say; but little space is available.

Under New Canaan's zoning covenants, only seventy-seven acres of land—or roughly twenty-four not-so-square blocks—are open to commercial development. Offices are severely curtailed in the choicest territory, the six-square-block "magic circle" composed of colonial-style, two-story stores.

New Canaan has always been adamant about its idiosyncrasy. Religious dissidents first settled the region early in the 1700's and sought to form their own parish because they disdained walking to church in Stamford and Norwalk. New Canaan Parish was founded in 1731; the town incorporated seventy years later.

Miles off the main roads to New York City, inland from the maritime routes and without a major supply of waterpower, New Canaan watched much of the Industrial Revolution pass it by. A shoemaking industry did develop in the village, sending its wares as far as Georgia; brick and tool factories also grew up, and a stagecoach link to New York began in 1821.

But it was the opening of the railroad spur to Stamford and New York, on July 4, 1868, that shaped today's New Canaan more than any other event. It made the village accessible to wealthy urbanites as a rural retreat and, later, a suburb.

New Canaan remains a haven for affluent families. Estimates from the 1980 census put average family income for the 17,931 residents at $54,000, second only to Darien in the state. Nearly 85 percent of households are made up of families. Owners far outnumber renters.

Most of the newcomers are executives and middle-level managers who work for such companies as Xerox, General Telephone and Electronics, and I.B.M. The older New Canaan families include their own notables: Eileen Heckart, the actress; Rawleigh Warner, Jr., the chairman of the board of Mobil; William Attwood, the former publisher of *Newsday;* and Jack Paar, the television personality.

"There are two reasons why people want to live in New Canaan—zoning and schools," said Mabel Lamb, president of Mabel Lamb Inc., a real-estate agency in business in New Canaan since 1950. To those, other brokers and residents add transportation and the downtown district.

Nearly two thirds of New Canaan is zoned for four-acre or two-and-a-half-acre lots. The most common home, realtors say, is the four-bedroom, two-and-a-half-bath colonial, selling for $350,000 to $450,000. There are many contemporary and ranch-style houses in the same price range. But a family willing to forgo the acreage sometimes can find a two-bedroom "starter house" near downtown for $150,000 to $200,000. Such houses exist, but they are hard to find.

Nearly all of New Canaan's 700 condominium and co-op apartments, making up 10 percent of the housing stock, are occupied. Condominiums range in price from $225,000 to $350,000, co-ops somewhat less. Conversions have removed all but about a hundred apartments from the rental stock.

The public schools are a principal attraction for newcomers. The 2,500-student system receives 55 percent of New Canaan's $20 million budget, and by most statistical measures it delivers on the investment. Nearly all of New Canaan's ninth graders score at or above "levels of expected performance" on statewide tests. Upperclassmen average better than the national norms on the Scholastic Aptitude Test.

Just behind schools in the hearts of New Canaanites is the shopping district. Restaurants, taverns, groceries, antique stores, a theater, pharmacies, and clothiers all operate within walking distance of one another on tree-lined streets. Each morning, shopkeepers sweep their walks or, with a cloth and their own warm breath, clean the windowpanes corner to corner.

For about 1,100 residents, morning means boarding Metro-North's New Haven division commuter trains for Manhattan. Three direct trains go and return each weekday, taking about sixty-five minutes each way. Other trains run only as far as Stamford, where passengers transfer. By car via the Merritt Parkway, New Canaan is about forty miles from midtown Manhattan.

Most commuters prefer the railroad to driving, and, in a rarity in Connecticut, praise the service. "The line is generally very good, converse to what you hear about Metro-North," said Thomas Goodale, an executive with the Philip Morris Company. "It's on time, clean, not overly packed."

For all its advantages, New Canaan is hardly immune to suburban stresses. Public school enrollment has fallen by about 15 percent since 1977, and an elementary school may have to be closed in coming years, according to Dr. William C. French, the superintendent.

Crime is rising, although New Canaan's crime rate is low in comparisons with national averages for communities its size, according to the Federal Bureau of Investigation. Affluence, privacy, and access to the Merritt Parkway—three of the things homeowners like about New Canaan—attract criminals, the police point out. "The pickings are good," noted Police Chief Ralph Scott. Hundreds of homeowners have responded by installing home-security systems, Mr. Scott said.

Like crime, a resident-turnover rate of 30 percent a year has begun to transform New Canaan. Newcomers can find acceptance hard in a village with private clubs for golf, tennis, winter sports, and shooting.

Some longtime residents say newcomers have to work at making friends in the town; others say the transient nature of the population makes it easy. Almost all agree, however, that the easiest way in is through volunteer activities in such places as the Silver Hill Foundation, a psychiatric hospital, or the Waveny Care Center, a skilled nursing facility. And New Canaan has three clubs for newcomers, offering a range of activities.

If anything, said Mary Louise King, the author of the historical *Portrait of New Canaan,* the newcomers are the most adamant in defending the village against change. "People want the town to remain the way it was when they moved in," she said. "That's been the pattern for one hundred years."

—SAMUEL G. FREEDMAN

NEW MILFORD

To midtown Manhattan: Train or bus 120 minutes

In 1882, as he was chronicling the first 170 years of New Milford's history, Samuel Orcutt could not resist adding a bit of chest-puffing to his scholarship. Having seen New Milford become "in some mercantile respects the center for the whole county," he wrote, "it merits particular consideration as to the causes of its growth and prosperity."

A century later, New Milford merits "particular consideration" for another reason: it is molding a reputation as the home-buying and home-building bargain of suburban Connecticut. Acre lots can still be had here for $25,000 to $30,000 and dozens of houses for less than $100,000.

"New Milford is the first place for the last hope" of home ownership, said Clifford Chapin, the first selectman. He called his town "the last frontier when you leave the 'Gold Coast'" of the Westport-to-Greenwich shoreline.

Contrasts abound. The Grange lodge shares an intersection with a modern professional office building; Cliff & Jean's Old Town Cafe, where breakfast still costs less than a dollar, sits down Bank Street from Bobbitt's Health Food Emporium.

With 19,420 residents spread over sixty-four square miles of the Housatonic River valley and the Litchfield Hills—this is the largest town by area in Connecticut—New Milford has been able to absorb blue-collar workers, executives transferred to Fairfield County corporations, and New York City expatriates seeking a quieter life.

This has resulted in changes that most would agree enrich the fabric of the community—live theater, film revivals, and fine restaurants. But there is considerably less agreement on the three shopping malls that have sprung up on Route 7, housing developments that rose on hills stripped of foliage, and the fact that, while there were 160 farms in the 1940's, there are perhaps only a dozen today.

"People don't wish to change New Milford to Stamford or Long Island or wherever they're from," maintained Mr. Chapin, who, as a lifelong resident and a working farmer, might be expected to revere tradition. "They just want to season it. The only difference is more business and more traffic."

But Roger Richmond, who, as the vice president of the DeVoe Realty Company here, makes his living from growth, voiced concern. "The character of the town is changing. It is becoming a sort of bedroom community for the towns to the south—something we're not crazy about."

The change itself, however, is consistent with New Milford's historic role: a home to generations of newcomers. When the first Europeans settled here in 1706, no others lived within fourteen miles. When it was incorporated six years later, only a dozen families were in the community.

The Housatonic Railroad made its first trip—to Bridgeport—in 1840 to the echo of New Milford's church bells and volleying cannons; tobacco-curing operations, foundries, and pipe-making factories all grew along the rail's spine. But the town remained largely farm-oriented, with Main Street, as Mr. Orcutt recounted, "an irregular cart path winding in and out of the stumps of trees," and inhabited by geese, pigs, and cows bound for grazing grounds on the nearby Village Green.

The Green remains the centerpiece—in geography and ambience—of colonial New Milford. The locals brag that the three-block Green is the longest in New England. The young and amorous find the bandstand, built in 1896, the ideal setting for twilight courting. Offices now occupy most of the four-dozen former homes—dating as far back as 1730—that line the Green. A town declaration of the area as a historic district forbids substantial "exterior change" to the houses.

As residents recall, the most enduring change in the community began in 1957, when Kimberly-Clark opened a diaper and tissue plant that now has 1,200 employees. "The real change commenced then, and it hasn't stopped yet," said David Murphy, a realtor and lifelong resident of New Milford.

Developers erected hundreds of starter homes for the plant's workers. "We as natives said, 'Who's going to live in those? They're so close together,'" Mr. Chapin recalled. "At $10,000 to $12,000 apiece, lots of people. Now the same homes bring upward of $85,000 to $90,000."

Still, New Milford remains a bargain. According to Mr. Richmond, the average price of houses offered for sale is $90,000 and the average price for a condominium unit is $50,000. Those prices are a half to a third of prices in some Fairfield County communities. The average rent for apartments is $425 to $450 a month. Apartments, however, are scarce and hard to find.

Annual taxes on a typical $100,000 home would be between $1,000 and $1,400.

New Milford also has distinctive estates, several of which are usually for sale at any time, say real-estate brokers. A nineteenth-century manor house on thirty to fifty acres, for example, may be offered from $500,000 to $1 million.

The Mathews family bought such a property in 1982 for about $300,000. They got a house built around 1700, a barn, and an indoor pool, all on 5.7 acres of land bordered by the Housatonic River and Route 7. "This property cannot be duplicated anywhere, anyhow," said Scott Mathews. "It's priceless. We were looking for a New England type of setting and New Milford is almost a replica of Vermont."

Lawrence and Barbara Servoss, who moved from Denver in 1982, expressed delight with the mix of low price and small-town ambience. They paid $87,000—"much less than we would have for a comparable home in Colorado," Ms. Servoss said—for a two-year-old, three-bedroom, two-and-one-half-bath colonial on two acres.

For dining out, restaurants range from the French cuisine of the Booth House, the Swiss specialties of Rudy's, and the Italian seafood of Joey's to the forty-two-year-old institution that is Clamp's hamburger stand.

There are two theater companies, the Connecticut Stage and Creative Arts, which operate year-round; and the Housatonic Art League has its headquarters in town.

Among the town's other cultural and entertainment amenities are the Bank Street Theater, which has revived such films as *City Lights* and *The Grapes of Wrath;* the annual town fair in July; and the traditional Christmas tree-lighting and concert, which is presided over by Skitch Henderson, a town resident. In addition, there are sports leagues for young people and activities in nine town parks and on nearby Candlewood Lake.

The 4,300-student public school system, according to its superintendent, Dr. Edward Center, is not as "pressured as in some suburban communities."

Ninth graders in the high school score at or above the statewide level of expected performance more than 96 percent of the time on

Connecticut's achievement tests. Student scores on the Scholastic Aptitude Test are close to the national averages. About 30 percent of high-school graduates go directly to work and about 50 percent go on to four-year colleges.

Commuting to New York, Danbury, or the Stamford area can be a problem. Commuters can drive or take a bus to Danbury, where they can board Metro-North trains to Grand Central Station. There are also three buses a day to and from Manhattan. Average commuting time by train or bus is about two hours.

And then there is the problem of Route 7, a two-lane road that runs through town and is still awaiting a widening promised a quarter of a century ago. Commuters say that it can take as long to reach Stamford, thirty-five miles away, on Route 7 as it can to reach Manhattan, eighty miles distant, on Routes 84 and 684.

—SAMUEL G. FREEDMAN

N E W T O W N

To midtown Manhattan: Train 120 minutes

When prospective home buyers want to check out the towns of northern Fairfield County in Connecticut, Gil Bastos, a real-estate broker, makes a special point of driving them through Newtown's Main Street, past the colonial houses, the old churches, and the flagpole. "When you drive down Main Street, the charm really grabs you," said Mr. Bastos, former president of the Newtown Board of Realtors. "That catches them, right there."

Newtown, a triangular-shaped town bordering the Housatonic River about seventy miles northeast of midtown Manhattan, is a mix—part old New England, as reflected by Main Street and the eighteenth-century houses that are scattered around the countryside; part rural, with a few working farms and some open land; and part suburban, with the housing developments that have crept over the rolling hills in the 1960's and 1970's.

"We're just beyond the expensive Fairfield County towns, such as New Canaan, Darien, and Fairfield," said R. Scudder Smith, editor and publisher of *The Newtown Bee,* the town's weekly newspaper. At the same time, he added, Newtown is more accessible to employment centers, such as Stamford, Greenwich, Danbury, and even New York City, than the more rural towns to the north and east. "We're sort of a halfway point."

Houses, however, still are somewhat cheaper in Newtown than

417

they are in the more affluent towns of lower Fairfield County, with the average price of a single-family house around $130,000, Mr. Bastos said. And it still is possible to find a summer cottage converted to year-round use for $70,000 to $85,000.

But a sampling of recent house sales indicates that most transactions involve substantially higher amounts. For example, a two-year-old four-bedroom colonial on a bit more than an acre sold not long ago for $175,000. It has an annual tax bill of $2,300.

The rental market in town is tight, and, as it still is in a lot of the more rural towns in Connecticut, the construction of apartments and condominiums was generally prohibited until 1984 by Newtown's zoning laws. Some residents complained that young people who grew up in Newtown, as well as some elderly people with limited incomes, could not afford to live there. But now the municipality has an ordinance that allows accessory apartments to be built in residential zones. By some estimates, as many as 400 such apartments had been created illegally before the ordinance was passed.

Newtown has a population of more than 19,000, and it covers 60.38 square miles of wide valleys and rolling hills, making it the fifth largest town in Connecticut in area. The area, once known as Quanneapague, was purchased in 1705 from the Pohtatuck Indians by land speculators from Stratford. The price was "four guns, four broadcloth Coats, four blankitts, four ruffelly Coats, four Collars, ten skirts, ten pair of stockings, forty pounds of lead, ten pounds of powder and forty knives." It took until 1711, however, before the General Court of the Connecticut Colony incorporated the "new town."

Early in the Revolutionary War, Tory sentiment was strong in Newtown, and the town's best-remembered incident of the war occurred in 1781 when the French general Rochambeau and his troops camped in town on their way to Yorktown, Virginia.

The two best-known landmarks are the rooster weathervane on the Congregational Church on Main Street (the rooster is on the town seal) and the flagpole in front of the church in the middle of the intersection where Church Hill Road meets Main Street.

A flagpole has been there since 1876 (the present steel one was erected in 1950), and directions to most locations in town usually start at the pole. The State Department of Transportation, however, regards the flagpole as a traffic hazard because it stands in the middle of Main Street, which is also Route 25. So far, the residents have resisted all attempts to move it. "Save the Flagpole" bumper stickers, one manifestation of the resistance, abound.

At one time, a section of Newtown known as Hawleyville was a thriving railroad center, but commuters now have to drive elsewhere to catch a train. Some go to Bethel or Danbury to a branch line connecting with Metro-North's New Haven division. The commuting time to Grand Central Terminal is about two hours. A few commuters shorten the trip by driving across I-84, which cuts through the town, to catch the Harlem division trains at Brewster, New York. I-84 connects with I-684, a direct link to Westchester County and New York City; the drive to Manhattan takes a minimum of ninety minutes.

Newtown residents generally have a high regard for their school system, although fights to get the town budget approved, either at a town meeting or by a referendum, have become more difficult in recent years. The six public schools (one high school, one middle school, and four elementary schools) have an enrollment of almost 4,000. The average class size is twenty-three at the elementary and twenty-two at the secondary level. About 60 percent of high-school graduates go on to college, and about 10 percent pursue other training in such fields as nursing and business.

John Reed, the superintendent of schools, said the high-school students who take the Scholastic Aptitude Test score, on average, well above the national norms in both verbal and mathematical skills.

Dr. Reed described the school population as a "unique" combination, with short-term students whose parents are frequently transferred by their corporations, as well as a stable population of students from families who have lived in Newtown for generations.

Mr. Bastos, who has real-estate offices in both Newtown and Danbury, said Newtown has two major assets—"New England colonial charm and shopping nearby for the daily needs."

But Mr. Smith, whose family has run the weekly newspaper for several generations, noted that there were still gaps in the town's available shopping. For major purchases, and even to get a pair of shoes repaired, residents often go to Danbury, he said. He also remarked that there seemed to be less participation in town affairs than in the past. "People come here and are either totally involved, or don't want to be interested at all."

In addition to the schools, recreation facilities are often cited as an attraction. There is an active library with more than 10,000 cardholders and more than 31,000 volumes. There are two lakes—Lake Lillinonah and Lake Zoar—with boating and swimming. There is a busy town park with swimming and tennis courts and a second park under construction.

The biggest bargain in town, however, is at the Edmond Town Hall, the handsome brick municipal building on Main Street. There is no commercial movie house in town, so first-run motion pictures, which have usually made the rounds of the area theaters, are shown nightly at Town Hall. The admission charge is $1.

—RICHARD L. MADDEN

NORWALK

To midtown Manhattan: Train 90 minutes

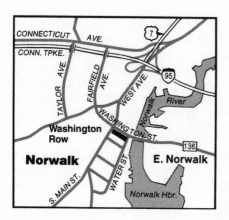

N orwalk would probably win the diverse city award for the State of Connecticut—if there was one," said its three-term mayor, William A. Collins. "That makes it a really nice place to live for those of us who cherish diversity, but it also makes it difficult for Norwalk to develop a strong image."

Despite residential areas in backcountry Silvermine and shore-front Rowayton that are indistinguishable from Wilton, Westport, or Darien, it is the depressed South Norwalk industrial district that has dominated the city's image for decades. Known as the "hole in the doughnut," Norwalk is supposedly the gap in a circle of wealthy residential towns.

But the era of decline brought about by the flight of commerce and industry to outlying malls and the Sun Belt appears to be coming to an end. Beginning with SoNo—the name given to South Norwalk by a colony of artists who moved there in the mid-1970's when it was cheap and are moving out now that it has become too expensive—Norwalk is reclaiming itself.

A collection of dilapidated, abandoned hat and underwear factories, ship chandleries, and six rare iron-front buildings on Washington and South Main streets were placed on the National Register of Historic Places a few years ago and rehabilitated. Now young, mostly single professionals who work for Fairfield County's corpo-

420

rations live in the enclave of condominiums, offices, boutiques, art galleries, and restaurants, which has been named Washington Row.

Arthur Collins (no relation to the mayor), the developer selected by the city to plan and execute the $10 million project, retained a turn-of-the-century flavor in the facades and streetscapes while modernizing the interiors. "I appreciate what Norwalk is, as opposed to the high-income, transient life of Greenwich, Darien, and New Canaan," said Mr. Collins, who grew up in Norwalk.

The charm and marketability of the restoration sparked similar projects in the immediate area and along Route 7, a busy north-south commercial artery, where the Yankee Metal building will soon become 132 apartments renting for about $800 a month. The plan to extend four-lane Martin Luther King Drive to give access to Interstate 95 from Route 136 is a strategy to attract light industry back to South Norwalk.

A recent surge in demand for housing in Norwalk, a city of 26.6 square miles with a population of 78,000, resulted from what Mayor Collins called "an invasion of office buildings" pushing north from Stamford and Greenwich. Examples include Prudential Insurance's 400,000 square feet in River Park and G.T.E.'s world training center in West Norwalk.

Norwalk is almost fully developed, predominantly with single-family homes. But Patsy Brescia, twenty-year resident and manager of William Pitt Realty, believes it to be the prime remaining lower Fairfield community "with the product people are looking for." She cited the stock of 3,000 condominium units, from efficiencies at $50,000 to luxury town houses with private marinas at $350,000, plus starter homes and homes for established families priced up to 20 percent less than in Darien, New Canaan, Wilton, and Westport. The average family income in those communities exceeds $41,000, almost twice that of Norwalk.

The cost of housing is highest around the perimeter of the city, declining in concentric circles to the lowest-cost industrial section. At the southwestern tip is Wilson Point, where waterfront estates go for $1.4 million and up. Sasqua Hills, the southeast area that includes Calf Pasture Beach, has condominiums costing up to $350,000 and houses starting at $175,000. House prices in the northwestern and northeastern sectors of Silvermine and Cranbury, above the Merritt Parkway, range from $150,000 to $400,000.

East Norwalk, south of the Thruway from the Norwalk River to Westport, is a mixed commercial, residential, and light-industrial area with houses and condominiums at $95,000 and up. In West Norwalk from Scribner Avenue north to the Merritt, and in Brookside, from Scribner Avenue south to the thruway—both extending to the Darien line—houses are in the $100,000 to $200,000 range.

Small homes in Rowayton, bordering Five Mile River on the

southwestern border, are priced higher than comparable homes would be in other parts of the city.

Property in Norwalk is assessed at 70 percent of fair-market value. The owner of a house sold for $125,000 would be assessed at $87,500 and pay taxes of $2,500.

Norwalk began in 1640 as a 16,000-acre tract bought from the Indians for $60 worth of clothing and a few trinkets by Roger Ludlow, a Massachusetts Bay Colony magistrate. The city prospered as a seaport and agricultural center until the mid-1800's, when railroads enabled it to expand into manufacturing.

By the 1920's, it had acquired a reputation as a summer resort for New Yorkers, many of whom traveled up by yacht, and fashionable shops and hotels thrived along West Avenue. By the 1950's, however, commerce and industry had begun their flight. In the face of air-conditioning and growing world travel, summer cottages lost their charm and were sold off as small year-round homes.

Nevertheless, as summer approaches, Norwalk's island-dotted harbor and Five Mile River still come alive with thousands of boats. Sport and professional fishermen go after "flats" (Norwalkese for flounder), striped bass, "frostfish" (cod), bluefish, and mackerel. Oysters and clams can be bought on Water Street at Bloom Brothers, which has its own beds.

Of the city's 1,000 acres of parkland, thirty-three are devoted to Calf Pasture and Shady beaches at Calf Pasture Point, where picnic tables and a children's playground are free to residents. The town's fifty tennis, paddle tennis, and basketball courts are also free. Bailey's Beach in Rowayton is restricted to residents of that district, and the municipal Oak Hills Golf Course charges an $8 annual fee plus greens fees of $5 to $7.

Norwalk restaurants tend toward plain, moderately priced food attuned to the neighborhood. Judy's, on South Main Street, caters to the City Hall crowd. The General Putnam Inn on the town green recalls the city's colonial beginnings, and the 200-year-old Silvermine Tavern on Silvermine Road serves leisurely meals amidst early American paintings and furniture.

The Norwalk Symphony Orchestra attracts world-class guest artists, as do the Westport Country Playhouse, the Darien Dinner Theater, and two playhouses in Stamford, none more than twenty minutes away. The Silvermine Guild of Artists, the Rowayton Arts Center, and the Lockwood-Mathews Mansion Museum are among the arts institutions.

For 2,000 New York commuters, Metro-North has twenty-eight trips each weekday from the East Norwalk, South Norwalk, or Rowayton stations. The trip takes an hour and a half.

Public safety is in the hands of a 154-member police force and a fire department of 155 professionals, in contrast to the volunteer fire services in many other Connecticut towns.

Opinions vary about Norwalk's fully integrated 11,000-student school system. Wendy Baker of Wilson Point took her two daughters out, she said, "for lack of challenge." But Harriet Haffner of Haffner Real Estate stated that her children "learned to live in the real world with all sorts of socioeconomic groups, and they had no trouble getting into Wesleyan and Yale."

Sixty-five percent of high-school graduates go on to some form of higher education. Eighth-grade reading scores show well over 85 percent of the students reading and doing math at or above grade levels.

Norwalk's image soon may be brightened by development of a Maritime Center on Washington Street. The $22 million center, scheduled for completion in 1987, will have an aquarium, exhibits, children's educational programs, boat-building and sea-skill courses for adults, a theater with a five-story screen, restaurants, promenade decks, and marine-related shops. In addition, the Oceanic Society of Stamford will relocate at the center with its research vessel *The Oceanic,* and the Norwalk Seaport Association's oyster sloop *Hope* will be docked nearby for environmental voyages on Long Island Sound.

—ELEANOR CHARLES

RIDGEFIELD

To midtown Manhattan: Train 90 to 120 minutes

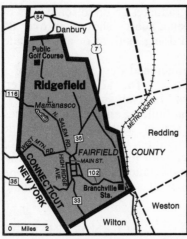

Many of its neighbors in Connecticut's Fairfield County are changing from sleepy suburban towns to busy corporate headquarters, but one of Ridgefield's proudest claims is that it has stayed more or less the same for more than 275 years.

Along Route 7 lie Danbury and Norwalk, so flooded with new businesses that what was once a pleasant rural roadway framed by trees has become a miles-long parking lot during rush hour, and Stamford has become a major office center. Main Street in Ridgefield, however, is lined with historic colonial homes with white picket fences, old taverns turned into inns, and the occasional clothing store, newsstand, or pharmacy. A "Greening of Main Street" volunteer committee plants trees and even encases garbage pails in wooden boxes with geraniums planted on the tops.

Away from Main Street, off back roads where sunlight filters through the trees, estates built by wealthy families at the turn of the century still stand—some subdivided, some intact—their mansions adorned with columns, gables, and stone towers.

Ridgefield's population has swelled from 8,500 twenty-five years ago to 20,000 today, but residents say it retains the atmosphere and scale of exurbia, with a small-town sense of community.

"The New England village atmosphere of the town is really charming," said James Sandy, who moved to Ridgefield in 1973.

424

RIDGEFIELD

"The people are very friendly, very open. When my son was in the Boy Scouts and going on an overnight campout, I called the guy in charge of it to offer to help supervise and he told me they were overbooked with fathers. That's the kind of thing you run into all the time."

"Overall, this is still a small New England town," stated Elizabeth Leonard, Ridgefield's first selectman. "Our development has not been haphazard. We have not ruined a beautiful community. We're dead serious about planning and zoning discipline."

This emphasis on conservation has preserved parts of Ridgefield since its founding in 1708. Twenty-two settlers traveled from Norwalk, seventeen miles to the south, in search of farmland and arrived in what is now Ridgefield after dark. They spent that first night perched on a rock to avoid wolves and the Ramapoo Indians, from whom they later bought 20,000 acres for the equivalent of about $300.

Settlers Rock still stands on North Salem Road. The house of Ridgefield's first minister, Thomas Hauley, built in 1713, is still on Main Street.

Ridgefield grew so that it was able to supply 275 soldiers in the Revolutionary War, some of whom fought in the town's only battle. On April 27, 1777, British and Americans who had been fighting at sea to get through to New London disembarked and fought hand to hand in the Battle of Ridgefield. The British won.

The War of 1812 touched Ridgefield much more peripherally when Sarah Bishop, a young woman from Long Island, fled to a cave after being jilted by a British soldier and froze to death.

Ridgefield remained a quiet farming town until the beginning of the twentieth century, when wealthy families from New York City began to see its possibilities as a summer retreat, according to Richard E. Venus, a lifelong resident and former postmaster who served as historian for the town's 275th anniversary celebration in 1983.

Many of the large estates these families built still stand along High Ridge and West Mountain roads. A president of Standard Oil employed fifty men to tend his estate and help care for orchids that were among the first grown in this country. The presidents of Underwood Typewriter, Ingersoll Rand, and several other corporations built houses on grounds ranging from 500 to 1,500 acres.

Many of these estates have been subdivided, with corporate executives living in what were once caretakers' cottages. Some mansions have been razed to make way for smaller homes or condominiums. But many remain, and the town is largely made up of subdivisions with two-acre zoning that retain a backcountry flavor.

This atmosphere is Ridgefield's strongest selling point, said Lillian

Moorhead, a broker with Heritage Properties who served ten years on the Board of Selectmen. Although it boasts the suburban amenities of low crime, good schools, convenient commuter transportation, acres of sports fields, and local arts activities, the town still seems more country than suburb.

But the amenities are not cheap. Home prices average $150,000, ranging from $80,000 to more than $3 million, Ms. Moorhead reported. The tax rate is $45.10 for each $1,000 of valuation and houses are assessed at 36 percent of market value; the owner of a house with a market value of $100,000 would pay taxes of $1,600 a year, according to Alfred Carzi, the town assessor.

The taxes go in part to support recreational facilities such as a municipal golf course, public tennis courts, bridle paths, and more than 4,000 acres of farmland, forestland, and open space such as Hemlock Hills with hiking paths cut through it. Swimming, fishing, and boating are available on Lake Mamanasco, and the Ridgefield Y.M.C.A. has recently been renovated.

Ridgefield has six public schools—four elementary, one junior high, and one senior high school—with an average class size of about twenty. On national standardized tests, students at all levels average in the 87th percentile, according to Joseph Leheny, assistant superintendent for instruction. About 85 percent of high-school graduates go on to higher education.

In the last quarter century there has been an influx of corporate executives who commute to New York and the new corporate centers in Danbury, Norwalk, and Stamford. When Union Carbide moved its headquarters to Danbury a few years ago, several executives settled in Ridgefield, a fifteen- to twenty-minute commute on Route 7.

The Metro-North railroad's Branchville station, on the Danbury line, serves Ridgefield. Passengers must change at Norwalk for the main line into New York City. The trip takes from one-and-a-half to two hours. Many commuters choose to drive to neighboring Katonah, New York, where the trip to Grand Central takes an hour and fifteen minutes, or to New Canaan, where express trains take slightly more than an hour.

Corporate executives make up about a third of Ridgefield's population, Ms. Moorhead estimated. The balance are descendants of the original settlers, descendants of the staffs of the big estates—many of whom are doctors and lawyers—and a large number of artists and writers drawn by the bucolic setting.

Eugene O'Neill wrote *Desire Under the Elms* while living in a farmhouse on North Salem Road with two large elms in the front yard. A strong interest in the arts has spurred such organizations as the Ridgefield Guild of Artists, the Ridgefield Workshop for the Performing Arts, the Ridgefield Ballet, and the Ridgefield Orchestra.

R I D G E F I E L D

Ridgefield also houses the Aldrich Museum of Contemporary Art, a building dating back to the 1700's with modern sculpture on its lawn, and the Keeler Tavern, an eighteenth-century inn turned into a museum of colonial life.

The town has modern inns and restaurants as well. The Inn at Ridgefield, The Elms, Stonehenge, and Le Coq Hardy are among the best known.

"People move here because they love this atmosphere," said Ms. Leonard, "but it is very hard for them to adjust to the fact that it's not an urban area." For example, she noted, there is no municipal bus service and the sewer system dates to 1902. In addition, rising property values have made it harder for the town's elderly residents living on fixed incomes to maintain their homes, she added. Ridgefield has built sixty units of housing for the elderly but has more than fifty people on a waiting list.

—SUSAN CHIRA

WESTPORT

To midtown Manhattan: Train 60 minutes

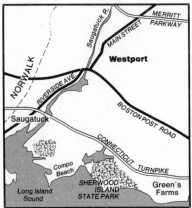

In the 1930's and 1940's, when a colony of affluent artists and writers settled in what was then the quiet summer resort of Westport and New York's Theatre Guild established the Westport Country Playhouse, the town acquired a lively, arts-oriented ambience that set it apart from its more sedate neighbors. That ambience persists, and today's residents characterize the town as cosmopolitan, relaxed, worldly, and liberal.

Ann Chernow, an artist who moved to Westport twenty years ago, said "it's more like New York than the other communities, while maintaining much of the village charm that Greenwich relinquished when it became citified with large office buildings." Ms. Chernow, whose husband, Burt, is an artist and writer, is thankful that they came in the 1960's. "We couldn't afford to buy our house today."

Although most can well afford them, many Westporters eschew private clubs and schools in favor of an unstructured social and cultural life. But a population boom from 11,000 in the 1940's to 25,500 today and the sprouting of small downtown office buildings has old-timers mourning for the "sweet little country town" of fifty years ago.

The so-called Gold Coast towns of Greenwich, New Canaan, Darien, and Westport are almost interchangeable in terms of prestige, fine homes, extensive recreational facilities, and efficient town services. All are expensive, but in Westport, where the median price of

428

a house is $212,000, houses equivalent to those in Greenwich may be a bit cheaper. Brokers attribute the difference to the additional fifteen minutes' travel time to Manhattan. The ride to Grand Central Station on Metro-North takes about sixty minutes.

Westport is on Long Island Sound and is abutted by the city of Norwalk to the west and the towns of Weston and Fairfield to the north and east. Its twenty square miles are almost fully developed, mostly with single-family homes that range from colonial cottages to baronial estates.

The inhabitants—among them Paul Newman and his wife, Joanne Woodward, the actors; Robert Ludlum, the novelist; and Steven Dohanos, the artist—represent a broad mix of national and religious backgrounds but a somewhat narrow economic one. A 1983 Chamber of Commerce survey found that the median household income exceeded $40,000. The survey also found that the vacancy rate among the town's 9,200 houses and half-dozen condominium developments was less than 5 percent.

Condominiums, for which zoning was approved only recently, range in price from $125,000 to $500,000, while houses are priced from $150,000 to $5 million. Rents start at $550 for a studio or $1,900 for a modest four-bedroom house. Small beach cottages may be rented, often to groups, for about $8,000 from June to September.

The owner of a typical three-bedroom house on one acre, priced at $250,000, would pay annual taxes of about $3,400.

Home seekers may choose a water or woodsy setting, an in-town or a secluded location. "Westport has no wrong side of the tracks," said Dorothy Williams, a former assistant to the selectmen and staff member of the Chamber of Commerce. Modest houses on small lots are tucked in among imposing homes on large parcels all over town.

Most houses are on lots of a half to two acres, but larger acreages are prevalent north of the Merritt Parkway and around the town's perimeter. Stabling a horse at home is not uncommon; unlike other communities, Westport has no ordinances governing the practice. The town's average density of 1,250 persons per square mile increases somewhat along the Saugatuck River, between the Merritt Parkway and the Post Road, and on the Longshore peninsula.

Bordering the Sound are the homes and marinas of Saugatuck Shores at the western end, then Longshore with the town-owned Longshore Country Club and Compo Beach. On the eastern end are 250-acre Sherwood Island State Park and the elegant homes of Green's Farms, site of the original settlement of the area by John Green and a group of English farmers in 1645, almost 200 years before the town was incorporated in 1835.

Boutiques clustered on Main Street, off the western end of the Post Road, do a brisk business in rather expensive merchandise. Department stores were excluded by zoning years ago, but many

Manhattan stores—among then Bloomingdale's, Macy's, Saks Fifth Avenue, and Lord & Taylor—have branches nearby in Stamford.

For recreation, there are three town beaches, twenty-six tennis courts, an eighteen-hole golf course, and two marinas. Recreation ID cards cost $15 and there are greens and tennis fees; beach parking stickers are $15 for one car, $20 for a second.

From the end of June through September, there are a variety of free concert, dance, and children's programs every evening at the Levitt Pavilion on a grassy bank of the Saugatuck River. The Nature Center for Environmental Activities on Woodside Lane provides a wide range of field trips and other activities for both children and adults.

The Westport Country Playhouse offers a full summer season, and there are many art galleries, among them one in the Town Hall, run by the Westport-Weston Arts Council.

For dining out, there are such notable restaurants as Le Chambord, featuring *nouvelle cuisine;* the Arrow, which serves freshly made pasta; and Manero's Steak House.

To the dismay of many residents, a half-dozen corporate offices and about thirty small commercial buildings have been put up in recent years, but such development is small compared with what has taken place in Greenwich and Stamford. The town's 1.2 million square feet of commercial space (none in industrial use) is limited to the Post Road and Riverside Avenue. "There is continued demand and room for another million square feet in those two corridors," according to Melvin Barr, the planning director.

Westport is governed by a Board of Selectmen and elected members of a representative town meeting. Public safety is provided by fifty full-time police officers, forty-three special and twenty-seven auxiliary officers, and three marine patrol boats, along with forty paid firemen and about 200 volunteers. Almost 150 physicians, surgeons, psychiatrists, and dentists attend to medical needs, and free ambulance service is available.

The schools are well regarded. About 90 percent of the students who are graduated from Staples High School go on to college, and their Scholastic Aptitude Test scores are well above national averages. The almost all-white school population of about 4,200 has been augmented for several years by seventy-five black children bused in voluntarily from Bridgeport.

There are workshops for gifted children in all grades, foreign languages begin in fifth grade, and advanced college-placement courses are given in high school. Westport is the regional headquarters for children with learning disabilities and other handicaps.

The one private school in town is Green's Farms Academy on forty-two acres off Beachside Avenue, founded in 1925. The school, which is on the former Robert T. Vanderbilt estate, has an enrollment of 438 day students. Tuition ranges from $2,500 a year in kindergarten to $6,100 in the twelfth grade.

The arts remain a strong component of town life, although nowadays artists are far outnumbered by business executives. Because of its liveliness, Westport has attracted many young professionals who work in nearby offices. Unable to afford most housing in Westport, some have been moving into illegal "accessory apartments," usually offered by older people with room to spare in their homes. "Studies are being done to decide what to do about it," said Mr. Barr, who indicated that legal zoning for such accommodations would be proposed.

—ELEANOR CHARLES